CLAS

MW00780029

General Editors
Lorna Hardwick   James I. Porter

CLASSICAL PRESENCES

Attempts to receive the texts, images, and material culture of ancient Greece and Rome inevitably run the risk of appropriating the past in order to authenticate the present. Exploring the ways in which the classical past has been mapped over the centuries allows us to trace the avowal and disavowal of values and identities, old and new. Classical Presences brings the latest scholarship to bear on the contexts, theory, and practice of such use, and abuse of the classical past.

The dissemination of classical material to children is a major form of popularization with far-reaching effects, but until very recently has received little attention within the growing field of classical reception studies. This volume explores the ways in which children encountered the world of ancient Greece and Rome in Britain and the United States over a century-long period beginning in the 1850s, as well as adults' literary responses to their own childhood experiences of antiquity. Rather than discussing the role of classics in education, it focuses on books read for pleasure, and primarily on two genres of children's literature: the myth collection and the historical novel. The tradition of myths retold as children's stories is traced in the work of writers and illustrators from Nathaniel Hawthorne and Charles Kingsley to Roger Lancelyn Green and Ingri and Edgar Parin D'Aulaire, while the discussion of historical fiction highlights the roles of nationality and gender in the construction of an ancient world for modern children. The book concludes with an investigation of the connections between childhood and antiquity made by writers for adults, including James Joyce, Virginia Woolf, and H.D. Recognition of the fundamental role in children's literature of adults' ideas about what children want or need is balanced throughout by attention to the ways in which child readers have made such works their own. The formative experiences of antiquity discussed in this book help explain why, despite growing uncertainty about the appeal of antiquity to modern children, the classical past remains a perennial object of interest and source of inspiration.

Childhood and the Classics

Britain and America, 1850–1965

Sheila Murnaghan and
Deborah H. Roberts

OXFORD
UNIVERSITY PRESS

OXFORD
UNIVERSITY PRESS

Great Clarendon Street, Oxford, OX2 6DP,
United Kingdom

Oxford University Press is a department of the University of Oxford.
It furthers the University's objective of excellence in research, scholarship,
and education by publishing worldwide. Oxford is a registered trade mark of
Oxford University Press in the UK and in certain other countries

First published 2018
First published in paperback 2020

Published in the United States of America by Oxford University Press
198 Madison Avenue, New York, NY 10016, United States of America

British Library Cataloguing in Publication Data
Data available

Library of Congress Cataloging in Publication Data
Data available

ISBN 978–0–19–958347–8 (Hbk.)
ISBN 978–0–19–885921–5 (Pbk.)

For our families

Preface

This book is the result of a long friendship and many conversations about ancient and modern literature. What began as a project on twentieth-century women writers and the classics gradually evolved into a study of writing about antiquity for children and the lifelong consequences of childhood encounters with the Greco-Roman past. As we became more deeply involved with both classical reception studies and children's literature studies in our teaching and scholarship, we were often struck by a fundamental affinity between the two fields, both of which are concerned with the construction of a past that is inaccessible but still with us, at once alien and familiar.

As our work progressed, we were pleased to find an emerging community of scholars working at the intersection of classics and children's literature, brought together through a series of conferences: the pioneering "Asterisks and Obelisks" (2009), organized by Owen Hodkinson and Helen Lovatt at the University of Wales at Lampeter, and "Our Mythical Childhood" (2013) and its successors at the Faculty of Artes Liberales of the University of Warsaw, part of an ongoing international project under the tireless and inspirational direction of Katarzyna Marciniak. The connections made on those occasions have been cemented and extended through important essay collections edited by the organizers and by Lisa Maurice.

We benefited significantly from the questions and comments of audiences at Lampeter and Warsaw and in other settings where we have presented our work, including Bryn Mawr College, Boston College, Hamilton College, Swarthmore College, Rutgers University, Northwestern University; meetings of the American Philological Association (now the Society for Classical Studies), the Classical Association of the Atlantic States, the American Comparative Literature Association, and the International Society for the Classical Tradition; and conferences on classical reception in Milton Keynes, Hay on Wye, and London. We are especially grateful to those friends and colleagues who read all or part of our manuscript and provided incisive, informative comments: Catherine Butler, Robert Germany, Jane Gordon, Michael Hearn, Hannah Kosman,

Bettina Kümmerling-Meibauer, Vicki Mahaffey, Alison Poe, and Rebecca Resinski. For generously sharing their unpublished work, we thank Gillian Bazovsky, Rachel Bryant Davies, Catherine Butler, Pamela Gassman, Jacob Horn, Anne Morey and Claudia Nelson, Hallie O'Donovan, Yopie Prins, Rebecca Resinski, and Andelys Wood. And for useful documents, suggestions, reminiscences, and anecdotes, we are indebted to Amy Gordon, Shirley Pomeroy Herndon, Dennis Nolan, and Lee Pearcy.

The editors of the Classical Presences series, Lorna Hardwick and James Porter, offered welcome encouragement at the outset; the anonymous readers for Oxford University Press gave useful advice; and the OUP staff, especially Georgina Leighton, have been a source of expert editorial guidance. The librarians at Haverford College and at the University of Pennsylvania supported us; at Haverford College, Terry Snyder assisted us in tracking down permissions and Margaret Schaus helped us time after time with recalcitrant bibliographical issues. We have had excellent research assistance from Florencia Foxley, Jacob Horn, Matthew Liscovitz, and Jeffrey Nolte. We also thank George Gordon and Jeffrey Nolte for their hard work in preparing our final bibliography and Jeffrey Carnes for his excellent index. Research funding from Haverford College and the University of Pennsylvania supported our various travels and the acquisition of many out-of-the-way children's books, and our respective departments have been exceptionally stimulating and collegial environments in which to develop our ideas. Thanks as well to the Ardmore Station Café, where we met so often to discuss the book over breakfast that they simply brought us "the usual."

Finally, for their good-humored interest and support throughout its creation, we gratefully dedicate this book to our families: to our husbands, Hugh Gordon and Aryeh Kosman, and to our children, George Gordon, Jane Gordon, and Hannah Kosman.

Acknowledgments

An earlier version of portions of Chapter 1 was originally published as D. H. Roberts, "From Fairytale to Cartoon," *Classical Bulletin* 84 (2009), 58–73.

An earlier version of a section of Chapter 4 and part of Chapter 7 was originally published as S. Murnaghan and D. H. Roberts, "Armies of Children: War and Peace, Ancient History and Myth in Children's Books after World War One," in K. Marciniak, ed., *Our Mythical Childhood* (Leiden: Brill, 2016).

An earlier version of a section of Chapter 4 was originally published as D. H. Roberts, "Reconstructed Pasts: Rome and Britain, Child and Adult in Kipling's *Puck of Pook's Hill* and Rosemary Sutcliff's Historical Fiction," in C. Stray, ed., *Remaking the Classics: Literature, Genre and Media in Britain 1800–2000* (London: Duckworth, 2007) and is used here by permission of Bloomsbury Academic, an imprint of Bloomsbury Publishing Plc.

An earlier version of portions of Chapter 6 was originally published as S. Murnaghan, "The Memorable Past: Antiquity and Girlhood in the Works of Mary Butts and Naomi Mitchison," in C. Stray, ed., *Remaking the Classics: Literature, Genre and Media in Britain 1800–2000* (London: Duckworth, 2007), and is used here by permission of Bloomsbury Academic, an imprint of Bloomsbury Publishing Plc.

The brief quotation from p. 7 of *Proofs and Theories: Essays on Poetry by Louise Glück*, copyright ©1994 by Louise Glück, is reprinted by permission of HarperCollins publishers.

Despite extensive enquiries we have been unable to locate the copyright holder for the image in Plate 5. Should the copyright holder be in contact after publication, we would be happy to include a suitable acknowledgment on subsequent reprints.

Contents

List of Illustrations

No epoch of time can claim a copyright in these immortal fables. They seem never to have been made; and certainly, so long as man exists, they can never perish; but, by their indestructibility itself, they are legitimate subjects for every age to clothe with its own garniture of manners and sentiment, and to imbue with its own morality... In performing this pleasant task... the Author has not always thought it necessary to write downward, in order to meet the comprehension of children... Children possess an unestimated sensibility to whatever is high, in imagination or feeling...

—Nathaniel Hawthorne, Preface to
A Wonder-Book for Girls and Boys

Introduction

> My mother read to us, then taught us to read very early. Before
> I was three, I was well grounded in the Greek myths, and the figures
> of those stories, together with certain images from the illustrations,
> became fundamental referents.
>
> —Louise Glück, "Education of the Poet"[1]

This book concerns the widespread and formative reception of classical
antiquity that takes place in childhood. Experiences like Louise Glück's
have long played an indispensable role in the continued cultural impact of
the Greco-Roman world. The dissemination of classical material to children is a major form of popularization, with far-reaching effects: where the
classical languages are not an inevitable part of formal education (as
increasingly now, and for many children in earlier periods), other kinds
of early exposure have provided access to the ancient world and the
impetus to seek out further encounters in various settings. (How many
classics students in our own day began with a favorite book of mythology?)
Of the countless writers and artists who, like Glück, have appropriated and
reworked classical material, many trace their inspiration to childhood. To
choose just one contemporary example, Adèle Geras, in a prefatory note to
Ithaka, a work of young adult fiction based on the *Odyssey* myth published
in 2005, explains that "This book is not a version of Homer nor a retelling
of the *Odyssey*, but a novel written under the influence of stories that I read
as a young child and that I've loved ever since." Until very recently,
however, children's experiences of the classical tradition have received
almost no attention within the growing field of classical reception studies.

---

[1] Glück 1994: 7.

We help to fill that gap by investigating works that contributed—or responded—to this form of reception in Britain and the United States over a century-long period beginning in the mid-nineteenth century, with special attention to the first half of the twentieth century. As Glück's account illustrates, modern children typically meet the ancient world first through mythology, and myth is both our starting point and a persistent concern throughout. We begin in the 1850s with the reworking of classical mythology into a new form of pleasure reading for children and trace the development of that form in ever-proliferating myth collections through the middle of the twentieth century. But any consideration of myth is always bound up with questions of history and of the relationship between the imaginary and the real. We show how myth has been presented to children not only as a timeless possession of the human race but also as the prelude to history, and we give particular attention to historical fiction for children during the same span of time. Despite its contrasting aim of communicating factual information about the past, historical fiction is aligned with myth in its openness to invention and its designs on the child reader's imagination and capacity for identification, and it too is seen as a form of pleasure reading.

Pleasure reading that takes place privately or within the family rather than as part of formal education (whether in schools or at home) is our principal focus: we are not centrally concerned with the role of the classics in school curricula, a subject which has already received considerable attention.[2] But as we will show, pleasure reading is variously and inescapably bound up with education. Most of the writers we discuss assume that the kinds of children who enjoy books about the classical past will either go to school or be educated at home (though in the earlier part of this period only boys are regularly expected to learn Latin and Greek) and many of their books are explicitly intended as preludes or supplements to schoolwork. They may be presented as breaks from study, but they are also often enlisted in its service, as when teachers give children stories they hope will engage an imaginative interest in the classical past.[3] In addition to

---

[2] For Britain, see Stray 1998, a study that covers roughly the same time span (1830–1960), and for the United States, Winterer 2002.

[3] Such books are frequently offered as prizes for educational achievement; students who excel in Latin, for example, may be rewarded with works of historical fiction that will build on what they have learned from reading Caesar.

complementing instruction in ancient languages and ancient history, such imaginative works may be seen as playing a role in children's moral education and psychological development. It can be argued that all works for children have the effect, whether explicit or implicit, of imparting adult perspectives, so that the distinction critics draw between pleasure reading and instructional reading (though historically important) is conceptually problematic as well as often blurred in practice.[4]

While our primary concern is with myth collections and historical novels for children, we take note along the way of other genres of children's literature that also engage with classical antiquity, especially versions of Aesop's Fables, retellings of the Homeric epics, and works of fantasy in which classical figures play a part. Along with works that are clearly intended for children, we also pay attention to crossover books of both kinds: books intended for adults but often read by children and books ostensibly for children that in some way seek or find an adult audience.[5] And we move beyond children's literature to consider adults' memories of their own childhood encounters with antiquity and the uses and meanings assigned to those encounters in memoirs and other genres of adult literature during the same period.

Glück's internalizing of Greek mythology at an early age dramatizes the natural connection that, as we will see, is often thought to exist between children and the classical past. But this connection is necessarily activated by her mother, who has already identified the myths as promising early reading and presented them to her daughter. The place of classical material among the pleasures of childhood is the result of adult intervention and has a specific history, which originates in the conjunction of mid-nineteenth-century conceptions of childhood with developments in writing and publishing for children. Since adults' ideas about what is appropriate or desirable for children are shaped by their own experiences, the bringing together of children and antiquity is a self-perpetuating phenomenon: the transmission of the classics is often bound up with a return to the author's own childhood, as in the case of Charles D. Shaw, author of a 1903 collection *Stories of the Ancient Greeks*.

---

[4] For a critique of the "education–amusement divide" in children's literature criticism, see Lesnik-Oberstein 1994: esp. chs. 2 and 3.

[5] On this phenomenon, see esp. Beckett 2009, 2012a, 2012b; Falconer 2009.

But there is always a new generation to whom the ancient stories must be told; and the author has spent pleasant hours in trying to retell some of them for the boys and girls of to-day.

He remembers what joy it was to him to read about the Greek gods and heroes; and he knows that life has been brighter to him ever since because of the knowledge thus gained and the fancies thus kindled. It is his hope to brighten, if possible, other young lives by repeating for them the immortal fictions and the deathless histories which have been delivered to new audiences for thousands of years.   (Shaw 1903: iii)

Even as he presents the retelling of these stories as a delightful return to his own childhood, Shaw reveals the gap between himself as author and both his own childhood self and the children he is writing for. His childhood belongs to the past, subject to nostalgia and accessed through memories and legacies that persist into a later stage of life. In the meantime, childhood itself has changed, so that material that is "immortal" and "deathless" has to be updated for "the boys and girls of to-day." Offering his readers a form of pleasure that will increase their knowledge while it stimulates their imagination, Shaw aims not only at sharing his childhood experience with them but also at turning them into adults like himself, who have had their lives brightened by the same past experience.

Over the last several decades, theoretical discussions of children's literature have drawn attention to the distance between adult writers and their child audiences that Shaw implicitly acknowledges. Since the seminal work of Jacqueline Rose, first published in 1984, which takes J. M. Barrie's various versions of Peter Pan as a case study, it has been a widely held tenet of children's literature studies that the child addressed by children's literature is always to some extent an adult projection; authors write from an adult perspective for and about children as they now imagine them and as contemporary cultural discourse constructs them.[6] The very idea of childhood as a distinct time of life, and of children as markedly different kinds of people, is produced by adult

---

[6] Rose 1992. Important theoretical discussions along similar lines include Lesnik-Oberstein 1994, Nodelman 2008; for critical assessments of Rose's book and its impact, see especially the special issue of *Children's Literature Association Quarterly* (2010: 35/5) that appeared on the twenty-fifth anniversary of its first publication and Rudd 2013. The story of Peter Pan may as some critics contend be an imperfect example, but the disconcerting prominence of adult concerns and adult designs on child readers in Barrie's story allows it to be read as a paradigmatic case of the adult presence Perry Nodelman and others consider a definitive feature of books for children.

awareness of different experiences and different states of mind that arrive at a later stage—that are necessarily outside the ken of children.

Rose stresses in particular the investment of children's writers and other adults in nostalgic and idealized conceptions of childhood as a distinct, undifferentiated, and unchanging time of life, associated with pure origins and prelinguistic states of mind. Some of the critics who have extended or revised Rose's ideas have focused instead on the way adult writers approach their child readers as future adults, seeking to move them out of their childish state and prepare them for what lies ahead.[7]

It is telling that Rose's chosen exemplar is a figure based on a classical prototype, since the classical world is itself envisioned as a special, simpler age and the source of timeless wisdom that counters the decay of modern culture. As a result, antiquity has often been figured as the childhood of humanity and viewed as an era to which all children have a natural connection. The authors who seek to realize and perpetuate this connection reveal the points of intersection between ideas about childhood and ideas about the classical past. And, as they make the ancient world suitable and accessible for children and elicit children's identification with figures from that earlier period, they generate new and overlapping chronologies: the ancient past is assimilated to various other times, including the more recent pasts of the author's own childhood, of definitive earlier retellings, and of national history; the present time inhabited by "the boys and girls of today"; and the future, which child readers are expected to create and for which they are being prepared.

At the same time, these works define—and seek to foster—the kinds of children who will respond to antiquity's appeal. Some are directed at all children in their distinction from modern adults, while others provide reconstructions of the ancient past tailored to children of a particular gender or class. There can be different versions of antiquity for girls and for boys, or versions in which children of one gender are implicitly the intended audience. Because classical material is often associated with schooling, the presumed audience for books about antiquity is sometimes elite or exclusive. But in other ways, classics for children can have an inclusive effect. Because such works often constitute a first exposure

---

[7] See esp. Nodelman 2008.

to an unknown or less fully mediated past (as may also happen in works for a popular audience), they may be more readily available to a range of readers than works with contemporary settings which treat the conditions of a particular social milieu as normative and self-evident, never explaining what the child is assumed to know.[8] And because antiquity's "immortal fictions and deathless histories" are often understood to transcend local differences, exposure to classical material can be seen as uniting children of various nationalities and classes.

Our main subject, then, is a set of adult ideas about childhood and adult expectations and hopes concerning child readers, registered in works that implicitly address other adults even when ostensibly directed only to children. But we do also acknowledge and seek to capture, to the extent that we can, the ways in which the children who receive these works make them their own, in a dialogic process that, as David Rudd has suggested, necessarily qualifies Rose's account of children's literature as wholly dominated by adults. Each of our chapters begins with a reminiscence that testifies to children's reading in one way or another, and we also consider the role of adult memories of childhood in adult writing. Such memories are inevitably reconstructions by the remembering adult, but many of their features offer plausible tokens of childhood experience: attention to the appearance and feel of the physical book; vivid recollection of the particular time and place of reading or being read to;[9] indifference to the mediating role of the author;[10] an instinctive assimilation of the historical past to the child reader's present; or an explicitly drawn contrast between the remembered childhood reading and the adult's current understanding.[11]

We see the child's bypassing of the author, and the fusing of ancient practices with personal experience, in the historical novelist Rosemary

---

[8] In *What Books to Lend and What to Give*, written primarily for those involved in the education of non-elite children in parish schools, the novelist Charlotte Yonge lists works of Greek mythology and historical fiction set in antiquity, but does not recommend "Drawing-Room Stories" (including her own *Countess Kate*) because "they deal with a way of life . . . so much out of the line of the ordinary clients of the parish library" (Yonge 1887: 35).

[9] See Rudd 2013: 89 on the importance for children of "rituals of reading (up trees, under bedclothes with torches, comfort eating"), and Ch. 1 on the dialogic nature of children's reading.

[10] See e.g. Eudora Welty's memory that "It had been startling and disappointing to me to find out that story books had been written by *people*, that books were not natural wonders, coming up by themselves like grass" (1984: 5).

[11] For a selection of memories of childhood reading, see Tatar 2009: 205–38.

Sutcliff's recollection of her childhood reading of Kipling's stories about a young centurion in Roman Britain:

Parnesius gave me my first feeling for Roman Britain, filling my small opening mind with a splendour as of distant trumpets, long before I had the least idea what the Roman Empire was all about, and when I pictured Maximus's white buckskin leggings laced with gold as being exactly like the knee-high gaiters with buttons all up the sides, in which my own unwilling legs were encased in the winter. (Sutcliff 1960: 53)

And the Australian novelist David Malouf, whose works include a retelling of the final book of the *Iliad*, offers this highly circumstantial account of how he first heard of the Troy legend.

In 1943, to be precise, in Brisbane, a wartime city, where as a nine-year-old, I heard the Troy story for the first time on a rainy Friday afternoon when we were unable to go out in the playground as usual for our period of tunnel-ball, and our teacher, Miss Findlay, read to us instead. I immediately identified Troy, under the threat of imminent fall, with our own sand-bagged and blacked-out city that was waiting then, with the outcome of the war still unknown, for the Japs to arrive, and my own childish fears with the horrors of that earlier war. On several occasions afterwards, those old emotions rose up and haunted me in the shape of poems. (Malouf 2009: 13)

Works from this period that represent the classical past for children or evoke childhood experience of that past are far too numerous to allow for complete coverage even of the genres on which we primarily focus; our aim is rather to sketch general trajectories, identify persistent challenges and strategies, and highlight particularly telling or interesting examples. In doing so we place texts that are well known and much discussed alongside others, once widely read, that have now dropped out of sight.

Our starting point is the three myth collections produced by Nathaniel Hawthorne in America and Charles Kingsley in England between 1851 and 1855, which represent a new departure in their deliberate reworking of classical myths as enjoyable stories for children. We situate these innovative works in relation to contemporary ideas about childhood and set them against the background of earlier handbooks of mythology for children, which typically focus on the Greco-Roman divinities, carefully identified as "heathen" or as "fabulous," and offer an array of informative (if often selective) detail with little attention to narrative form. Although Hawthorne and Kingsley confront the same culturally problematic elements these earlier texts had to deal with—paganism, sex, violence, and magic—they do so through an assimilation of myth to fairy tale, whose (contested) emergence as a form of children's literature is an important part of the story we tell. Both of these writers inaugurate central and persistent elements of the tradition with which we are concerned; at the same time, their approaches to childhood and to antiquity diverge in significant ways, and the differences between them introduce a set of variables to which we will attend throughout. These include varying formulations of the relationship between childhood and antiquity (in some instances archetypal, universalizing, and transnational, in others historically specific and bound up with national identity), and varying conceptions of the child audience, including different expectations of age, gender, and nationality (though rarely of class).

After a preliminary chapter on Hawthorne and Kingsley, we trace their legacies and other manifestations of the association of children and antiquity, with a particular focus on the end of the nineteenth century and the first half of the twentieth century. These decades saw important developments in thinking about antiquity (with both archaeology and anthropology fostering a turn to prehistory), in the availability and cultural standing of classical education, in views of childhood, in ideas about gender, in children's reading practices, and in the technologies of book production, especially where illustration is concerned. All of these—along with broader geopolitical events, and especially the twentieth century's two world wars—reshaped the representation of antiquity for children.

Our second and third chapters are concerned with the development of a tradition of myth for children. In Chapter 2 we discuss the ongoing reception of Hawthorne's and Kingsley's work, as their books took on the status of classics in their own right, to some extent displacing their ancient sources. We see this status reflected in accounts of children's reading, in the cultural currency of Hawthorne and Kingsley's works, and especially in a continuous stream of new and reissued editions, most of them illustrated, often by distinguished artists of their day. The images in these editions variously support, contest, or bypass the text, shift the balance between adult and child addressees, and reflect changing ideas of how the ancient world should be represented to modern audiences. In Chapter 3, we discuss Hawthorne and Kingsley's successors, the authors and illustrators of new works that present classical mythology to children from the late nineteenth to the mid-twentieth centuries. We pay particular attention to the impact of developments in anthropology and folklore studies on children's myth books, to the new dominance of America in children's book publishing following World War I, to debates about the proper place of myth in modern children's reading, to the role of nostalgia in shaping the presentation of myth for children, and to the ever-increasing role of illustration and the emergence of the picture book as a favored form for the retelling of myth.

In our fourth and fifth chapters, we turn to the historical novel, long viewed both as appropriate entertainment and as a source of education for children. In doing so we also take on works largely addressed to older children than the intended readers of many myth collections; many of the works we discuss would now fall into the category of young adult literature. Children's historical fiction is marked by constant negotiation of the competing claims of historical difference and transhistorical continuity; that continuity is often presumed to underlie the modern child's ability to identify with characters from other times and to profit from the lessons of the past. We explore the issue of identification and the particular ways in which the ancient past is remade in relation to child audiences distinguished first by nationality and then by gender. In Chapter 4 we examine the specifically American inflection of Roman history as depicted in books published in the United States between the two world wars, against the background of British historical fiction. In Chapter 5, we consider the ways in which representations of ancient girlhood during the same period are variously designed to appeal to modern female readers. These two forms of remaking involve somewhat different concerns or projects: the first seeks to connect the child with the classical past through evocations of the national past and present, while the second is largely concerned with the challenge posed to such a connection by the limited female presence in our ancient sources and the limitations on female roles in the ancient world.

In Chapter 6, we move away from children's literature to consider the impact of childhood encounters with antiquity as they are recalled in works addressed to adults and situated within broader reflections on the shapes of individual lives. Heinrich Schliemann and H.D. provide contrasting accounts of the significance of such encounters and the kinds of experiences and achievements they lead to. Their divergent visions recapitulate the contrast between a historical and an archetypal view of antiquity, while also reflecting the gender differences that we discuss in relation to historical fiction. The ramifications of these two conceptions are then traced in a range of modernist writers and thinkers, including Freud, Joyce, H.D., Jane Harrison, Naomi Mitchison, Mary Butts, and Virginia Woolf, with attention to the Greek language as both an educational attainment that marks the transition from childhood to adulthood and as a key to the transition within antiquity from prehistory to history, which may be mapped onto the successive life stages of the modern individual.

Finally, in Chapter 7, we focus on a novella by H.D., *The Hedgehog*, a work that straddles the boundary between children's and adult literature and that thematizes the central issue of the adult's stake in a child's relationship to the classical past. It does so through a story about a girl whose "fundamental referents" are shaped (like Glück's) by her mother's transmission of classical mythology. H.D. presents an idealistic view of the child's relationship to a universal mythical tradition (and its implications for the future), which can be traced back to Hawthorne, but is formulated here specifically in response to World War I. She also explores the question of children's autonomy as they come to terms with the versions of antiquity produced for them by adults.

Our story ends in the mid-twentieth century, with the dropping off of new editions of Hawthorne and Kingsley and the emergence (with the D'Aulaires) of copiously illustrated texts and picture books as the preferred medium for myth. Historical fiction set in the ancient world continues to proliferate, but we are also on the brink of new developments in children's fiction that is based on or somehow incorporates classical material. We conclude with an Epilogue in which we first look back at the tradition of classics in childhood and at what the works we have discussed imply about the kind of child who should be reading about the classical past and about adult desires for that child. We then turn to a brief exploration of recent and current trends; these reflect both a growing uncertainty about the appeal of antiquity to modern children and an ongoing conviction that the classical past is of perennial interest. In contemporary representations of that past for children we find an ever greater stratification of the child audience in terms of age, an increasing embrace of the comic or parodic, the influence of new genres like the comic book and the video game, changing attitudes to the place of sex and violence in children's literature, and increased concern with the treatment not only of gender but of other forms of difference.

1

"Very Capital Reading for Children"

Hawthorne, Kingsley, and the Transformation of Myth into Children's Literature

As a schoolboy at the end of the eighteenth century, the English poet and essayist Leigh Hunt (1784–1859) found pleasure in classical mythology despite an unpromising source.

> But there were three books which I read in whenever I could, and which often got me into trouble. These were Tooke's *Pantheon*, Lempriere's *Classical Dictionary*, and Spence's *Polymetis*, the great folio edition with plates. Tooke was a prodigious favorite with us. I see before me, as vividly now as ever, his Mars and Apollo, his Venus and Aurora, which I was continually trying to copy; the Mars, coming on furiously in his car; Apollo, with his radiant head, in the midst of shades and fountains; Aurora with hers, a golden dawn; and Venus, very handsome, we thought, and not looking too modest, in "a slight cymar" [Dryden, "Cymon and Iphigenia," l. 100]. It is curious how completely the graces of the Pagan theology overcame with us the wise cautions and reproofs that were set against it in the pages of Mr. Tooke. Some years after my departure from school, happening to look at the work in question, I was surprised to find so much of that matter in him. When I came to reflect, I had a sort of recollection that we used occasionally to notice it, as something inconsistent with the rest of the text,—strange, and odd, and like the interference of some pedantic old gentleman.   (Hunt 1850: 131–2)

Hunt's "prodigious favorite" was Andrew Tooke's frequently revised and reprinted translation, first published in 1694[1], of François Pomey's

---

[1] Tooke's authorship of the 1694 translation and other early editions has been questioned; see Treadwell 1985: 290–1.

Pantheum mythicum seu fabulosa deorum historia (Lyons, 1659); on the title page of the 1781 edition Hunt might have read, the work is described in full as *The Pantheon, Representing the Fabulous Histories of the Heathen Gods, and Most Illustrious Heroes; in a Short, Plain, and Familiar Method, by Way of Dialogue. Revised, Corrected, Amended, and Illustrated with new Copper cuts of the several Deities: For the Use of Schools.* This compendium, whose nod to "dialogue" takes the form of a highly artificial conversation between the questioning Palaeophilus and the informative Mystagogus, is organized in encyclopedic fashion around the principal Greco-Roman ("heathen") gods, lesser divinities, and heroes; it firmly identifies ancient beliefs and practices as false and idolatrous, but provides copious and detailed information from a variety of ancient sources, sometimes organized by subheadings such as "Image," "Qualities," and "Actions." Here, for example, is the first paragraph of the entry for Proserpine or Proserpina,[2] which has footnotes citing Virgil, Pausanias, Hesiod, Arnobius, and Eusebius:

> She, who sits next to Pluto, is the Queen of Hell, the Infernal Juno, the Lady (as the Greeks commonly call her) and the most beloved Wife of Pluto, the Daughter of Ceres and Jupiter. She is called both Proserpine and Libera. Jupiter, her Father, begat her, when he was disguised in the Shape of a Bull; and after she was born and grown up, he debauched her himself in the Shape of a Dragon: whence it came to pass, that, in the Mysteries of the Sabazia, a Golden Snake, folded in a Circle, was produced; which, when any were initiated, was usually put into their Bosoms, and received again, when it slid down from them below.   (Tooke 1781: 254)

In what follows, Mystagogus offers a brief account of the abduction and restoration of Proserpine and two interpretations of the myth as an allegory of the natural world. Palaeophilus responds both with questions and with exclamations of sympathy ("O! poor Lady!," 255).

Hunt's experience with Tooke's *Pantheon* points to the perennial resourcefulness of child readers as they make what they wish of the books they meet: their opportunistic selectivity, their indifference to the role of the author, and their particular attunement to images. His recollections and those of others show that a dry schoolbook like Tooke's could at one time seem a diverting alternative to (and respite from) the

---

[2] Where there is a difference between Greek and Roman nomenclature for mythical figures, we follow the usage of the author under discussion.

study of antiquity through the acquisition of the ancient languages.[3] Thomas Keightley (1789–1872), an early folklorist and author of an 1831 mythology which proposed to "initiate" secondary school and university students into a philosophical approach based on German scholarship (1831: v), paints a similar picture when he writes in a later edition of "those blissful days when I drew food for the imagination even from Tooke's Pantheon" and notes that "in writing this volume I had myself and my younger days always in my mind, and thought what would have interested me at the time when I was able to extract pleasure even from such a book as Tooke's Pantheon" (Keightley 1886: viii).

Despite Keightley's hopes of improving on Tooke, the successive editions of his mythology are still essentially handbooks intended for use in schools, where an acquaintance with classical mythology was considered during this period a necessary part of education.[4] It is only in mid-century that we find a transformative turn to works of mythology cast as storytelling and designed to give child readers the pleasure that Hunt and Keightley managed to extract from Tooke: Nathaniel Hawthorne's *A Wonder-Book for Girls and Boys* and *Tanglewood Tales* (1851, 1853), Charles Kingsley's *The Heroes: or, Greek Fairy Tales for My Children* (1855), and their successors and imitators. Hawthorne in particular is generally said to have revolutionized the treatment of myth for children by presenting it as entertainment, rather than as a source of information (on a par with history and geography) whose pleasures are incidental or instrumental.[5] But both Hawthorne and Kingsley gave new impetus and a lasting impact to the idea that classical myths, if properly conceived, have a natural appeal to children. And both advanced the claim that myths are inherently suited to children because they belong to

---

[3] On children's reading in Hunt's day, see Grenby 2011. As late as 1935, "a Hospital Librarian" recalls that his interest in the classics began in "early childhood when Tooke's Pantheon at my mother's knee was the most absorbing and delightful of books" (Compton 1935: 111).

[4] For girls as well as boys: in Jane Austen's *Mansfield Park*, published in 1814, the Bertram sisters boast that by the age of ten they knew "the Roman emperors as low as Severus; besides a great deal of Heathen Mythology" (Austen 1953: 33). Cf. Fletcher 2008: 227, 242. Keightley (1866: v) notes that some of his most enthusiastic readers have been "of the gentler sex" and cites one "young lady" who read his book four times before she turned 16.

[5] Richardson 1979; MacLeod 1995: 115; Donovan 2002; Wadsworth 2000; Horn 2013. Bulfinch's *Age of Fable*, designed for family reading, and first published in 1855, also played an influential role in subsequent presentations of myth (Feldman and Richardson 1972: 506–7).

a childlike time in human history; in doing so, they articulated key assumptions underlying the many efforts to bring together children and antiquity that we explore in the course of this book. At the same time, their visions differed in important ways, presenting a set of variables—pertaining to the relationship between myth and history, to gender, and to national identity—that also shape our discussion.

Antecedents and Beginnings

The identification of myth as children's proper pleasure reading was unquestionably a decisive shift, but it was also the outcome of developments that, over the half century between Hunt's reading of Tooke and Hawthorne's *Wonder-Book*, laid the groundwork for an approach to myth that would at once cater to children's perceived tastes and protect them from the dangers to which Hunt was so happily exposed. We cannot be sure why Tooke, Lempriere, and Spence got Hunt into trouble; the most likely explanation is that they were viewed as a distraction from proper studies focused on the ancient languages.[6] But we can see from the "wise cautions and reproofs" tuned out by Hunt that Tooke's *Pantheon* itself reflected concerns about myth's suitability as reading for modern children.

Children in antiquity undoubtedly heard and read versions of these stories and encountered depictions of mythological subjects in daily life. But given that the classical myths as transmitted in the sources that survived antiquity were not written with children in mind and reflect the values and beliefs of a different era,[7] their suitability for children has been a perennial issue, and every retelling is shaped, whether explicitly or not, by the need to adjust the myths to ever-changing ideas about what children should and should not be exposed to—from Tooke/Pomey's wariness towards heathen "idolatry," to recurrent concerns about sexuality and violence, to present-day discomfort with ancient views of gender, class, and status. Tooke's translation, like its original, reflects

[6] Nicholas Roe goes further, arguing that books like Tooke's were viewed as scandalous for their revolutionary democratization of education (Roe 2003); but he cites no direct evidence for this, and handbooks of mythology were evidently widely used in schools, or at least so their publishers and authors claim (Tooke 1819: v; Keightley 1838: iv).
[7] The discussion in Plato's *Republic* bks. 2–3 makes clear that even in their own day myths might be regarded as both natural and problematic stories for a young audience.

the attitudes of his seventeenth-century milieu both in its concern with the myths' role in supporting pagan religious beliefs and in the freedom with which it refers to sexual activity even when it expresses disapproval. The consequent accessibility of sexual content was in fact one of Tooke's main attractions for Hunt, who relished the introduction to the erotic afforded by subjects such as Venus, "very handsome," and "not looking too modest."[8] Hunt's lifetime, however, spanned an era of increasing constraints (both social and legal) on sexual language and content in texts intended for the general public, and especially in those whose readership might include women and children; we find a growing demand for alternatives that would provide the crucial acquaintance with mythology but be less likely to corrupt—and in particular, for alternatives that could be safely offered to girls as well as boys.[9]

Mary Monsigny's *Mythology, or, a History of the Fabulous Deities of the Ancients: Designed to Facilitate the Study of History, Poetry, Painting, etc.* (1794, first American edition 1809) was intended specifically for "young persons of our sex"; in an introductory note Monsigny explains that she felt an acquaintance with mythology was "absolutely necessary" for the comprehension of works of literature and art, but that she had found no book she could "with propriety put into [girls'] hands."[10] And when in 1806 the novelist and philosopher William Godwin (writing as Edward Baldwin) produced a *Pantheon* intended to remedy Tooke's "imperfections," he made explicit that this book was written "for the use of young persons of both sexes" while suggesting distinct concerns depending on the reader's gender: "I trust that nothing will be found in it, to administer libertinism to the fancy of the stripling, or to sully the whiteness of mind of the purest virgin" (Baldwin 1806: vii). It was perhaps in response to competition from such cautious offerings that Tooke's *Pantheon* was revised in 1810 (the 33rd edition) and again in 1817 with an eye both to changing times and to a changed readership,

---

[8] Hunt elaborates on this topic elsewhere in his *Autobiography* (Hunt 1850: 115, 168–9).

[9] On the history of such censorship and expurgation, see Boyer 1968, Bristow 1977, Hyland and Sammells 1992, Lewis 1976, Perrin 1969.

[10] Monsigny 1794: 1–2. On classical learning and mythology in girls' education in the United States during the late 18th and 19th centuries, see Winterer 2007: 146–55, and on Monsigny's bowdlerization, see Winterer 2007: 152. Aaron Burr's classically educated daughter Theodosia Burr Alston thought of writing her own myth book for children, but seems never to have completed it; see letters from Burr to his daughter, Van Doren 1929: 117–65; Winterer 2007:115.

dropping the dialogue form, adding study questions, and changing the wording of the more risqué passages. The 1817 Baltimore edition carries the subtitle, *Revised for a classical course of education, and adapted for the use of students of every age and of either sex*, and promises "chaste diction" that will make the book useful for both "young ladies and young gentlemen" at a time when "classical learning has of late become an object of considerable importance in female education" (Tooke 1825: iii–iv).[11] Jupiter is here said to have "imposed upon" Alcmena, not "defiled" her, and to have "deceived," not "debauched" Calisto (Tooke 1781: 14–15; 1825: 27–8); and instead of being "passionately in love with Cyparissus, another very pretty boy" (Tooke 1781: 33), Apollo is merely "passionately fond of Cyparissus, another boy" (Tooke 1825: 43). Hunt's own favorite, Venus, rather than being "infamous for so many Whoredoms, Rapes, and Incests" and "Mistress and President of Obscenity" (Tooke 1781: 108) is "mistress, president and patron of all manner of licentiousness" (Tooke 1825: 100).

The continuing presentation of myth in this period primarily as useful instruction may reflect a prevailing prejudice against the fantastical in children's literature. Collections of French fairy tales—popular with adults in the aristocratic circles of the seventeenth century—had been translated into English starting in the early eighteenth century. Some of these then appeared in versions specifically for children and (along with traditional English folk tales) in inexpensive chapbooks that aimed at a popular audience but were widely read by the young.[12] It is clear that fairy tales continued to be available to child readers in the late eighteenth and early nineteenth century;[13] as M. O. Grenby notes, "many of the condemnations of children's use of fairy tales are premised on the proposition that children avidly read them."[14] But during these decades there was a strong current of opinion, influenced by the educational theories of Locke and Rousseau and reinforced by religious concerns, that children's reading should not include fairy tales and other imaginative forms but only factual and morally uplifting material rooted in reason and everyday experience.[15] Critics found fault with fairy tales

---

[11] See Winterer 2007: 146–55.
[12] Darton 1982: 85–91; Kinnell 1995: 28–9; Grenby 2011: 102–11.
[13] Jackson 1989: 196–7.   [14] Grenby 2011: 105.
[15] Darton 1982: chs. 9–11; Jackson 1989: ch. 7; Avery and Kinnell 1995.

and folk tales as frightening, misleading, excessively adult in theme, unedifying, and vulgar; and although myth was largely exempt from the last two charges because of its association with the cultural and educational canon of classical literature, its pagan, fantastical, and horrific elements might raise similar concerns.[16]

Critics of imaginative literature had their opponents, some of them influenced by early Romantic views of folk tale and folk poetry as the proper reading for children;[17] among these was Charles Lamb, whose *The Adventures of Ulysses*, an extended retelling of most of Homer's *Odyssey* published in 1808, was an important forerunner of later attempts to turn classical texts into recreational reading for children.[18] His publisher, William Godwin, had two years before in his own pseudonymous myth collection championed the place of imagination in children's reading as the "great engine of morality" (Baldwin 1806: x) and attacked Tooke and others whose combined "dullness" and "malice" had made the subject "repulsive" to the young (vi). Godwin made a point, however, of distinguishing Greek myths from "the unsubstantial creations of a fairy region" (v), and as publisher, he urged Lamb to remove some of the *Odyssey*'s more lurid supernatural features, such as the blinding of the giant Cyclops, citing the squeamishness of the parents to whom he must necessarily seek to sell his publications.[19] Lamb resisted most of Godwin's suggestions; but he did also go out of his way to portray Ulysses as a morally exemplary figure, and he framed the book as a sequel to the Abbé Fénelon's educational *Adventures of Telemachus* (published in France in 1699 and immediately translated into English), a highly popular work that turned Telemachus' quest for his father into a series of instructive visits to diverse lands undertaken under the tutelage of Minerva disguised as Mentor.[20]

The opposition to imaginative literature for children was an even stronger factor in America, where publishers (in what Anne Scott McLeod

---

[16] See Watson 2009: 14–25 and works cited in n. 15.

[17] Jackson 1989: ch. 9; Kümmerling-Meibauer 2008; O'Malley 2003: 126–8; Watson 2009; Richardson 2009.

[18] In a famous letter to Coleridge written in 1802, Lamb deplores contemporary works that convey "knowledge insignificant and vapid" and asks, "Think what you would have been now, if instead of being fed with Tales and old wives' fables in childhood, you had been crammed with geography and natural history?" (Marrs 1975: 81–2); see also Watson 2009: 25–6.

[19] Marrs 1975: 278.   [20] Murnaghan 2015b and bibliography cited there.

identifies as a period of "sharpened nationalism" from the 1820s on) were relying less on reprints of English children's books and turning increasingly to the largely didactic work of American writers.[21] One of the central figures was Samuel Goodrich, best known for the Peter Parley books, which sought to offer young children information in an appealing and age-appropriate form.[22] Goodrich was strongly opposed to fantasy and fairy tale, and most of his titles (*The Tales of Peter Parley about America*, 1827; *Peter Parley's Method of Telling about Geography*, 1830) promise the acquisition of general knowledge.[23] His publication history is complicated, but among the works ascribed to him (as copyright holder) was the 1832 *A Book of Mythology for Youth, Containing Descriptions of the Deities, Temples, Sacrifices and Superstitions of the Ancient Greeks and Romans*.[24] Goodrich's book, like those of Tooke and Monsigny, is essentially an instructive handbook, organized by types of divinity and by individual divinities, and with little attention to narrative; it too begins by explaining the origins of idolatry and of pagan belief in "fabulous divinities" (Goodrich 1832: 11).

Goodrich goes even further than Monsigny and the revised Tooke in avoiding "the indelicacies which are introduced into almost every book of Mythology" (vi). But his book is designed to please children as well as to provide them with an education that is free from such indelicacies; he presents it as "an entertaining little volume" (vi) and seeks to make it "acceptable to young readers" by using "a familiar style," and including both "many engravings" and "a variety of curious anecdotes" (v). Meanwhile, his views on imaginative literature were by no means universal,

---

[21] MacLeod 1994: 87–98; cf. MacLeod 1995: 106–14; Marcus 2008: ch. 1; Avery 1994: 65–92.

[22] Goodrich also published an annual gift book, *The Token*, to which assorted writers including Nathaniel Hawthorne contributed sketches. On Hawthorne's relationship to Goodrich (he acted as ghostwriter, with his sister Elizabeth, for one of the Peter Parley books), see Wadsworth 2000.

[23] Marcus 2008: 21–30; Avery 1994: 78–81. In his autobiography, Goodrich describes his own childhood dislike of fairy tales, which he found false, frightening, and conducive to wickedness (Goodrich 1856: 166).

[24] The popularity of Goodrich's Peter Parley books led to the appearance of a large number of false "Parleys," especially in England, some of which Goodrich then republished (Marcus 2008: 25). In the appendix to his autobiography, Goodrich identifies *Peter Parley's Mythology of Greece and Rome* as an English counterfeit (Goodrich 1856: 551); *A Book of Mythology for Youth* is not listed among the genuine ones (537–43), but the copyright is in his name.

and two American contemporaries recall Godwin's defense of the imagination and further anticipate later developments in the presentation of myth for children: although both Eliza Robbins (*Elements of Mythology*, 1830) and William Darlington (*A Catechism of Mythology*, 1832) reiterate the educational importance of a knowledge of mythology and the necessity of avoiding "licentious and indelicate stories" (Darlington 1832: v), they also see myth as a means of developing the child's imagination, and Darlington cites entertainment as one of his chief goals.

By the middle of the century, the resistance to imaginative works for children had slackened considerably, though America continued to lag behind Britain in this respect. This change was partly a result of shifting attitudes, partly the result of accommodations that made fairy tales more acceptable to a middle-class audience.[25] The Brothers Grimm, who had originally seen the stories they collected as having "the same purity that makes children appear so wondrous and blessed to us" without being *for* children,[26] rewrote and revised their work several times to produce narratives increasingly accessible to children in both style and content.[27] A selection of their work first appeared in England in 1823–6 as *German Popular Stories* and was well received; the translator, Edgar Taylor, not only selected but revised, removing the more violent or otherwise problematic episodes.[28] Sir Henry Cole, under the pseudonym "Felix Summerly," began in 1843 to publish a series of well-designed illustrated books which he intended as a direct counter to the works of "Peter Parley"; these included a number of familiar fairy tales, but with an increased didactic emphasis; and in 1846 the first English translations of Hans Christian Andersen's literary fairy tales appeared.[29] It was in this

[25] On the development of a "safe place for fantasy" specifically in the context of "middle-class ideology and pedagogy," see O'Malley 2003: 124–35. On the complicated history of the fairy tale as literature for children, and especially on developments in the 19th century, see Darton 1982: 85–101, 214–15, 241–2; Jackson 1989: 64–6, 116–17, 196–7, 219–23, 236–7; Avery 1994: 123–6; Butts 1995: 86–90; Briggs and Butts 1995: 137–40; Schacker 2003.

[26] From the preface to volume 1 of the first edition, translated and cited by Tatar (1987: 206).

[27] On the evolution of the Grimms' work see Tatar 1987: esp. ch. 1; Zipes 1988; Blamires 2003: 72–83. The success of the Grimms encouraged not only the collection of folk tales in other countries but also the rewriting of these stories for children (Kümmerling-Meibauer 2008: 189–90).

[28] On the nature and effect of Taylor's transformation and "domestication" of the Grimms, see Schacker 2003: ch. 2.

[29] Andersen 1846a, 1846b, 1846c, 1846d. See Butts 1995: 87–91; Darton 1982: ch. 12, pp. 233–5; Jackson 1989: chs. 9, 10, esp. pp. 219–21, 225–8; O'Malley 2003: 124–35.

more favorable climate that the two myth collections that most clearly anticipate Hawthorne and Kingsley in their adoption of an engaging narrative form were published in England.

J. M. Neale's *Stories from Heathen Mythology and Greek History* (1847) justifies itself as a necessary prelude to later education, but in place of a catalogue of gods, demigods, and heroes, offers its readers a series of stories, identified as such, beginning with "The Story of Perseus and the Gorgons," and drawing on Homer, Herodotus, Greek tragedy, and other ancient sources. Neale was a High Church Anglican priest and a prolific church historian, translator, and writer of sermons, now best remembered as the author of the carol "Good King Wenceslas."[30] In his efforts to present myths as appealing stories, he is hampered by the same issue that Tooke's *Pantheon* seeks to address through authorial admonitions: the myths his readers need to know because of their importance for the understanding of both Greek and Latin, without which "no *man* among the upper classes can be properly educated" (italics original), and English literature (which even girls will read) are pagan falsehoods (Neale 1847: 2–3), manifesting a "disturbed" form of "truth and beauty" (vii–viii).

Beyond the necessity of understanding the classical references which authors have regrettably included in their literary works, Neale manages to find other advantages in reading these dangerous tales: to understand myth is to know the darkness over which the Early Church triumphed, and so to understand what we have gained (4); some of the stories, though unhappily misunderstood by "the common people" as factually true, are really parables intended by the wise to pass down truths lost after Babel (4–5). In keeping with this understanding of myth as in origin allegorical, he tries to provide at the end of each story an interpretation that (whether intended by its authors or not) will allow us "to turn it to good account."

Neale retells the myths in a straightforward, mildly archaizing style, selecting and even introducing elements that will forward his Christianizing aims. In the Perseus story, Polydectes is not Perseus' tormentor but a kind and generous ruler whose affectionate support Perseus seeks to repay by the gift of Medusa's death. He responds to the arrival of Danae

---

[30] For a memoir of Neale's life, see Towle 1906.

and her son on Seriphos in terms that recall the other "good king" whose story Neale famously told:

"Bid them come in," said good king Polydectes; "they shall fare no worse than we do. Or stay, they are strangers; I will go myself and comfort them: it is a sad thing to be a stranger in an unknown country." (10–11)

This noble figure then enables the allegorical interpretation that Neale gives the story.

This is, when rightly explained, a very true story; and what is stranger, it is or ought to be true of every one of those who read it. We have all of us a Medusa, against whom we are bound to go forth, and whom we must kill, if we would not have her kill us.... And why are we bound to fight manfully against ourselves? Why, but for the same reason as the hero of my story had? To shew our love to the Great King That made us His own when we were infants, and has all our lives long fed, and guarded us. (18–19)

But even after he has purified the myths through morally instructive readings and demonstrations that they prefigure a Christian truth, Neale remains troubled by one "greatest danger," that the presence of "so much truth and so much beauty in the fables of a vile and false religion" will lead to an ecumenical conclusion:

that, after all, a man's faith cannot matter so very much; that there is some truth in all forms of belief, and that, so long as a man lives a virtuous life according to his creed, it is no great matter what that creed is. (186)

It is hard to imagine a more conflicted retelling of myth.

No such anxiety reveals itself in two contemporary translations of a myth collection that, like the Grimms' and Andersen's stories, was rapidly domesticated as recommended reading for English-speaking children. The historian B. G. Niebuhr's *Griechische Heroengeschichten*, based on stories he wrote for his young son while stationed in Rome as Prussian ambassador, was published posthumously in 1842. Niebuhr reports in a letter that the "free and picturesque style" he adopted made the myths "as exciting as poetry" for his son, who read them with "cries of joy."[31] His manner of telling reflects the age of his reader (who was not quite 5 when Niebuhr began to write): "The Voyage of the Argonauts" begins with the words "There was a king in Greece whose name was Athamas" (Niebuhr 1843b: 1)

---

[31] Letter to Mme Hensler, Rome, 19 January 1822 (Niebuhr et al. 1854: 417).

and omits or glosses over the more problematic episodes, such as Medea's murder of her brother. Both in this story and in the one that follows we get some light moralizing of a kind that seems especially aimed at children. The narrator comments approvingly that Phrixus and Helle were "very good, and loved each other very much" (1), and we learn that Hercules, who commendably "ate much roast meat and bread but no dainties" (23–4) and was generally "very good-natured,"

had only the one fault, that he became furious when he was angry, and then he did bad things, though afterwards he wept sorely for what he had done, but it came too late, and could not undo what he had done. Alcmena and Amphitryon had not punished him for it when he was little. (24)

Niebuhr's collection was translated into English the following year, first by Lucie Duff Gordon, as *Stories of the Gods and Heroes of Greece* and then, as *Heroic Tales of Ancient Greece*, by "Felix Summerly" (Henry Cole), the champion of imaginative literature for children.[32] As an epigraph to his translation, Cole quotes an article from the *Westminster Review* in which the historian George Grote declares that "More interesting narratives for boy as well as man, no book of fairy tales can supply" (G.G. 1843: 285–6, Niebuhr 1843b: ii), and Cole too asserts that myth is as intensely appealing as fairy tales to very young children:

These tales have been found to have great charms for a child, and during their translation they were listened to with as wrapt attention as fairy tales by a little girl of five years of age, who had never before heard a word of mythology.
(Niebuhr 1843b: v–vi)

In emphasizing the "charms" of myth—for girls as well as boys—and in comparing the attraction of myth to that of fairy tales, Cole here anticipates the transformative developments in the presentation of mythology to children that were to follow in the next decade.

Old Greek Fairy Tales

While Cole sees myths as resembling fairy tales in their capacity to enchant child readers, Hawthorne and Kingsley treat classical mythology as itself a species of fairy tale and as peculiarly suited to children. Both

---

[32] Niebuhr 1843a, 1843b; Duff Gordon's name does not appear on her translation; her mother Sarah Austin, an established translator, is named as editor.

explicitly identify the myths they tell as fairy tales and recast those myths in ways that support the comparison, capitalizing on the contemporary popularity of fairy tales and their position within the lucrative and expanding market for children's books on both sides of the Atlantic.[33]

In Hawthorne's case, the affinity with fairy tales is advertised in the title of his first myth book, *A Wonder-Book for Girls and Boys*, which offers an enticing suggestion of the pleasures of fantastic literature in order to attract readers for what he hoped would be a profitable venture.[34] As early as 1838, Hawthorne had discussed with Henry Wadsworth Longfellow a collaborative book of fairy tales that he thought might "make a great hit, and entirely revolutionize the whole system of juvenile literature" and also "put money in our purses."[35] But a notebook entry for the same year ("Pandora's box for a child's story") indicates that he was also thinking about the myths as a subject, and in a letter of 1846 he mentioned his longstanding "idea of some stories to be taken out of the cold moonshine of classical mythology, and modernized, or perhaps gothicized, so that they may be felt by children of these days."[36] This thought had by the spring of 1851 become a definite plan, as he wrote to the publisher J. T. Fields:

I mean to write . . . a book of stories made up of classical myths . . . As a framework I shall have a young college student telling these stories to his cousins, brother and sister, during his vacations, sometimes at the fireside, sometimes in the woods and dells . . . Unless I greatly mistake, these old fictions will work up admirably for the purpose; and I shall aim at substituting a tone in some degree Gothic or romantic, or any such tone as may best please myself, instead of the classic coldness, which is as repellant as the touch of marble. The book, if it comes out of my mind as I see it now, ought to have pretty wide success amongst young people; and, of course, I shall purge out all the old heathen wickedness, and put in a moral wherever practicable.[37]

---

[33] For a critique of this shift of genre, see Richardson 1979; on Hawthorne's frame story as reflecting 19th-century fairy stories rather than traditional folk tales, see Donovan 2002. On the rapid growth of children's book publication in America in the second third of the 19th century, see Marcus 2008: 16–31; on developments in Britain, see Briggs and Butts 1995: 162–5.

[34] In a letter to Horatio Bridge, Hawthorne describes his title as "an *ad captandum* one"—one designed to take in ignorant hearers (Bridge 1893: 127). Hawthorne's children's books were generally more profitable than his works for adults (Laffrado 1992: 135). On the role of writing for children in Hawthorne's career, see Sánchez-Eppler 2004.

[35] Pearce 1972: 298.

[36] Letter to Evert Duyckinck, Apr. 15, 1846 (Hawthorne 1885b: 153).

[37] Cited by the recipient in Fields 1900: 59. See also Hawthorne 1985: 436–7.

The book appeared later that same year with a preface declaring that "The author has long been of opinion that many of the classical myths were capable of being rendered into very capital reading for children" (Hawthorne 1982: 1163).[38] The identification with fairy tales is made clear in the frame story: the internal narrator, a Williams College sophomore with the luminous name of Eustace Bright, turns to myths when he has exhausted his supply of fairy tales; these myths, he says, are "the nursery-tales that were made for the amusement of our great old grandmother, the Earth, when she was a child in frock and pin-a-fore" (1168).[39] Hawthorne further evokes the atmosphere of the fairy tale by giving Bright's young listeners names he explicitly identifies as suited to fairies (and that clearly recall the fairies of *A Midsummer Night's Dream*): Primrose, Cowslip, Squash Blossom, etc. (1166). The book contains six discrete myths (indebted to Ovid and other ancient sources, though more immediately to Charles Anthon's widely influential *Classical Dictionary*, first published in 1841[40]) with titles such as "The Golden Touch" (Midas), "The Three Golden Apples" (Hercules and Atlas), and "The Miraculous Pitcher" (Baucis and Philemon). The sequel that followed two years later, *Tanglewood Tales* (named after the country house in western Massachusetts where *A Wonder-Book* is set), contains another six, including one of Odysseus' adventures ("Circe's Palace") extracted from the *Odyssey* and treated as a separate tale. Here the frame is dropped, but in his preface Hawthorne continues the fiction that Bright is the teller of these tales.[41]

The myths in both volumes are chosen for the resemblance of their plots to fairy tales, not only through the presence of magic, but also because of certain familiar narrative elements: the prohibition, the wish gone wrong, the mysterious helper, the miraculous object, the witch, the monster. These magical elements are presented in the spirit of playful delight that the books are designed above all to elicit, as in this

---

[38] References for both of Hawthorne's myth books are to the 1982 Library of America edition.

[39] On the role of this frame story see Laffrado 1992, Donovan 2002, Horn 2013.

[40] On Anthon's *Classical Dictionary* and the sources from which he compiled it, see Sypher 2015: 81–94; on Hawthorne's use of Anthon, see esp. McPherson 1969.

[41] On the change in the narrator–author relationship between Hawthorne's two books, see Baym 1973 and Laffrado 1992: 66–131.

account of the slippers given to Perseus by Quicksilver (Hawthorne's translation of Mercury).

So Perseus proceeded to put one of the slippers on, while he laid the other on the ground by his side. Unexpectedly, however, this other slipper spread its wings, fluttered up off the ground, and would probably have flown away, if Quicksilver had not made a leap, and luckily caught it in the air . . .

When Perseus had got on both of these wonderful slippers, he was altogether too buoyant to tread on earth. Making a stop or two, lo and behold! upward he popt into the air, high above the heads of Quicksilver and the Nymphs, and found it very difficult to clamber down again.   (1181–2)

Hawthorne's books were generally well received on both sides of the Atlantic,[42] but one British reader, Charles Kingsley, found them distasteful and countered with another widely read and influential retelling, *The Heroes: or, Greek Fairy Tales for My Children* (1855). Kingsley, a British clergyman, historian, novelist, poet, and amateur naturalist, now best known for his later children's book, *The Water-Babies*, had written several historical novels, one of them (*Hypatia*) set in antiquity; his poems include a version in English dactylic hexameters of the story of Andromeda.[43] An early biographer claims that Kingsley found Hawthorne's works "distressingly vulgar" and it seems likely that he was put off by their irreverent treatment of classical material.[44] In a letter to Hawthorne's publishers he describes himself as covering some of the same ground as Hawthorne, but in a "more classical fashion."[45]

Kingsley's book differs from Hawthorne's in its narrative mode—he represents himself as the narrator and his own children as his listeners (without Hawthorne's elaborate frame story, though still evoking a vision of myth as transmitted orally between friends and family members)—and in its selection of material: rather than giving a series of self-contained highlights of Greek myth, he tells in full the stories of three heroes, Perseus,

[42] For contemporary reviews see Idol and Jones 1994: 179–83, 235–9.

[43] On Kingsley's career as a Victorian "public intellectual" (256), especially in relation to his historical fiction, see Goldhill 2011: chs. 6, 7.

[44] Margaret Farrand Thorp (who had access to a wide range of Kingsley material including family letters) describes his reaction to Hawthorne's work in these words (Thorp 1937: 170), which many subsequent accounts of Kingsley's writing of *The Heroes* cite without reference.

[45] Kingsley's motives may have been in part financial; *The Heroes* was to come out in time for the Christmas gift sales and Kingsley's communications with publishers in both Britain and America show an interest in the book's prospects for earning (Klaver 2006: 410).

Jason, and Theseus. But Kingsley is even more explicit than Hawthorne in making the identification with fairy tales: the subtitle of his book is *Greek Fairy Tales for My Children*, and in his introduction he describes the Greeks as his "old friends" who come to tell the children "some of their old fairy-tales, which they loved when they were young like you" (Kingsley 1859: xi). Although his focus is on heroes, he chooses three cycles in which fairy-tale elements are prominent, and begins his first story, the tale of Perseus, with the evocative words "Once upon a time there were two princes who were twins" (1).

This shared strategy of assimilating Greek myths to fairy tales is at once an implicit defense and a form of advertisement. Like the title of Hawthorne's first book, it positions both writers on the side of fantasy at a time when, as we have noted, imaginative literature for children had gained new acceptance, and children were regarded as both a natural and an unproblematic audience for fairy tales. Since fairy tales had been widely written or rewritten with a child audience in mind, and since the fairy world was at this point associated with Romantic ideas of childhood innocence, the description of myth as fairy tale reassures adults that these books will not include anything inappropriate for children.[46] This comparison may also be a way of palliating the fact that these stories belong to a pagan religious tradition. If they are merely fairy tales (and Kingsley suggests that this is really what they were for the Greeks as well as for us) then the issue of serious belief does not arise.

Hawthorne and Kingsley, however, make still more of the comparison. Both of them suggest that myths conceived of as fairy tales are particularly suited to children because myth itself belongs to a childlike stage in human history. Hawthorne's Eustace Bright claims to be telling nursery tales that stem from the childhood of the Earth; in his preface, Kingsley explains that "while they were young and simple [the Greeks] loved fairy tales, as you do now" (1859: xviii). In making this claim, these authors elaborate what has been a recurrent rationale for the long and varied tradition of bringing together children and antiquity that they themselves helped to foster.

---

[46] On contemporary fairy literature and the adult interest in fairies see Donovan 2002: 24–5. An unsigned review by H. F. Chorley compares Hawthorne's work to that of Hans Christian Andersen and speaks of its appeal to all ages (Idol and Jones 1994: 182).

In asserting that the Greek myths are natural reading for children because they are the products of a childlike time, Hawthorne and Kingsley both reflect what was by the mid-nineteenth century (in Daniel Hoffman's words) "a commonplace made attractive both by Romantic idealization of the child and by progressive theories of cultural evolution."[47] The period was marked by a widespread identification between the life of the individual, beginning with childhood as a distinct phase, and the course of history.[48] But this identification took many forms in accord with individual interests and allegiances, and there were significant differences between Romantic and progressive formulations of the idea; these differences are mirrored in Hawthorne and Kingsley, who start from different conceptions both of the childlike setting in which the myths originated and of the kind of childhood that setting resembles.

According to Hawthorne's version, which is rooted in Romanticism, the myths emanate from an idealized golden age, "the pure childhood of the world," that predates any known civilization, including that of the Greeks.[49] When Mr Pringle, the classically educated father of some of his listeners, complains that Eustace Bright's exuberant versions depart too far from their classical models, Bright responds that the Greeks did not create their myths but inherited and distorted them.

My own opinion is, that the Greeks, by taking possession of these legends (which were the immemorial birthright of mankind,) and putting them into shapes of indestructible beauty, indeed, but cold and heartless, have done all subsequent ages an incalculable injury.   (1255)

A similar point occurs in the preface of A Wonder-Book, where Hawthorne stresses in his own voice that the myths are a universal possession.

---

[47] Hoffman 1964: 199.

[48] For "a comparison with the life cycle of the individual" as "the most common metaphor used by Victorians in discussing the process of historical development," see Bowler 1989: 10, and for further discussion of this "pervasive paradigm" (280), Culler 1985; Rowland 2012: 25–157.

[49] On Romantic conceptions of childhood, which originated with such thinkers as Locke, Rousseau, and Herder, and were notably developed in England by Wordsworth, Coleridge, Blake, and Lamb, and in America by Hawthorne's friend Bronson Alcott and the theologian Horace Bushnell, see Plotz 2001; Brown 2004: 145; Mintz 2004: 76–7; Cunningham 2005: 69–72; Kümmerling-Meibauer 2008; Rowland 2012; McGavran 2012. On the continuing impact of Romantic conceptions on children's literature throughout the 19th and 20h centuries and into the present day, McGavran 1991, 1999; Rose 1993.

No epoch of time can claim a copyright in these immortal fables...they are legitimate subjects for every age to clothe with its own garniture of manners and sentiments, and to imbue with its own morality.   (1163)

Hawthorne's sidelining of Greek civilization is in keeping with Romantic ideas of children as identified with nature and the primitive. The primordial age in which the myths originated belongs to the past, but an unsituated, essentialized past that is everyone's heritage and that is accessed, not through particular texts, but through the mentality of childhood, which recreates its spirit. According to Bright, "children are now the only representatives of the men and women of that happy era; and therefore it is that we must raise the intellect and fancy to the level of childhood, in order to re-create the original myth" (1310). Addressing a child audience does not mean generating simplified half-truths, but rather achieving a more complete and authentic vision, not writing down, but writing up.

Hawthorne makes this point while also addressing the problem of mythology's unsuitable subject matter. In the preface to *Tanglewood Tales*, he presents himself as Eustace Bright's editor and reports a conversation between them in which he raises the issue.

These old legends, so brimming over with everything that is most abhorrent to our Christianized moral sense—some of them so hideous, others so melancholy and miserable, amid which the Greek Tragedians sought their themes, and moulded them into the sternest forms of grief that ever the world saw;—was such material the stuff that children's playthings should be made of! How were they to be purified? How was the blessed sunshine to be thrown into them?   (1310)

Bright's answer is that elements unsuitable to children are not really intrinsic to the myths.

But Eustace told me that these myths were the most singular things in the world, and that he was astonished, whenever he began to relate one, by the readiness with which it adapted itself to the childish purity of his auditors. The objectionable characteristics seem to be a parasitical growth, having no essential connection with the original fable. They fall away and are thought of no more, the instant he puts his imagination in sympathy with the innocent little circle, whose wide-open eyes are fixed so eagerly upon him. Thus the stories (not by any strained effort of the narrator's, but in harmony with their inherent germ) transform themselves, and reassume the shapes they might be supposed to possess in the pure childhood of the world.   (1310)

Myths here acquire independent agency, as they spontaneously recapture their true form when redirected to their natural audience. The modern

author is occluded, becoming simply a reflex of his auditors, the astonished observer of a process that he facilitates by entering into the
imagination of his audience but does not himself control. This reflects
in part a common conception of children's literature for, as Karin
Lesnik-Oberstein observes, "children's literature is often spoken of as if
it has been written by children expressing their needs, emotions, and
experiences."[50] But in this case, the denial of authorship is also the denial
of history: the revision of material from the past to meet the needs of a
particular modern audience is reconceived as the recovery of timeless
lost originals, in keeping with a Romantic conception of children as
mediators, prophets, and poets of what adults have lost and hope to
regain: the divine, the natural world, the golden age.

Kingsley's vision, by contrast, is tied to a view of history that is not
cyclical and recurrent but linear and progressive. The childlike era in
which the myths arose is identified specifically with an early phase of
Greek culture that also corresponds to a stage in the development of all
nations. "While they were young and simple [the Greeks] loved fairy
tales, as you do now. All nations do so when they are young" (1859:
xviii). For him, childhood is not the idyllic state that it is for Eustace
Bright; it is primitive as well as primal, and in their early days nations
display the faults as well as the virtues of children:

For nations begin at first by being children like you, though they are made up of
grown men. They are children at first like you—men and women with children's
hearts; frank, and affectionate, and full of trust, and teachable, and loving to see
and learn all the wonders round them; and greedy also, too often, and passionate
and silly, as children are.   (xii)

Accordingly, Kingsley finds in the Greeks a mixture of merits and
limitations. He stresses as the reason children should read the myths the
debt modern people owe to the Greeks' many accomplishments, a debt
that pervades every aspect of their cultural and intellectual lives and
extends, because the New Testament is written in Greek, to the Christian
religion that he and his presumed readers share (vii–ix).[51] Kingsley

---

[50] Lesnik-Oberstein 1999: 23.
[51] On Kingsley's role in promoting a progressive vision allied specifically with liberal
Anglicanism and closely associated with Thomas Arnold, see Bowler 1989: 56–7.

declares his own love for the Greeks and assures his readers that even though the Greeks were heathens, God loved them too:

For you must not fancy, children, that because these old Greeks were heathens, therefore God did not care for them, and taught them nothing... For Jesus Christ, remember, is the Light who lights every man who comes into the world.
(xiii–xiv)

In spite of their polytheism the moral teachings of myth are unfailingly wise and noble:

there are no fairy tales like these old Greek ones, for beauty, and wisdom, and truth, and for making children love noble deeds and trust in God to help them through... The stories are not all true, of course, not half of them; you are not simple enough to fancy that; but the meaning of them is true, and true forever, and that is—"Do right, and God will help you."   (xix–xx)

In Kingsley's progressive view of historical development, the age of Greek myth is a phase that humanity has outgrown, especially with the coming of Christianity. Children can enjoy and benefit from the myths that arose at that time, and may find in them an especially congenial medium for simple moral lessons, but will also move on to more advanced encounters with classical culture. This is clear from the opening words of his preface:

My dear children,
Some of you have heard already of the old Greeks; and all of you, as you grow up, will hear more and more of them. Those of you who are boys will, perhaps, spend a great deal of time in reading Greek books; and the girls, though they may not learn Greek, will be sure to come across a great many stories taken from Greek history, and to see, I may say every day, things that we would not have had if it had not been for those old Greeks.   (vii)

Kingsley anticipates that his readers, as they move into new stages of their own lives, will acquire a deeper knowledge both of the Greeks themselves and of their contributions to modern culture. But addressing them in their current state, he is as open as Hawthorne about the deliberate rewriting required if the myths are going to send the right message. When introducing the Argonauts and their quest for the Golden Fleece, he suggests that the ancient sources paint their motives as purely material: "some say that it was to win gold" (71). But after adducing a list of ancient and modern examples (including Christ, the Spartans at Thermopylae, Socrates, New World explorers, and "the ladies who went out last year to drudge in the hospitals of the East") to prove that "the noblest deeds that have been done on earth have not been done for gold" (71–2), he declares his intention to remake the ancient myth in accord with his own values: "Therefore we will believe—why should we not?—of these same Argonauts of old, that they too were noble men," a position expressed even more cavalierly when he begins his narrative, "And what was that first Golden Fleece? I do not know, or care" (73). With his "some say," Kingsley projects a reductive and amoral account of the original myth (in which the Argonauts are not generally motivated by pure greed) all the better to allegorize it: "for each of us has a Golden Fleece to seek, and a wild sea to sail over ere we reach it, and dragons to fight ere it be ours" (73). Later in "The Argonauts," he suggests his own stories' role in eliciting such heroic behavior when he revises the received account of Orpheus and the Sirens; Kingsley's Orpheus does not rescue the Argonauts from the Sirens simply by singing louder and better, he gives them "the song of Perseus"—with which Kingsley's book began— and they respond not just to the music but to the story: "We will be men like Perseus, and we will dare and suffer to the last" (159). Less overtly, the myths are given a biblical coloration that reinforces the Greek world's anticipation of Christianity, as when we hear that, before the arrival of Jason, Phrixus could find no one to retrieve his fleece "for the man and the time were not come" (76).

These different conceptualizations of myth's relationship to history, and of children as the audience of myth, correlate with different modes of retelling. Hawthorne draws the myths into the sphere of their natural child auditors with versions ostensibly shaped by the interactions of a childlike narrator with a group of high-spirited middle-class contemporary children at play in a series of idyllic natural settings. The independence from the ancient sources that Bright defends to Mr Pringle is openly linked to the bold imaginative freedom that was for the Romantics a prized feature of childhood: we are told that Bright's mind was "in a free and happy state" very different from "the trained diligence of maturer years" (1193) and that he "disregarded all classical authorities, whenever the vagrant audacity of his imagination impelled him to do so" (1168).[52]

---

[52] The connections between Hawthorne's subversion of classical authorities and his aim of educating his readers in a form of spirituality distinct from Puritanism and rooted in nature and the imagination are explored in Resinski 2009, 2011a, 2011b.

Bright's stories are directly inspired by the landscapes in which they are told: the story of Midas' Golden Touch "had come into his mind, as he lay looking upward into the depths of a tree, and observing how the touch of Autumn had transmuted every one of its green leaves into what resembled the purest gold" (1194).

As he reworks the myths, Bright often tailors them to his audience by turning them into stories about children. This happens most pointedly in the version of the Pandora myth that appears in A Wonder-Book, which is also assimilated to the biblical story of Adam and Eve.[53] Epimetheus and Pandora are young playmates living in a golden age that is equated with the Garden of Eden, as the story's title, "The Paradise of Children," signals. This golden age is a literal "childhood of the world": in those days, he tells us,

everybody was a child. There needed no fathers and mothers, to take care of the children; because there was no danger, nor trouble of any kind, and no clothes to be mended, and there was always plenty to eat and drink.   (1215)

Furthermore, the children in this primal world "never quarreled among themselves; neither had they any crying-fits; nor, since time first began, had a single one of these little mortals ever gone apart into a corner and sulked!" (1216). The inevitable fall is the result of childish naughtiness and curiosity rather than adult sinfulness, brought about by Pandora's "vexation" at not knowing what is in the box, exacerbated by too much idleness; the transposition of the original myth into the realm of childhood facilitates that falling away of objectionable elements that occurs (Bright insists) when the myths are told to children.[54] In other myths, the transgressions even of evil adults are cheerfully assimilated to childishness. The villagers in the Baucus and Philemon story who teach their children to be rude to strangers are "naughty." The misdeeds of figures like Medea or King Minos are often labeled "mischief"; the terrible monsters whom they unleash are described as their pets.

---

[53] For the longstanding tradition of equating Pandora and Eve and for the influence of Milton's Paradise Lost on Hawthorne's version, see Doudna 1985; on the critique of this identification by Hawthorne's source Charles Anthon, see Horn 2013: 71–2; Resinski 2009.

[54] In The Water-Babies, Kingsley offers a revised reading of the Pandora story in which Epimetheus and Pandora are quite right to open the box, "for, else, of what possible use could it have been to them"; Epimetheus thus gets not only trouble, but "a good wife, experience, and hope," and it is his and Pandora's descendants, not those of Prometheus, who are inventors and scientists and "get good lasting work done in the world" (Kingsley 2013: 148–50).

In Hawthorne's retelling of the rape of Proserpina, the original myth is redeemed from its darker significance as an account of sexual violence through the conversion of Proserpina into a little girl who herself plays a redemptive role. She is snatched by Pluto not because he seeks a wife but because he wants "a merry little maid, to run up stairs and down, and cheer the rooms with her smile" (1413). The innocence of Pluto's intentions is underscored when Proserpina is playing in his hall and we learn that he "gazed after her, and wished that he, too, was a child" (1432). Proserpina both stands up to Pluto, refusing to be reconciled to the loss of her mother and rejecting all the rich food he offers her, and responds to him with warm-hearted pity, learning to love him a little and, in the end, accepting her role as his companion for half the year. The myth has been effectively reconceived as a type of children's story (best known from later versions such as Frances Hodgson Burnett's *Little Lord Fauntleroy* (1885–6) or Johanna Spyri's *Heidi* (1881)) in which an affectionate child brings happiness into the life of a disagreeable and lonely old person.[55] The theme of rape is similarly circumvented in Hawthorne's account of Europa, whom he turns into a little girl mysteriously carried away from her playmates by an alluring bull; those playmates include her brothers who, along with her mother, embark on a long fruitless search for her.

Elsewhere, Hawthorne foregrounds the redemptive power of children by inserting new child characters into the myths. A small boy plays a decisive role in the story of Bellerophon: his belief in the winged horse he has seen reflected in the Fountain of Pirene inspires Bellerophon to persist in his hunt for Pegasus. The value of his faith in the imaginary is confirmed when we learn at the end of the tale that he grows up to be a poet. King Midas is given a daughter, Marygold, who finally cures her father of his love of gold when his golden touch turns her into a statue; even before that, his greed is distinguished from hard-hearted avarice because he wants gold only so he can give it to her. Throughout, there is

---

[55] Hawthorne anticipates this plot type in his own earlier sketch, "Little Annie's Ramble," in which a little girl explores the world in the company of the narrator, who "walks in black attire, with a measured step, and a heavy brow, and his thoughtful eyes bent down," and says of himself "I delight to let my mind go hand in hand with the mind of a sinless child" (1982: 228). Children who play a similar role in fiction for adults include Eppie in George Eliot's *Silas Marner* (1861) and Phoebe Pyncheon in Hawthorne's own *House of the Seven Gables* (1851).

an emphasis on the bonds between parents and children and between siblings and playmates. Even the coming-of-age adventures of young male heroes stop short of leading to romance or marriage. Perseus never encounters Andromeda and simply returns to his mother; Ariadne declines to leave Crete with Theseus, preferring to stay with her old father; Jason recognizes Medea as a dangerous "enchantress" whom he is happy to leave behind; when Cadmus is presented with his wife Harmonia, his first thought is that she might be his long-lost sister and playmate Europa.

The children who populate this mythic world not only resemble Bright's auditors but are also openly modeled on them, as he indicates at the end of the Pandora story:

"Primrose," asked Eustace, pinching her ear, "how do you like my little Pandora? Don't you think her the exact picture of yourself? But you would not have hesitated half so long about opening the box."   (1230)

Bright, who is "as light and active as if he has wings to his shoes" (1166, cf. 1193) is himself represented within the myths by the figure of Quicksilver, the playful, buoyant version of Mercury who accompanies the characters on their adventures, sees into their hearts, and intervenes with magical solutions to their problems.[56]

Bright addresses himself to "the imagination and sympathies of the children" (as he puts it to Mr Pringle, 1235) through an ironical, self-conscious narrative mode that minimizes the myths' mysterious and frightening features, as in his introduction of the Gorgons: "I hardly know what sort of creature or hobgoblin to call them. They were three sisters and seem to have borne some distant resemblance to women, but were really a very frightful and mischievous species of dragon." After describing their various attributes, he adds that "They had wings too, and exceeding splendid ones, I can assure you; for every feather in them was pure, bright, glittering burnished gold, and they looked very dazzlingly, no doubt, when the Gorgons were flying about in the sunshine" (1171). This light-hearted tone is complemented by the liberal use of familiar modernizing details. Musing on what it would have been like to have a Centaur for a schoolmaster, Bright adds "I wonder what the blacksmith

[56] These identifications were anticipated in the games of Hawthorne's own children. In a notebook entry from 1849, his wife Sophia records that she acted out Greek myths with them: their daughter Una played Pandora, their son Julian played Hermes, and she herself was cast as Minerva (Valenti 1996: 158).

charged him for a set of iron shoes!" (1438); Jason sows the dragon's teeth with the help of a "brush-harrow" (1461); Midas has a pair of spectacles and, in a celebrated passage, sits down to a breakfast that epitomizes prosperous New England domesticity: "hot cakes, some nice little brook-trout, roasted potatoes, fresh boiled eggs, and coffee" (1201). Bright's young listeners are invited to understand the stories in relation to their own experiences: the men who spring from the dragon's teeth are encrusted with dirt "just as you may have seen it clinging to beets and carrots, when pulled out of their native soil" (1379); Metanira catches Demeter putting her baby in the fire when it is "crowing and clapping its fat little hands and laughing in the nurse's face, (just as you may have seen your little brother and sister do, before going into its warm bath)" (1428).

Hawthorne's idealization of childhood and foregrounding of childish perspectives are not, however, unqualified. Bright's self-conscious narrative mode, which includes many claims of forgetfulness and ignorance, provides frequent reminders of what has been left out, some clearly directed at more knowledgeable readers: Jason has an encounter with a mysterious figure who is never named as Juno, but is accompanied by a telltale peacock; Cadmus and Harmonia find themselves "with a group of rosy little children (but how they came thither, has always been a mystery to me)" (1381). The questions Hawthorne has himself pose to Bright in the preface to *Tanglewood Tales*—"How were [the myths] to be purified? How was the blessed sunshine to be thrown into them?" (1310)—spell out the authorial intervention required to make the myths suitable for children. While Bright presents himself as merging into a process of spontaneous oral storytelling, the figure of Hawthorne, his nominal editor, remains a visible presence, who stands for that purposeful reworking and for an inescapable adult sensibility. This is especially the case in *Tanglewood Tales* where Hawthorne as "editor" smiles at Bright "commencing life with such confidence in himself and his performances," observing that "A few years will do all that is necessary towards showing him the truth, in both respects" (1310).

Even when writing for children, Hawthorne does not lose sight of the human capacity for greed, selfishness, cruelty, and sexual transgression, which he attributes to the Greek myths in their undoctored state and which he himself explored in his works for adults, most famously in two romances written close in time to his myth books, *The Scarlet Letter* (1850), and *The House of the Seven Gables* (1851). As in Ovid's

Metamorphoses, the magical transformations of myth sometimes show up the inherent depravity of human adults. Quicksilver turns Baucus and Philemon's inhospitable neighbors into fish, proclaiming "They needed but little change; for they were already a scaly set of rascals, and the coldest-blooded beings in existence" (1273). When Circe turns Odysseus' gluttonous men into pigs, she commands, "You are already swine in everything but the human form . . . assume your proper shapes, gormandizers, and begone to the sty!" (1396–7). When Cadmus sows the dragon teeth, he is puzzled by the creatures who spring up and "hardly knew whether to consider them as men, or some odd kind of vegetable; although, on the whole, he concluded that there was human nature in them, because they were so fond of trumpets and weapons, and so ready to shed blood" (1379). The sexual element in the Persephone myth does make its way indirectly into Hawthorne's version, displaced, as it is in the classical version told in the *Homeric Hymn to Demeter*, onto Persephone's furtive ingestion of pomegranate seeds.[57]

At various points, Hawthorne reveals the limits of carefree, childish merriment. When Ceres in her search for Proserpina visits Apollo, the embodiment of happy sunshine, he is too preoccupied with his own pleasure to help her and happily turns the story of Ceres' grief into a song that shows he has "a harp instead of a heart" (1425). The vision of childhood in "The Paradise of Children" is so patently idealized that Bright himself speculates that Pandora would have better off with a few more chores to keep her busy and in the end "cannot help being glad that our foolish Pandora peeped into the box." Although Hawthorne seems at times to distance himself from the concerns of a believing Christian (he speaks lightly of "old heathen wickedness" and describes the "moral sense" of his day as "Christianized" rather than Christian), his golden age is an essentially Christian one, in which the inevitable fall is ultimately fortunate, since the arrival of the Troubles is outweighed by the presence of Hope, which "spiritualizes the earth" and "shows it to be only the shadow of an infinite bliss hereafter" (1229).[58] Beyond that, it is not even really a fall, since it simply takes the form of Pandora and

---

[57] Laura Laffrado sees the sexual innuendo in this passage as in keeping with "a movement towards denial, not purification" characteristic of the stories in *Tanglewood Tales* (Laffrado 1992: 110–11, 122).

[58] Hathaway 1961: 171; Laffrado 1992: 83–4; Stephens and McCallum 1998: 80–1.

Epimetheus growing up as they are destined to do.[59] In keeping with this vision, Hawthorne recognizes, and incorporates into his narrative, the benefits of an adult outlook that includes deeper knowledge and understanding as well as a loss of innocence. When he engages in the kind of moralizing allegory favored by Neale ("We have all of us a Medusa... whom we must kill, if we would not have her kill us" (Neale 1847: 18), he links it specifically to the expanded sympathy and moral consciousness that come with experience:

And, Oh, my good little people, you will perhaps see, one of these days, as I do now, that every human being, who suffers anything evil to get into his nature, or to remain there, is a kind of Minotaur, an enemy of his fellow-creatures, and separated from all good companionship, as this poor monster was!
(Hawthorne 1982: 1333)

In this passage, and in similar observations throughout the two collections, Hawthorne highlights and promotes virtues, such as imaginative sympathy, sociability, and love of nature, that are rooted in Romanticism and its particular vision of childhood (Donovan 2002: 35).[60]

In keeping with his more reverent attitude to the Greeks, Kingsley tells the myths in a consistently dignified manner, with diction that is characteristic of mildly archaizing Victorian prose, reminiscent in places of the King James Bible ("now it came to pass"), with a touch of Malory ("smote", "slew", "that he might go"); he describes himself in a letter as having "adopted a sort of simple ballad tone, and tried to make my prose as metrical as possible."[61] Rather than bring the world of myth closer to his readers by playful anachronism, Kingsley regularly reminds children that they are in the presence of the old and lofty, as when the fairy-tale opening of the story of Perseus gives way to a more biblical solemnity:[62]

But there came a prophet to that hard-hearted Acrisius and prophesied against him, and said, "Because you have risen up against your own blood, your own blood shall rise up against you; because you have sinned against your kindred, by your kindred you shall be punished. Your daughter Danae shall bear a son, and by that son's hands you shall die. So the Gods have ordained, and it will surely come to pass." (1859: 2)

---

[59] Resinski 2009, 2011b.
[60] On Hawthorne's moralizing in these tales, see also Billman 1982.
[61] Letter to J. Ludlow, Dec. 1856 (Kingsley 1899: 389).
[62] Brian Alderson, recalling his childhood pleasure in *The Heroes*, comments on Kingsley's "patina of age and dignity" (Alderson 1995: 75–6).

The passages in which Perseus first meets Minerva/Athené provide a good example of the contrast between Hawthorne's modernizing or domesticating and Kingsley's archaizing:

"She is a very accomplished person, I assure you," continued Quicksilver, "and has all the arts and sciences at her fingers' ends. In short, she is so immoderately wise, that many people call her Wisdom personified. But, to tell you the truth, she has hardly vivacity enough for my taste; and I think you would hardly find her so pleasant a traveling companion as myself . . . " (Hawthorne 1982: 1176)

And as [Perseus] slept, a strange dream came to him; the strangest dream which he had ever had in his life. There came a lady to him through the wood, taller than he, or any mortal man; but beautiful exceedingly, with great gray eyes, clear and piercing, but strangely soft and mild. (Kingsley 1859: 11)

Where Hawthorne offers in contemporary idiom a jocular account of an unusually talented "person," and slips in a witty allusion to Minerva's chief divine attribute in the guise of a figure of speech, Kingsley's goddess appears (as Homeric gods often do) in a dream, described as "a lady" but clearly distinguished from "any mortal man."

In places, however, Kingsley goes beyond archaizing to describe a world that seems designed to strike readers as fantastical, alien, and emotionally evocative in ways they may not be completely ready to grasp. In the story of Perseus, when the hero is sent to seek directions from the Graiae, who share a single eye and a single tooth, Kingsley represents the three Grey Sisters as articulating their own archaism; they sit chanting "a low song: 'Why the old times were better than the new'" (Kingsley 1859: 27).

The contrast with Hawthorne is again striking. Hawthorne's narrator provides the "poor old ladies" with new names (Scarecrow, Nightmare, and Shakejoint), represents them as much given to bickering, and offers mock-advice to his young hearers:

As a general rule, I would advise all people, whether sisters or brothers, old or young, who chance to have but one eye among them to cultivate forbearance and not all insist upon peeping through it at once. (Hawthorne 1982: 1181)[63]

---

[63] As Katharine Lee Bates (whose own views of myth will be discussed in Chapter 7) puts it, Kingsley's Graiae are "frost-bound spirits, kindred of the Titans," recalling in their hatred of the new the conflicts between older and younger generations of gods in Aeschylus' *Eumenides* (150, 163) and *Prometheus Bound* (148–51), while Hawthorne "concerns himself not at all with nature-myth or spiritual significance. He is intent on amusing the children with the best story possible" (Hawthorne 1897: xi).

Kingsley's three Grey Sisters, who inhabit the "Unshapen Land," are characterized through an evocation of their barren setting and a formulaic, almost incantatory expression of a pitiable lack they do not themselves acknowledge:

There was no living thing around them, not a fly, not a moss upon the rocks. Neither seal nor sea-gull dared come near, lest the ice should clutch them in its claws. The surge broke up in foam, but it fell again in flakes of snow; and it frosted the hair of the three Grey Sisters, and the bones in the ice-cliff above their heads. They passed the eye from one to the other, but for all that they could not see; and they passed the tooth from one to the other, but for all that they could not eat; and they sat in the full glare of the moon, but they were none the warmer for her beams. And Perseus pitied the three Grey Sisters; but they did not pity themselves.   (Kingsley 1859: 27–8)

Rather than follow Hawthorne in representing mythical characters as actual children, Kingsley focuses on young male heroes entering adulthood who, like the "teachable" early Greeks, learn from experience—and whom he describes as like schoolchildren, with a schoolchild's supposed sense of natural hierarchy:

So that a man was honoured among them, not because he happened to be rich, but according to his skill, and his strength, and courage, and the number of things which he could do. For they were but grown-up children, though they were right noble children too; and it was with them as it is now at school, the strongest and cleverest boy, though he be poor, leads all the rest.   (xviii)

While Hawthorne, with a characteristically Romantic devaluing of formal education, lampoons classical scholarship and portrays the telling of myth as a vacation pastime, Kingsley anticipates in multiple ways the future education of his readers, depicted in his preface as inescapable: "So as you must learn about [the Greeks], whether you choose or not, I wish to be the first to introduce you to them" (xi). He gives considerable attention to Cheiron's training of the future Argonauts in a setting that suggests a boy's school, in which future leaders master valuable skills and form lifelong friendships—while playing games, eating their fill, and drinking clear spring water, "for wine is not fit for growing lads" (83). This nostalgic vision of school and schoolchildren is further incorporated in the story and explicitly mediated by adult memory when the Argonauts, near the start of their voyage, pass the site of Cheiron's school:

their hearts yearned for the dear old mountain, as they thought of pleasant days gone by, and of the sports of their boyhood, and their hunting, and their schooling in the cave beneath the cliff. And at last Peleus spoke, "let us land here, friends, and climb the dear old hill once more. We are going on a fearful journey; who knows if we shall see Pelion again." (110)

Later in the story, Kingsley offers his girl readers a similar glimpse of the nostalgia they may some day feel for their (very different) present lives, when Medea envisions going into exile with Jason:

Medea wept, and shuddered, and hid her face in her hands; for her heart yearned after her sisters and her playfellows, and the home where she was brought up as a child. (142)

Kingsley's interest in his reader's future education, reinforced by his sense of responsibility to the Greek literary tradition and to the partial historicity of these legends, also makes itself felt in his deployment of archaeological and historical facts or suppositions, of puzzling or excessive detail, and of digressions that might be at home in an ancient author (such as Ovid) but are oddly out of place in a supposed fairy tale—all of which are of no concern to Hawthorne, whose attention to historical context never goes beyond the occasional place name. Kingsley mentions the Cyclopean stone walls of Tiryns and evidently identifies Andromeda's people with the Canaanites, later to meet with destruction at the hands of "a strange nation . . . out of Egypt" (59); he not only gives a full account of Theseus' adventures, but also adds the odd (and apparently irrelevant) story of his mother Aethra's later fate; and an allusion to the fine weather that accompanies Danae's journey in the chest with her child leads to a brief account of the story of Halcyone and Ceyx (4–5).

Kingsley regularly reminds his reader that the stories he is telling are partial and temporary, and points to the deferral of full understanding. He refers to things that children "would not understand," and that are "too terrible to speak of here," mentions "ancient songs" they will later read, and characters—such as Aeneas—of whom they will hear "many a noble tale" (188, 108, 86). These comments suggest a particular version of the implied dual audience characteristic of most literature for children: they are directly addressed to the child reader, but only the adult reader (or the older child) will understand what is being talked about. In the story of Perseus Kingsley seems to be offering not so much isolated allusions as a kind of puzzle, with pieces the reader may some day put together. He never explicitly speaks of Jupiter's love for Danae, much less of Perseus' conception. But someone who knows the traditional story will be struck by several moments in the narrative that clearly point to what has been suppressed. For example, although Perseus seems originally to have appeared from nowhere, Danae refuses to marry Polydectes not only because she does not love him but also because "she cared for no one but her boy, and her boy's father, whom she never hoped to see again" (10), and there are several allusions to his divine parentage.

As this last example suggests, Kingsley's respect for his Greek sources and for his readers' future education also affects his treatment of material considered problematic or inappropriate for children. Whereas Hawthorne, through his playful, iconoclastic narrator, either avoids the more questionable episodes, revises them, or transforms them altogether, Kingsley is more likely either to hint at the tradition or to offer some kind of palliative commentary or alternative reading, as when he assimilates the Argonauts to other heroes with loftier goals. When he comes to the end of that story, however, he regretfully has to relinquish any hopes for the outcome, and defers his readers' encounter with what he represents as a terrible truth mitigated by the nobility of its representation.

And now I wish that I could end my story pleasantly; but it is no fault of mine that I cannot. The old songs end it sadly, and I believe that they are right and wise . . . Jason could not love [Medea], after all her cruel deeds. So he was ungrateful to her, and wronged her; and she revenged herself on him. And a terrible revenge she took—too terrible to speak of here. But you will hear of it yourselves when you grow up, for it has been sung in noble poetry and music . . . (188)[64]

Hawthorne is untroubled by the quest for gold and avoids the problem of the outcome by ending his story as the Argonauts leap aboard, their mission accomplished.

The two authors' treatment of a troublesome element in the story of Theseus offers an even more striking contrast. Whereas Kingsley uncomfortably provides two versions of Theseus's abandonment of Ariadne and passes on as hastily as his hero, Hawthorne never lets his heroine leave Crete in the first place (casting her, like Proserpina, as a girl who willingly brings cheer to a lonely old man) and ascribes the story that appears in his sources to what some "low-minded" (and inaccurate) people say.

---

[64] This passage is omitted in some abridged versions of Kingsley; see e.g. the version in the "Told to the Children" series, rewritten by Mary MacGregor (Kingsley 1905) and in Kingsley 1961.

But that fair Ariadne never came to Athens with her husband. Some say that Theseus left her sleeping on Naxos among the Cyclades; and that Dionusos the wine-king found her, and took her up into the sky, as you shall see some day in a painting of old Titian's, one of the most glorious pictures upon the earth. And some say that Dionusos drove away Theseus, and took Ariadne from him by force: but however that may be, in his haste or in his grief, Theseus forgot to put up the white sail.   (Kingsley 1859: 251)

Now, some low-minded people, who pretend to tell the story of Theseus and Ariadne, have the face to say that this royal and honorable maiden did really flee away, under cover of the night, with the young stranger whose life she had preserved. They say, too, that Prince Theseus (who would have died sooner than wrong the meanest creature in the world) ungratefully deserted Ariadne, on a solitary island . . . Here is what Ariadne answered, when the brave Prince of Athens besought her to accompany him. "No, Theseus!" the maiden said, pressing his hand, and then drawing back a step or two, "I cannot go with you. My father is old, and has nobody but myself to love him . . . "   (Hawthorne 1982: 1336)

Where Hawthorne dismisses the prior tradition as mere gossip, Kingsley feels obliged to report its variants; but here as with the ending of the story of the Argonauts, a doubly proleptic glimpse of the story's later artistic reception by "old Titian" and of his readers' later encounter with "one of the most glorious pictures upon the earth" serves somehow to mitigate the inglorious truth.

As they jointly championed the idea of classical myth as a fitting subject for children, Hawthorne and Kingsley also defined contrasting visions of the relationship between children and the ancient times in which the myths originated. According to one, that past is a privileged moment of purity and wholeness, whose essence is captured in timeless myths; its spirit is dulled for the human race through the transition to modernity and for individuals through the transition to adulthood, but children have a natural and perennially renewed connection to it. According to the other, antiquity is one point on a historical continuum, out of which the modern world evolved; children can benefit from learning about the classical past from adults and in educational settings; their first encounters will properly be with its most child-pleasing products (which emerged from a time that was, as children are, both endearing and immature) but they will progress to more serious study of classical languages and/or ancient history.

We will see these two visions recurring over the century that followed the publication of Hawthorne's and Kingsley's books, sometimes in competition, sometimes in combination, variously shaping the presentation of both myth and history for child audiences and defining the ways in which childhood encounters with antiquity are related to the life stories of individuals. Two additional factors that distinguish the two authors will also be in play throughout our discussion. One is the gender of the child reader to whom classical material is directed. In keeping with the prevailing educational practice of nineteenth-century England, Kingsley's addressees are on the brink of a divide: the boys will go on to learn Greek and Latin and to have a full classical education while the girls most likely will not. For Hawthorne, it is not so clear that such future schooling conveys advantages over the privileged state of childhood, at least where the all-important virtues of imagination, sympathy, and attunement to nature are concerned, and girls are conspicuously prominent in his imagined audience. They come first in his title, *A Wonder-Book for Girls and Boys*, and among the group of children who form the internal audience of that volume, a girl, Primrose, is the oldest, the most assertive in teasing and challenging Eustace Bright, and the one who displays the most advanced understanding of human behavior.[65] That is not to say, of course, that access to education is not an essential feature of the Tanglewood setting: Mr Pringle's resistance to Bright's retellings is based in his own classical education; Bright is a college student for whom visits to Tanglewood are a welcome break from his studies; and Primrose already knows enough from other sources to point out that "the story of Midas was a famous one, thousands of years before Mr. Eustace Bright came into the world" (1210).[66]

The other factor is that of nationality. Hawthorne is clear that his free, child-friendly versions of the myths are distinctively American

[65] In the golden age portrayed in "The Paradise of Children," Epimetheus is able to make a creditable wreath for Pandora, even though this is a skill at which girls excel, because "boys could do it, in those days rather better than they can now." On the notable gender equality among the vigorously active Tanglewood children, see Peck 1985; for the view that Primrose is positioned on the verge of a less emancipated adult state, see Ginsberg 1993. On the diminution of gender differentiation and, in some cases, a preference for girls as characteristic of Romantic views of childhood, see Cunningham 2005: 70.

[66] Not only is the Tanglewood setting itself a kind of fairy tale, as the names of the house and the children who frequent it indicate, but the idyllic life of these children is both tied to their middle-class status and nostalgic, evoking an idealized pre-industrial world at time when American society was experiencing rapid industrialization and increased child labor (Pfister 1996: 246).

reinventions. In Bright's dispute with Mr Pringle, he declares his independence from the classical sources by asserting that "an old Greek [has]
no more exclusive right to [the myths], than a modern Yankee has"
(1255). His versions are rooted in the beautiful, fertile American landscape and in an idealized vision of prosperous American family life. The
tales are full of references to New World flora and fauna: the golden
apples retrieved by Hercules are "as big as pumpkins" (1251); among the
crops cared for by mother Ceres is "Indian corn" (1409); the houses in a
pygmy village are "about as big as a squirrel's cage" (1338). The terrain
around Tanglewood is the natural setting of legendary marvels: admiring
the vivid leaves of a New England autumn, Eustace laughingly asks,
"Why did I not tell you how old King Midas came to America, and
changed the dusky Autumn, such as it is in other countries, into the
burnished beauty which it here puts on?" (1211). The creatures of myth
are measured by local landmarks: when one of the children wants to
know the size of a certain giant, Bright places him in Massachusetts:
"I suppose he might be from three to fifteen miles straight upward, and
that he might have seated himself on Taconic, and had Monument
Mountain for a footstool!" (1254). Tales of ancient kings can point to
democratic lessons. After being turned into a woodpecker as punishment
for his excessive pride in the trappings of royalty, King Picus "felt himself
merely the upper servant of his people, and that it must be his life-long
labor to make them better and happier" (1407).

Bright's stories are allied to the American tall-tale tradition as well as
to the European fairy tale. As they look out over the Catskills, he
mentions the presence there of Rip Van Winkle, the children ask to
hear about this "wonderful affair," and he declines only because it has
been so well told already (1278). This unspoken reference to the work of
Washington Irving connects the myth books to the development of a
specifically American literature in the early decades of the nineteenth
century. The cheerful tenor of the myths, as well as the Tanglewood
context, reflect Hawthorne's own efforts to define American cultural
values by countering the rigidity, self-righteousness, militarism, and
emotional severity of the Puritans through the recovery and importation
of English traditions of merry-making, domestic comfort, aesthetic
exuberance, and warm-heartedness that had been too readily left behind.
In this context, the Greeks, whose versions Eustace rejects because they
are "cold and heartless," resemble the Puritans, while Eustace's own

reworkings, whose effect Mr Pringle compares to "bedaubing a marble statue with paint" (1254–5), are like the rich scarlet embroidery with which Hester Prynne, the outcast adulteress of *The Scarlet Letter*, answers her judges.[67] The telling of classical myths in an American setting brings renewal at once to those myths and to that setting.

It may be that the "distressing vulgarity" that supposedly moved Kingsley to compete with Hawthorne was related to a distaste for certain products of American culture.[68] In any case, the selfless heroism that Kingsley hoped to inspire in his readers, especially his male readers, is tied to his conception of the destined roles of Englishmen as fighters against tyranny, explorers, naturalists, social reformers, and energetic defenders of Protestantism. True heroism, he says in his preface, is that of men who "left their country better than they had found it;" the apparently offhand remark on linguistic usage that follows, "And we call such a man a hero in English to this day," identifies this view of heroism with a specifically national perspective (1859: xx). In Kingsley's vision of history, it took the arrival of the Teutonic northern races to rescue Christianity from its Catholic past. In the *Heroes*, with its focus on Greek mythology, and therefore on pre-Christian Greek history, he is able to occlude the story of the Christian Church in antiquity, which he had portrayed only a few years earlier in his controversial adult novel *Hypatia* (1853) as corrupted by elements of priestly asceticism and power-seeking that clearly evoked nineteenth-century Catholicism.[69] The assimilation of mythological heroes to modern English boys allows him to project a smooth trajectory from pre-Christian antiquity to modern Anglicanism: as recapitulated in the lives of his readers, the history of Christianity plays out exclusively within the noblest and most successful of the northern races.

[67] On Hawthorne's cultural project of tempering Puritan extremism with Old World traditions, see Newberry 1987: esp. 174 for discussion of Hester's embroidery.

[68] Kingsley may have had a general distaste for American literary imports for children; in a passage in *The Water-Babies* he satirizes a number of the best-known under titles like "Squeeky" (for Susan B. Warner's *Queechy*) and "the Narrow Narrow World" (for *The Wide, Wide World*, by the same author) (Kingsley 2013: 155).

[69] Bowler 1989: 56–7; Goldhill 2011: 203–7.

2

Classics in Their Own Right
Visions and Revisions of Hawthorne and Kingsley

In his introduction to *Pegasus, The Winged Horse*, a version of Hawthorne's "Chimera" published as a separate illustrated volume in 1963, the poet Robert Lowell recalls his own first encounter with Hawthorne's tales.

> The stories of the Greek heroes are endless, and almost as endless is the number of their storytellers. Where should one start? For me they began thirty-five years ago, when Herbert Hoover was President of the United States, and radios ran on batteries, and ladies were beginning to cut their hair short, and people traveled long distances by train and not by air. My mother used to read to me from a lyre-stamped and wilted tan-covered book of Hawthorne's Greek tales that had been given her as a child. Hawthorne had been dead only about thirty-five years when the book was first bought for her and read to her.
>
> (Hawthorne 1963: n.p.)

A century after their first publication, Hawthorne's retold myths had assumed the classic status of their ancient sources. Lowell presents them as timeless works with the power to preserve and awaken memories of the past—not the remote past of the classical world but a more recent and personal American past. They take him back to his own childhood in the 1930s, which he makes into "the olden days" for his child readers and then, via the material book which so often figures in such reminiscences, to his mother's childhood at the end of the nineteenth century, within striking distance of Hawthorne's long-ago lifetime. In this chapter, we turn to the cultural legacy of Hawthorne's and Kingsley's myth collections as they were received from generation to generation and became classics in their own right, at once capable of inspiring nostalgia for earlier times and subject to continuous renewal through a long series of fresh editions—from traditional classicizing volumes like the one given to Lowell's mother to the stand-alone illustrated storybook that he himself was introducing.[1]

Influence and Afterlife

Hawthorne and Kingsley not only inaugurated the tradition of classical mythology as children's pleasure reading; they themselves remained prominent figures within that tradition for at least a century, during which time their books were repeatedly reissued in a wide array of formats. Their works outlasted the several other myth collections that also appeared in the mid-nineteenth century and that were viewed as comparable by reviewers and critics of that time. Those included the earlier books of Neale and Niebuhr discussed in Chapter 1, and two collections of stories from the 1860s by George William Cox (1827–1902), a disciple of the prominent theorist of myth Max Müller: one designed to introduce myth to very young children (*Tales from Greek Mythology*, 1861) and one that combined the myths themselves with a grounding in Müller's view that they derived from the animistic beliefs of the original Aryans (*Tales of the Gods and Heroes*, 1862).[2]

When in 1887 the novelist Charlotte Yonge published a survey of suitable reading for students in parish schools (*What Books to Lend and What to Give*), she mentioned all five writers, recommending both Niebuhr and Neale along with Hawthorne and Kingsley, but dismissing Cox on the grounds that his Aryan theory interfered with the pleasure of reading the myths.[3] Niebuhr's stories were still popular enough in 1903 to appear in an edition with illustrations by Rackham, but were no longer

---

[1] *The Winged Horse* resembles a picture book in its brevity, its proportions (flat and thin), and its many illustrations, but most contemporary critics would exclude it from that category because its pre-existing text can stand on its own and takes up much more space than the pictures. On definitions and typologies of the picture book, see Kümmerling-Meibauer 2017, Nikolajeva 2006, Nikolajeva and Scott 2006, D. Lewis 2001.

[2] A reviewer writing in the *Saturday Review* for Dec. 29, 1860 groups Cox, Kingsley, and Neale together as authors who adapt Greek legends to "the understandings of English children" by telling "their stories, as stories, in a clear and interesting way," but prefers Cox because of the absence, due to his scientific approach, of "any moral purpose whatever" (842) and reports that a group of children exposed to Neale's and Cox's versions of the same stories unanimously preferred Cox.

[3] But see also her earlier recommendation of Cox's scientific approach along with Hawthorne and Kingsley (Yonge 1869b: 456).

republished after the start of World War I.[4] During the same decades, however, Hawthorne's and Kingsley's versions had become recognized staples of children's literature. For example, the publisher's note to Josephine Preston Peabody's *Old Greek Folk Stories*, published in Boston in 1897, indicates that the stories included are "designed to serve as a complement to the Wonder-Book and Tanglewood Tales." Hawthorne's works were at once a foundation on which later writers might build and a still-contemporary presence with which those writers had to reckon.

For children who read or heard their books, as well as for adult authors who followed in their footsteps, Hawthorne's and Kingsley's retellings of the myths became the definitive versions; this had been predicted by another English novelist, Mary Mitford, who wrote to Hawthorne after the publication of *Tanglewood Tales*, "How many thousands will think of you as the name of some glorious old legend comes to them!"[5] Along with Bulfinch's 1855 *Age of Fable*, designed for family reading, they displaced for the general reader both their ancient sources and the handbooks of the more recent past. Many later myth books were based, often tacitly, on these influential predecessors, and aspects of the myths that Hawthorne and Kingsley emphasized, or even invented, became canonical. One often-noted example is Midas' daughter Marygold: added by Hawthorne out of an interest in children who enliven and instruct their elders, she is now widely assumed to be an essential element of the myth.[6]

The authority that these authors derived from their foundational role—and, presumably, from their stature as writers for adults—was amplified by the very fact of being encountered in childhood. As Lowell goes on to add,

> If I read some false, modern retelling of the old stories, I say to myself, "This isn't the way it happened. I was there. It wasn't a wall that Lynceus could see through, but a millstone!" Hawthorne's fables are history to me, and just as much fact as the earth, the water, and the sky.   (Hawthorne 1963: n.p.)

---

[4] The Rackham edition of Niebuhr was reprinted in 1910; an illustrated selection of Cox's retellings appeared as *Dwellers on Olympus* in 1913 as part of Thomas Nelson's "Children's Bookshelf" series, but was never reprinted (Cox 1913).

[5] Quoted in J. Hawthorne 1885: 2. 35. On Mitford's response to Hawthorne's work, see Idol 1999.

[6] On the afterlife of Midas's daughter in myth books for children, see Roberts 2015. On the similar impact of narrative details in Howard Pyle's retelling of the story of Robin Hood, see Stephens and McCallum 1998: 5.

Experienced early and with the immediacy and conviction that are often recalled as features of childhood reading, Hawthorne's and Kingsley's versions became (to recall Louise Glück's formulation) "fundamental referents," shaping lifelong conceptions of the myths as their successors' versions do today.

The constant republication of these works was partly driven by their suitability as gifts. The adults who presented them to children may have been motivated by nostalgia, whether for their own childhood or for the two illustrious eras with which these books were associated, classical antiquity and the nineteenth century.[7] But the books they bought were new ones, produced to meet an ongoing demand. The myth collections joined other recognized classics in a flourishing gift-book market that publishers had fostered and exploited since the inception of the children's book industry in the late eighteenth century. By the Victorian period, both expensive and cheaper editions of approved children's books were often advertised as "suitable for presents, school prizes, or rewards," and both authors appeared in special gift-book and prize editions.[8] A Wonder-Book, Tanglewood Tales, and The Heroes were all initially published late in one year and given a publication date in the next, a standard practice known as "postdating," which allowed publishers to advertise books for Christmas two years running.[9] The long history of these books as gifts is recorded in the many inscriptions in surviving copies, ranging from "Fanny Lovekin from her affectionate friend Charlotte Gibson, August 13th—1864" (in an 1859 edition of The Heroes) to "Kirsten from Grandma Bernice" (in an edition published in 1968).[10]

[7] As Geoffrey Trease observes, "Amiable aunts tend to give as presents the books which they have enjoyed themselves in that improbable youth they must once have experienced" (Trease 1964: 11).

[8] Goldman 1994: 72. On the gift book in this period, see esp. Felmingham 1988; cf. also Ray 1976: 206–7; on the earlier gift-book tradition, see Grenby 2011: 168–78; on the Victorian gift book, see Goldman 1994: 66–75; on developments at the turn of the 20th century, Hearn 1996: 21; Kooistra 2002: 206–9.

[9] For example, Macmillan's first edition of The Heroes is dated 1856, but was already reviewed in The Spectator for Dec. 19, 1855 as "well adapted for a gift-book to the young" (17).

[10] Examples of prize inscriptions in the early 20th century include "Mr. Guy Baskett, A Reward for superior spelling. W. F. Cuberly, Teacher" (in a reprint of A Wonder-Book) and, in The Heroes, "Lloyd Park U.M. Church Sunday School, Presented to Stanley Discon on promotion to the Upper Junior Department, Easter 1927. Superintendent A.M. Ascoli."

The end of copyright protection around the turn of the twentieth century made Hawthorne's and Kingsley's texts widely available for reprinting in new editions of all kinds; many of these involved fresh illustrations, which were also fostered by the development of new color printing processes at about the same time.[11] The fashion for lavishly illustrated gift books that flourished from the 1890s through the early decades of the twentieth century generated some especially distinguished editions, particularly of Hawthorne, whose collections of discrete tales of wonder offered classical analogues to other popular choices such as *Grimm's Fairy Tales* and *The Arabian Nights* and to other works featuring fairies, such as Christina Rossetti's *Goblin Market*.[12] But there were many cheap editions as well; one striking example, apparently intended for the boy's adventure market, is a volume issued by an American publisher sometime between 1900 and 1912 in which the text of *Tanglewood Tales* appears with no illustrations at all except for a cover featuring a scene of Native Americans in canoes.

The myth collections were also included in the complete multivolume sets of their authors' works that appeared from the 1860s and 1870s on, and these editions were read by children even if they were not marketed primarily to them. For the children's book historian Brian Alderson, the memories stored in Kingsley's *The Heroes* are tied to its presence in one such set:

Charles Kingsley's *The Heroes* was at the right-hand end of the book-case, just above the carpet, where one could lie and read it in comfort. It was the three-and-sixpenny standard edition in dark maroon sand-grain cloth, lined up with companion volumes with unpromising titles like *Yeast* and *Hypatia*. But for all the dullness of its appearance there was nothing dull about its contents.

(Alderson 1995: 73)

If Hawthorne's books were especially favored for their resemblance to fairy-tale collections, Kingsley's gained extra appeal from their emphasis on classical heroism and its modern lessons. This reflects Kingsley's own conception, set forth in his title, confirmed in his introduction ("we call such a man a hero in English to this day, and call it a 'heroic' thing to suffer pain and grief, that we may do good to our fellow men," Kingsley

---

[11] Kooistra 2002: 206–9.

[12] On the prominence of fairy subjects and on illustrators who specialized in them, see Kooistra 2002: 206–7.

1859: xx) and reiterated in his accounts of the heroes themselves and in references to their later analogues (the Spartans at Thermopylae, the British in the Crimea). But Kingsley's orientation to heroism also resonated with a general emphasis on heroic self-sacrifice in British fiction for children during the years leading up to World War I, and there were a number of new editions of *The Heroes* between 1900 and 1915.[13]

Kingsley's formative role for those who fought in World War I is affirmed by two writers looking back at the war from different perspectives. In her memoir *Testament of Youth*, the disillusioned pacifist Vera Brittain associates Kingsley with a pernicious classical ideal that motivated many young British soldiers. Contrasting the messy death of her fiancé Roland Leighton with the fantasies that propelled him to the front, she writes that it was "so painful, so unnecessary, so grimly devoid of that heroic limelight which Roland had always regarded as ample compensation for those who were slain, like Kingsley's *Heroes*, 'in the flower of youth on the chance of winning a noble name'" (Brittain 1933: 241). In *Books, Children, and Men*, first published in French in 1932, the historian Paul Hazard hopefully envisions an end to such conflicts through natural alliances among children, fostered by their common reading. He concludes with a section on heroism, still for him a noble trait, as especially inculcated by Kingsley:

> The finest and noblest of the books intended for children tell of heroism. They are the inspiration of those who, later in life, sacrifice themselves that they may secure safety for others.
>
> Charles Kingsley wrote a book for his own children, Rose, Maurice, and Mary, and called it *Heroes*. He drew his characters from the Greek epic and they stand out in his book, bathed in the clear light of the Mediterranean, as though they were living statues of humanity's benefactors.   (Hazard 1944: 170)

This view of Kingsley's work persisted through successive decades of the twentieth century and shaped what appears to be the last new English-language edition of *The Heroes*, published in the United States in 1968. Here Kingsley's own preface is moved to the back, and followed

---

[13] Kingsley's status as the purveyor par excellence of the heroic is reflected in the publisher's description of C. A. Kincaid's 1915 *The Indian Heroes*: "The author has followed the style of Kingsley's *The Heroes* not only in the spirit in which he has treated his materials, but also in his style, which is both simple and worthy of the subject." On the increased emphasis on mythological hero stories in the US from the turn of the century on, see Brazouski and Klatt 1994: 5–6.

by a brief biography of Kingsley as social reformer and "Father of Heroes"; readers then learn about heroes in other eras ("Heroes are Here to Stay"), including a number of figures from American history "and a handful of 'Ace' pilots from World War One," and are told what it means to be a hero in the twentieth century:

What *is* important is that a person can and *should* try to act like a hero in his daily life. All it takes is courage and a willingness to accept the challenges of life without flinching or backing away.   (Kingsley 1968: 207)

The English traveler and writer Patrick Leigh Fermor (1915–2011) offers a quirkier account of Kingsley's role in his own military career, as well as a reminder of the link between childhood pleasure reading (or listening) and the choice to study ancient languages despite their diminishing status. Looking back on his time living in mountain caves on Crete and fighting with the Greek partisan resistance in 1942, he comments on how he and his comrades were selected.

With an insight once thought rare, the army had realized that the Ancient tongue, however imperfectly mastered, was a short-cut to the Modern: hence the sudden sprinkling of many strange figures among the mainland and island crags. Strange, because Greek had long ceased to be compulsory at the schools where it was still taught; it was merely the eager choice—unconsciously prompted, I suspect, by having listened to Kingsley's *Heroes* in childhood—of a perverse and eccentric minority: early hankerings which set a vague but agreeable stamp on all these improvised cave-dwellers.   (Leigh Fermor 2005: 5)

Leigh Fermor first presents ancient Greek as a useful skill for operations in Greece but an unlikely qualification for combat. But the introduction of Kingsley brings a further twist. In the post-World War I period, exposure to *The Heroes* leads to learning Greek as a spirited, unconventional choice rather than as the natural next step in a boy's traditional formation. Greek inspired by Kingsley is not a spur to straightforward heroism like that sought by Roland Leighton, but a token of readiness for unexpected adventure and suitability for a scrappy band of unconventional warriors.

The classic status assumed by these myth collections, as well as their implication in both world wars, is further highlighted in an another evocative mid-twentieth-century reminiscence. *Betsy and Tacy Go Downtown*, published in 1943, is one of a series of fictionalized accounts by Maud Hart Lovelace (1892–1980) of her own childhood in a small town in Minnesota. In an episode that takes place in 1904, when the author's fictional stand-in Betsy is 12, *Tanglewood Tales* figures, not as a gift or a prized possession, but as a library book (Lovelace 1979: 83–7). Betsy is an aspiring author and enthusiastic reader; when her parents discover that she has been enjoying the hired girl's sensational novels, they arrange for her to go downtown to the "new Carnegie library" to read more highbrow, canonical works ("Good books. Great books. The classics.") as preparation for her future as a writer. When she gets there, she explains to the librarian that she might not find what she needs in the Children's Room because she wants to read the classics, although she is not certain she will like them. But the librarian answers, "I know a few you'll like ... And they happen to be in the Children's Room" and leads her there, explaining that "There's nothing more classic than Greece" and that the place to start is Greek mythology. She then produces *Tanglewood Tales*, which Betsy spends the rest of the day happily reading, oblivious to the passage of time.

Tanglewood Tales here represents "Greece," serving as a child-friendly surrogate for classical literature and, in the setting of the library, as an emblem of turn-of-the-century American cultural aspirations. Between 1883 and 1917, the philanthropist Andrew Carnegie endowed hundreds of libraries throughout the United States, requiring that they be partly supported by the community and that they provide free service to all. These libraries helped to spread high culture beyond such established settings as Hawthorne's New England, making prosperous Midwestern towns like Betsy's into new, proudly democratic centers of civilization. The building that Betsy approaches is described as "this small white marble temple ... glittering with newness"; the role of the Children's Room as the proper place for a foundational first encounter with classical Greece is signaled by a painting on the wall "of a rocky island with a temple on it, called *The Isle of Delos*." The adventure that takes Betsy to Greece via the library is also a first foray into what is referred to throughout the series as "the great world." Recalled in the context of World War II, this represents an important step towards the kind of world citizenship manifested in America's involvement in that war—and expressed in the final book in the series (*Betsy's Wedding*) by the characters' shared commitment to the country's entry into World War I. As she immerses herself in a book of Greek myths, Betsy joins the international community that, according to Paul Hazard (whose book was translated into English and published in America in 1944), is fostered by childhood reading of shared classics.[14]

As time went on, Hawthorne's and Kingsley's myth collections were subject to various forms of revision and updating. Both authors appeared in annotated editions for use in schools, with glosses on mythical and historical references and difficult words, and by the early twentieth century both had been rewritten in simplified versions; this presumably reflects a growing awareness that the audience of younger children addressed by Hawthorne and Kingsley (whose own children were all under 10 when the books were published) might in fact find their language too difficult, as well as the fact that they were becoming increasingly old-fashioned and a belief that the stature of the two writers called for the widest possible access.[15] Individual myths were excerpted for anthologies of myths, legends, and fairy tales, which could reflect changing views of such material.[16] One anthologist of the 1920s, Romer Wilson, pokes fun at the traditional association with fairy-tale magic. She includes Kingsley's "Perseus" in her *Green Magic: A Collection of the World's Best Fairy Tales from All Countries* (1928), but prefaces the myth with a description of ancient Greece as a time "when our forefathers were still troubled with dragons and mammoths in everyday life," assimilating two rather different non-classical conceptions of the primal (Wilson 1928: 323). She strikes a more serious note in her introduction to Hawthorne's "The Miraculous Pitcher" in *Silver Magic* (1929), comparing the poverty of Baucis and Philemon to the "wretched state" of "millions of Europeans in our time" (Wilson 1929: 15).[17]

---

[14] On Carnegie Libraries, see Van Slyck 1995; on the significance of Betsy's visit to the library, Sweeney 2005. As Sweeney notes (43), the libraries that brought cultural opportunities to immigrants and members of the white working class were less inviting to African Americans.

[15] See *Saturday Review* for Dec. 29, 1860: 842 and Cox 1861: v on the difficulty for the very young of mid-century writers. Both *The Heroes* and a selection from Hawthorne's two books appeared in the "Told to the Children" series: Mary MacGregor retells Kingsley's stories, full of strange things and unfamiliar names, "so simply that even small boys and girls will learn to love these brave men" (Kingsley 1905: vii), and C. E. Smith, who has "changed all the big words . . . and made some of the sentences easier," hopes that younger children "will be able to enjoy every word in the book" (Hawthorne 1906: vii).

[16] Such collections include Shahan 1901; Tappan 1907; Mabie 1913; R. Wilson 1928, 1929.

[17] Not everyone admired Hawthorne and Kingsley; in *Literature for the Elementary School* (1907), to take one example, Porter Lander MacClintock (who believed that to offer

The mythographer Marina Warner recalls that as a child in the 1950s, she was "enthralled" by both Hawthorne and Kingsley, "devouring the stories under the bedclothes by torchlight" (Warner 2010: 24), but by that time the books were less widely read and the form in which children might encounter these stories was changing. By the middle of the twentieth century, picture books, which typically have fewer pages and in which the verbal and the visual elements of the text create an intertwined and interdependent narrative, were playing an increasingly important role in the children's book market; influenced by this trend, a number of illustrated editions of single stories by Hawthorne and Kingsley appeared during this period, including several versions of Hawthorne's "The Golden Touch"[18] and the version of his "Chimera" introduced by Lowell. Although their pre-existing and thus independent texts meant these were not true picture books by current definitions, they could be similarly marketed and might be seen as the same by purchasers. These illustrated single-myth storybooks are among the last really distinctive new editions of Hawthorne's and Kingsley's myths; the versions issued since that period are reprints of earlier editions.[19]

A single-story illustrated edition of Kingsley's *Theseus* published in 1964 reframes the myth from a mid-twentieth-century perspective. An afterword entitled "How Much is True?" by Mary Renault, who had recently published two historical novels based on the legend of Theseus, supplements Kingsley's text with knowledge gained in the intervening century. Renault rejects Kingsley's label of "fairy tale," which she attributes to ignorance and excessive rationality rather than a desire to accommodate pagan traditions within a Christian framework. For her, what matters is that the legends have been shown to have a factual basis, and she gives a romanticized account of the archaeologists Heinrich Schliemann and Arthur Evans, who recognized in them the "smell of

---

myth to young children is to misunderstand both myth and children) accuses Hawthorne of covering up "the grim Titanic story" of Pandora with "mere babble" and "flippant detail" and declares that the faults of "inanity . . . sentimentality . . . cynicism and cheap satire . . . poison practically everything done for children by Kingsley and Hawthorne" (MacClintock 1907: 113, 122, 98).

[18] See Brazouski and Klatt 1994: 74–5.
[19] What appears to be the last new edition of Kingsley's complete text is the 1968 version mentioned earlier; an inexpensive edition designed for schools and school libraries, it includes marginal illustrations of glossed words and objects and full-page black-and-white illustrations that recall the poster art of the late 1960s.

truth" (Kingsley 1964: 44) and went on to prove their historicity. These researchers are as heroic to her as Theseus, whom she praises primarily as a champion of the oppressed. In keeping with this orientation, the illustrations are strongly influenced by Minoan art.

Reception through Illustration

As this last example suggests, Hawthorne's and Kingsley's texts were significantly transformed in the course of their long history of republication through ever-changing sets of illustrations, a feature that generally plays an especially important role in books for children. It is clear from adult reminiscences that images often make as strong an impression on child readers as the texts they accompany; we have already seen one example of this in Leigh Hunt's recollections of the engravings included in Tooke's *Pantheon*.[20] The use of illustrations in books for children goes back at least to the early modern period, and John Locke's influential *Some Thoughts Concerning Education* (1693) includes the recommendation that the first books given to children should contain illustrations to entice their readers and make them more eager to learn (Locke 1889: 133). Throughout the nineteenth century, when adult books were also often illustrated, images were presumed to have a particular appeal for children; Lewis Carroll has Alice think, as she looks at the book her sister is reading, "what is the use of a book . . . without pictures or conversation?" (Carroll 1953: 1).[21]

Accordingly, both Hawthorne and Kingsley conceived of their books from the outset as including illustrations. Writing to his publisher about his plan for *A Wonder-Book*, Hawthorne was already suggesting that they should be illustrated by Hammatt Billings (1818–74), a well-known artist and architect, then at the height of his career as an illustrator (other notable commissions included the original editions of *Little Men* and *Uncle Tom's Cabin*).[22] Kingsley, an experienced amateur artist, himself

[20] A more recent example is the historical novelist Barry Unsworth (1930–2012), who vividly recalled a volume of myths he received for his sixth birthday: "I could read by then, after a fashion, but it was . . . the pictures that enthralled, beautiful colour plates" (2005: 100).
[21] For overviews of the history of illustration in children's books see Kümmerling-Meibauer 2006: 276–81 and Whalley 2004: 381–427.
[22] Eustace Bright expresses surprise that the myths "have not long ago been put into picture-books for little girls and boys" and later tells Primrose that Mr J. T. Fields will publish his stories and "get them illustrated, I hope, by Billings" (Hawthorne 1982: 1168, 1302).

supplied the line drawings that were used in the first edition of *The Heroes* and in a number of reprints.[23] Unlike *Alice in Wonderland* and the works of Beatrix Potter, however, Hawthorne's and Kingsley's stories had no lasting association with their original illustrations. In common with many other collections of traditional material (such as fairy tales, Aesop's Fables, or the Arthurian legends), these books attracted a long series of illustrators, including some of the best known of their day, who supplied anything from a single frontispiece to dozens of separate images.[24] As we have noted, there was a proliferation of beautifully illustrated versions of both authors in the late nineteenth and early twentieth centuries, many designed for the gift market. These had begun to decrease both in number and in quality by 1930;[25] although there were some new illustrated editions in the 1950s and 1960s, subsequent editions generally reprint earlier editions in facsimile or reuse their illustrations.

Illustrations of Hawthorne's and Kingsley's works vary in the degree to which they share the text's orientation to children. Illustrators were often selected on the basis of their independent stature and marketing appeal and were not necessarily expected to subordinate their own agendas to the text. In many instances, the artist appears to be illustrating the myth in general rather than the author's particular version, often drawing on longstanding traditional iconography. This is the case with Billings's illustrations for Hawthorne, which are mostly static, generic images of mythical scenes and figures: for example, Perseus holding the

[23] Kingsley learned drawing from his father and sketched throughout his life (Colloms 1975: 25); on his drawing class for the young men of Bideford, see Kingsley 1899: 380–1; on his erotic drawings, Colloms 1975: 77, 80–1; Goldhill 2011: 252–3. He evidently disliked the engravings made from his drawings for *The Heroes*, calling the results "a brutal mess" (letter to T. Hughes, Klaver 2006: 414–15).
[24] Illustrators of Hawthorne include: Hammatt Billings (1851, 1853), Frederic Church (1883), George Wharton Edwards (1888), Walter Crane (1892), Howard Pyle (1900), V. W. Burnand (1903), Olive Allen (1906), Lucy Fitch Perkins (1908), Willy Pogany (1909), H. Granville Fell (1910), Maxfield Parrish (1910), Elenore Plaisted Abbott and Helen Alden Knipe (1911), Milo Winter (1913), Edmund Dulac (1918), Arthur Rackham (1922), Gustaf Tenggren (1923), Fern Bisel Peat (1930), Frederick Richardson (1930), Salomon Van Abbé (1949, 1950). Illustrators of Kingsley include: Charles Kingsley (1855), Maud Hunt Squire and Ethel Mars (1901), Jessie M. King (1903), T. H. Robinson (1903), Rose le Quesne (1905), Wal Paget (1909), George Soper (1910), William Russell Flint (1912), Sybil Tawse (1915), Harry G. Theaker (early 1900s), H.M. Brock (1928), Helen Kihn (1930), Helen Monro (1933), Howard Davie (1934), Salomon Van Abbé (1955), Charles Keeping (1961), Joan Kiddell-Monroe (1963), Ron King (1968).
[25] Felmingham 1988: 2.

Gorgon's head, with his shield, winged slippers, and helmet at his feet. Billings could as well have been illustrating Tooke's *Pantheon* and, at a time when publishers often supplied illustrators with subjects to depict rather than actual manuscripts or galleys, he may never have seen Hawthorne's text. The book does include, however, a frontispiece of a type long common in fairy-tale collections, a scene of the storyteller surrounded by his child audience, for which Hawthorne supplied a drawing of the Tanglewood porch.[26] A number of Hawthorne's illustrators simply disregard his innovative conversion of mythical adults into children, instead supplying conventional images of full-grown Pandoras and Proserpinas.

The question of what makes an illustration suitable or appealing to children is in any case a complicated one. One account of the desired qualities can be found in Thackeray's review of Cruikshank's illustrations for the first English edition of *Grimm's Fairy Tales*: "the first real, kindly, agreeable, and infinitely amusing and charming illustrations in a child's book in England."[27] But those qualities are hard to pin down and children's own responses are variable and unpredictable. Their tastes may be formed to some extent by what adults offer them, but they are not limited by those choices and, as the example of Leigh Hunt indicates, they can take pleasure in illustrations that seem unlikely to appeal to the young. [28] There has long been a general tendency to eschew violence and sexuality in images for children, but with considerable variation over time. It would be surprising to find the horrific image of the Scissor-Man from E. T. A. Hoffmann's 1845 *Der Struwwelpeter* (*Slovenly Peter*) in a twenty-first-century book for children, but in the middle of the nineteenth century that illustration and others almost as disturbing could be presented as "funny pictures" ("drollige Bilder"), as they are in Hoffmann's subtitle. As with the stories themselves, the fact that certain images are the first a child encounters may outweigh other considerations. In her autobiography, *A Mid-Century Child and Her Books*, the pioneering American children's librarian Caroline Hewins reveals her

---

[26] J. Hawthorne 1885: 459, 475. For examples of frontispiece images in German, French, and British fairy-tale collections, see Tatar 1987: 108–13.

[27] The *Westminster Review* for June 1840, quoted in Hearn 1996: 8.

[28] On the unpredictability of children's emotional reaction to images, see Tucker 1976: 115–17. On child viewers (implied and actual) of picture books, see Nodelman 1988: ch. 1; Evans 2009; Arizpe and Styles 2003; and D. Lewis 2001: esp. ch. 7.

lifelong attachment to Billings even when compared to famous later illustrators whose images are more colorful and ostensibly inviting:

> The "Wonder Book" was on my pillow when I opened my eyes on the morning of my seventh birthday. The purple-covered "Tanglewood Tales" with Proserpine and Europa, Theseus, Jason and Circe is still mine; but the dear green "Wonder Book" with the Hammatt Billings pictures of the groups of children on Tanglewood porch, Perseus holding up the Gorgon's head, King Midas, Pandora, the three Golden Apples, Baucis and Philemon and the Chimera vanished long years ago, and not even the Walter Crane or Maxfield Parrish editions will ever take its place.   (Hewins 1926: 66)

In the case of Hawthorne and Kingsley, the situation is further complicated because some editions of their works were intended primarily for adults. Both authors were published in fine art editions aimed at collectors, and illustrated gift-book editions of children's literature were known to be attractive to adults as well.[29] Such books may reveal their orientation in the telling choice of which moment in a myth to illustrate.[30] That choice may be driven less by an episode's centrality to the story or interest to the child reader than by its susceptibility to the artist's style or to contemporary taste; it is remarkable how many illustrations feature nymphs who are at best secondary figures in their tales. The sometimes surprising amount of nudity or partial nudity, both male and female, presumably reflects an adult aesthetic that finds the nude acceptable when mythological or historical—or in some cases a once acceptable adult delight in the supposedly innocent bodies of young children that now seems to us disconcertingly voyeuristic.

Out of this rich and impressive history, we have chosen a selection of examples for each author that translate distinctive features of their texts into visual terms, providing a kind of pictorial narrative that may reflect, complement, or comment on the verbal one.[31] In the case of Hawthorne,

---

[29] For example, the illustrations by Maxfield Parrish in a 1910 edition of Hawthorne's two books appeared first in 1909 as a series on Greek mythology in *Collier's* magazine (Yount 1976: 75). See also on William Russell Flint later in this chapter. On the relationship between illustration and audience in crossover and repackaged books, see Beckett 2009: 234–6. On contemporary crossover picture books, see Beckett 2012b.

[30] On the "moment of choice" in illustration, see Hodnett 1982: 6–10.

[31] Although in illustrated books the pictorial narrative is generally subordinate to the text rather than on an equal footing (as in picture books), the reader's experience of the text is nonetheless conditioned and transformed by different sets of illustrations. For a survey (and some typologies) of the ways in which the verbal and the visual interact in picture

we focus on his persistent and self-conscious appeal to the child readers of his own day, and discuss three illustrators who engage in various ways with his playfulness, his conversion of mythical women into girls, and his time-blurring identification of figures from myth with modern children. In the case of Kingsley, we focus on the centrality of heroism in his retellings, and consider five illustrations of the myth of Theseus and the Minotaur, from the time of *The Heroes'* first publication until the mid-twentieth century, whose diverse representations of the classical past and responses to Kingsley's narrative create different images of ancient heroism for modern audiences.

The frontispiece to an 1885 edition of *A Wonder-Book* illustrated by Frederick S. Church (1842–1924) introduces Hawthorne's text with a witty, updated visual analogue to his identification of mythical characters with modern children, in particular Eustace Bright's comparison of his boldest auditor Primrose to Pandora (Fig. 2.1). Adapting a canonical depiction of the Pandora myth, in which Pandora kneels beside an ornately decorated chest and the evils emerge in swirling clouds, Church conflates the child reader with Pandora and the book itself with her box.[32] While Billings's more conventional frontispiece for the first edition presents Hawthorne's text as a record of spontaneous storytelling, Church treats it thirty years later as an established book (now *The—* rather than *A—Wonder-Book*) to be experienced by a girl of his own day, who is clearly dressed in late nineteenth-century clothes.

Although this reader seems, like her mythic counterpart, more perplexed than enchanted by what she has released, the parallel with Pandora also highlights her curious interest, and the vignettes that replace the original evils indicate the pleasures and lessons ahead (as well as the capacity of illustrations to stand for the myths on their own). Church's substitution redefines Hawthorne's "wonders" as "the

books, see Lewis 2001: ch. 2; for a discussion of the transformation of a single text by different sets of illustrations, see Nikolajeva and Scott 2006: 41–51 on versions of Andersen's *Thumbelina*.

[32] The kneeling pose and swarming evils, which had already appeared in illustrations of Hawthorne's Pandora by Billings and by Church himself, go back at least to John Flaxman's depiction of "Pandora Opening the Vase" in his 1817 *Compositions from the Works, Days, and Theogony of Hesiod* (Panofsky 1956: 93–102). The ornate chest reflects Hawthorne's extended description (Hawthorne 1982: 1218) and possibly Rossetti's famous painting of 1870, in which Pandora holds an embossed gold casket. The depiction of the evils in many versions as stinging insects and bats also derives from Hawthorne (1224).

Fig. 2.1. Frontispiece by Frederick S. Church from Nathaniel Hawthorne's *The Wonder-Book for Girls and Boys* (1885).

forbidden—yet *humanizing*—contents of Pandora's box"[33] and recapitulates what Hawthorne has done in turning "legends . . . brimming over with everything that is most abhorrent" (Hawthorne 1982: 1310) into lightly moralized pleasure reading.

Among subsequent illustrators, the American Milo Winter (1888–1956) stands out for his close responsiveness to Hawthorne's reconception of the myths. In his illustration of the Proserpina myth from an edition of *Tanglewood Tales* published in 1913, Winter follows Hawthorne's conversion of Proserpina from an abducted bride into a little girl kidnapped by Pluto in the hopes that she will enliven his gloomy underworld existence (Plate 1). Like most of Hawthorne's illustrators, Winter does not depict the actual abduction, a scene that has a long illustration tradition going back to antiquity but that may be viewed as too scary and suggestive for children. Taking his lead from Hawthorne's title, "The Pomegranate Seeds," he illustrates instead the scene in which Proserpina, ravenous because she has been refusing the excessively rich food that Pluto's cooks have prepared, is tempted by a servant bearing a withered pomegranate on a golden salver.

The particular details of the oppressively opulent setting and its modern furnishings are Winter's invention, but they are very much in accord with Hawthorne's playful elaboration and recasting. The absence of sunlight—an important theme for Hawthorne, who stresses Pluto's aversion to natural light and Proserpina's resemblance to a sunbeam— is indicated by a conspicuously ornate chandelier. Scary features of the underworld setting have been domesticated: the three-headed dog Cerberus reappears as a wall ornament, and Hawthorne's benign Christianizing is echoed in the appearance of the Devil as a deferential servant. Proserpina is clearly a child and resembles a nineteenth-century girl known for her strong-minded views and unintended travels to the underworld, the Alice of *Alice in Wonderland*, especially as envisioned in John Tenniel's illustrations. When Winter himself illustrated that book two years later, in 1910, he gave Alice the same flowing golden hair and chaste white dress as Proserpina.

Winter has also captured the subtle presence of more adult themes in Hawthorne's narrative. Critics have drawn attention to the symbolic

---

[33] Pfister 1996: 251.

reemergence of the sexuality Hawthorne elsewhere suppresses in his description of Proserpina's eating of the pomegranate (which has had that connotation ever since antiquity):

So she took up the pomegranate, and applied it to her nose; and somehow or other, being in such close neighborhood to her mouth, the fruit found its way into that little red cave. Dear me, what an everlasting pity! Before Proserpina knew what she was about, her teeth had actually bitten it, of their own accord!

(Hawthorne 1982: 1433–4)

Winter suggests the sexual threat represented by the pomegranate through Proserpina's defensive body language—her decidedly proper straight back, crossed ankles, and hands clasped across her lap. And there is a further hint in the snaky-tailed devil who offers the long-haired heroine an apple-like piece of fruit with winning words ("the only one in the world").

Winter's composition tacitly evokes the iconographic tradition of the Adam and Eve story. He has integrated into his portrayal of a stubborn child conventional imagery of the biblical fall, in which the Devil frequently appears as a snake with a human head and Eve is regularly portrayed with long hair and crossed legs—as, for example, in the version of Eve's temptation by John Stanhope painted in 1887 (Plate 2). This identification of Proserpina with Eve is an unspoken echo in a different medium of Hawthorne's identification of Pandora with Eve in *A Wonder-Book*; it highlights the underlying similarities between these two retold myths, both of which Hawthorne transforms into the story of a little girl's half-conscious, seemingly involuntary surrender to temptation.[34] With the multiple associations of his Proserpina, Winter captures the simultaneous modernizing and Christianizing of Hawthorne's narratives.

The extensive range of images included in the celebrated 1922 edition of *A Wonder-Book* illustrated by Arthur Rackham (1867–1939) gives a particularly rich visual account of the several layers of reception involved in the reissuing of Hawthorne's texts for new audiences. This is a lavish gift book, intended at least as much for display and admiration among adults as for actual use by children.[35] While many such books make no

---

[34] Cf. Pandora untying the cord: "It had disentangled itself so suddenly, that she could not in the least remember how the strings had been doubled into one another; and when she tried to recollect the shape and appearance of the knot, it seemed to have gone entirely out of her mind" (Hawthorne 1982: 1222).

[35] On the dual audience of gift books and on Rackham's particular mastery of this market, see Kooistra 2002: 206; Felmingham 1988: 56–7.

overt reference to children or their presumed tastes, Rackham's illustrations are closely engaged with the idea of children both as protagonists and as consumers of Hawthorne's text.

Rackham was clearly given ample scope by his publisher, and the book incorporates illustrations in three media: pen-and-ink line drawings, part-color prints influenced by Japanese woodblocks, and full-color glossy plates based on watercolors. Deploying a range of styles, Rackham illustrates not only Hawthorne's text but also (in an expanded version of what Church accomplishes in his frontispiece) the phenomenon of twentieth-century children (and their adult observers) encountering Hawthorne in a new edition produced by himself in a later period. His "List of Illustrations" is headed by a drawing of himself with pen and paper, in an explicit nod to the creation of the physical illustrated book. And, like Church but in a different configuration, he conflates the myths and the book in which they appear: in a small vignette, the imps and fairies that populate the text are seen playing with the book (but, as its pages are blank, apparently indifferent to its contents).

A line illustration strategically placed just before the opening of the narrative offers a visual manifesto for the volume (Fig. 2.2). A girl and boy dressed in somewhat prettified clothes in the style of the 1920s are positioned by "The Hawthorne Tree." In keeping with Hawthorne's title and the tenor of his frame narrative, the girl is placed in the foreground and in closer contact with the tree.

The conversion of Hawthorne into a tree is not just a visual pun. It is also an emblem of this prominent artist's appropriation of Hawthorne's text, since the tree, with its twisted gnarled trunk, its emerging gnome's face, and its branches turning into arms, is one of Rackham's most frequently used and widely recognized images—a recurrent feature of his work that serves as a kind of hallmark or signature.[36] The image presents children being drawn into the magical world of the book and identifies that world with the fairy realm of little people and dark forests derived from the European fairy tale. Rackham in effect foregrounds those aspects of Hawthorne's text—the fairy-tale comparison and the

---

[36] This tree type is often recognized as Rackham's virtual signature: "The trees we have come to know as 'Rackham trees'" (Baughman 1967: 8); "Rackham's gnarled and sometimes frightening trees, like the limbs of witches, have permanently entered the imagination of those who first saw them in childhood" (Harthan 1981: 241). On the relationship between such tree imagery and folklorists' interest, beginning in the late 19th century, in tree animism, see Peppin 1975: 20.

¶ The Hawthorne Tree

Fig. 2.2. Illustration by Arthur Rackham, "The Hawthorne Tree," from Nathaniel Hawthorne's *A Wonder-Book for Girls and Boys* (1922).

associations of a setting known as the Tanglewood—that make it most amenable to the English fairy-tale atmosphere that he imparted even to works with quite different settings, such as *A Midsummer Night's Dream*, also set in ancient Greece. This is fitting for an edition in which his illustrations are the main selling point. At the same time, through the suggestion of a talking tree, he presents Hawthorne's stories as unmediated expressions of a magical natural world. The message of this introductory image is reinforced in subsequent illustrations of the myths: the golden-age children of the Pandora story swarm over a tree, and Baucis and Philemon are shown transformed into trees of the same twisted, partly embodied type as "The Hawthorne Tree."

Rackham does not, however, wholly bypass Hawthorne's own vision of the myths as transmitted in a nineteenth-century American context. In other images, differently dressed children represent the book's internal audience. One of the line drawings in the text illustrates a particularly exuberant episode of the frame story: when Eustace Bright returns from college for the Christmas holidays, there is an enormous snowstorm, in which the children rejoice "tumbling head over heels into its highest drifts, and flinging snow at one another" (Hawthorne 1982: 1212) before returning to their playroom and fantasizing about being snowed in until spring. The style of Rackham's portrayal is modern in its loose lines and open composition, but the children are conspicuously old-fashioned in their dress, especially the girls with their full, flounced skirts (Fig. 2.3). Further, this image closely recalls in its layout and style another which portrays the naked frolicking inhabitants of the mythic "paradise of children."

From Rackham's twentieth-century perspective, Hawthorne's mid-nineteenth-century setting is its own mythic "Paradise of Children," to which gently falling snow and playful skirmishes bring nothing but added pleasure, a world now not only idealized (as Hawthorne himself acknowledges) but viewed through a further layer of nostalgia and perhaps, for English readers, somewhat exotic. This rendition of the setting in which the stories were first told reinforces the message that the book will take its readers to a delightful, unfamiliar world.[37]

---

[37] Similar connections between the myths and the internal setting are made by parallel scenes of the mythical children and the Tanglewood children sitting on fallen tree trunks, and by an image in which a girl in a flounced dress and a goblin walk side by side carrying

Fig. 2.3. Illustration by Arthur Rackham from Nathaniel Hawthorne's *A Wonder-Book for Girls and Boys* (1922).

Rackham's atmospheric full color plates situate the myths themselves in mysterious, otherworldly settings. He places Pandora and her box in a misty void, abstracted from any context beyond what is suggested by a set of floorboards and a kind of magic carpet, on which she kneels in her traditional pose, releasing a swarm of bat-like spirits (Plate 3). This figure is not, however, entirely timeless in either historical or personal terms: the few objects around her answer to the decorative tastes of the early twentieth century; her nudity places her in prelapsarian mythic time, answering to Hawthorne's statement that she lived when children had "no clothes to mend," but her bobbed hair suggests the 1920s.

dandelion torches. Rackham's attention to the American setting of Hawthorne's frame story is in contrast with the lack of any American coloration in his illustrations for narratives set in America, such as *Rip Van Winkle* and *The Legend of Sleepy Hollow*.

Rackham's Pandora could not be naked if she were not understood to be a child, and yet she is not wholly asexual. Her long limbs and swelling chest suggest the onset of maturity, pointing to the transformation that she is bringing on herself through her action. In this respect, her portrayal connects her to the more decidedly nubile but clothed Pandoras and Proserpinas of other illustrators such as Walter Crane and Maxfield Parrish and (for twenty-first-century viewers at least) raises a question about how this figure, with her creamy bare skin lit from an unseen source, may have been viewed by some of Rackham's adult readers. To his child audience, he offers a girl who looks like one of them, but transposed to another world, without the grounding in the here-and-now provided by clothes, on the brink of mysterious new experiences.

Kingsley's illustrators respond to his exploration of mythical heroism as a model for modern times, but rarely address themselves in any obvious way to a child viewer. Kingsley's efforts at "translating the children back into a new old world" rather than remaking the old world for present-day children, his formal, even (in his words) "metrical" prose, and his many classical allusions[38] evoke from most of his illustrators various modes of classicizing, and favored subjects typically include those moments most emblematic of heroic achievement: Perseus with the Gorgon's head or rescuing Andromeda, Jason retrieving the Golden Fleece, and Theseus battling the Minotaur—which will be our focus here. If, however, these illustrators refrain from self-conscious play, they do in some instances complicate or question the heroic paradigm Kingsley makes of Theseus' victory over his monstrous opponent, a process that begins with Kingsley's own illustration.

Kingsley's line drawing of Theseus and the Minotaur has an apparent naivety that seems to allow for child readers though not actively to invite them; the figures are centered against a very lightly sketched background, and Theseus' tunic and headband signify antiquity without any more extensive stage-setting. The image (Fig. 2.4) forms a surprising contrast with the violence of the narrative: Kingsley chooses to show not the moment when Theseus "caught [the Minotaur] by the horns, and forced his head back, and drove the keen sword through his throat" but the moment just before the killing, when "at last Theseus came up with

<hr />

[38] Letter to J. M. Ludlow, Kingsley 1899: 389–90.

Fig. 2.4. Illustration by Charles Kingsley from *The Heroes* (1859).

[the Minotaur] as he lay panting on a slab among the snow" (Kingsley 1859: 250). Or is it the moment just after the killing? The sword is clean, but Theseus' posture suggests that the struggle is over. In either case, though, by depicting a moment not described in the narrative—whether between overtaking and killing or between killing and departure—Kingsley has opened up a space of reflection for both his hero and his reader, thus supplementing his own text through his illustration.

In this simply rendered physical setting (snowy peaks, rocky slab), Theseus stands with his foot on the Minotaur's back and his sword pointed at the creature's throat, but his stillness is striking, and his mournful expression transforms what might have been an iconic posture of triumph.[39] The Minotaur's "teeth of a lion, with which he tore his prey" (249) are not visible, and his bull's head is simply animal-like without being monstrous; his human hands, protruding tongue, and exhausted limpness lend an air of pathos to the hero's victory, whether imminent or achieved.

Kingsley's illustration, in its contrast with his text, thus anticipates the moral he draws at the very end of *The Heroes*. Having told us that "after his triumph [Theseus] grew proud, and broke the laws of God and man" (253) and came to a sad end, Kingsley concludes with a prayer and a warning: "God help us all, and give us wisdom, and courage to do noble deeds! But God keep pride from us when we have done them, lest we fall, and come to shame!" (254–5). The Theseus in Kingsley's text performs a noble deed by killing the Minotaur, but the Theseus in his illustration better exemplifies the Christian hero who—however triumphant—feels no pride. This visual supplement thus suggests a kind of correction, a glimpse of what the Greeks might have been had they outgrown the childlike phase of humanity to which Kingsley assigns them.

Many later editions of Kingsley's by then classic text, reflecting the trend towards elegant (and lucrative) gift-book editions, replace his simple line drawings with elaborate full-color or black-and-white images of noble youths or men and beautiful women.[40] Most of his illustrators were known in part for their work on other children's books, and without seeming in any way to address or call for a child viewer, the illustrations are compatible with the kind of art children would have seen in other

---

[39] In Billings's illustration for Hawthorne's *Tanglewood Tales*, Theseus poses with his foot on the Minotaur's severed head. Like Winter's Proserpina, Kingsley's Theseus recalls a familiar scene in Christian iconography, here the representation of St Michael standing with his foot on the fallen Satan as dragon.

[40] Very occasionally a non-classical image of the heroic impinges, as in the 1915 edition illustrated by Sybil Tawse, whose cover depicts an ancient hero in a forest on the verge of spearing a deer, his location and pose evocative of images of Native Americans in adventure stories.

works. But one notable edition, published in 1912 by the Medici Society and "illustrated after the watercolour drawings by W. Russell Flint" (1880–1969), evidently envisions among its primary purchasers adult connoisseurs of art and of the printed book. Flint's depiction of Theseus' battle with the Minotaur (in stark contrast with Kingsley's own illustration) makes this deed horrific as well as heroic through its fidelity to a dramatic moment of violence in the text, which also serves as the caption for this final illustration in the volume: "[Theseus] caught him by the horns, and forced his head back, and drove the keen sword through his throat" (Kingsley 1912: 164) (Plate 4).

Here as in Kingsley's drawing we see the snowy ridges and the slab of rock, but the setting is less schematic and more atmospheric, partly obscured by mist from which the almost sculptural dimensions of the figures emerge. The Minotaur has the head of a bull and the body of a human, but the lion's teeth of Kingsley's text, here clearly displayed, add to his monstrosity, and Flint emphasizes the contrast between man and beast-man by a contrast in skin color that also evokes racial difference, with Theseus as white, and by Theseus' slighter and nimbler frame. Theseus' posture recalls the iconography of scenes in ancient art and in classicizing sculpture in which a hero subdues a wild creature by lunging between its legs or pressing his knee against its body.[41] As in Kingsley's text, Theseus forces the Minotaur's head back; his sword's striking vertical enters the monster's mouth in a particularly brutal and invasive reading of the phrase "through his throat." At the same time the savagery of Theseus' expression and the pathos of the Minotaur's human hand, grasping the hero's knee at the center of the image, offer a disquieting image of heroism and threaten to complicate the reader's expected sympathies—an effect Kingsley's own illustration avoids by a less faithful rendition that lends to Theseus himself an air of sympathy for the Minotaur.

We find a more unambiguously celebratory depiction of Theseus' heroism in the Macmillan Children's Edition of 1928, illustrated by H. M. Brock (1875–1960).[42] Brock's brightly colored plate (Plate 5) is

[41] See e.g. Étienne-Jules Ramey's 1826 statue group *Theseus and the Minotaur* in the Tuileries.

[42] Brock was a prolific illustrator (in a somewhat nostalgic mode) of 19th-century fiction who also illustrated children's gift books, school books, and magazines. On Brock and on his brother C. E. Brock, see Hodnett 1988: 195–7 and Felmingham 1988: 42.

in the classicizing tradition familiar from Flint and other predecessors, but his illustration is simpler and more stylized than Flint's: it has a certain flatness, and is framed as an illustration, with decorative borders and a caption that is part of the picture. Several of these features apparently reflect the publisher's views about what was appropriate to child readers: when Macmillan earlier reissued Kingsley's own illustrations in its "Books for the Young Series," his drawings were "re-engraved in simpler style, placed within decorative borders, and printed in color" (Alderson 1995: 81–2).[43]

Brock's depiction of the struggle between Theseus and the Minotaur offers a more straightforward response to Kingsley's text than Kingsley's own surprisingly complicated image, while sparing the child reader the disquieting brutality of Flint's illustration. This Theseus is obviously a classical hero: he wears sandals and a headband, and his body is barely concealed by a loose tunic-like garment. His sword is still at a distance from the Minotaur's gaping mouth, and his face as he holds the Minotaur's horn and prepares to strike reveals no savagery, only heroic determination. The Minotaur is not only bull-headed and dark where Theseus is pale—with racial overtones, as in Flint—but strikingly, almost ludicrously monstrous; to the "lion's teeth" of Kingsley's text Brock has added hands with long sharp claws, and these hands are not humanized (as in Flint's picture) by any suppliant grasp. The reader's sympathies are thus very clearly directed.

Brock's approach is also subtly synoptic. Rather than leave the illustration's relation to the narrative ambiguous (as Kingsley's drawing does) or key the illustration, like Flint's, to a specific moment, Brock's caption, "Theseus Slays the Minotaur," which echoes Kingsley's title for this part of the story ("How Theseus Slew the Minotaur"), suggests that the image here stands for the episode as a whole. As part of the frame, the caption fulfills this function visually as well: for, as J. R. R. Tolkien observes, in a book of myths or fairy tales the frame around an illustration serves (like such verbal formulas as "once upon a time") to mark off a particular segment of the endless "World of Story."[44] And indeed, the

---

[43] See Kingsley 1875. The somewhat luridly colored illustration in this edition disambiguates the narrative moment by adding blood to the tip of Theseus' sword.

[44] Tolkien 1994: 188. On framing and frame-breaking in the picture book, see Moebius 1996; Nodelman 1988: 50–3; Nikolajeva and Scott 2006: 62–3, 224–7; Smith 2009; Scott 2010.

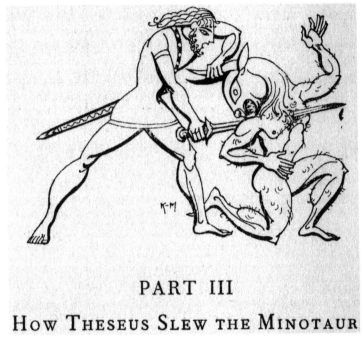

PART III
HOW THESEUS SLEW THE MINOTAUR

Fig. 2.5. Illustration by Joan Kiddell-Monroe from Charles Kingsley's *The Heroes, or, Greek Fairy Tales for My Children*, originally published by J. M. Dent, © 1963 Joan Kiddell-Monroe. Used by permission of Euan Murray.

illustrator has compressed the changing landscapes of Kingsley's narrative to show at once the "arches and galleries" of the man-made structure where Theseus' adventure begins, the "black cliffs" where he meets the monster, and the "edge of the eternal snow" where the final battle takes place (Kingsley 1928: 206–7).

The illustration by Joan Kiddell-Monroe (1908–72) (Fig. 2.5) for a 1963 edition of *The Heroes*, also seems to stand—though in a somewhat different way—for the story as a whole, since it takes the form of a black-and-white vignette that accompanies the chapter heading and serves as its visual correlative. Kiddell-Monroe's image is at once modernizing and archaizing: she disregards the European tradition of classical history painting and looks to antiquity not just for isolated motifs or for type scenes but also for stylistic models. As the illustrator of the Oxford Myths and Legends series, she typically drew on the traditions of the different cultures whose tales she was illustrating. Here, the influence of Greek black-figure vase painting can be seen in her depiction of animals like horses and bulls and in the clothing, hairstyles, and oval eyes of her humans, and her version of the death of the Minotaur recalls specific representations of this scene on vases of the Archaic period. The effect of this, and of other choices Kiddell-Monroe makes, is to disrupt Kingsley's links between ancient and modern heroism.

Like Flint and Brock, Kiddell-Monroe depicts the moment when Theseus is about to finish off the Minotaur, but she reduces the scene to its central actors (no snowy peaks, no stone slab); both the lack of context and the flat side-by-side depiction of the central actors are characteristic of her models. This Minotaur has the bull's head, lion's teeth, and human body of Kingsley's text; the body is also naked where Theseus is clothed, and hairy where he is smooth. In a composition that may be indebted to a number of vase paintings but seems most closely adapted from the Theseus Amphora in the Boston Museum of Fine Arts (Fig. 2.6), Theseus is standing in the dominant position, and the Minotaur kneeling with one hand raised; rather than force the Minotaur's head back and drive the sword down its throat, Theseus pulls the Minotaur's head sideways and drives the sword into its back and through its chest. Kiddell-Monroe's version departs from its chief model in two respects: no grasping hand lends pathos or suggests human contact, and the sword emerges, its point dripping with blood. But this gruesome image is presumably mitigated for young readers by the use of black and white, by a distancing archaism that represents Theseus as a hero from a very different time and place, and by a stylization that (as with puppetry and animation) accommodates violence.

At about the same time we find a very different vision of Kingsley's Greek past and of what matters in his stories—one that, like Kingsley's own illustration, is in tension with the text it accompanies, but to different effect—in the work of Charles Keeping (1924–88), who was commissioned to provide the illustrations for an abridged edition of *The Heroes* published by Hutchinson Educational (Kingsley 1961). Keeping's black-and-white line drawings, variously placed on the page, share with Kiddell-Monroe's vignettes a focus on the human figure rather than on its setting, but where she distances her figures from the viewer through a combination of archaism and stylization, Keeping charges his figures with emotion and creates an invented past whose people look familiar as well as other.

Fig. 2.6. Two-handled jar (amphora), Greek, Archaic period, about 540 BCE, ceramic, black figure, by the British Museum Nikosthenes painter. Height: 39.2 cm (15 7/16 in); diameter: 22.5 cm (8 7/8 in); diameter (lid): 7.2 cm. Museum of Fine Arts, Boston; Otis Norcross Fund, 60.1.

Photograph © 2018 Museum of Fine Arts, Boston.

It is somewhat surprising that Keeping, whose work was regarded as controversial and unorthodox, should have been asked to illustrate a simplified edition evidently intended for younger readers. He had already illustrated many of Rosemary Sutcliff's historical novels and was later to provide a particularly striking set of pictures for Leon Garfield and Edward Blishen's innovative retelling of Greek myth, *The God Beneath the Sea* (1970), but he resisted suggestions that he had an affinity for the ancient world or an interest in historically accurate representation.[45] He disowned any source whatsoever for his depiction (in historical novels) of how people dressed and what they looked like in the past ("I wasn't around, I made it all up");[46] and in his illustrations for Garfield and Blishen's myth books rejected "any of the conventional marks of Greekness, in dress or otherwise."[47] Keeping also rejected the traditional association of illustration with significant narrative moments:

Many people believe that an illustration should illustrate the story. This is something I don't really believe. I'm sick to death of the illustration that just shows an incident. It bores one doing it. I would much sooner make a drawing that has an evocative mood.[48]

Despite these disavowals, Keeping's illustrations for *The Heroes* include both conventional images (a shield, a helmet, a ship) and "incidents" (Perseus' flight from Medusa's sisters, Theseus' defeat of Sciron), perhaps as required by the publisher. But his own preference for the evocative mood rather than the obvious plot moment is also clear, especially where he reanimates the traditional vignette, using sequences of separate drawings to bring out sequences of mood in Kingsley's narrative. When (for example) Theseus finally uncovers the sword and sandals that will reveal his father's identity (and thus his own),

he caught them up, and burst through the bushes like a wild boar, and leapt to his mother, holding them high above his head.
But when she saw them she wept long in silence, hiding her fair face in her shawl; and Theseus stood by her wondering and wept also, he knew not why.
(Kingsley 1859: 198)

Kingsley's own drawing has the two standing together quietly in the aftermath of the discovery; but Keeping gives us, on separate pages, the Theseus who leaps and holds high what he has found, and the mother weeping with bent head.

---

[45] He told an interviewer that his first thought on being offered Sutcliff's *The Silver Branch* was "Romans, oh no! Last thing I want to do!" and, according to Edward Blishen, he "didn't particularly care for the Greeks" (Martin 1993: 55, 129).

[46] Interview quoted in Martin 1989: 41.   [47] Blishen quoted in Martin 1993: 126.

[48] Keeping 1970, cited in Martin 1989: 43.

Keeping's resistance to typical illustration protocols also in places expresses his resistance both to this edition's oversimplification and to the myths themselves as celebratory portraits of heroism. In a telling sequence, he subordinates the encounter with the Minotaur to Theseus' relationship with and loss of Ariadne. (This edition suppresses Kingsley's acknowledgment that he may have abandoned her as she slept.) First we see Ariadne and Theseus, looking like two teenagers from Keeping's day in spite of their vaguely classical clothing, and seated on the ground in a pose that is notably modern in its informality and intimacy. The way in which Keeping depicts this intimacy suggests a kind of narrative substitution: the two are face to face, with limbs apparently intertwined, as Theseus is with the Minotaur in many earlier illustrations, and the pairing of boy and girl thus not only precedes but in some sense displaces the hostile pairing of hero and beast (Fig. 2.7).

We do see the Minotaur on the next page (Fig. 2.8) rushing forward with head down, just as in Kingsley's narrative, as if to grapple with Theseus. But Theseus himself, for all his prominent place in the

Fig. 2.7. Illustration by Charles Keeping from Charles Kingsley's *The Heroes* (abridged edition), originally published by Hutchinson Educational, © 1961 Charles Keeping.

Permission is granted for the use of illustrations by Charles Keeping by B. L. Kearley Ltd for the estate of Charles Keeping.

CLASSICS IN THEIR OWN RIGHT 79

Fig. 2.8. Illustration by Charles Keeping from Charles Kingsley's *The Heroes* (abridged edition), originally published by Hutchinson Educational, © 1961 Charles Keeping.

Permission is granted for the use of illustrations by Charles Keeping by B. L. Kearley Ltd for the estate of Charles Keeping.

adjoining text, is missing from this picture. The hero's absence, and the consequent incompleteness of the visual narrative, are striking: Keeping shows neither the battle that follows nor the killing nor the moment of triumph. Theseus is also missing from the next illustration (Fig. 2.9), which shows the sleeping Ariadne. Here, however, Theseus'

Fig. 2.9. Illustration by Charles Keeping from Charles Kingsley's *The Heroes* (abridged edition), originally published by Hutchinson Educational, © 1961 Charles Keeping.

Permission is granted for the use of illustrations by Charles Keeping by B. L. Kearley Ltd for the estate of Charles Keeping.

absence is not an elision of events in the story but an acknowledgment of a separation that is itself part of the story: Keeping's illustration offers a visual suggestion of the abandonment this edition suppresses.

Keeping's visual narrative thus deprives Theseus of a moment of individual heroism and reminds readers of a moment of shame, the abandonment of the friend and ally with whom an earlier image showed him so closely and touchingly linked. In so doing it provides a partial counter-narrative to the ameliorative and simplified version offered by the abridged edition, which also suppresses Kingsley's concluding account of Theseus' pride-driven downfall and ends with the words, "And now Theseus was king of Athens, and he guarded it and ruled it well" (96). Keeping's illustrations further suggest a critique of the heroism central to Kingsley's book, and one quite different from the Christian critique of heroic pride implicit in Kingsley's own illustration of Theseus and the Minotaur. Keeping's drawings of two women in isolation—first Theseus' mother and then Ariadne—not only provide the discrete images of evocative moments he prefers, but also tell a story about separation and abandonment and point to the ways in which heroic endeavor destroys human bonds.[49]

Although in his introduction to *Pegasus* Robert Lowell declares Hawthorne's myths to be the right versions and identifies more modern retellings as false, he nonetheless looks ahead to his readers' future encounters with other versions as they grow older and celebrates the reception of myth in all its variety.

Later, you will read these stories as the Greeks wrote them, and as others have rewritten them, and you will see scenes from the stories as many artists have painted them. You will be surprised to discover how differently the best minds of the ages saw the same persons and plots.   (Hawthorne 1963: n.p.)

In Chapter 3, we consider the ways in which writers and artists other than Hawthorne, Kingsley, and their illustrators re-envisioned these same persons and plots in the continued reception of myth for and by children from the last years of the nineteenth century through the middle of the twentieth.

---

[49] Keeping's use of sequences of illustrations that both enhance the emotional impact of Kingsley's story and counter its emphasis on heroism creates a kind of intertwined narrative or "composite verbal-visual narration" that is particularly characteristic of the picture book but that Joseph Schwarcz and others also see in "the profusely illustrated book" (Schwarcz 1982: 11).

"*It is the only one in the world,*" said the servant

Plate 1. Illustration by Milo Winter from Nathaniel Hawthorne's *Tanglewood Tales* (1913).

Plate 2. *Eve Tempted* (1887) by John Roddam Spencer Stanhope.
Manchester Art Gallery UK/Bridgeman Images.

Plate 3. Illustration by Arthur Rackham from Nathaniel Hawthorne's *A Wonder-Book for Girls and Boys* (1922).

[Theseus] caught him by the horns, and forced his
head back, and drove the keen sword through his throat

Plate 4. Illustration by William Russell Flint from Charles Kingsley's *The Heroes, or, Greek Fairy-Tales for My Children*, published by the Medici Society, © 1912 William Russell Flint. Used by permission of Susan Russell Flint.

THESEVS SLAYS THE MINOTAVR

Plate 5. Illustration by H. M. Brock from Charles Kingsley's *The Heroes* (1928).

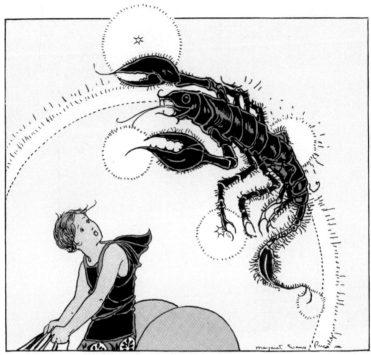

The Scorpion reached his great claws toward the chariot

Plate 6. Illustration by Margaret Price from *A Child's Book of Myths*, published by Rand McNally, © 1924 Margaret Evans Price. Used by permission of Denise Bergne on behalf of the estate of Margaret Evans Price.

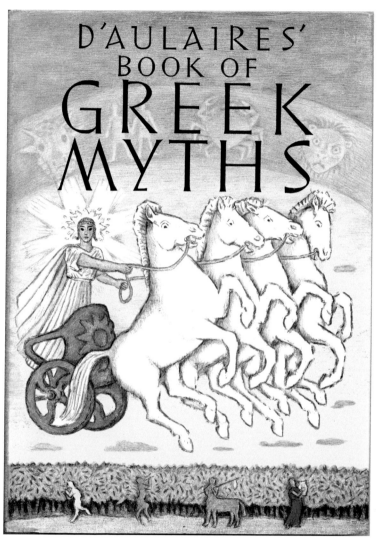

Plate 7. Front cover of *D'Aulaires' Book of Greek Myths* (1962) by Ingri and Edgar Parin D'Aulaire.

Plate 8. Illustration from *D'Aulaires' Book of Greek Myths* (1962) by Ingri and Edgar Parin D'Aulaire.

3

"Steeped in Greek Mythology"
The First Half of the Twentieth Century

Looking back at her childhood as an English expatriate in Egypt in the 1930s and 1940s, the novelist Penelope Lively recalls an especially absorbing book.

I was steeped in Greek mythology by way of Andrew Lang's *Tales of Troy and Greece*. That late Victorian retelling was central to my imaginative life: I re-enacted the stories, reconstructing them to suit my circumstances, because of course I was right in there anyway—Penelope—but with the wrong part, since it is made clear that she is far less beautiful than Helen, and all that shilly-shallying with the suitors is tiresome. So I made various adjustments but, crucially, the narratives and the characters became deeply familiar, and have remained so. I was lucky and wish that all children had such exposure; unless you know that mythology, much of western art and literature will be baffling to you later in life.[1]

Like Leigh Hunt in his recollections of reading Tooke, Lively describes a child's encounter with mythology in which the modern reteller plays only an incidental role. At once timeless and malleable, the myths transcend the particular features of a given retelling. As they are freely appropriated by the child reader, they provide an adaptable template for individual experience and transmit a cultural legacy that is valued in retrospect as a lifelong benefit. Lively also tells a version of the story we traced in Chapter 2, of nineteenth-century myth collections achieving the status of classics and being read by new generations of children well into the twentieth century.

Lang's late Victorian collections were among the hundreds of new myth books for children published in Britain and America (alongside

---

[1] Greenway 2005: 103. Lively has repeatedly returned to the formative influence of Lang's book in interviews and other reminiscences. Cf. esp. Lively 2005: 201–3.

new or reissued editions of Hawthorne and Kingsley) from the late nineteenth through the mid-twentieth century.[2] This outpouring was fostered by the inclusion of such storybooks in place of the old handbooks in school curricula, by the appeal of myth as a subject for illustration, and by the open availability of ancient material to modern retellers, who also felt free to borrow from their predecessors within the developing modern tradition. As a common heritage, belonging to everyone and needing to be acquired by all educated people, classical mythology was (and still remains) a reliable low-cost standby for publishers and a topic to which a wide array of writers, including established children's authors and specialists in other areas, repeatedly turned.[3]

In these books, myth is recurrently justified as a subject for children by its educational value, whether as the gateway to the subsequent study of history (about which we will have more to say in Chapter 4) or as the foundation for a broader cultural literacy which we have seen acknowledged by the early handbooks, embraced by Kingsley, and celebrated by Penelope Lively among countless others.[4] But those promised benefits regularly coexist, as they do in Lively's recollection, with a strong affirmation of myth as a source of pleasure, through its capacity to stimulate the imagination and its appeal to a child's natural sense of wonder and attunement to nature.

Working in the tradition inaugurated by Hawthorne and Kingsley, retellers of myth pursued a range of agendas, many of them invisible or immaterial to their child readers. With the growth of anthropology and folklore studies, fresh versions were underwritten by more fully elaborated historical schemes aligning classical culture with childhood and by

---

[2] A bibliography listing British and American versions through 1994, but drawing mainly on American sources, includes 381 items (Brazouski and Klatt 1994).
[3] Some examples: Enid Blyton (1930, 1939); Catherine Gasquoine Hartley (1909), author of *Cathedrals of Southern Spain, Divorce To-day and To-morrow*, and *Mind of the Naughty Child*; Sally Benson (1940), author of *Junior Miss* and *Meet Me in St. Lewis*; the American essayist and critic Clifton Fadiman (1959, 1960); the Scottish novelist Compton Mackenzie (1972).
[4] One example, James Baldwin's *A Story of the Golden Age of Greek Heroes* (1887), is designed "to pave the way . . . to an enjoyable reading of Homer, either in translations or in the original" (1905: viii). Odysseus' childhood is used as a frame for bringing together myths that provide background to Homer. Less predictably, K. D. Cather's *Pan and His Pipes and Other Tales for Children*, published in 1916 by the Victor Talking Machine Company of Camden, New Jersey, tells the myths of Pan and Syrinx and of Hermes' invention of the lyre to interest children—or their parents—in the Victrola phonograph.

new formulations of the romantic association between children and popular culture. In the years following World War I, the United States overtook England as the center of children's book publishing and was the site of important innovations in the presentation of myth, especially in the turn from illustrated book to picture book—and also of renewed challenges to fantasy as appropriate material for children. By mid-century, there were on both sides of the Atlantic new myth collections that were themselves shaped by nostalgia for the now-classic versions of the nineteenth century, including those of Andrew Lang. Over the same period, encounters between modern children and ancient myths were not only promoted through retellings but also incorporated into fictional narratives: mythical figures emerged from anthologies to play a role in stories about contemporary British children, and fictional American children were portrayed as reenacting Greek legends in a New World setting.

Myth as Folklore and Fiction in Turn-of-the-Century Britain

Lang's *Tales of Troy and Greece* (1907) was not the first work in which he retold Greek mythology for child readers. It was preceded by almost two decades by *The Blue Fairy Book* (1889), the first of the "Coloured Fairy Books," a series of compendia of magical tales for children, which included, under the title "The Terrible Head," a version of the myth of Perseus. That he retold the same myth twice is one manifestation of Lang's immense productivity over a long career as a classical scholar and a versatile man of letters, but the differences between his two versions also reflect developments within the new science of anthropology, in which Lang was a leading figure.[5]

As a series of regularly appearing volumes suitable for gift-giving, Lang's highly profitable fairy books helped to bring about a resurgence of the fairy tale as children's literature at a time when it was once again threatened with eclipse by realistic family stories.[6] Each book brought

---

[5] For overviews of Lang's life and works, see Lancelyn Green 1946; Langstaff 1987.

[6] Lancelyn Green 1946: 81–2; Hearne 1988: 221. This was noted at the time by Mrs E. M. Field in her survey, *The Child and His Book* (1892: 235, 242) On the many British books featuring fairies in the opening decades of the 20th century, see Eyre 1973: 19–20.

together stories from diverse traditions. Although European fairy tales predominate, the first volume also contains tales from the *Arabian Nights* and a retelling of part of *Gulliver's Travels* as well as the Perseus myth, and the later volumes include African and Native American folk tales; here Greek myth's similarity to fairy tales places it in the context of worldwide folklore, which was a major concern of late nineteenth-century anthropologists such as Frazer, whose *The Golden Bough* was first published in 1890.[7] Most of the retellings in the fairy books were composed not by Lang himself, but by a group of largely female writers and translators whom he supervised, prominent among them his wife Leonora.[8] Lang did, however, write the version of the Perseus myth that appears as "The Terrible Head."

For this tale, Lang draws on material from classical sources including Pindar, Simonides, and Apollodorus, but so fully assimilates the story to the fairy tales among which it appears that an uninformed reader would not recognize it as a Greek myth. The particular names of people and places are replaced with generic designations: Perseus is "the boy," Danae "the Princess," the Graiae "The Three Gray Sisters," the Hesperides "The Fairies of the Garden," the Gorgons "The Dreadful Women."[9] Like some fairies in European fairy tales—and like the series of books in which they are to be found—the "Western Fairies" are each associated with a separate color: "dressed one in green, one in white, and one in red." Lang also gives the story a vaguely northern location and makes Perseus a northern European type with "short curly yellow hair, and blue eyes" (Lang 1965: 190). Magical elements are accentuated, with emphatically capitalized labels for Perseus' talismanic objects: "a Cap of Darkness," "a Sword of Sharpness," "Shoes of Swiftness"—all of which recur within the same collection in the tale of Jack the Giant Killer. And the song sung by Danae to the baby Perseus in a surviving fragment of the classical poet Simonides becomes a charm-like lullaby.

---

[7] Thomas Keightley, whose handbook of mythology is mentioned in Chapter 1, anticipated this cultural range in his earlier *Fairy Mythology* (1828).

[8] The irony that Lang is now best known for works he did not write is often noted; on Lang's own frustration with this misattribution, see Lancelyn Green 1946: 96; on the translators who contributed to Lang's volumes and their relative invisibility, see Lathey 2010: 102–9; on Leonora Lang's role, see Hearn 1986: 487.

[9] On this change and on the adaptation in general, see Lancelyn Green 1946: 81–3; Jiang 2011.

Child, my child, how sound you sleep!
Though your mother's care is deep,
You can lie with heart at rest
In the narrow brass-bound chest . . . [10]

In contrast, the book that Lively read, *Tales of Troy and Greece*, resembles Kingsley's volume in that fairy-tale elements are integrated into a series of hero tales with a clear historical context. Published in 1907 (and so technically not "late Victorian"), it reflects the same increased interest in hero tales in the years before World War I that also led to a cluster of new editions of Kingsley's own work.[11] The title seems to promise discrete "Tales," but most of the book is a continuous narrative of the Troy legend, drawn largely from Homer and other epic sources. Three further stories, those of Jason, Theseus, and Perseus, are appended and situated within that framework. The "Nymphs of the Isle of the West," still have their special colors, but they also introduce themselves as "Aegle," "Erytheia," and "Hesperia" (Lang 2006: 272). The magic items Perseus carries are so closely identified with their owner Hermes that the Nymphs mistake him for the god; and while one of those objects is still called the Sword of Sharpness, we are also told that "the name of it was Herpê" (269).

It may seem that Lang has simply chosen to employ for different publishing projects two different generic models for recasting myths for children, both of which emerged from the works of Hawthorne and Kingsley and their contemporaries: the fairy tale and the more extended heroic narrative. But the differences between these two versions also reflect different sides of Lang's intellectual identity. As his biographer

[10] Lang 1965: 182–3. This is a close translation of the Greek original (itself possibly the reworking of a subliterary form) into the idiom of English folk poetry, much like the idiom Lang uses for his wholly invented "Song of the Western Fairies": "Round and round the apples of gold, | Round and round dance we; | Thus do we dance from the days of old | About the enchanted tree . . . "

[11] In the US, this trend may have been stimulated by the publication of Civil War stories such as Stephen Crane's *The Red Badge of Courage* (1895). Thus in 1905, shortly before Lang's book appeared, Hamilton Wright Mabie published *Heroes Every Child Should Know*, which begins with Perseus (adapted from Kingsley's version) and Hercules and includes both Robert E. Lee and Abraham Lincoln. While Lang himself deplored Kingsley's moralizing tendencies and anti-Catholic preoccupation, he admired him especially as a writer for boys, who could best appreciate "this really great and noble and manly and blundering genius" (Lang 1901: 155).

puts it, "we feel that it is Lang the classical scholar rather than Lang the folklorist who is telling 'Odysseus the Sacker of Cities' or 'The Story of the Golden Fleece.'"[12] And, especially where the use of proper names is concerned, those differences also answer to some of Lang's most strongly held views as a pioneering and combative figure in the emerging field of anthropology.[13]

Like such contemporaries as Edward Burnett Tylor and William Robertson Smith, Lang responded to the striking similarities among myths and folk tales from all parts of the world with an evolutionary explanation, according to which every race progresses through a set of stages marked by distinct types of mythical narrative: (1) "popular tales of the lower and more backward races," (2) "the *märchen*, or *contes*, or household tales of the modern European, Asiatic, and Indian peasantry," and (3) "the romantic and heroic tales of the great civilised races, or races which have proved capable of civilisation" found in "epic poetry and legend" (Lang 1913: 302–6).[14]

It is the use of names that distinguishes Lang's most advanced stage from the intermediate second stage: "in the popular tales of the peasantry ... the story is not localized, and the characters are anonymous." Legends that have

won their way into the national literatures and the region of epic ... attach themselves to the dim beginnings of actual history, and to real personages like Charlemagne ... The characters are national heroes, such as Perseus, Jason, Œdipus and Olympian gods ... Their paths and places are not in dim fairyland, but in the fields and on the shores that we know. (304)

The contextualized versions of such common tales retold by Homer represent a high point of cultural development: "then we recognise the effect of race upon myth, the effect of the Greek genius at work on rude material" (Lang 1884: 28). This evolutionary scheme was at the heart of Lang's ongoing polemic against the dominant myth theory of the mid-nineteenth century, the philological approach of the Indo-Europeanist

---

[12] Lancelyn Green 1946: 84.

[13] On Lang's role as one of the "founding fathers of British anthropology," see Ackerman 1991: 33–6.

[14] Cf. on folk tales as "fiction in its childhood," MacCulloch 1905: 1, and on the contrast between such views and the Grimms' view of folk tales as the remnants of lost poetic traditions, Schacker 2003: 17.

Max Müller (1823–1900).[15] Müller situated myth in a narrative of decline: the original Aryans had an intense, animistic relationship to the natural world, expressed through their powerful and concrete language; the myths of the Aryans' descendants, with their specific names and their narrative sequences often containing dark, disturbing elements, were deformations (produced, in a famous phrase, by "a disease of language") based on misunderstandings of the Aryans' live metaphors.

If, in their general style, Lang's retellings continue and update those of Hawthorne and Kingsley, they are based on a different and more fully elaborated conception of the connections between childhood and the times in which the myths were generated. His more systematic model of human evolution aligns his two ways of telling the Perseus myth with different historical eras whose modes of storytelling speak to child readers of different ages. The fairy-tale version belongs, not to a lost golden age of which children are "the only representatives," but to an intermediate stage of cultural history still manifested by the modern peasantry of Europe and elsewhere, which is to be treasured for its childlike freshness and directness—as it was by Lang himself, who retained throughout his life a deep love of fairy stories dating from his own childhood.[16] In casting a Greek myth in this form, Lang is in effect reversing what he understands to be the historical sequence, translating his literary sources back into the traditional unlocalized, anonymous tale that lies behind them. The heroic version of the same myth, being explicitly grounded in the culture that produced it, belongs to a more advanced stage than the fairy tale; it is accordingly aimed at older children who can be expected to take an interest in the historical details that distinguish it.

Even more than Kingsley, Lang envisions for his hero tales a reader who is already an incipient student of Greek history, and his narrative is

---

[15] As noted in Chapter 2, Müller's disciple George William Cox had written several well-received myth books in the 1860s. In addition to the two storybooks mentioned there, Cox published *A Manual of Mythology in the Form of Question and Answer* (1867), which provides a grounding in solar mythology and a survey of Greek myth from that perspective. Another predecessor of Lang in his interest in folklore was Thomas Keightley, discussed in Chapter 1.

[16] Lang cites a French predecessor in the study and composition of fairy tales to make this point: "We can never quite recover the old simplicity, energy, and romance, the qualities which, as Charles Nodier said, make Hop o' my Thumb, Puss in Boots, and Blue Beard 'the Ulysses, the Figaro and the Othello of children'" (Lang 1895: xv–xvi).

filled with nuggets of information relating to the language and context of his Greek sources. In addition to his magic sword, Perseus is provided by his protector Dictys with more mundane equipment: "three weighed wedges of gold (which were called 'talents' and served as money)" (Lang 2006: 266). A first chapter recounting Ulysses' coming of age through his fight with the boar is followed by a second on "How People Lived in the Time of Ulysses." Writing only a few years after Arthur Evans's discoveries at Knossos in 1900, Lang is one of the first of many writers for children to ground the awe-inspiring features of Greek civilization in the new findings of archaeology. Describing the furnishings of Minos' palace, he mentions huge vases "like the pots in the story of Ali Baba and the Forty Thieves in the Arabian Nights," inscribed tablets from Egypt, and gold and silver cups, then adds, "We know that this is true, for the things themselves, all of them, or pictures of them, have been brought to light, dug out from under ground; and, after years of digging, there is still plenty of this wonderful palace to be explored" (Lang 2006: 242).

The hero tale offers more extensive treatments of motivation and moral character than are found in *The Blue Fairy Book*, with an explicit orientation to Greek religion rather than the proto-Christian values promoted by Kingsley. In the fairy tale, Danae's father casts her out in the chest because "cowardly as he was, he had not quite the heart to kill the Princess and her baby outright" (Lang 1965: 182), while in the heroic version Lang introduces the Erinyes and explains that Acrisius was afraid they would attack him if he killed his own kin. After defeating the Minotaur, Theseus "kneeled down and thanked all the gods, and promised rich sacrifices, and a new temple to Pallas Athênê, the guardian of Athens" (Lang 2006: 249).

The historical specificity of the hero tales also tallies with a gender difference in the assumed audience of each retelling. The fairy books were aimed at a younger, undifferentiated readership in which girls played at least as important a part as boys; Lang himself viewed girls as the natural audience of fairy tales.[17] Not only does *Tales of Troy and Greece* introduce historical facts such as boys would learn at school, but

---

[17] In his preface to Irene Maunder's *The Plain Princess* (1905), he comments: "When I was a little boy it is to be supposed that I was a little muff; for I read every fairy-tale I could lay my hands on . . . and I hated machinery of every description. These tastes and distastes I have never overcome, but I am pretty sure they are unusual in little boys" (Lancelyn Green 1946: 9).

the book is dedicated to the adventure writer H. Rider Haggard, and there is an emphasis throughout on boys growing up with a vocation for adventure and heroism. Theseus is trained by his mother Aethra to lift large objects, so that he will be able to roll away the stone under which his magical shoes and sword are hidden. Perseus listens with fascination to the story of Bellerophon and aspires to perform similar deeds. In the fairy tale, "a young man like a king's son" and "a tall and beautiful lady" simply give Perseus the Shoes of Swiftness along with instructions on how to obtain the other objects he needs (Lang 1965: 184–5). In the later version, Athena reveals herself and explains why the gods are helping him: "We have watched you long, Perseus, to learn whether you have the heart of a hero...We have seen that your heart is steadfast, and that you have sought through hunger and long travel to know the way wherein you must find death or win glory" (Lang 2006: 268). Of course, this orientation to boy readers does not mean that the book was not read and enjoyed by girls; as we have seen, Penelope Lively found plenty of material in Lang's narrative on which to base her own fantasies of female experience (including an account of the rivalry between Penelope and Helen (11)).

Lang's treatment of tales drawn from worldwide traditions as similar manifestations of a universal and childlike cultural stage correlates with the view that stories and the love of storytelling unite children of all cultures—a view that, as we will see in Chapter 7, came to be tied in the early decades of the twentieth century to a redemptive vision of children as the key to overcoming international conflicts. As he put it in the preface to *The Brown Fairy Book*,

All people, black, brown, red, and yellow are like each other when they tell stories; for these are meant for children, who like the same sort of thing, whether they go to school and wear clothes or, on the other hand, wear skins of beasts or even nothing at all, and live on grubs and lizards and hawks and crows and serpents, like the little Australian blacks. (Lang 1904: viii)

In Lang's works this stress on similarity motivates a project in which the tales are essentially homogenized, appearing between the same covers and told in a similar style, and this effect is powerfully reinforced by the accompanying illustrations. All of the fairy books and *Tales of Troy and Greece* were illustrated by Henry Justice Ford (1860–1941).[18] Like his

---

[18] On Ford's career and his influential illustrations for Lang's books, see Gessert 2017: 78–86.

slightly older contemporary Walter Crane, Ford was squarely within the tradition of Pre-Raphaelite artists such as Rossetti, Burne-Jones, and Holman Hunt whose depictions of classical scenes and figures were inflected by a strong interest in medieval art and culture. In Ford's illustrations, supernatural creatures are often vaguely classical in appearance while the human characters are more fully medieval. And while details vary according to the story's setting, most of the characters appear dressed in tunics, caps, and boots that suggest northern Europe, and are located in settings that involve dark forests and Gothic architecture. Just as Perseus acquires "short curly yellow hair, and blue eyes" in Lang's text, so in Ford's illustrations ancient heroes wield the weapons of medieval knights and appear among tangled thorny thickets and pointed arches. In his depiction of Theseus and the Minotaur (Fig. 3.1), which captures the moment when, in Lang's version, Theseus has blinded the Minotaur with a vial of poison, Theseus' tunic is embellished with chains and a patterned border, and the labyrinth suggests both a castle and a forest. A distinctively northern ambiance that had developed within British visual culture, and which had been made familiar through Pre-Raphaelite iconography and illustrations of European fairy tales, became by implication the natural habitat of figures from Greek mythology.

A similar conception of Greek myth as naturally at home in a British setting underlies a notable cluster of children's books from the first decade of the twentieth century, in which figures from myth are displaced from their ancient contexts and relocated in contemporary England. Among these, Pan plays a particularly important role.[19] J. M. Barrie borrows Pan's name for the immortal and unaging boy who in a series of texts published between 1902 and 1911 appears first in Kensington Gardens and then in the Darling family's London nursery; in Francis Hodgson Burnett's *The Secret Garden* (1910 as adult serial, 1911 as children's book), set among the Yorkshire moors, the Pan-like Dickon plays his pipe and draws wild animals to his side; and when the pointy-eared Puck appears in the Sussex countryside in Kipling's *Puck of Pook's Hill* (1906), a young Roman centurion who arrives from the past addresses him as "faun."[20] Pan himself, as protector of wild things,

---

[19] On Pan and the motif of the puer aeternus, see Kümmerling-Meibauer 2012. For further discussion of the figure of Pan in children's fiction, see Chapter 7 and works cited there.

[20] Puck was identified with Pan as early as the 17th century. Bazovsky 2018.

HOW THESEUS SLEW THE MINOTAUR

Fig. 3.1. Illustration by Henry Justice Ford from Andrew Lang's *Tales of Troy and Greece* (1907).

makes a notable appearance in Kenneth Grahame's *The Wind in the Willows* (1908), where Rat and Mole, drawn irresistibly by his music, encounter the god on an island in the river that is at the heart of the story;[21] and in E. Nesbit's *The Enchanted Castle* (1907), four children encounter the Greek gods in the form of statues come alive on the grounds of a great English estate; they feast with several Olympians and with Psyche, Eros, Hebe, and Ganymede.[22]

As these writers construct narratives in which English children (or animals) encounter the mythical in their own world, they resemble the anthologists in suggesting a particular affinity between childhood and myth, often attributing to children an openness to encounters with mythical figures that is in one way or another denied to adults.[23] It is only children who can follow Peter Pan to the Neverland; the children who meet with Puck are magically prevented from sharing what he shows them with grownups; in *The Secret Garden*, the children Mary, Colin, and Dickon inhabit a secret Arcadian world of their own, and in Nesbit's book adults who encounter the marble pantheon believe they have gone mad. In *The Wind in the Willows*, though adult animals catch a glimpse of Pan, it is a lost otter pup who evokes his presence and sleeps between his protective hooves. And just as myth is regularly said (by adult writers) to awaken and develop the child reader's imaginative powers or sense of the classical past, so these fictional encounters with domesticated mythical beings convey a sense of something beyond the everyday reality into which they have been introduced: the historical or mythical past, the natural world, the realm of the imagination, the realm of the divine.

These assorted manifestations of the mythical are not only alike in being very much at home in their English setting, but all of them also magically point beyond or transform that setting in ways that answer to children's heightened imaginative powers and may also have a lasting

---

[21] On readings of Pan in *The Wind in the Willows*, see most recently Rudd 2010.

[22] On the classical gods in Barrie, Hodges, Grahame, Nesbit, and others, see Hale 2015, Brown 2017; on the experience of the ancient past in Nesbit's *The Story of the Amulet*, *The Magic City*, and *The Enchanted Castle*, see Paul 2015.

[23] See Hale 2015 on the classical elements in Barrie, Hodges, Grahame, and Nesbit's books as generally expressing the division between childhood and adulthood, and reflecting an Edwardian vision of childhood as "separate and superior, attuned to a pastoral and nostalgic spirit of nature presided over by pagan, rather than Christian gods" (Hale 2015: 25).

impact on their inner lives or alter their present circumstances. Peter Pan takes Wendy and her brothers to the Neverland, presented as a realization of childhood imagination, while Puck introduces two English children to people summoned from the past and thus extends their understanding of the land and its history. In Nesbit's *Enchanted Castle*, the children who picnic with the gods find that they are at once in the grounds of the estate and in another world; the gods themselves alternate between the quotidian and the sublime; in the space of a few pages Apollo addresses Hermes as "old chap" and says to one of the children that "The span of your life, my earth-child, would not contain the words I should speak, to tell you all I know" (Nesbit 1979: 234, 237).[24] This juxtaposition of worlds enables the gods to pluck pomegranates from willow trees and golden dishware from ash and oak:

It was a celestial picnic. Then everyone sat or lay down and the feast began. And oh! the taste of the food served on those dishes, the sweet wonder of the drink that melted from those gold cups on the white lips of the company! And the fruit! There is no fruit like it grown on earth, just as there is no laughter like the laughter of those lips, no songs like the songs that stirred the silence of that night of wonder.   (233)

The music of Pan has a similarly otherworldly effect on its hearers in *The Wind in the Willows*, which is fantastical only in being populated by animals who speak, have nicely furnished homes, drive motorcars, and so on:[25]

"Now it passes on and I begin to lose it," [Rat] said presently. "O Mole! the beauty of it! The merry bubble and joy, the thin, clear, happy call of the distant piping! Such music I never dreamed of, and the call in it is stronger even than the music is sweet! Row on, Mole, row! For the music and the call must be for us."   (Grahame 1982: 111)

Even in *The Secret Garden*, an almost entirely realistic work of fiction, the Pan-like Dickon assists a process of growth and regeneration which is described by one of the other children, Colin, as "the Magic" and which

---

[24] Sarah Annes Brown sees this "code-switching" (Brown 2017: 192) as one of a number of ways Nesbit undercuts the authority and majesty of the gods, in keeping with a pervasive marginalization and diminution of the Greek pantheon in fantasy fiction.

[25] The chapter in which Pan appears, "The Piper at the Gates of Dawn" is generally noted as an intrusion into the two central narrative strands, Mole's story and Toad's story; but see Rudd 2010 for the view that Pan in fact pervades Grahame's text.

leads to spiritual rebirth not only for Colin and his cousin Mary, but also for Colin's miserably grieving father.

Myth in America after World War I

In the early decades of the twentieth century, Lang's role as the chief popularizer of classical mythology for English-speaking children was taken over by Padraic Colum (1881–1972), whose works were based on an even more unified and thoroughgoing identification of ancient myths with popular folklore. Unlike Lang, Colum was not a scholar, but came to myth fortuitously, in the course of a literary career.[26] A poet and playwright associated with the Irish Renaissance and the Abbey Theater, he emigrated from Ireland to New York in 1914 to try his luck as a freelance writer. His subsequent career as a children's author was shaped by the circumstances he encountered there. In the years following World War I, America overtook England, where the aftereffects of the war were more severe and long-lasting, as the source of the most original and distinguished English-language children's books.[27] Among the many factors that contributed to this flowering of American children's publishing in the 1920s and 1930s were the first children's bookstores, the first separate reviewing of children's books, the first training school for children's librarians, the institution of the Newbery Medal (an annual award for the best children's book given by the American Library Association), new printing techniques, the influence of high quality European books, and a climate of renewed peace and prosperity.[28]

This impressive expansion was accompanied by the desire to create a distinctively American children's literature (much as there had been in the early decades of the nineteenth century), written by American authors, promoting American values, and set in the American landscape, and by the ambition of making America an international center for the production of books that could compete with those produced

---

[26] For overviews of Colum's life and career, see Bowen 1970, Sternlicht 1985.

[27] Eyre 1973: 12–13, 23. A Boston bookseller, Bertha Mahoney, commented in 1928 that "ten years ago . . . the height of our expectations lay with the coming of an attractive new edition of a favorite or classic, usually an importation from England" (Mahoney 1928: 2–4, quoted in Marcus 2008: 71).

[28] On these developments, see Bechtel 1969; Bader 1976: 23–3; Hearn 1996: 27–8; Marcus 2008: 71–83.

in Europe.[29] This second goal was aided by a large concentration of European émigré artists, who spurred the development of innovative illustration and picture-book design, in many cases drawing on the native folk traditions of the artist's country of origin. Those artists also made use of transformative new lithographic technologies, first introduced by Ingri and Edwin Parin D'Aulaire with *The Magic Rug* in 1929, that allowed texts and images to be printed together on the same page so as to form a unified whole.[30]

It was one of these émigré artists, the Hungarian Willy Pogany, who recruited Colum to write a book of Irish stories that he could illustrate, a commission that led to further collaborations between the two of them and to Colum's adaptations of Greek myth. After the appearance of *The King of Ireland's Son* (1916), Colum was offered a regular contract for two books a year—a children's version of a myth cycle or saga and a collection of stories for younger children—by Macmillan, a leading children's publisher which was soon to establish (in 1919) the first independent children's division in an American publishing house.[31]

Through these developments, Colum unexpectedly became a children's writer, and even more unexpectedly an acknowledged expert on folklore. "I began by telling the stories I remembered from my grandmother's house in *The King of Ireland's Son* and then I was labeled a folklorist and mythologist and I went on with it."[32] Colum's storytelling is rooted in the stories and songs he heard as a child in Ireland, but he assumed that such stories represent a universal medium. It seemed a natural progression to him, as well as to his publisher, for *The King of Ireland's Son* to be followed by *The Adventures of Odysseus or The Children's Homer* (1918) and *The Golden Fleece and the Heroes Who Lived Before Achilles* (1921), as well as *The Children of Odin* (1920).

In his comments on storytelling, Colum articulates a frequently made connection between child audiences and popular audiences.[33] In this he

---

[29] Schmidt 2013: xvii–xix.   [30] Eyre 1973: 42; Bader 1976: 38–59.
[31] Hearn 1996: 27.
[32] Bowen 1973: 26. In that capacity, Colum was commissioned by the Hawaiian legislature to produce a volume of authentic Polynesian legends to be used in schools; he based his work on extensive research into Hawaiian traditions, but with strategic reworking on the model of the European folk tale (Bowen 1973: 27).
[33] On the affinities between children's literature and popular literature, see Murnaghan 2011; Nodelman 2008: 3–5.

recalls Eustace Bright's championing of the "modern Yankee" in the face of the more refined and scholarly Mr Pringle in *A Wonder-Book* and Lang's association of fairy tales with "the peasantry," but without Lang's interest in identifying Greek myth as a distinct and higher form belonging to a more civilized people. On this understanding, myths retold for children in effect reproduce the popular oral tales that lie behind our written sources; it makes sense for modern writers to imitate stories they themselves heard from humble sources when they were children—in the case of Colum from his own relatives, in the case of others from servants.[34]

In asserting the popular roots of his own art, Colum lays particular stress on the common experiences of oral audiences. Thus his response when asked about the differences between his works for children and for adults:

They're all folklore. If you sat in a house the children would be listening to the man who was telling the story, but so would the adults. They are children's in the sense that they are told very simply and straight-forwardly, and they're about wonders, which children like. But who is to say what a children's story is?[35]

For Colum, oral narrative is especially suited to the kind of archetypal wisdom with which children are often associated: "for the human voice . . . can put into our deeper consciousness those lasting patterns that belong to the deeper consciousness of the race" (Colum 1968: 21).[36]

In terms of style and subject matter, Colum stresses that "both children and the lower class of reader hate books which are written down to

---

[34] Lang's biographer links his success with the fairy books to the influence of his nurse "Old Nancy," who told tales of "Whuppity Stoorie and the Red Etin" on long winter evenings (Lancelyn Green 1946: 80). The implicit corollary is that modern retellings replicate stories told in similar situations in antiquity. Cf. the preface to *Greek Tales for Tiny Tots* (1929), discussed later in this section, and W. H. D. Rouse in the preface to *Gods, Heroes and Men of Ancient Greece*: "If I have sometimes drawn on my imagination for the dialogues, so did Homer and Nonnus [Rouse's acknowledged sources]; and so did the Greek nannies when they told the stories to their nurslings" (Rouse 1957).

[35] Bowen 1973: 32–3.

[36] Earlier in the same essay, he identifies "reverie" as the shared quality that distinguishes oral narratives and good childrens' stories (8). In describing a storyteller of his youth, he identifies oral communication with especially direct and even preverbal signification (often associated with children): "He had a language that had not been written down; he had words that had not been made colorless by constant use in books and newspapers. He was free to make all sorts of rhymes and chimes on the language he used, and to use words that were meaningless except for the overtones of meaning that were in their sounds" (2).

their capacity" (13).[37] Writers who respect "the child's mind and the child's conception of the world" can use mature language as long as the action and the sentences are clear. The work should be infused with a "mood of kindliness" (meaning especially kindliness on the part of the teller towards the characters) and a "mood of adventure" (15), and should retain the archaic figures of romance, including Kings, Queens, and Princes as well as witches and trolls. There should be an element of magic that answers to the child's—and the humble person's—sense of the possibilities that inhere in the material world: "For children feel, as people with few possessions feel, the adventure and the enchantment that are in things" (18). Colum's deep connection to storytelling is reflected in his habitual use of internal narrators and frame stories. His most extended account of Greek myths, *The Golden Fleece and the Heroes Who Lived before Achilles*, offers a continuous account of the Argonaut legend, but includes many inset stories told by various members of the expedition along the way.

The opening of the Persephone story in *The Golden Fleece* (told by Orpheus to the Lemnian women because they do not want to hear stories about men) illustrates Colum's storytelling principles in practice: his swift-moving action, sympathy for his characters, and a style marked by lightly elevated diction and the fullness of oral narrative (e.g. "sown," "mounted up," the triple reference to Persephone at the end).[38]

Once when Demeter was going through the world, giving men grain to be sown in their fields, she heard a cry that came to her from across high mountains and that mounted up to her from the sea. Demeter's heart shook when she heard that cry, for she knew that it came to her from her daughter, from her only child, from young Persephone. (Colum 2004: 67–8)[39]

---

[37] This is a frequent refrain among writers for children; see Ransome 1937 (cited in P. Hunt 1990: 33–4); Lewis 1966: 22; Trease 1973: 102 (cited in P. Hunt 1990: 49).

[38] Colum's style has been considered especially suited to his subject matter even by critics writing several decades after him. For Lionel Trilling (who finds Hawthorne's works arch, facetious, and evidently directed to girls), "His language is vigorous and straightforward, yet sufficiently formal and literary to keep the old stories at their proper distance" (Trilling 1956: 12); to Rosemary Sutcliff, Colum's style is "lively, with the sound of the spoken word, and with the faintest lilt to it—never strong enough to be at odds with the subject matter—of the Celtic tongue" (Sutcliff 1963: 431).

[39] The language here recalls the language of God's command in the story of the sacrifice of Isaac: "Take now thy son, thine only son Isaac, whom thou lovest" (Genesis 22:2, King James Version).

A similar note of pathos colors Theseus' return from his adventures, shadowed by Aegeus' suicide.

> The men and women who came to the beach wept and laughed as they clasped in their arms the children brought back to them. And Theseus stood there, silent and bowed: the memory of his last moments with his father, of his fight with the Minotaur, of his parting with Ariadne [called back to Crete to reign with her father]—all flowed back upon him. He stood there with head bowed, the man who might not put upon his brows the wreath of victory that had been brought to him. (240)

Colum emphasizes Theseus' personal story and subjectivity, without the attention to history that marks Lang's account of the same moment:

> The shore was dark with people all dressed in mourning raiment, and the herald of the city came with the news that Aegeus the King was dead . . . Theseus wished to die, and be with Ariadne [in this version carried away by "a grievous sickness"] in the land of Queen Persephone. But he was a strong man, and he lived to be the greatest of the Kings of Athens, for all the other towns came in, and were his subjects, and he ruled them well. His first care was to build a great fleet in secret harbours far from towns and the ways of men, for, though he and Minos were friends while they both lived, when Minos died the new king might oppress Athens. (Lang 2006: 252)

Lang acknowledges Theseus' grief, but moves swiftly to the manly self-mastery that allows him to play his part in early Athenian history, notably the unification of the surrounding region and the development of a strong navy.

The illustrations by Pogany that accompany *The Golden Fleece* match the studied simplicity of the narrative. Pogany was an extraordinarily versatile artist, and some of his work is highly ornate, but for this book he produced line drawings which are relatively plain though not markedly oriented to children, except possibly in his choices of which moments to illustrate: episodes involving violence and sexuality are represented obliquely rather than directly. Pogany's version of Theseus with the Minotaur (Fig. 3.2), for example, presents a point in their battle at which Theseus' decisive victory is not in doubt (so that the threat presented by the Minotaur is muted) but the actual killing has not begun.

The viewer is placed slightly behind Theseus as he moves decisively into the pictorial frame and forces the Minotaur back out on the other side, his upraised sword countering the even level of their heads. There is none of the northern European ambiance or surrounding detail of Ford's

Fig. 3.2. Illustration by Willy Pogany from Padraic Colum's *The Golden Fleece and the Heroes Who Lived Before Achilles* (1921).

version for Lang's *Tales of Troy and Greece*, (Fig. 3.1) with its strewn bones and elaborate arched cave framing the figures. Pogany's figures move freely and energetically through space that is uncluttered and devoid of cultural associations. It is only within the frame itself that the Minotaur is literally cornered by Theseus, the bulky, gaping monster clearly overmatched (as also in Ford's version) by the trim, closed-mouthed, determined hero.

While many editions of mythology for children appeared in the US during the years between the world wars, often with impressive illustrations, there was also considerable resistance to this material. Hawthorne's playfully retold classics had fostered an American identity typified by leisured, privately educated nineteenth-century New Englanders freed from the constraints of Puritanism. But drawing on Greco-Roman traditions did not so clearly forward the twentieth-century goal of reflecting a society characterized by westward expansion and new waves of European immigration, with literature that stressed American innovation, orientation to the future, and down-to-earth, egalitarian values. Figures from classical mythology did not so naturally inhabit a landscape that was regularly portrayed as a virgin wilderness conquered and shaped by hardy pioneers.

In the progressive educational climate of the period, the value of fantasy for children, and especially for very young children, was once again a matter of spirited debate (as it had been several times before in other times and places, including, as we saw, both England and the United States in the early nineteenth century). A key figure in that debate was a pioneering educator, Lucy Sprague Mitchell, who argued that children were most interested in the objects and activities of their own familiar world and therefore needed stories that would reflect and stimulate that interest; the myths and fairy tales given to children, she claimed (anticipating a central tenet of children's literature studies), really reflected the tastes and assumptions of adults (Mitchell 1921: 23).[40] Without dismissing myths, Mitchell resisted the idea that their portrayals of adult issues could be understood by or made suitable to children: "Hardly before the involved introspections of adolescence can we expect the real beauty and poignancy of a genuine myth to be even dimly understood. And why offer the shell without the spirit?" (34–5).[41]

Mitchell's views put her at odds with many children's librarians, and several figures who were in sympathy with Mitchell's progressive views and advocacy of realistic and child-centered books nonetheless rose to

[40] On Mitchell's life and career, see Antler 1987; on her views about children's literature and the controversy they sparked, see Antler 1987: 247–55; Hearn 1996: 32–5; Marcus 1992: 47–58; Marcus 2008: 100–3, 129–30; Mickenberg 2006: 40–6.

[41] Mitchell also anticipates later critiques in questioning the values reinforced by myth, especially in the treatment of women. See Antler 1987: 251.

the defense of myths and fairy tales.[42] Colum's publisher, Louise Seaman Bechtel, a strong admirer of Mitchell and herself the publisher of many realistic works, felt constrained to defend Colum's books in an essay in the Macmillan's fall catalogue for 1930, asserting that they create their own version of the here-and-now: "Some have thought this writing somewhat 'special' for the average American child. That is not the feeling of those who have been led into the books with story-telling . . . He has so arranged his tellings that we move back easily into other worlds, and think, as we read, that they are almost our own" (Bechtel 1930: 58).

Collections of classical myth could be differentiated from the pure fantasy of fairy tales through their connections to history and Western literature, but they were nonetheless under a similar cloud (as Bechtel's defense of Colum indicates) and, with some exceptions, were generally not among the most innovative or celebrated children's books of the period. While Colum's *The Golden Fleece and the Heroes who Lived before Achilles* was a runner-up for the inaugural Newbery award in 1922, no other book of mythology has been honored since then.[43] Many myth books of those decades were uninspired reworkings of earlier versions, sometimes serving as vehicles for fresh, and considerably more distinguished, illustrations.[44]

Despite Colum's achievements, classical myth did not play a leading role in works inspired by folklore: those more often drew on European traditional tales, often from an émigré artist's own tradition, or—in keeping with the quest for an indigenous American literature—American tall tales, as in Carl Sandburg's 1922 *Rootabaga Stories*.[45] A more congenial

[42] Mitchell's chief adversary was Anne Carroll Moore of the New York Public Library, who especially prized traditional tales and featured them prominently in her collections and story hours, reflecting her more conservative, romantic view of childhood as a special time that could and should be protected from the encroaching world (Marcus 1992: 57).

[43] By contrast, several works of historical fiction set in antiquity (to be discussed in Chapters 4 and 5) have been "Honor Books," though not outright winners: Caroline Dale Snedeker's *The Forgotten Daughter* and Erick Berry's *The Winged Girl of Knossos* in 1934 and Olivia Coolidge's *Men of Athens* in 1963. Colum was honored again in 1926, for *The Voyagers*, a book about Atlantic discoverers, and in 1934 for a book of Irish stories, *Big Tree of Bunlahy: Stories of My Own Countryside*.

[44] Anne Carroll Moore, writing in 1919 about an *Aesop's Fables* illustrated by Milo Winter, praised the exceptional illustrations but deplored the unsigned, "attenuated and modernized" fables: "Hands off Mother Goose and the old fairy and folk tales, the poetry, and the great traditions of the race, unless the work is signed and there is fair evidence of competent literary treatment" (Moore 1939: 53).

[45] Mickenberg 2006: 33–6; Bechtel 1969: 249.

classical analogue was *Aesop's Fables*, which had a strong association with non-elite culture, as well as a longstanding place alongside myth in anglophone children's literature.[46] One of the most distinguished American illustrated books for children from this period is a compilation of previously published Aesop's Fables issued in 1933, with wood engravings by the Russian émigré Boris Artzybasheff.[47] Artzybasheff's depiction of "The Lion and the Mouse" (Fig. 3.3) well illustrates his

Fig. 3.3. Illustration by Boris Artzybasheff, "The Lion and the Mouse," from *Aesop's Fables* (1933).

[46] See Lerer 2008: 35–56. Hall 2016, 2018; Mickenberg 2006: 33–6; Bechtel 1969: 249. *Aesop's Fables* was recommended as children's reading by Locke in 1693 and appeared in a pioneering version for children published pseudonymously by William Godwin in 1805, a year before his *Pantheon*.

[47] On Artzybasheff's career as a children's illustrator and especially his innovative illustrations for Colum's *The Forge in the Forest* (1925), a collection of retold tales that includes the myths of Phaethon and Bellerophon, see Bader 1976: 187–96.

strong lines, bold proportions, stylized, almost tropical foliage, and—in the quizzical expression of the lion who pauses mid-pounce to listen to the arguments of the diminutive mouse—his subtle humor.

In some cases an illustrator would also provide the text, as in *A Child's Book of Myth* (1924), by Margaret Evans Price (with an introduction by Katherine Lee Bates, author of "America the Beautiful," which will be discussed in Chapter 7). Possibly because the impetus came from Price's role as illustrator, her book, which was very successful and has been repeatedly reissued, is closer than most myth collections of its time to a picture book (as the term is now understood). The text is still dominant, but Price's book has the picture book's large, flat format, and her many illustrations (one or two for almost every pair of facing pages) are all in full color; some are full-page illustrations, conventionally listed in a separate table of contents, but many share the page with the text and often playfully escape their bounds. Price goes out of her way to include depictions of mythical figures as children, as in her image of Phaethon on the verge of losing control of his father Apollo's chariot (Plate 6). With open mouth, the boy gazes in childish dismay at one of "the monsters of the sky" (Price 1924: 83), which is at once a giant, threatening scorpion, and a constellation of stars that break the frame at the top of the image; meanwhile, as he shrinks from this threat, he and his horses sink beneath the frame at the bottom.[48]

At the same time, several works of this period do find ways of connecting classical mythology to the world of modern American children, fulfilling Bechtel's claim that effective storytelling could make the world of myth "almost our own." One unusual myth collection, published in 1929, offers (whether intentionally or not) a strong implicit counter to Mitchell's views: *Greek Tales for Tiny Tots*, "told by John Raymond Crawford, drawn by Pauline Avery Crawford." This version is not based on earlier books, but on the stories that Raymond Crawford (1886–1929), a professor of classics at Lafayette College in Easton, Pennsylvania, told (in a situation reminiscent of Hawthorne's frame story) to his two sons and the children of friends; the drawings are by his wife Pauline (1890–1952), an accomplished artist.[49]

---

[48] On frames and frame-breaking in the modern picture book see Moebius 1996; Nodelman 1988: 50–3; Nikolajeva and Scott 2006: 62–3, 224–7; Smith 2009; Scott 2010.

[49] For the eventful lives of the Crawfords, in which the preparation of this book coincided with a brief happy period, and especially for Pauline Crawford's subsequent career as a poet and contributor to the *International Herald Tribune* in Paris, see Robertson 2001.

In a preface addressed with mock-humility *"To The Presbyteroi"* ("To the Elders"), the Crawfords justify their enterprise by claiming to reenact the original telling of these myths to ancient children and by citing (in a somewhat tongue-in-cheek mode) the pleasure and the better understanding of human relationships (one of Mitchell's main educational goals) gained from them by their own children:

We do not believe that little Pericles at four or little Alcibiades at five had begun getting the myths direct from Homer and the dramatists. We venture to suppose that it was some dark-eyed Aglaia in the nursery who gave the youngsters of old Greece their first introduction to the lore of their race—and that informally, colloquially, in much her own language and manner, and with here and there a touch of her own invention.

It is in some such spirit that these tales have been set down, and it is in the spirit of the humble illustrator of the Greek pottery that they have been drawn. Our compensation, and in a way our justification, have already come in the delight of seeing our own children, while still very young, enthusiastically interpreting human relationships in terms of Perseus and Atalanta and the rest of that heroic crew.   (Crawford 1929: 5)[50]

The inventive touches that mark the book as intended for small children involve both the omission of unsuitable features, including some regularly found in versions for older children, and the addition of details that bring the stories closer to the here-and-now of the modern child, with a jokey effect reminiscent of Hawthorne's modernizing. Pandora has become an American child of the 1920s: "a little girl with bobbed hair" (11). The siege of Troy occurs under twentieth-century urban conditions: the Greeks infiltrate Troy, crawl "into the kings' palace through the kitchen window, which the cook had left open," and hustle Helen out again. "But the Trojans put their wooden horse in the Zoo, and went to see it every Sunday afternoon, and fed it peanuts, which it loved" (34). Icarus falls into the arms of a mermaid who saves him from drowning. Apollo chases Daphne

---

[50]   There is a similarly jocular and personal preface by the publisher, whose firm, Public School Publishing Company, specialized in textbooks, works of pedagogy, and classics revised for young readers, including *Grimms' Fairy Tales* (1894), *Robinson Crusoe for Boys and Girls* (1894), and *Tales of Troy for Boys and Girls* (1898). He draws attention to the inclusion of Camilla, adding that "the late Mr. Publius Virgilius of Rome wrote about her. I fell in love with her and that's why we published the book" (3). The book ends with some half-hearted instruction in the form of a "Pronouncing List": "It doesn't really matter very much how you pronounce the names in this book if you only love the stories. But this list (if you can make anything of it) shows how some people think they sound best" (83).

in order to pinch her ears. The story of Oedipus ends when he solves the riddle of the Sphinx and the grateful Thebans make him their king and give him "a beautiful golden cushion to sit on" (52). Circe's enchantments are followed by a party at which cake and ice cream are served; once Perseus marries Andromeda, he gives her "a five pound box of chocolates every morning for breakfast" (46).

The tales are given folk-tale titles ("The Girl who Wanted to Peek," "The Boy who Flew Too High") and begin "Once" or "Once upon a time." The style is simple, even childlike, with repetition and short sentences: "Once there was a little boy with freckles, named Theseus. Only, he didn't have any daddy, because his daddy was dead" (9). In this respect, the book recalls a more earnest precursor, Helen Beckwith's *In Mythland* (1896), which uses myths to teach reading to kindergarten-age children through similarly simplified diction:

> Theseus lived with his mamma.
> They lived in his grandfather's house.
> One day she said,
> "Come with me, my boy.
> Do you see that large stone?
> Can you turn it over?"
> "Yes, indeed," said Theseus.
> And he turned it over.   (54)

Beckwith also eliminates the darker aspects of myth in view of her young audience, changing the Minotaur to a dragon.

Crawford's versions include playful turns of phrase that, like the patently child-oriented revisions of the plot, convey to the book's adult readers an adult's knowing sense of the disparity between ancient myths and modern idioms. On hearing Ulysses' idea of the wooden horse, "Nestor wagged his head, and said most impressively, '*I* believe the honorable gentleman is quite right'" (33). To Ariadne's suggestion that they should get married, "Theseus said that would be charming" (73). Similarly, the book's title, with its reference to "Tiny Tots," speaks to the adult who might read the book to a child rather than directly to the child.

If the tales are "told by" Raymond Crawford, they are equally "drawn by" Pauline Crawford, who illustrates each story with a comic strip on the facing page that offers a telegraphic alternative narrative (Fig. 3.4) and makes this book (like Price's) very similar to a picture book. The comic form is a borrowing from more popular genres, imported into a

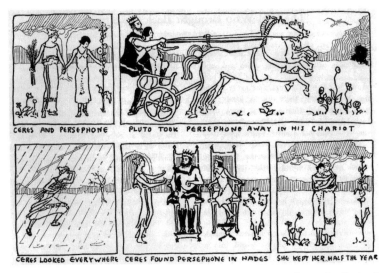

Fig. 3.4. Illustration by Pauline Crawford from John Raymond Crawford's *Greek Tales for Tiny Tots* (1929).

myth book for the first time, presumably because of the very young audience, but destined (along with various cartoon-like styles of illustration) to become a significant feature of the genre beginning in the second half of the century.[51] The treatment is conspicuously modernizing in places; here, in Crawford's illustration for "The Girl Who Brought Back the Summer (*Persephone*)," Ceres' clothing and hairdo are classical, but Persephone has the dress and bobbed hair of a flapper. In keeping with the narrative, in which Persephone is eager to accept a ride in the chariot of the "young and handsome" King Pluto and (apart from her homesickness) is "very happy" as his Queen (29), this illustration transforms the traditional iconography of the abduction scene in ancient art and in the subsequent European tradition.[52] Where Hades typically appears as a frightening figure, grasping Persephone by the waist and either lifting her from the ground or carrying her off in his chariot as she raises her arms

---

[51] This particular form of comic strip (with accompanying text rather than speech balloons) is known as a "text comic"; another example from the same period may be found in the Rupert Bear stories, created by Mary Tourtel in 1920 and taken over by Alfred Bestall in 1935.

[52] On the iconography of this episode in antiquity, see Lindner 1984.

in supplication and terror, Pauline Crawford's King Pluto is a dashing and attractive figure, and Persephone seems to be enjoying her ride behind four prancing white horses. In a later panel, the underworld, though it lacks flowers, is otherwise nearly as bright and pleasant as the world above, and Cerberus seems more like a three-headed pet than a guard dog. The style is deliberately amateurish, aiming to evoke a child's drawing much as the narrative style evokes a child's telling (as both are envisioned by adults).[53]

The Mythical Adventures of American Children

Beyond the genre of the myth collection, there was in America no wave of fictional encounters with figures from classical myth as there had been in Edwardian England. Neither Pan (whom Robert Frost pictured in a New England pasture, tossing away his pipes as "too hard to teach | a new-world song") nor the Olympian gods were found to be at home in America.[54] The best-known exemplars of American fantasy, L. Frank Baum's Oz books, also written during the first decade of the twentieth century, deliberately avoid European traditions, including those of Greco-Roman antiquity. Some of the books in the series have been read as recalling mythic plots (the abduction of Persephone, the return of Odysseus), but Dorothy and her friends never encounter Greek gods, either in Kansas or in Oz.[55]

One book published in 1924, Mary Dickerson Donahey's *Peter and Prue*, does put American children in contact with figures from mythology, although not in an American setting. Two habitual runaways find themselves traveling to the moon and the planets, where they encounter the Greek gods, who have been forced to live up in the sky by the fact that

[53] On deliberately childlike drawings in 20th-century children's books in general, see Eyre 1973: 53.

[54] "Pan With Us," 16–17, in Frost 1915.

[55] Levy and Mendlesohn 2016: 59–62; Tuerk 2007: chs. 10, 11, 13; on American elements in *The Wizard of Oz*, see Attebery 1980; on the reception of the Oz stories as "American myth," Zipes 1994: ch. 5. On Baum's 19th-century American predecessors, some of whom draw largely on European fairy-tale traditions, and some of whom endeavor to transplant the fairy tale to American settings, see Attebery 1980: ch. 4. None of these predecessors, except for Hawthorne, makes significant use of Greek myth.

the Greeks no longer believe in them or give them presents, leaving them "dreadfully poor" (Donahey 1924: 64). The children make the acquaintance of various divinities (both Greek and Norse), who take them traveling and tell them myths, including the stories of Arachne, Phaethon, Proserpine, Cupid and Psyche, and the Trojan War. Peter and Prue's journey, although ostensibly a means of teaching them the true merits of home, thus also constitutes the same sort of introduction to Greek mythology they might have found in Price or Hawthorne; the educational value of their journey is further enhanced when they are given bits of astronomical information about the planets they get to visit.

Far from being especially attuned to figures from the classical world, these children view them with unabashedly contemporary and American attitudes, including condescending views of recent immigrants and admiration for technical and industrial progress. When they first hear about the ancient Greeks, Prue comments that her father "goes to a Greek to get his shoes shined" (63) and Peter has heard from an uncle "that the Greeks were going to conquer America by buying up all the restaurants" (63). When they meet Vulcan, Peter suggests that he come down to earth and set up a factory, adding, "My father's an advertising man. He'd help you with your ads, and that's the most important part of any business" (141). At one point Peter uses the expression "step on the gas" which proves incomprehensible to the Four Winds: "It was queer to be among people who never talked automobile!" (219).

Two of the most celebrated and distinguished children's author-illustrators of the first half of the twentieth century did, however, produce works that fully integrate the cultural heritage of classical antiquity into a vision of down-to-earth American life as typified by white, non-urban communities—in both cases by situating classical myths and fables in archetypal small towns and allying them with the American tradition of the tall tale. The tall tale tradition, which features implausible events in ordinary settings, was in favor with progressive educators and publishers and grew in popularity during the Depression.[56] The first of these authors, James Daugherty (1889–1974), published towards the end of that period, in 1938, a picture book based on an ancient fable, *Andy and the Lion: A Tale of Kindness Remembered or the Power of Gratitude,*

---

[56] Hearn 1996: 35.

which was widely acclaimed and named a Caldecott Honor Book (a runner-up for an annual prize for best children's picture book) in 1939.

As an artist and illustrator, Daugherty was decisively influenced by his reading of Walt Whitman and dedicated himself from an early age to the representation of American themes and values.[57] During the 1930s he painted murals for public buildings under the auspices of the Works Progress Administration (WPA), depicting scenes from American history and showcasing American technological progress. He wrote and illustrated children's books that stressed the energy, courage, ingenuity, and self-reliance of the early settlers, including a biography of Daniel Boone, which won the Newbery Medal in 1940 (but is now viewed more critically for its positive treatment of the eradication of Native Americans). In his Newbery acceptance speech, entitled "Children's Books in a Democracy," Daugherty trumpeted the superiority of American reality over classical myth: "Certainly the vast and fantastic epic of America is a rich storehouse of true stories that make the legends of Greece and old Europe seem trivial and tame."[58]

Daugherty's picture book *Andy and the Lion* draws not on a classical myth but on the more demotic fable of Androclus and the Lion, which concerns a runaway slave who helps a lion by removing a thorn from its paw; after he has been recaptured and included in a wild animal show before the emperor Caligula, Androclus' life is saved when the same lion refuses to attack and devour him.[59] Daugherty turns the hero of this fable into a barefoot American boy in overalls. Andy takes a book about lions out of the Andersonville Public Library, reads about lions all evening (as his father reads a paper whose headline proclaims "Lion Escapes Circus"), listens to his grandfather's "tall stories" about shooting lions in Africa, dreams about lions, thinks about lions all morning, and finally encounters the escaped circus lion with a thorn in its paw—which he removes with the pair of pliers he carries "in the back pocket of his overalls." The following spring, Andy goes to the circus; when the lion charges the crowd, he and Andy recognize each other, and the lion stops his rampage.

---

[57] On Daugherty's career and especially his mission of creating children's books that would instill and reinforce American values, see Schmidt 2013: 33–58.

[58] Daugherty 1940: 233, echoing the title of James Truslow Adams's 1931 bestseller *The Epic of America*, in which the term "American dream" was coined.

[59] This story first appears in Aulus Gellius, *Attic Nights* 5.14.

Then the next day Andy led the lion and all the people in a grand parade down Main Street to City Hall. There the Mayor presented Andy with a medal for bravery. And the lion was very much pleased.

The slave hero of the ancient fable has been reinvented as a pint-sized citizen with the practical skill and resourcefulness of his pioneer ancestors; the cruel and hierarchical Roman games have been transformed into a traveling circus, which is construed as a benign public entertainment that brings together the inhabitants of a small town and provides the occasion for another unifying and celebratory civic ritual, a parade.

The illustrations, which take up whole pages and appear opposite brief bits of simple text, are bold pen-and-ink drawings in black, white, and sepia.[60] They share the energy and monumentality of Daugherty's large-scale murals, in which his realistic subjects take on a mythic grandeur. For example, the final image, in which Andy, still reading, but now with the lion on a leash, returns his book to the library (Fig. 3.5), is dominated by the massive lion as he strides upwards, with his tail swinging and—like Artzy-basheff's lion—showing a sympathetic rapport with a smaller, weaker figure. This illustration and the almost identical one at the beginning of the book frame the story with the image of an imposing neoclassical library on a hill, its sunlit pillared porch standing next to the silhouette of a man hard at work mowing the lawn. Daugherty thus figures the library as a temple on a hill, the shrine, perhaps, of the classical literary tradition from which his plot is taken. But this library, like the "small white marble temple" visited by Betsy in Maud Hart Lovelace's *Betsy and Tacy Go Downtown*, is a public institution, an expression of America's commitment to universal cultural literacy and self-improvement, and the book Andy himself reads is not the story of Androclus, or a collection of Aesop's Fables, but a book of natural history—science, not myth.[61] The juxtaposition of the pillared building on a hill with American labor and American technology point to the absorption and democratization of European culture—as does

---

[60] On the relative weight of the images, which "form a self-contained, self-explanatory sequence," making this a picture book in the fullest sense, see Bader 1976: 151–4.

[61] In his Newbery acceptance speech, given during World War II, Daugherty celebrated the power of libraries to open children's eyes, but also to preserve American values in the face of hostile propaganda: "when, as it is said, ideas are bullets, then our libraries become munition plants for democracy, and power plants for freedom" (Daugherty 1940: 231).

ANDY TOOK THE BOOK BACK TO THE LIBRARY.

Fig. 3.5. Illustration from *Andy and the Lion* (1938) by James Daugherty.

Daugherty's dedication, in which a pair of lions with aristocratic English names act as guardians of a more famous American public library:

> To Lady Astor and Lord Lenox, the library lions
> who have so long sat in front of the New York Public Library
> and with such complacent good nature and forbearance
> looked down on Manhattan parade

In a review written a few years later, Daugherty hailed the arrival of a new addition to "Tom Sawyer's gang, that immortal and formidable band of boys of American fiction": Homer Price, the hero of a book published in 1943 by Robert McCloskey (1914–2003).[62] *Homer Price* combines the adventures of a modern boy who resembles Tom Sawyer or Booth Tarkington's Penrod or Daugherty's own Andy with a witty and self-conscious assessment of the relevance of classical myth to the lives of American children. The book is initially framed as a rejection of ancient myths and European fairy tales in favor of more familiar material. The publisher's promotional material locates its inspiration in an anecdote about McCloskey's early days as an aspiring author.

While in New York he went to call on an editor of children's books, with his portfolio under his arm. "She looked at the examples of 'great art' that I had brought along (they were woodcuts, fraught with black drama). I don't remember just the words she used to tell me to get wise to myself and to shelve the dragons, Pegasus, and limpid pool business and learn how and what to 'art' with. I think we talked mostly of Ohio."[63]

The immediate outcome of this advice was *Lentil* (1940), a picture book about a boy in a small Ohio town such as the one that McCloskey himself had grown up in, and the first of several celebrated children's books rooted in particular American places, including *Make Way for Ducklings* (1941), set in the Boston Public Gardens, and *One Morning in Maine* (1952), based on the experiences of McCloskey's own daughters.

Homer Price, which followed soon after *Lentil*, also features an ordinary American boy, who lives in the Ohio town of Centerburg. The implications of this choice of subject matter are made clear in the book's frontispiece (Fig. 3.6).

---

[62] Daugherty 1943: 425.

[63] A different version of this anecdote in a memoir by McCloskey's daughter identifies the editor as his longtime editor May Massee and makes *Homer Price* the immediate outcome (J. McCloskey 2011: 18).

Fig. 3.6. Frontispiece from *Homer Price* (1943) by Robert McCloskey.

By calling his hero "Homer," which happens to be a familiar, unpretentious American name, McCloskey neatly suggests the displacement of the legendary by the real.[64] But that gesture is less dismissive than it first appears and, like Daugherty, McCloskey reappropriates what he seemingly rejects. As the stories unfold, the modern Homer emerges as a spokesman for his ancient namesake, whom McCloskey embraces as a model even though he turns away from classical subject matter. Classical myths are reclaimed as the property of modern American children, as they had been reclaimed before by more straightforward retellers such as Hawthorne or the Crawfords, but in this case, as in *Andy and the Lion*, those myths are recast as modern children's own quasi-mythic experiences.

Like Daugherty, McCloskey invests his tale with mythic significance: the ordinary hero and his small-town surroundings are conspicuously archetypal, as the name Centerburg suggests, and their portrayal is shaped by nostalgia.[65] As the publisher indicates, "Mr. McCloskey looks back with humor and affection at the Midwest America of his childhood" (a period when Homer was a more common name than in 1943); written during World War II, the book offers a secure, innocent, idealized vision of America at a time of heightened patriotism.[66] For example, Homer captures a band of robbers with the help of his pet skunk, and an unstoppable machine produces thousands of doughnuts.

These "preposterous stories" (to quote the publisher again) are identified as down-to-earth New World counterparts of classical myths.[67] Several are sly appropriations of famous episodes from the *Odyssey*, which McCloskey, like Hawthorne, draws on as a source of discrete tales. Homer's relatives include "Uncle Ulysses," a name that similarly

[64] As was later to be the case with the animated cartoon character Homer Simpson (named for the creator's actual father), who first appeared on American television in 1989. The name Homer was inspired by a childhood friend of McCloskey's; his editor added "Price" to avoid publishing the book with a confusing title (Schmidt 1990: 35–6). An earlier example of the playful use of a classical name is "Agamemnon John," a character in Lucretia Peabody Hale's comic tales about a foolish American family, *The Peterkin Papers* (first collected in 1880, though appearing in periodicals from 1867 on).

[65] Schmidt 2013: 218–19.

[66] One of the book's first reviewers found there a welcome echo of his own boyhood. Gugler 1943: 425.

[67] The tall tale connection is even stronger in the sequel, *Centerburg Tales* (1951), reflected in the book's title and in the chronologically impossible stories told by Homer's "Grampa Hercules." The frontispiece of *Centerburg Tales* shows a bust of Homer sharing a shelf with a bust of Mark Twain. On the reception of *Homer Price* as a celebration of American values, see Schmidt 1990: 29.

reflects American custom, but also "Uncle Telemachus," which does not. In one episode, "Nothing New under the Sun (Hardly)," Homer out-does the town's adults as a reader of myth, employing a tactic borrowed from a Greek model. A reclusive wanderer comes to town, whom the residents identify as a latter-day Rip Van Winkle. When he is dis-covered to have a musical mouse-trapping machine, they hire him to drive it through the town, but then panic when all the children follow him: "*We guessed the wrong book! . . .* not *Rip Van Winkle* but *another book, The Pied Piper of Hamelin!*" (McCloskey 1943: 118). All is well, however, because Homer has anticipated this danger and has arranged for the local doctor to stuff all the children's ears with cotton: "You know, just like Ulysses, not you, Uncle Ulysses, but the ancient one—the one that Homer wrote about. Not me but the ancient one" (121). Another episode is an unstated reworking of the Penelope myth, as a strong-minded spinster controls a contest for her hand by unraveling a piece of her own knitting.

In this projection of simpler and more authentic American past, Homer himself is not only Centerburg's best reader of myth but also its most astute critic of twentieth-century progress, which beguiles the more benighted adults in such forms as mechanization (various machines eagerly acquired by Uncle Ulysses), advertisement, and the cookie-cutter suburb.[68] In his moral clarity and his attunement to time-less old-fashioned values, Homer resembles the child readers that retel-lers of myth have traditionally sought to address and to shape. The classical Homer may be pushed off his pedestal, but his place is taken by a clear-eyed child who is at home in mythology and can rescue his elders from the corrupting forces of modernity.

New Classics: Optimism and Nostalgia in the Mid-Twentieth Century

A more straightforward affirmation of the ongoing value of classical myths can be found in the several updated versions of Bulfinch's *Age of*

---

[68] Schmidt 2013: 221–6. The clever hero of classical epic is also shown to be a more reliable model than the superhero of the popular comic book. The movie actor who plays the comic-book hero "the Super-Duper" comes to town and ends up needing Homer's help when his car breaks down. On this episode as part of a heated debate about comic books as suitable reading for children, see Marcus 2008: 153–4.

Fable (1855) published at around the same time as *Homer Price*. Bulfinch's collection, not aimed specifically at children, was nonetheless intended to have "the charm of a story-book," and had long been read by younger readers; now, however, it was regarded as in need of revision or replacement. In 1942, Macmillan published a simplified edition of Bulfinch for children, with elegant, sophisticated illustrations by Helen Sewell (*A Book of Myths*, 1942).[69] Two other updated versions of Bulfinch from the same period were both illustrated by Steele Savage (1900–70),[70] who had already worked on other volumes of traditional tales, including the *Arabian Nights* (1932). *Stories of the Gods and Heroes*, by Sally Benson (1897–1972, better known as the author of *Junior Miss* and *Meet me in Saint Louis*), published in 1940, is now no longer read. But Edith Hamilton's *Mythology*, which appeared in 1942, remains one of the most enduring myth collections of the mid-twentieth century.

Unlike Sewell's and Benson's versions, *Mythology* was not intended solely as a work for children or younger readers; it was commissioned in 1939 by the Boston publisher Little, Brown as a replacement for Bulfinch for a general audience. But Hamilton's work has come to be read almost exclusively by children and teenagers, whether on their own or at school. Hamilton (1867–1963) herself was a schoolteacher and headmistress before she became an author, and the book has been widely used as a first introduction to mythology—and often to the classical world—for American middle- and high-school students. And her conception of myth, rooted in her own childhood encounters with the Greeks, inspired a retelling with the qualities generally sought in versions suitable for children.[71]

Testimony to *Mythology*'s widespread association with childhood, and its continued appeal some thirty years after its first appearance, comes in a 2002 interview by the journalist Bill Moyers with Mary Zimmerman, a playwright known for her adaptations of Homer and Ovid, born in 1960.

---

[69] On Sewell's career as an illustrator, see Bader 1976: 81–7; Bechtel 1969: 102–17, esp. 109–11 for appreciative comments on *A Book of Myths* as "an outstanding book of our time."

[70] For a biographical sketch, see Viguers et al. 1958: 174.

[71] On Hamilton's life and career, see Bacon 1980; Hallett 1996–7, 2009a, 2009b; Reid 1967.

MOYERS: How did you come to love these stories?

ZIMMERMAN: I'll tell you, I read Edith Hamilton's *Mythology* when I was a child...

MOYERS: So did I.

ZIMMERMAN: ...and yes, those little pen and ink drawings are engraved on my heart.[72]

Hamilton based *Mythology* directly on the ancient sources rather than simply revising Bulfinch's text; writing in her early seventies, she drew on a long history of reading, teaching, and storytelling that was more personal than scholarly and untouched by the intellectual currents that, as we have seen, inspired such predecessors as Lang and Colum.[73] *Mythology* is grounded in wholesale rejection of any connections established by anthropologists and archaeologists over the previous seventy years between the historical Greeks and prehistoric or primitive cultures.[74] Hamilton does not avail herself of any of the strategies by which a suitably tailored primitivism serves to identify childhood with the classical past: Lang's understanding of myth as an advanced form of the fairy tale, to which it can be reduced again for child readers; Colum's absorption of the Greeks into a romanticized and universal oral culture; or the projection of societies congenial to modern adolescents onto prehistoric cultures known only through material evidence, to be explored in Chapter 5.

Nor, despite her deep admiration for the Greeks, does Hamilton associate their myths with a primordial golden age, as Hawthorne does. For her, "Nothing is clearer than the fact that primitive man, whether in New Guinea today or eons ago in the prehistoric wilderness, is not and never has been a creature who peoples his world with bright fancies and lovely visions. Horrors lurked in the primitive forest, not nymphs and naiads" (1942: 4). Hamilton has to admit that the Greeks had a prehistory, but she maintains that their mythology had nothing to do with it. "Of course they too once lived a savage life, ugly and brutal. But what the myths show is how high they had risen above the ancient filth and fierceness by the time we have any knowledge of them" (7).

---

[72] Moyers 2002.

[73] Bacon 1980: 307–8; Casazza 2003; Reid 1967: 66, 153–4. See Hamilton 1930 for her highly idealized and in its day widely popular account of Greek culture.

[74] On Hamilton's views in relation to the enthusiastic primitivism that animates Robert Graves's roughly contemporary *The Greek Myths* (1955), see Murnaghan 2009.

On Hamilton's account, the historical Greek world, while not figured as humanity's childhood, is markedly child-friendly in character. Its most salient feature is an enlightened humanism, through which the Greeks replaced terrifying, ritual-exacting divinities with gods in their own image, who were "normal and natural," "friendly," and "companionable" (9). These gods are cast as adults of the kind that children need to have around them. This is suggested by her explanation of why the Greeks preferred versions of the story of Iphigenia in which Artemis does not require Iphigenia's sacrifice: "Never would such a demand have been made by the lovely lady of the woodland and the forest, who was especially the protector of little helpless creatures" (364). And it is made explicit when she comments on the tendency in Greek myths for supernatural figures to be linked with specific familiar locations:

A familiar local habitation gives reality to all the mythical beings. If the mixture seems childish, consider how reassuring and how sensible the solid background is as compared with the Genie who comes from nowhere when Aladdin rubs the lamp and, his task accomplished, returns to nowhere.   (10)

Accordingly, she produced versions of the Greek myths that have readily been found suitable for children and adolescents in their reassuring content as well as their accessible style.[75] True to her conviction that anything alarming is alien to Greek culture, Hamilton downplays elements of sexuality, violence, and danger. She does include the story of Ariadne's abandonment by Theseus, but stresses the happy outcome: "She was asleep and he sailed away without her, but Dionysus found her and comforted her" (215), almost as if Dionysus were a babysitter who is reassuringly present when a child wakes up from a nap. In her version of the Pygmalion myth, she appeals to the idea of child's play as an alternative to the unnerving sexual obsession described by her classical source. While Ovid depicts the frustrated Pygmalion as a human wanting to make love to a statue (*Metamorphoses* 10.252–69) Hamilton reconceives him as an adult trying to believe, as a child does (and for good measure a female child), that a doll is real. "For a time, he tried to pretend, as children do with their toys . . . He put her to bed at night

---

[75] In her foreword, she compares the differences among her sources to those between *Cinderella* and *King Lear*. On Hamilton's marked preference for some of her sources over others, and especially for Greek sources of the classical period, see Murnaghan 2009: 82.

and tucked her in all soft and warm, as little girls do their dolls. But he was not a child; he could not keep on pretending" (148–9).[76]

When Hamilton's Theseus meets the Minotaur, he has no reason to be afraid and dispatches him easily (if brutally): "certain that he could retrace his steps whenever he chose [because of Ariadne's thread], he walked boldly into the maze looking for the Minotaur. He came upon him asleep and fell upon him, pinning him to the ground; and with his fists—he had no other weapon—he battered the monster to death" (215).[77] Hamilton gives more space to Theseus' activities after his return from Crete than to his undemanding encounter with the Minotaur, painting him as the George Washington-like founder of a proto-American democracy:

So Theseus became King of Athens, a most wise and disinterested king. He declared to the people that he did not wish to rule over them; he wanted a people's government where all would be equal. He resigned his royal power and organized a commonwealth, building a council hall where the citizens could gather and vote. The only office he kept for himself was that of Commander in Chief. Thus Athens became, of all earth's cities, the happiest and most prosperous, the only true home of liberty, the one place in the world where the people governed themselves.   (216)[78]

In keeping with its conservative conception and orientation to readers of all ages, Hamilton's *Mythology*, like Lang's and Colum's collections, is in the tradition of the illustrated book rather than the picture book. But by the middle of the twentieth century, there were also myth collections that reflected the flowering of the children's picture book in that period, a development that we have seen anticipated in the collections illustrated by Margaret Evans Price and Pauline Crawford and fully realized in Daugherty's *Andy and the Lion*. The most notable and lastingly influential of these is the work of the husband-and-wife team Ingri and Edgar Parin D'Aulaire (1904–80, 1898–1986). *D'Aulaires' Book of Greek Myths* appeared in 1962 and remains, at least in the American market, the most

[76] See discussion in Hallett 2009a: 128.

[77] Hamilton's sleeping Minotaur may go back to one of her more obscure ancient sources: in a version preserved in a scholium to Homer's *Odyssey*, Ariadne instructs Theseus that if he comes across the Minotaur asleep he should lay hold of the hairs of his head and sacrifice him to Poseidon.

[78] Cf. Hamilton's conversion of Prometheus into "an icon for American freedom" (Prins 2017: 107) in her translation of Aeschylus' *Prometheus Bound*.

enduring myth collection of this period, still widely bought and read amid a full and diverse array of more recent alternatives.[79] Compared to many of its predecessors, the D'Aulaires' volume manifests an unusually strong complementarity between its text and its illustrations and a decisive shift in pictorial style towards a more overtly child-oriented presentation.[80] The illustrations reflect familiar, longstanding iconographic traditions, but with an unusually bright palette, free treatment of proportion and perspective, elements of jokiness and caricature, and allusions to children's experiences.[81]

The staying power of this collection may be especially correlated with its success in satisfying adult notions of what appeals to children, since it has survived a major shift, in the 1970s, in which decreased funding for school libraries made gift-giving friends and relatives the predominant purchasers of children's books.[82] In this respect, the book undoubtedly benefits from its literally sunny cover, which depicts Phaethon driving the horses of his father Helios (though with some hints, especially in the expressions on the faces of his horses, of the fall to come) (Plate 7).

Inside that cover, readers encounter a text that also fulfills Hawthorne's stricture that for myths to be acceptable for children, sunshine has to be let into them, an achievement that is attributed to the Greeks themselves in the opening paragraph:

In olden times, when men still worshipped ugly idols, there lived in the land of Greece a folk of shepherds and herdsmen who cherished light and beauty. They did not worship dark idols like their neighbors, but created instead their own beautiful, radiant gods.   (D'Aulaires 1962: 9).

---

[79] A slightly earlier compendium in the same physical format is *The Golden Treasury of Myths and Legends*, published in 1959, with prominent, but not markedly child-oriented illustrations by another husband-and-wife team, Alice and Martin Provensen (1918–2018, 1916–87), which have equal weight with (and sometimes overwhelm) the straightforward text by Anne Terry White (White 1959).

[80] The D'Aulaires' responsibility for both text and pictures undoubtedly contributes to the overall harmony of the book; in a documentary on their work, Ingri D'Aulaire describes the relationship of the words and images as "a complete marriage" (Morrison 1976). Yet it would not have turned out that way if a projected collaboration with Robert Graves had not fallen through due to strong differences over the interpretation of particular myths (O. D'Aulaire 1996: 5).

[81] On the D'Aulaires' freedom from traditional proportion and perspective as reflecting at once "the decorative, often dramatic stylization of folk art and the willful, often expressive distortion of modernist art," see Bader 1976: 43.

[82] Hearne 1988: 223.

Here the Greeks are idealized and contrasted with their neighbors in space much as in Hamilton's account they are contrasted with their predecessors in time. As the book ends with the disappearance of the classical world, the ancient myths survive in a luminous form: "the Muses fell silent, but their songs live on to this very day, and the constellations put up by the gods still glitter on the dark blue vault of the sky" (189).

The D'Aulaires' retold myths generally share the optimistic tone of the many children's books that they had published since their emigration to America from Europe in 1929, beginning with *The Magic Rug* (1931), a landmark for its introduction of color lithography into American children's publishing; those books included depictions of a boy's life in Norway based on Ingri's own childhood memories and a series of biographies of important Americans, including *George Washington* (1936) and *Abraham Lincoln* (1939), treated in a way that has invited the label "mythic."[83] The *Book of Greek Myths*' plentiful illustrations, in black-and-white, sepia, and full color, present a world of marvelous, larger-than-life creatures, often with touches of humor: Ares crammed in a jar, nervous sailors diving off Dionysus' ship, Pandora surrounded by odd little monsters labeled "scheming," "drudgery," and "gossip," a fisherman hauling in a catch that includes Danae in her chest but also a wealth of lobsters, crabs, squid, and jellyfish. There are two depictions of the baby Hermes, introduced as "the merriest of the Olympians" (50).

Despite its striking coherence and overall lightheartedness, this book was, according to Ingri D'Aulaire, the most drawn out and contentious of their joint projects, involving five years of "hard battles" over masculine versus feminine elements of the myths.[84] It is impossible to trace this struggle with confidence in the finished product (though we are told by

---

[83] On the D'Aulaires' lives and careers, see Mahoney and Mitchell 1940, Foster 1970; on their lithography technique, Massee 1935; for the mythic character of the American history books, Schmidt 2013: 163–72. Notably, *Abraham Lincoln* ends before the assassination with his successful defense of the Union. In their joint acceptance speech when the book won the Caldecott Medal in 1940, Edgar D'Aulaire traces the roots of this myth-making to his childhood. Because they had not met these figure in their schooling, "we had to approach the subjects as children"; his American grandmother introduced him to Lincoln as a "huge figure towering over everything" (252), whom he and Ingri came to depict as (in her words) "the shining symbol of democracy, fairness and tolerance" (247).

[84] Morrison 1976.

the D'Aulaires' son Ola that his father specialized in illustrating monsters (1996: 7)), but the violent character of many myths is simultaneously acknowledged and mitigated, especially in the illustrations.

The D'Aulaires' picture of the abduction of Persephone (Plate 8) includes Pluto's powerful black horses, but shows them neither hastening through the meadow nor charging into the abyss, as in more traditional versions; instead, they seem to be almost helplessly falling downwards. Persephone's upflung arms are a traditional motif, found already in ancient depictions of the scene, but here they pull her back up and away from Pluto and his underworld destination into the sunlit realm of blue skies and tumbling flowers, from which she now departs but to which she will certainly return. The composition of this image recalls that of Frederic Leighton's well-known 1891 painting *The Return of Persephone*, and Persephone appears in the same pose, seen from a different angle, in a subsequent illustration in which she rises out of the earth to rejoin her mother; her facial expression here could as easily belong to that moment, and the instantly drooping flowers at the earth's edge anticipate Demeter's strategy for securing Persephone's release. Meanwhile the pigs that fall along with Persephone add a jaunty, comical note, and their wildly gesturing swineherd takes the place of Persephone's bereft companions.

But the D'Aulaires' most striking conversion of myth into suitable material for children comes in their presentation of the Minotaur's conception, a subject so sensitive that their predecessors either omit it altogether or nervously gloss over it. Perhaps because her book was aimed at a general audience, Hamilton does casually explain that the Minotaur was "the offspring of Minos' wife Pasiphaë and a wonderfully beautiful bull" (Hamilton 1942: 212), but Lang darkly suppresses this detail (with Medea telling Theseus, "Whence this evil beast came I know, but the truth of it may not be spoken" (Lang 2006: 236)) while Colum and others leave it out altogether. In the text, the episode is finessed in keeping with the D'Aulaires' generally evasive treatment of sexual content (Cronus "fell upon his father" (12); Zeus sneaks to earth to "marry mortal girls" (24)). It starts with Pasiphaë's misguided admiration for the bull and refusal to sacrifice it despite Poseidon's command. She persuades Minos to spare the bull and, "She admired the bull so much that she ordered Daedalus to construct a hollow wooden cow, so she could hide inside it and enjoy the beauty of the bull at close range." The consequence of this enjoyment is recast as Poseidon's reaction to the bull's preservation: "To punish the king and queen, Poseidon caused Pasiphaë to give birth to a monster, the Minotaur" (149).

The accompanying illustration (Fig. 3.7) makes the episode even more child-friendly by turning the characters into toys, with the cow on a wooden platform with wheels like a pull toy and Pasiphaë climbing into it like a little doll. As in the nursery, model animals and model people conventionally and innocently commingle. Critics have pointed out that the D'Aulaires' books about American history include illustrations in which the figures suggest dolls and toy soldiers, conveying the image of a toy world that "seems well suited to a young child's first encounters with

Fig. 3.7. Illustration from *D'Aulaires' Book of Greek Myths* (1962) by Ingri and Edgar Parin D'Aulaire.

the abstraction of the 'past.' "[85] Here that strategy is taken a step further as the troublesome characters of mythology become nothing other than toys (much as Galatea is assimilated to a child's doll for Hamilton's Pygmalion). Once again, the D'Aulaires fulfill Hawthorne's programmatic vision for the conversion of myth into children's literature, giving a literal answer to his rhetorical question: "was such material the stuff that children's playthings should be made of!" (Hawthorne 1982: 1310).

This application of the most obvious markers of childhood to one of the darkest, most shocking stories in classical mythology highlights the full integration of myth into children's literature by the mid-twentieth century. The D'Aulaires here set the tone for subsequent directions in children's mythology, in particular mythology for an increasingly demarcated audience of very young children: the embrace of mythical monsters as lovable figures, sometimes resembling stuffed animals, and the use of imagery from games and cartoons to render disturbing events appealing and inconsequential.

Britain at Mid-Century

In the years following World War II, there was renewed interest in mythology for children, not only in the United States, but also in England, where during the first half of the century, even while new anthologies of myth continued to appear,[86] a strong tradition of fantasy works for children had also developed, culminating in mid-century with Tolkien's *The Hobbit* (1937) and *Lord of the Rings* cycle (published 1954–5) and C. S. Lewis's *Chronicles of Narnia* (1950–6).[87] Classical myth tends to play a smaller role in such works than northern European myth and folklore,[88] but figures from the Greco-Roman mythical tradition are nonetheless a recurring presence in various kinds of fantasy fiction. Tolkien sought to produce through what he called "sub-creation"

[85] Marcus 1980: 18. Cf. Mahoney and Mitchell's observation that the picture of Washington taking command of his army in Cambridge at the end of *George Washington* is "such a scene as a child might set up with his tin soldiers, toy buildings and trees" (1940: 262).

[86] See e.g. Buckley 1908; Hutchinson 1925; Blyton 1930, 1939; Rouse 1934. Levy and Mendlesohn suggest that the interest in classical mythology between the wars "reflected a growing desire to foster a greater sense of national identity" by promoting "a sense of common heritage in European culture" (2016: 82).

[87] Cook 1976: 2; Eyre 1973: 19–20, 30, 59; Levy and Mendlesohn 2016: ch. 4.

[88] See Brown 2017: 189.

a "Secondary World, into which both designer and spectator can enter," a world so separate from our own that it excludes even previously known elements of fantasy.[89] Lewis, in contrast, freely allowed elements from the primary world's varied imaginings to enter his invented world. It is thus in Lewis, rather than Tolkien, that we again find English children encountering mythological figures such as fauns, dryads, and centaurs—not (this time) in Britain but in an invented realm, which is itself, however, expressive of nostalgia not only for a mythical Arcadian past and for childhood but for an earlier Britain.[90] The most prominent British author of classical myths for children in the postwar period—and one whose works, like Hamilton's, are still being read—was a close friend of both Tolkien and Lewis, Roger Lancelyn Green (1918–87).[91] Lancelyn Green's work, like that of Lewis, is pervaded by nostalgia: for classical antiquity, for childhood, and for writers encountered in childhood.

Like Hamilton, Lancelyn Green based his versions directly on the ancient sources but also saw himself as updating modern retellings, in his case those of Andrew Lang. Lancelyn Green read Lang's works intently during his bookish and often solitary childhood,[92] and his own first book, published in 1946, was a critical biography of Lang. Following Lang's example, he retold myths in two formats. In 1958, he published both *Old Greek Fairy Tales* and *Tales of the Greek Heroes*.[93] *Old Greek Fairy Tales* is dedicated to his wife, "For June, who complained that there were too many names in Greek Mythology," and includes a preface in

[89] Tolkien 1994. But see Stevens 2017 on Tolkien's debt to Vergil's conception of the Underworld.

[90] On classical elements in the Narnia books see Maurice 2015b, Slater 2015.

[91] Others between 1945 and 1970 include Graves 1962; Seraillier 1965; Reeves 1969a, 1969b.

[92] Described in terms reminiscent of a children's book in the front matter of a Puffin Classics reprint: "Roger Lancelyn Green . . . became interested in myths and legends at an early age. His boyhood schooling was interrupted by bouts of illness, which kept him at home in Poulton Hall, Cheshire, where he browsed continually in the magnificent Queen Anne library. Andrew Lang's fairytales, H. Rider Haggard's adventure stories—these were his early influences." Among the later influences also mentioned are "an abiding love for Greece" cultivated through frequent visits (Lancelyn Green 1994).

[93] Lancelyn Green's many other publications include a children's fantasy of his own, *The Land of the Lord High Tiger* (1958); children's versions of Egyptian, Norse, and British traditional tales; additional versions of Greek myths, including *The Tale of Troy* (1958) and *Tales the Muses Told* (1965); *Mystery at Mycenae* (1959), a retelling of Helen's abduction by Theseus as a detective story for teenagers, and *The Luck of Troy* (1961), an adventure set in Troy featuring Helen's son Nicostratus.

which he explains that he is following Lang's lead in reconstructing the fairy tales behind the transmitted myths with their puzzling and confusing names, places, and genealogical connections. But stripping the stories of all markers of historical Greece does not eliminate, he insists, their essential Greekness, which he defines through a double expression of nostalgia, ending his preface with a quotation from Keats's 1819 "Ode to a Nightingale":

But about them all clings that magic of Ancient Greece—

> The same that oft-times hath
> Charm'd magic casements, opening on the foam
> of perilous seas, in faery lands forlorn.
>
> (Lancelyn Green 1958: 19)

If, as Lancelyn Green himself observed, Lang's *Tales of Troy and Greece* reflects "Lang the classical scholar" (1946: 84), *Tales of the Greek Heroes* reflects Lancelyn Green the enthralled traveler to Greece. When Lancelyn Green adds back the names and places left out of the fairy-tale versions, the result is not more historical and cultural information, but greater attention to the Greek landscape. After a dedicatory verse based on Euripides and a quotation from Matthew Arnold, the book begins: "If ever you are lucky enough to visit the beautiful land of Greece you will find a country haunted by more than three thousand years of history and legend" (Lancelyn Green 1994: 3). When we get to Theseus' adventures, we learn:

Theseus set out on the road to Athens, determined to clear the way of all evildoers: and he had not far to go before he met the first. A few miles from Troezen, where the most beautiful of ancient Greek theatres stands today, lived Periphetes the clubman. His only weapon was a mighty club shod with iron which was death to all passers by—until Theseus wrested it from his hands and paid him out in his own cruel coin.   (189)

As this passage illustrates, Lancelyn Green's style is straightforward and clear, with mild archaisms such as "mighty club" and "wrested." There are occasional modernizing touches, like the "band of desperadoes" (96) that interrupt the wedding feast of Perseus and Andromeda. Sex is treated with evasive decorum: When Danae gives birth to Perseus, her father "would not believe that Zeus was the child's father, but said that it was Proteus, his brother, whom he hated, who had stolen the key of the brazen tower and married Danae in secret" (88). In an afterword,

Lancelyn Green identifies as his particular innovation the fact that he has "tried to tell the tale of the Heroic Age as that single whole which the Greeks believed it to be" (267). Thus he takes pains to indicate relationships among the heroes and tie the various stories together.[94] He ends the Theseus story, not with the guilt and melancholy evoked by Colum or the history lessons offered by Lang and Hamilton, but rather breathlessly with connections to a knot of other stories (including one, the marriage of Theseus and Phaedra, whose sequel is better left unnarrated):

> Meanwhile Theseus had become King of Athens, and when he heard that Minos was dead, he made peace with the new king of Crete who sent him his sister Phaedra in marriage, so that, in spite of his loss of Ariadne, he still married a daughter of Minos.
> In time he grew weary of his peaceful life, and longed for further adventures. So he was overjoyed when a message reached him from a young Prince called Jason urging him to join an expedition in search of the Golden Fleece from the Ram which carried Phrixus and Helle over the sea from Greece many years before. (197–8)

Because Lancelyn Green gives his heroes names in order to place them in an absorbing system of interconnections rather than in a specific historical context, his hero tales differ less from his fairy tales than Lang's do; it is not surprising that in an afterword he cites both Hawthorne's *Tanglewood Tales* and Kingsley's *Heroes* as precedents. He also asserts once again the timelessness of these tales, which span the various stages both of human history (by which he means western history) and of an individual life:

> But indeed the gods and heroes of Ancient Greece can never seem as aliens to us. Their stories are part of the world's heritage, they are part of the background of our literature, our speech, our very thoughts. We cannot come to them too early, nor are we ever likely to outgrow them as we pass from such simple re-tellings as this to the Greek authors themselves . . . (270)

He concludes with a quotation from the dedicatory poem to *The World's Desire* (1890), an adventure novel co-authored by his two boyhood favorites, Lang and Rider Haggard: "*Old shapes of song that do not die | Shall haunt the halls of memory*" (270).

---

[94] This too can be traced to his childhood. According to the front matter of the 1994 Puffin edition, "From an early age he possessed a huge chart, like a family tree, which displayed and made sense of the complex relationships between all the Greek gods and heroes."

Lancelyn Green's conception of "simple re-tellings" of tales that belong to "the world's heritage" is more reminiscent of Hawthorne than of Lang the classical scholar or Lang the anthropologist; it epitomizes the romanticism that animates many children's myth books throughout the century between Hawthorne and Lancelyn Green. As reworked versions of earlier retellings, such tales affirm an unbroken continuity with the more recent past as well as with distant antiquity. With appropriate revision, they can keep alive not only the Greek world but also the author's childhood and the earlier times of the writers he encountered as a child, poets and novelists with their own nostalgic yearnings. Made suitable for child readers, retold myths preserve not only the past but also the stage of life at which they are first encountered, with its assumed innocence. Along with the suppression of unsuitable events, there is a tendency to hold strong emotion at arm's length through a summary, informational presentation that evokes the handbook, as in Lancelyn Green's conclusion to the Theseus story; children's versions can be conceived of as introductory or preliminary, with full experience of the myths deferred to a later time, when they can be encountered more deeply, often in poetry.

Lancelyn Green's approach receives a strong endorsement in Elizabeth Cook's *The Ordinary and the Fabulous: An Introduction to Myths, Legends and Fairy Tales*, an English educator's manifesto for "fabulous stories" as essential reading for children, first published in 1969 in the face of increased emphasis on "relevance" in education (in a later echo of Lucy Sprague Mitchell's stress on the here-and-now). Cook's defense restates the values that had been repeatedly associated with myths for children throughout the preceding century. "Childhood reading of symbolic and fantastic tales contributes something irreplaceable to any later experience of literature"; because these stories are "archetypal and anonymous," they teach patterns of experience through which the child can make sense of the world (Cook 1976: 4, 9). Especially for younger readers, Cook prefers a relatively detached presentation: "There is a hard, alert, often cheerful objectivity in the way in which most of them were told in antiquity, whether by early or late writers; it is congenial to many children between the ages of eight and eleven and the best modern versions manage to retain it" (10). Comparing different versions of selected episodes, she several times finds Lancelyn Green succeeding where Hawthorne or Kingsley no longer can; he operates with a similar conception of myth but lacks the old-fashioned, ornate style of the Victorians and avoids the sentimentality that is always a danger when myths are converted into fairy tales. "It seems to me that Hawthorne has fallen over the cliff, and that Roger Lancelyn Green manages very cleverly to stay on a safe cliff-path" (86). Judicious updating keeps an essentially unchanging enterprise alive.

4

"Be a Roman Soldier"
History, Historical Fiction, and National Identity

In his 1907 essay collection, *In a Nook with a Book*, Frederic W. Macdonald (a Methodist minister and Rudyard Kipling's maternal uncle) describes the childhood reading of "romance."

A child's adventures in the world of romance have infinite charm and reality. Long before he has seen the ocean, a mountain, a waterfall, or a foreign city, he has "travelled in the realms of gold." He has sailed with Columbus and Captain Cook, and wintered with Franklin in the Arctic seas. He has ridden through the desert on a camel, and slept by Indian camp fires. He has seen Horatius buffeting the waves of yellow Tiber, and the Black Prince charging at Cressy. By the time I was twelve years old I knew the pyramids and the Colosseum, I had seen Quintus Curtius leap into the gulf, and Caesar fall by Pompey's pillar. I had fought with the Crusaders, and retreated from Moscow with Napoleon.   (Macdonald 1907: 16–17)[1]

For the child reader, stories of other times and places offer an alternative existence in which "charm" and "reality" coexist, because children, Macdonald goes on to say, do not distinguish between the sacred and the secular, the allegorical and the real:

All things are sacred, then, for "Heaven lies about us in our infancy," and all things are secular, if that means real and actual. Crusoe is guarded and guided by God as truly as were the patriarchs in their wanderings. The lions between which Christian passed, have hair, and teeth, and claws like those we have seen in the menagerie. All is real and all is imaginary.   (15)

---

[1] On Macdonald's life (1842–1928) and work see his memoir, Macdonald 1919, and the account of his family circle in Flanders 2001.

Macdonald's description of his own early experience suggests that the allure of romance can be a path to historical knowledge, especially knowledge of individuals who play a significant role in national narratives of war, politics, and exploration.[2] The books Macdonald read during his childhood in the 1840s and 1850s were mostly not intended for children: his allusion to "the yellow Tiber" points to the most famous of Macaulay's *Lays of Ancient Rome*, "Horatius at the Bridge," and in the preceding paragraphs he recalls with nostalgia "*Robinson Crusoe* and the *Pilgrim's Progress...Don Quixote* and the *Arabian Nights*, and *Hans Andersen*, and the *Mutiny of the Bounty*" (15).[3] But writers for children who seek to convey historical information have regularly embraced the elements of romance that captivated Macdonald, soliciting their readers' interest through a similar blend of the imaginary and the real and through a similar focus on exciting adventures and memorable individuals.

The resemblance between history and fiction is a commonplace of postmodern theory, which calls attention to the role of narrative and plotting in both forms and to the constructed or fictive quality of what we read as historical fact.[4] Much of this theory is aimed at revealing the fictionality (shared with most forms of discourse) of contemporary historical writing that presents itself as rigorously factual and even scientific; in the earlier historical tradition, parallels between history and the novel are inescapable.[5] When children are the intended audience, moreover, history's reliance on fiction is more immediately evident: fictional elements are freely and overtly admitted in hopes of inspiring the pleasurable absorption that is often (as Macdonald's reminiscence attests) seen as belonging particularly to the child reader.[6] And so we find

[2] Geoffrey Trease gives a similar account: "At Henty's call I marched *With Roberts to Pretoria*, *With the Allies to Pekin*, *With Kitchener in the Sudan* and, I suppose, with almost every military expedition from Hannibal and his elephants onward" (Trease 1964: 19). Cf. Andrew Lang on "bookish children" who reenact what they read and on his own childhood play "as a Roman engineer, taking part in the siege of Jerusalem" (Lancelyn Green 1946: 8), and more recently Spufford 2002: 80 ("Be a Roman soldier, said a book by Rosemary Sutcliff").

[3] *The Mutiny of the Bounty* was presumably Sir John Barrow's account; *Hans Andersen* might be any of several collections available in English translation, including Andersen 1846a, 1846b, 1846c, 1846d, 1850.

[4] See esp. White 1978.   [5] LaCapra 1985: 122; cf. 1987: 8.

[6] On the role of vignettes drawn from legend in history for children see Maxwell 2009: 240. History and biography for children are less likely to include the narrative markers

many writers and educators in the century after Macdonald's own childhood teaching children about the ancient world by integrating myths into accounts of historical events, foregrounding biographical narratives, and exploiting the appeal of historical fiction.

Familiar Friends: From Romance to History

Older handbooks such as Tooke's *Pantheon* emphasize the importance of myth as a source of information ancillary to the reading of history, but in the wake of Hawthorne, Kingsley, and their successors, myth's appeal to the child's imagination played a role in its increased adoption as a curricular step for younger children towards the learning of ancient history, both in the United States and in Great Britain. In a chapter on Ancient History in the 1898 volume *Work and Play in Girls' Schools*, edited by three British headmistresses,[7] Mary Hanbidge recommends beginning with myth on the grounds that "With young children history proper is an impossibility, but an interest in the life of the past may be developed very early" (Beale, Soulsby, and Dove 1898: 161),[8] and adds a further rationale that recalls Kingsley: "The mental development of the child epitomises that of the race, and in the record of a nation mythology precedes history" (161). The familiar fairy-tale comparison also recurs, both as a supportive parallel (through the apt pairing of two figures famous for losing a shoe) and as a possible source of criticism, which Hanbidge counters.

Quite little children know Jason, with his one sandal, as well as they do Cinderella, and Athene is a familiar friend whose picture they recognize. Cavillers may say that we are only teaching fairy tales, but the same children grown a little older see their Athene the central point of all the glories of Periclean Athens, and find themselves in a world they know.   (161)

Dorrit Cohn sees as characteristic of "a scrupulous historian" when going beyond documentary evidence (Cohn 1999: 118).

[7] Beale, Soulsby, and Dove 1898. The authors were all leading figures in women's education, and Hanbidge herself was for three decades headmistress of the Central Foundation Girls' School in London.

[8] Similarly, in their introduction to *Greek Gods, Heroes, and Men* (1901), Caroline and Samuel Harding note "the value of the old Greek stories as material of the cultivation of the child's imagination and the development of the ethical perceptions" and cite "a report by the Committee of Ten appointed by the National Education Association" [of the United States] on "the necessity of basing the formal study of History on some sort of elementary studies in biography and mythology" (Harding and Harding 1906: iii).

The numerous histories and collections of lives that begin with myth
effectively treat myth as a part of history.[9] At the same time, ancient
history itself is sometimes treated almost as a collection of myths or
fairy tales: yet another source of delightful stories such as Hawthorne's
Eustace Bright tells in response to his young companions' requests.
In the dedication to her *Stories from Greek History* (1907), Ethelwyn
Lemon writes,

Do you remember that bright summer morning last year when we lay out on the
lawn and read together the "Labours of Heracles," and how you once interrupted
to ask "if the tales were true?"
  The tales in this little book *are* true, and beside the winter fire I wrote them,
fancying that I still had your eager face beside me, heard still your eager
demand for "another story." Will you like these as well, I wonder?

(Lemon 1907)

Mary Macgregor's introduction to *The Story of Greece* (1914), which
turns to history after a few opening myths, sees ancient Greece itself as a
"Wonderland"; a decade later, in 1922, Jeanette Rector Hodgdon entitles
her book ("written in the hope of stimulating interest in history, literature, religion, and art") *The Enchanted Past: True Stories of the Lands
Where Civilization Began*.[10] Like Lemon's dedication, Hodgdon's subtitle
assimilates history to myth, presenting it as a set of entertaining, even
magical tales, but with the added attraction of being true. The same
delightful fusion of the charming and the real is invoked when writers
explain to their child readers that certain myths have turned out (as a
result of archaeological excavations) to correspond with actual events. In
Greeks and Persians of Long Ago (1933), Louise Mohr invites her readers
to take particular pleasure in such revelations:

Even cities with great palaces and crowded market places have been so nearly
forgotten that men smile and say the bits of stories about them are only fairy
tales. Of all the tales about long-ago people, few are more interesting than those
in which half-forgotten people and places are proved to have been real.

(Mohr 1933: 15)

[9] See e.g. Yonge 1879, Macgregor 1914, Haaren and Poland 1904, Shaw 1903, and
Spickelmire 1911.
[10] Corinne Spickelmire's *Stories of Hellas* (1911) invites child readers to "sojourn a while
in Hellas" and enjoy "glad golden days...wandering through shadowy grottoes or dancing
with nymphs to the Pipes of Pan" (2).

Mohr's primary example is the myth of Theseus in light of Evans's discoveries at Knossos.[11]

For students who are "on the threshold of history," Hanbidge recommends biography, specifically "biographies introductory to history"—that is, the stories of "men who make or mark a period" (Beale, Soulsby, and Dove 1898: 161–2). Biography, which is closely allied to fiction by its strong narrative arc, its interest in character and motivation, and its emphasis on individual action, had a long-established place in children's reading by Hanbidge's day. The prominence of biography is reflected in the works of such prolific nineteenth-century writers for children as the English novelist Charlotte Yonge (1823–1901) and Jacob Abbott (1803–79), the American author of the "Rollo" books (realistic stories following the development of a typical boy), as well as in the many versions of Plutarch for children.[12] Yonge's *Book of Worthies* self-consciously follows a practice dating back to "old times" in providing "glorious examples ... on the way to deeds of virtue" (1869a: v); F. H. Weston's selection from Plutarch's lives is guided not only by their degree of interest for young readers but also by the clarity of their ethical teachings "either by example or contrast" (Weston 1900: v).[13]

Hanbidge and many of her contemporaries tend rather to see biography as offering the kind of intimate personal connection that Macdonald remembers from his reading and that is frequently associated with the experience of historical fiction. In making her recommendation she evokes a particular view of child development and emphasizes

[11] Cf. James Baikie (*Peeps at Many Lands: Ancient Greece*, 1920), who distinguishes the "fairy-tale" accretions of myth from a core that has "been proved, and that not many years ago, to be simple truth" (Baikie 2008: 13–14).

[12] See e.g. Kaufman 1884; Weston 1900; Gould 1910a, 1910b. An "insurance man," questioned in the early 1930s about his reading, recalls: "It would be a very difficult matter for me to tell why, or exactly when, I became interested in the classics, but I presume it happened in this way. I was born and reared on a Kansas farm. When a boy a Carnegie Library was opened at Manhattan, about ten miles from my home. I used to bring a load of wood or produce to town, sell it, and then spend the remainder of the day at the free library. On one of my trips I found Plutarch's Lives, took it home and, figuratively speaking, devoured it" (Compton 1935: 109). Abbott, who collaborated with his brother John on a series of biographies ("Makers of History") for somewhat older readers (aged 15 to 25), includes a number of figures from Greco-Roman antiquity.

[13] Each volume of F. J. Gould's *The Children's Plutarch* (1910a, 1910b) provides a topic index largely devoted to specific virtues exemplified by the different lives. On moral education by example in ancient biography, see also Guerber 1896: 5.

(in accordance with that view) the importance of individual persons in the child's experience: "since a child is naturally anthropomorphic, the personal element must be made the most prominent" (Beale, Soulsby, and Dove 1898: 161–2). Similarly, Alice Gardner (*Friends of the Olden Time*, 1891) seeks "to present before the eyes of children a few typical and significant characters in such way that their personality may be strongly realized and a living interest given to their history from the very first" (Gardner 1891: 3). John Haaren and A. B. Poland (*Famous Men of Greece* and *Famous Men of Rome*, 1904) spell out the crucial role of identification in this process, which is presented in a way that recalls the experience of fiction:

> Experience has proven that in order to attract and hold the child's attention each conspicuous feature of history presented to him should have an individual for its center. The child identifies himself with the personage presented. It is not Romulus or Hercules or Cæsar or Alexander that the child has in mind when he reads, but himself, acting under similar conditions.
>
> (Haaren and Poland 1904: 5)

Romulus will be more than a source of interest to the child reader, he will be the child's self.

When Hanbidge has students turn to "history proper" for the first time, she proceeds on the widespread assumption that children favor history that is shaped by storytelling, insisting on vividness and narrative continuity: "this must not be mere chronology, but a series of connected *pictures* of events" (Beale, Soulsby, and Dove 1898: 163). Some ancient histories for children aim to give the child reader not only a vivid image but also a kind of immersion in ancient reality, which at times is built into the historical narrative through fictional means. In *Friends of the Olden Time*, Alice Gardner asks her readers to imagine that they have fallen asleep and wake up in different places and at different times from 610 to 49 BCE. Her style is conversational ("Now that you are feeling exceedingly delighted and a little exhausted") and she also engages her readers in conversation with the people they encounter:

> But we ought to find out more about this great man, Pericles. Let us ask some questions of one of the gentlemen lounging in the porch. The Athenians are still, you see, fond of lounging.   (Gardner 1891: 30)[14]

---

[14] Cf. Baikie (2008) who takes his child readers to Athens to stay with a citizen.

In another variation, which instead of bringing the child reader into the ancient world offers the reader an ancient child's-eye view, Louise Mohr (*Greeks and Persians of Long Ago*, 1933) sets at the center of her account of ancient history from the Myceneans to Alexander a story (occupying several chapters) about the experiences of a fictional boy who lives in the Greek countryside. Imaginary children of the past may double as the audience for historical information, as in Norah MacKenzie's 1931 *Children of Athens, London, and Rome*, edited by Catherine B. Firth (a textbook for ages 7 to 11), which tells the stories of fictional children who listen to accounts of the past and of current political events as they go about their everyday lives in fifth-century BCE Athens, early nineteenth-century London, and first-century BCE Rome.

Bringing the Past to Life? Historical Fiction

We might appropriately describe these last examples as rudimentary works of historical fiction, and thus as belonging to a genre which has long served as both pleasure reading and approved educational fare for children.[15] Historical fiction, which (despite many earlier precedents) is often understood to begin with the works of Walter Scott (1771–1832), has been widely read by children from the outset.[16] Historical fiction specifically for children has been steadily produced (with some ups and down in popularity) since the second half of the nineteenth century, when it played a prominent role in the work of Charlotte Yonge, G. A. Henty, and Alfred Church, and has been regularly encouraged by teachers and parents.[17] Whether written ostensibly for adults or for

[15] The standing of the historical novel has been both varied and contested, and critics have raised and continue to raise questions of definition, categorization, and terminology. For earlier discussions of the genre, see Saintsbury 1975, Matthews 1901, Lukács 1982; for several recent considerations of the relationship between history and fiction in the historical novel and of subtypes and terminology, see Maxwell 2009, Hamnett 2011, and the essays in *Rethinking History* 9/2–3 (2005), esp. those by White, Shaw, Slotkin, and Demos; cf. also Goldhill 2011: ch. 5.

[16] For instances of children reading Scott with their governesses or parents, see Fletcher 2008: 229, 231, 296; cf. Maxwell 2009: 254; on Scott and girls' reading, see Flint 1993; on Scott as crossover fiction, Beckett 2009: 18.

[17] For a brief account of the development of historical fiction for children in Britain and the United States from the 19th through the late 20th century, see Rahn 1991; on Scott's increasing identification with childhood reading and on "juvenile" historical fiction in the late 19th and early 20th centuries and its influence on subsequent adult historical fiction, see

children, historical fiction shows up frequently in school libraries, on lists of appropriate reading, and as school prizes,[18] and historical novels or short stories originally written for adults have sometimes been repackaged as children's books.[19]

Historical fiction for children has been especially praised for giving earlier times a reality and a vividness history proper lacks,[20] and for connecting child readers with other eras through what Kim Wilson has called "the privileged position of personal re-experience."[21] But the rather slippery concept of "reality" at play in such formulations elides the question of historical difference: the success of such works in making the past immediate and accessible may work against their frequent claims to truthfulness, accuracy, and effectiveness in conveying the very different conditions and spirit of another era. Recent critical discussion has called attention to tensions that are inherent in the genre of historical fiction as a whole but particularly pronounced in works for children.[22] In particular, the premium placed on the modern child's identification with historical figures as a point of entry into the past complicates the definition suggested by Georg Lukács's still-influential argument that the genre begins with Scott because his work for the first time gives us "the specifically historical, that is, the derivation of the

Maxwell 2009: ch. 5; for recent work on historical fiction for children, see esp. Collins and Graham 2001, Lucas 2003, Wilson 2011, Butler and O'Donovan 2012.

[18] In a 1902 bibliography of the genre, J. Nield remarks: "In the last year or two there has been an almost alarming influx in this department of Fiction, and teachers in schools, besides readers in general, may be glad to be saved a somewhat tedious investigation" (Nield 1911: 2). By contrast, Arbuthnot (1947: 397) warns against an excessive emphasis on the use of realistic historical fiction in connection with social studies units.

[19] For example, Caroline Dale Snedeker's first book, The Coward of Thermopylae (1911), republished for children as The Spartan (1912), and the stories collected in Naomi Mitchison's The Hostages, discussed in Chapter 5. Maxwell 2009 suggests that Mitchison's historical novels for adults were themselves influenced by juvenile fiction and by "her own projects for classroom instruction" (260). On such rewriting and repackaging, see Beckett 2009: 61–83, 232–9.

[20] " ... peoples, places, and problems seem almost as real to us as those we know today" (Arbuthnot 1947: 411); the child "comprehends [past times] not as interesting historical settings and events but as vibrant moments of immediate reality" (Jacobs 1961: 191; cf. Jacobs 1952).

[21] Wilson 2011: 3. Wilson cites Lukács 1982: 42: "What matters [in the historical novel] is that we should re-experience the social and human motives which led men to think, feel, and act as they did in historical reality" (3).

[22] Stephens 1992: ch. 6; Wilson 2011; Butler and O'Donovan 2012.

individuality of characters from the historical peculiarity of their age."[23] There is a potential contradiction in what John Stephens cites as two of the standard "prescriptive, evaluative criteria for children's historical fiction": "Characters must be credible and invite reader-identification," and "Readers should feel they have learned more about a time and a place through the illusion that they have experienced them vicariously."[24]

The demand for characters in whom readers can see themselves inevitably introduces a present-day perspective and fosters forms of anachronism that extend beyond the circumstances, motivations, and emotional valences of individuals to include contemporary social values and political ideologies—which may be reinforced even as they draw the reader into another period.[25] In the case of works set in eras as far removed from their presumed audience in time and space as Greco-Roman antiquity, the distant past may be brought closer to home by assimilation to the more recent past of the reader's own culture. Yet, as the past undergoes multiple forms of identification with the here and now, a contrast between the two worlds is also established, whether that contrast is drawn implicitly or signaled explicitly by various modes of defamiliarization, by an implied judgment of relative merit, or by direct authorial intervention or commentary.[26] Catherine Butler and Hallie O'Donovan identify this coexistence of assimilation and contrast as a constitutive feature of the genre when they note at the outset of their *Reading History in Children's Books* that

---

[23] Lukács 1982: 19.

[24] Stephens 1992: 204. Although the second of these criteria "presumes that reader subjectivity is properly subordinated to a subject position inscribed within the text," the first suggests that the subject position is in part determined by the needs of the reader and in particular by the criterion of identification (204–5).

[25] For critiques of the incorporation of modern beliefs and feelings in the interest of reader engagement, see Barnhouse 2000 and Wilson 2011; Butler and O'Donovan (2012: ch. 4) offer a thoughtful defense of anachronism and an argument for compromise, treating the tension between authenticity and anachronism on the analogy of foreignizing and domesticating approaches to translation.

[26] On defamiliarization, especially in linguistic register, see Stephens 1992: 218–27; on the presumption of progress between past and present, Wilson 2011. Goldhill notes that in Victorian historical fiction the narrative voice frequently draws attention to the distance between present and past (2011: 184–5), a practice that persisted in some works of children's historical fiction into the first half of the 20th century.

historical books for children typically accommodate both a confidence in the essential continuity of human experience over time and an historicist insistence on the radical difference, and even inscrutability, of the past.[27]

Children's historical fiction set in classical antiquity, like other historical fiction, may feature real historical characters treated with freedom of invention, invented characters in historical settings, or both (with the former often as secondary characters).[28] It may focus on significant historical events (the Persian wars, the Catilinarian conspiracy, the invasion of Britain, the burning of Rome), but these historical settings often serve primarily as background for events in the lives of fictional characters in keeping with a general tendency, noted by John Stephens, for children's historical fiction to "displace macro-scale historical events into micro-stories of human relationships."[29] This is in part because such works tend to feature young protagonists who are not yet major players in the events of their day, supplying their readers with fleshed-out second selves who facilitate the absorption into the past that Macdonald achieved by imagination alone. Both limited and liberated by the relative paucity of detailed evidence for historical events (and its virtual absence for the daily lives of ordinary people), historical novels set in the ancient world sometimes draw on myth and legend to extend the narrative reach of history and on the findings of archaeologists to supplement the historical record.[30] But most novels set in the ancient world are broadly realistic, although they may include as part of the reality they depict divine or supernatural elements in which their characters believe.[31] There are a few examples of time travel to or from the ancient world in

[27] Butler and O'Donovan 2012: 1.
[28] Some critics would distinguish between fictional history (which features real historical characters and events) and historical fiction (where the focus is on invented characters); see Goodman 2005. On Victorian historical fiction set in antiquity (including some works read by and written for children), see Goldhill 2011: chs. 5, 6; Vance 1997: ch. 9; on historical writing for children set in antiquity after 1950, see Butler and O'Donovan 2012: ch. 2.
[29] Stephens 1992: 236.
[30] They may do both: Louise Lamprey's *Children of Ancient Greece* (1924) and Erick Berry's *The Winged Girl of Knossos* (1935) (discussed in Chapter 5) anticipate Mary Renault's work in rewriting and rationalizing the legend of Theseus in light of the archeological discoveries on Crete. On Crete, cf. also Naomi Mitchison's "The Prince" in *Boys and Girls and Gods* (1931a); for the use of myth and legend, see also Lamprey 1922; Crew 1927, 1928, 1929; Lancelyn Green 1959, 1961; Sprague 1947.
[31] In recent decades historical novels set in antiquity have played more freely with elements of fantasy. See the Epilogue and works cited there.

our period, but although these feature magic as the means of travel, the world to which the child characters travel (as in E. Nesbit's *The Story of the Amulet*) or from which people travel to speak to them (as in Rudyard Kipling's *Puck of Pook's Hill*) is itself for the most part non-magical. Plots vary considerably, from Victorian narratives of Christian suffering and conversion to the detective stories that become popular toward the middle of the twentieth century.[32] Among the most common in the first half of the twentieth century (which will be our focus in this chapter and the next) are tales of war, military service, and adventure, stories in which the central character overcomes some obstacle or deals with some past loss, and other coming-of-age stories. Protagonists may be children but are more often adolescents or young adults, especially in the narratives of maturation and adventure that have tended at least until recently to dominate the genre, and romantic love occasionally plays a role.

In the rest of this chapter, we explore the connections between past and present constructed in historical fiction (from the end of the nineteenth century to the middle of the twentieth) set in Rome and its empire and variously directed to British and American children. In particular, we show how the different cultural contexts of these intended audiences lead to different visions of the Roman world and different ways of relating Roman history to the reader's own national past. We begin with stories written by British authors for an audience of British children, but our ultimate focus will be the specifically American turn given to the treatment of ancient Rome in three novels written in the US between the two world wars.

Our Country Must Rule the World: Roman Past, British Present

In *Lucius: the Adventures of a Roman Boy* (1885), set in the first century BCE, A. J. Church describes a room in the villa in Arpinum, north of Rome, in which Lucius has grown up:

---

[32] On Christianity in Victorian historical fiction, see esp. Goldhill 2011: chs. 5, 6, and novels by Clarke (1890), Holt (1887), Leslie (2007a, b, c), Pollard (1892), Yonge (1890); for 20th-century novels in which Christianity plays an important role, see Bruce 1925, Mattingly 1928, Sagon 1907, Snedeker 1956, Malvern 1958, Speare 1961. For early examples of the mystery plot, see the novels of Jay Williams.

The apartment in which the household was collected was a long, low room, not unlike the kitchen of an old-fashioned English farmhouse. Hams and flitches of bacon hung from the rafters, and a great log of beech wood was burning cheerily in a large open fireplace. On the mantlepiece were quaint images of a highly antique appearance. These were the household gods, and were almost the only peculiar features of the room.   (Church 1960: 7)

Church's cautious "not unlike" introduces a description that so sub-sumes the Roman room into an English room which is at once old-fashioned and paradigmatic that its only specifically Roman features are explicitly marked by their individuality, quaintness, and antiquity. Like-ness serves as a foil for difference, and the reader's world is both compared with and distanced from the Roman past. There is a similar ambivalence in a passage in G. G. Manville Fenn's *Marcus, the Young Centurion* (1904), set in the same period. Fenn describes his protagonist as wearing "a loose, woolen, open-fronted garment, not very much unlike a tweed Norfolk jacket without pockets or buttons, very short in the sleeves" (Fenn 1904: 12). Fenn's even more qualified "not very much unlike" and his radical alterations of the Norfolk jacket create doubt about the resemblance even as it is offered.

We find a particularly playful evocation of likeness and difference in Rudyard Kipling's *Puck of Pook's Hill* (1906), in which figures from the English past are magically brought to present-day Sussex to tell their stories to two children, Dan and Una. One of the characters they meet is the young centurion Parnesius, a Roman whose family have lived in Britain for generations, and who is sent by the Emperor Maximus to serve on Hadrian's Wall, governing the Picts and resisting attacks from the north by the "Winged Hats." Here the Roman centurion Parnesius describes his own childhood in fourth-century Britain:

"Good families are very much alike. Mother would sit spinning of evenings while Aglaia read in her corner, and Father did accounts, and we four romped about the passages. When our noise grew too loud the Pater would say, 'Less tumult! Less tumult! Have you never heard of a Father's right over his children? He can slay them, my loves—slay them dead, and the Gods highly approve of the action!' Then Mother would prim up her dear mouth over the wheel and answer: 'H'm! I'm afraid there can't be much of the Roman Father about you.' Then the Pater would roll up his accounts, and say, 'I'll show you!' And then—then, he'd be worse than any of us!" "Fathers can—if they like," said Una, her eyes dancing. "Didn't I say all good families are very much the same?"
(Kipling 1993: 86–7)

Kipling's narrator begins with a statement not only of likeness but of universality; as the passage continues, however, the child reader is offered a glimpse of the ancient Roman law of *patria potestas*, and the evocation of the Roman father's distinctive powers is reinforced by the use of the Latin word for father. But though *pater* is Latin for father, "the Pater" is contemporary English colloquialism, and the father's traditional right of life and death over his children has become a family joke, clearly recognizable as such to Parnesius' modern audience within the text.

The traditional English farmhouse, the Norfolk jacket, and the reference to "the Pater" situate Rome in relation not only to the writer's own day but specifically to England and an English readership, calling on points of comparison presumed (whether rightly or wrongly) to be part of the young reader's everyday experience. Such parallels also extend to adult arenas of experience, especially warfare, which is prominent in accounts of Rome and its empire, bringing the romance of historical fiction to bear on a way of life that constitutes, for many readers of such books, their expected future. G. A. Henty's 1892 novel *Beric the Briton* tells the story of a young Briton who has lived for some years among the Romans. Upon his return, he endeavors to teach his people the Roman way of fighting, in order to improve their ability to resist the imperial power; after the failure of Boadicea's revolt, he spends time in Rome, where he is in turn a gladiator, Nero's guard, and an outlaw. He marries a Roman woman, and eventually returns to Britain to lead his people under Rome's rule, and become a Christian.[33] In this passage, near the beginning of the novel, he is trying to introduce the Britons to Roman tactics, and encounters some difficulty:

The manoeuvres to be taught were not of a complicated nature. To form in fighting order six deep, and to move in column, were the principal points... When, however, having arranged them at first in a line two deep, Beric proceeded to explain how the spears were to be held, and in what order the movements were to be performed,—the exercise answering to the manual and platoon of modern days,—the tribesmen were unable to restrain their laughter...To men absolutely unaccustomed to order of any kind, but used only to fight each in the way that suited him best, these details appeared absolutely ludicrous.   (Henty 1892: 57)

---

[33] On Henty and his influence, see Richards 1989, Reynolds 1990, Hoberman 1997, Vance 1997, Hingley 2000, Paris 2000, Goldhill 2011, Knuth 2012, and esp. Jones 2013.

This passage incorporates a commonplace in historical fictions of the Roman Empire: the contrast between the Roman mode of fighting (both unified and orderly) and the mode of fighting of their less civilized antagonists, who are individually brave and skillful but incapable of obedience and cooperation. But even as Beric is explaining Roman warfare to his fellow Britons—to whom it appears strange and ridiculous—the narrator briefly intervenes to offer young readers a comparison with the military training of their own day. The reader is evidently expected to understand the analogy, since the expression "manual and platoon" goes quite unexplained.[34] What's more, the modern British reader, unlike the ancient Britons, is expected to find Roman practices familiar: the British army of the reader's day is similarly trained, similarly unified, and similarly obedient to its commanders. Henty reinforces the analogy a little later when Beric divides his men into companies and appoints "sub-officers or sergeants" to serve under him (59); again, the narrative translates Roman practice (as adapted for Britons) into the language of the nineteenth-century British military.

The connection between past and present military service is subtler in Kipling's "A Centurion of the Thirtieth," the first of the three stories about Parnesius in *Puck of Pook's Hill.* When the young centurion tells the children how he decided to join the army, Dan asks him whether he had to pass an exam (Kipling 1993: 89). This is at once a marker of difference and an anticipation of similarity: Parnesius did not, of course, have to pass an exam, but he is an ancient analogue to those who trained at Sandhurst in Kipling's day and then served as junior commissioned officers in the army. Parnesius learns his "foot-drill," and then serves as a "probationer, waiting for a command" and training "a handful—and they were a handful!—of Gauls and Iberians" until (in part through his father's influence) he is made centurion (90–1).[35] In what follows he offers his listeners both the unfamiliar specifics of Roman military practice (how soldiers march, what they eat, how they carry shield and spear) and some apparently universal truths about military service ("a man doesn't forget his first march," 95). Parnesius' listeners, Dan

[34] On Henty's expectation that readers of his books will have "a familiarity with military terminology," see Jones 2013: 163.
[35] Foot-drill was part of the regular Sandhurst training, and cadets were given probationary commands.

and Una, who figure the reader within the text, do not always understand what he is telling them, but Dan, as a boy with the possibility of military life before him, has an intuitive grasp of Parnesius' reactions to events that Una lacks (101).

In fictions like Kipling's and Fenn's (in which the young Marcus, accompanied by an elderly veteran named Serge, joins Caesar's army in Gaul against his father's orders), military life is typically presented through the eyes of the young soldier, and thus obviously serves the purposes of the coming-of-age story. But the way in which writers represent the historical context of warfare also suggests comparisons with the larger historical and political context of writer and reader. Parnesius and his friend Pertinax are—in their comradeship, in their loyalty (even to a leader of questionable judgment), in their understanding of those they rule—like the best of young British officers serving the Empire in Kipling's tales of India, a link made perhaps most clearly by the poem "A British-Roman Song" that precedes the second of the three stories, and addresses Rome:

> Strong heart with triple armour bound,
> Beat strongly, for the life-blood runs,
> Age after Age, the Empire round—
> In us thy sons,
>
> Who, distant from the Seven Hills,
> Loving and serving much, require,
> Thee,—thee to guard 'gainst home-born ills,
> The Imperial Fire.   (96)[36]

The ending of Fenn's *Marcus, the Young Centurion*, in stating Rome's commitment to foreign rule and the cost of that commitment, also evokes Britain's imperial mission and the self-sacrifice of her soldiers. Warfare has its horrors as well as its moments of glory, but for the "old warrior" Serge, "our country must rule the world... And give up the bravest and the best of her sons to fight her cause!" (Fenn 1904: 392).

---

[36] On the analogy between Roman Britain and British India, see Rutherford 1964; Rivet 1976; Majeed 1999; Hingley 2000; Vasunia 2005; Roberts 2007, 2010; and works cited in these. For the view that Kipling's Roman stories depict Rome as a problematic and disturbing imperial paradigm, see Adler 2015. On the issue of empire in Kipling's work for children generally, see also Richards 1989, Kutzer 2000, Randall 2000, McBratney 2002.

The connection between ancient Rome and imperial Britain readers encounter in Henty, Kipling, and Fenn had become something of a commonplace by the later nineteenth century.[37] In Henty and Kipling, however, another parallel is also at work, one between modern Britain and its forerunner, the Britain of Beric and Parnesius. Because the period and place of Roman rule in Britain are part of British history as well as of Roman history, Roman Britain is a particularly frequent setting for historical novels for British children. Other examples are plentiful, in our period and afterwards, and even fictions that have little to do with Britain, like Amyot Sagon's *Under the Roman Eagles* (1907), Ioreth Evans's *Gadget City* (1944), and Geoffrey Trease's *Word to Caesar* (1955), may start in Britain, or feature a token British character, such as the faithful British (and Christian) slave in Marjory Bruce's *Maro the Lion-Keeper* (1925).[38]

Such fictions, whether written in the colonial period or in its immediate aftermath, seek to negotiate for the child reader a dual identification: with ancient Britain, conceived of as the ancestor of modern Britain and like modern Britain given to resisting would-be conquerors from across the channel; and with the Roman Empire, conceived of as the prototype of the British Empire, and like the British Empire seeking to impose the benign rule of law on a disorderly aboriginal people.[39] Henty's Roman-educated hero in *Beric the Briton* first seeks to use Roman military methods in support of his people's liberation, but in the end makes his peace with the Roman rule he perceives as superior; in Lydia Eliott's *Ceva of the Caradocs*, published sixty years later, the

[37] On the mid-century shift in Victorian discourse from republican Rome to imperial Rome as metaphor and paradigm, see Vance 1997: chs. 9–11; see also Betts 1971; Goldhill 2011: chs. 5, 6.

[38] Examples include Church 1887; Gullick 1926; Mattingly 1928; Mitchison, "Maiden Castle" in Mitchison 1929; Seaby 1943; Eliott 1953; Treece 1954 and 1965; Sutcliff 1954, 1955, 1993, 1959, 1961, 1965. On treatments of Roman Britain from 1950 to the early 21st century, and especially the representation of Roman Britain as a response to imperial and post-imperial Britain and the shift to a more critical perspective on Rome in recent fiction, see Butler and Donovan 2012: ch. 2. See also Butler 2015, and on the 1950s comic strip "Wulf the Briton," Keen 2015.

[39] See Hingley 2000: pt 2, chs. 5–8 on the gradual replacement of what he calls the Teutonic myth (the English as fundamentally Saxon, with the Roman past essentially lost and the British killed or driven out) by an understanding of Englishness as including elements of both the British (admirable in their resistance to the Romans) and the Romans (admirable for the culture they succeeded in transmitting to and through the British).

heroine wonders if it is "awful of [her]...to be glad that the Romans have made Britain a part of their marvelous Empire" (Eliott 1953: 9).[40] The young Romans of Kipling's *Puck of Pook's Hill* and Rosemary Sutcliff's many novels of Roman Britain, while enforcing Rome's rule and recognizing Rome as the source of civilization, also recognize the depth of their attachment to Britain, their home in some instances for many generations.[41] In A. J. Church's *The Count of the Saxon Shore*, Marion Mattingly's *Marcus the Briton*, and Rosemary Sutcliff's *The Silver Branch* and *The Lantern Bearers*, shifting alliances among Romans (typically of mixed ancestry) and Britons (some Romanized, some not) work to ward off new threats to Britain in the context of Rome's weakened power but persistent identification with the forces of civilization.

These texts envision a primary audience of British children who will see their own country both in the geographical space of ancient Britain and in the imperial power that rules it. E. Nesbit, whose novels for children both satirize and endorse her characters' patriotism, plays with this dual perspective in the *Story of the Amulet,* a novel of time travel, in a chapter in which the four protagonists, having traveled back to Roman Britain, then meet Julius Caesar on the eve of his invasion. Eager to save Britain, the older children play down its value as a prize, but the youngest, Jane, angry at being dismissed by Caesar as a barbarian, gives such an account of the glories of modern Britain (including its imperial claim to be, in Jane's confused version, "the country where the sun never sets") that Caesar makes up his mind to invade, if only out of curiosity, while acknowledging that if what he has heard (or dreamt) is true, "a hundred legions will not suffice" to conquer Britain (Nesbit 1959: 189, 193).[42]

The depiction of Rome in children's fiction is further complicated in works written in the context of the two world wars, where much of the action occurred in terrain fought over by the Romans, who might be

---

[40] See Butler and O'Donovan's discussion of this book and of the similar views of the Romanized Briton who is the hero of Treece's 1954 *Legions of the Eagle* (2012: 24–9).

[41] On "codes of manliness and concepts of national identity" in Rosemary Sutcliff's novels of Roman Britain, see Kennon 2007; on cultural identity in Henty and Sutcliff, see Johnson 2010.

[42] On Nesbit's treatment of ancient history, see Paul 2015.

variously identified with modern counterparts.[43] In I. O. Evans's *Gadget City*, a work for young readers published in 1944, Rome stands for the German invader. The novel is set primarily in Alexandria, where the hero, a "West Briton" named Morgan, works as a slave in the Museum, (here depicted as an institute for advanced scientific and technological research). The book opens with his capture in battle against the invading Romans, described in the language of World War II, with Britain in part assimilated to continental Europe:

> Thus our ancestors, nearly two thousand years ago, faced the blitzkrieg which the Romans launched against them, and which had already conquered the greater part of their island home. They were used to the idea that the greater part of the country formed a vast occupied zone. They were proud that their tribe, by fierce guerilla war in the mountains and forests, had kept their own region free. But now the Romans were advancing upon the Unoccupied Zone with an air of coming to conquer it at last. Streams of refugees fled before them, spreading tales of the most horrible atrocities. Above all, the refugees had spread rumours, all the more alarming because of their vagueness, of the dread Secret Weapon which had routed the United Nations of Britain at the battle of the River Thames.
>
> (Evans 1944: 10–11)

The Weapon in question proves to be an elephant, but when Morgan is captured he finds himself in a "concentration camp" before being sold as a galley slave and traveling to the Gadget City of the title.

In Allen Seaby's *The Ninth Legion* (1943), however, terms like "staff officers" and "military policeman" (as in Henty) inevitably identify the legionaries with British soldiers, in spite of the book's plentiful details about Roman military life. This does not mean that the ancient Britons are here equated with Germans; the British perspective is given equal weight and equal sympathy, and the only indication of the ongoing conflict is a paratextual one: the stamp that declares the book was produced in keeping with the "war economy standard." A more striking contrast with *Gadget City*'s vision of the Romans as Germans may be found in a contemporary American novel, Jay Williams's *The Counterfeit African* (1944), set not in Roman Britain but during Marius' campaign against Jugurtha. In his introduction, the author cites "the African campaign" as the testing ground for Marius's reorganization of the

---

[43] For the diverse uses of Rome as a possible parallel to British and American activities in World War I, see Vandiver 2010: 21–8.

"army of farmers" into "an army of professional fighting men" (Williams 1944: iii). To make the nature of this army clearer "to modern eyes," he uses contemporary military terminology (iv), and in this passage he clearly expects his young readers to catch an echo of the war currently in progress:

"Go on," Marius said softly. "What are they saying in Rome?"

"They're wondering why you haven't yet captured Jugurtha as you promised."

"So?" Marius flung himself into the camp chair and took his chin in his fist. "I almost had him near Cirta," he mused. "But the Desert Fox—that's what my boys call him—got away. He's a slippery one..." (5)

In giving Jugurtha the nickname of General Rommel, Williams recalls to his readers the recently concluded North African campaign of World War II, another testing ground and turning point. Here, then, it is Rome's enemies that are identified with the Germans, while the Romans recall the Allied forces. There are, however, indications that Williams expects his American readers to think of the Romans primarily as Americans: the emphasis is not on imperial ambitions but on "the cause of the plebeians" (16); the reference to Marius' "army of farmers" recalls as well a treasured trope of the American Revolution; and in assigning modern terms to ancient army officers Williams refers to "our armies." He concludes by thanking "Staff Sergeant Melvin Hess of the 260th Infantry Regiment for making it possible ... to finish this book while on active duty" (iii–iv).[44]

Citizen Soldiers and Pioneers: Roman Past, American Past

As this last example suggests, historical novels written in the United States, with its lack of a direct historical connection to the Roman Empire and its physical distance from the scenes of Roman history, offer different patterns of identification.[45] The American tenor of such works is

---

[44] For an American novel whose paratextual material identifies Rome with America's enemies, see Alfred Powers's *Hannibal's Elephants* (1944); the jacket blurb urges readers to buy war bonds and declares that "If the Carthaginians had done the equivalent" Rome would never have become "dictator of humankind" and all history since would have been "less dark."

[45] An earlier version of part of this section appeared in "Armies of Children: War and Peace, History and Myth in Children's Books After World War One," K. Marciniak (ed.),

especially pronounced in books written between the two world wars, a period that (as discussed in Chapter 3) saw a striking increase in the number of children's books published in the US and a renewed concern with the development of a specifically American body of children's literature. This literature celebrated and sought to inculcate definitive American values, particularly democracy, freedom, initiative, and self-reliance, which were regularly identified with the country's pioneer past, and which we find variously accommodated in works with Roman settings.[46]

Writing in the immediate aftermath of World War I, Reuben F. Wells presents his *With Caesar's Legions: The Adventures of Two Roman Youths in the Conquest of Gaul* (1923) as a pleasurable aid to the study of Latin and Roman history, expressing the hope that it will be "of value to those who are reading Caesar in school," for whom "the difficulty of translation" often impedes "a proper appreciation of the interest of the story" (8–9); at the same time, however, he refigures Rome's conquest of Gaul in terms of America's recent intervention in Europe.[47] In its general outline, the book represents a type familiar from Henty and many others: a tale of adolescent achievement and ultimate recognition by an admired leader in a historical context.[48] Two young cousins join Caesar's army, demonstrate their prowess, bravery, and cleverness, and come to the attention of Caesar. The author provides copious information about Roman military life and training, notes the continued importance of Caesar's tactics and includes comparisons with the military of his reader's day ("The cohort of Caesar's time corresponded very closely to

---

2016. *Our Mythical Childhood…: The Classics and Literature for Children and Young Adults.* Leiden: Brill. In the US as in Britain, the earlier sense of connection to republican Rome was to some extent displaced in the course of the 19th century; "Invocations of imperial Rome increased as America itself became a world empire by the 1890s, evoking military and cultural might rather than arcadian republican simplicity" (Winterer 2002: 143). But in the period we focus on, American expansionism is envisioned in children's books less as an imperial enterprise than as a pioneering movement inflected by democratic ideals (Schmidt 2013).

[46] See esp. Schmidt 2013; cf. also MacLeod 1995: 157–72; Murray 1998: 145–74; and on children's book publication in the US during this period, Marcus 2008: chs. 4, 5.

[47] For further discussion of Wells in the context of children's fiction after World War I children's fiction, see Murnaghan and Roberts 2016.

[48] Contemporary US examples of the same story type featuring Julius Caesar include Whitehead 1914; Wells 1960 (1st pub. 1923), 1925; Anderson 1929, 1935.

the modern company," 9). But here the point of reference is not British but American.

Wells prepares his reader (or perhaps his reader's parents and teachers) in his introduction:

> Another struggle ended only a few years ago on the same fields on which Caesar and his legionaries fought, a struggle that has some striking points of similarity to the former one. In the first century before the birth of Christ, as in the years from 1914 on, a great democracy fought with its allies to defend the latter's homeland and people from aggression. In both cases an invasion was threatened which, if not checked, would have brought destruction of property, the imposition of tribute, and the virtual enslavement of the people. In the World War more than one democracy was involved, and the fighting was on a far larger scale. In that, as in the campaigns with which this tale is concerned, the struggle ended with a host of threatening invaders driven back across the Rhine. (6)

Rome here resembles America, not as an imperial power, but as a democracy coming to the aid of European allies.[49] And although the two central characters, whose grandfather is a veteran of Marius' army, have been raised on stories of the building of Rome's empire, the emphasis in these stories is on the Roman legionaries as "citizen-soldiers," a term that evokes not only the idealized soldier of the Roman Republic and the conscripts and volunteers of World War I but the citizen-soldiers of the American Revolution. Wells further links these three historical moments when the legionary with whom the boys seek to enlist remarks that "A new Marius has come in our new leader, Caesar, I think, and the rights of the people will be restored. That is why I have rejoined the army" (32). Like "citizen-soldiers," "the rights of the people" evokes both the foundational values of the United States (themselves in part derived from an idealized vision of Rome), and the American War of Independence, recalled during World War I in such moments as General Pershing's visit, on July 14, 1917, to the tomb of Lafayette.[50]

Wells's narrative further develops the parallel between Roman citizen-soldiers and American enlistees by his depiction of his small-town protagonists, one the son of a farmer and the other of a merchant.

---

[49] For a similar vision during World War I of the Roman legionary as a soldier "whose duty led him to fight selflessly for the protection of a foreign people," see Vandiver 2010: 26.
[50] Farwell 1999: 93–4; Keene 2003: 107–8. (Note that Keene regularly refers to the (largely conscripted) armed forces of World War I as citizen-soldiers and that Farwell's last chapter is entitled "Return of the Legions.")

Their eagerness to join the legion they encounter at the outset of the novel is typical not only of the standard boy hero of adventure stories but also of the young American envisioned by World War I recruiting posters, eager to "see the world," and susceptible to promises of adventure and exotic travel. Titus and Julius "feel the thrill of tales of war," and when the legionary says "You want to join the army and fight, eh?" Julius replies, "Yes, and to travel... To go somewhere and see something. We can never amount to much in this cramped little town" (33).[51]

As the boys' adventures unfold, the reader's experience of this momentous struggle (where the Helvetians and Germans stand in for the German troops of 1917) is mediated through the day-to-day military life of two boys who seem little different from American small-town or farm boys.[52] The two friends compete with each other ("I'll bet you anything I can carry the pack as long as you can") and exclaim over the "fun" of training like the heroes of any adventure story (47), but their particular circumstances evoke both the way of life and the self-reliant ethos of the American frontier.

"Money," exclaimed Julius, his face falling. "Where can we get that? I haven't any." "Never mind," replied Titus. "I have some of my own with me, enough for us both. My father let me have all the pelts I got from the traps last winter, and I sold them for a good price the other day in town." (43)

Wells incorporates a few suggestions of earlier American types, such as the revolutionary citizen-soldier and the fur-trapping frontiersman, into a narrative that retells ancient history mostly in terms of recent events. We find a more sustained mapping of Roman history onto the American past in two novels that are partly set in Roman Britain: Paul Anderson's *Swords in the North* (1935) and Caroline Dale Snedeker's *The White Isle* (1940). In these books, Britain becomes a version of the New World and the American frontier in narratives that reflect American concerns with exploration, expansion, and the life of the pioneer; through this layering

[51] Cf. the popular 1918 song, "How Ya Gonna Keep 'Em Down on the Farm, After They've Seen Paree?" (words by Joe Young and Sam M. Lewis, music by Walter Donaldson). Motives for under-age enlistment in Britain during World War I included "boredom with work," "a longing for adventure" (Van Emden 2005: 3), and "an opportunity to travel" (Reynolds 2009: 256).
[52] There were evidently more farmers among American soldiers in World War I than members of any other occupational group (Farwell 1999: 62), although these were mostly conscripts, unlike Wells's enthusiastic enlistees (Keene 2003: 18–19).

of classical and national history, the Roman setting becomes both more familiar and better suited to the promotion of American values. As Roman Britain echoes, not just twentieth-century America, but also twentieth-century America's construction of the American past, Roman history is made to teach the same lessons that American history does—and America, as at many other junctures and in many other ways, rewrites the history of Britain as its own.

Swords in the North is one of five historical novels for children (or what we would now call young adults) set in Rome, Roman Gaul, and Britain during the first century BCE, and linked by shared characters (both historical and fictional), which Anderson (1880–1956) published between 1929 and 1939. These fall into a familiar "boys' story" mode, with central characters who are fighters (if thoughtful ones), who form strong bonds of friendship with other young men, and who are unfailingly loyal to the leaders they choose.[53] His stories reflect a familiar tension between admiration of Rome and sympathy for those freedom-loving peoples subjugated or enslaved by Rome. In *With the Eagles* (1929), a young Gaul enlists in Caesar's legions, while in *For Freedom and for Gaul* (1931), a friend of his joins Vercingetorix; the author declares his own even-handedness by dedicating each book in admiring terms to the general it features.

When Anderson shifts his focus from Roman Gaul to Roman Britain, we find a more overtly American turn in his narrative. This most distant of Roman provinces, instead of evoking the far-flung possessions of imperial Britain, recalls American myths of encounters with the New World,[54] and Roman expansionism is recast as a version of manifest destiny and the settlement of the frontier. The American subtext first emerges in Anderson's dedication to one of his own fictional characters, Tiberius Cornelius Rufus, the hero of his first book (*A Slave of Catiline*, 1930) and an influential presence in two others. Anderson represents

---

[53] There is copious evidence that these "boys' stories" were regularly read by girls; see for example on the popularity of "boys'" historical fiction and of Henty in particular among girl readers around the turn of the 20th century, Mitchell 1995: 111–15; cf. Reynolds 1990: 93, Flint 1993: 154–6. We also find the same story-type in writers like Rosemary Sutcliff who are not aiming specifically at a male readership.

[54] These are themselves based in part on the accounts of English explorers; indeed, the authors of early English accounts of America "likened themselves and the English enterprise in America to the Romans' invasion of England" (Kupperman 2000: 30).

Tiberius as both a personification of Roman virtue and a figure for the ideal American:

Although a character of fiction, the son of Flava Rufus typifies so well the qualities of courage, high patriotism, inflexibility of purpose, and a noble and lofty ambition—the qualities which not only made Rome great but which have animated the entire Western world in its rise from barbarism—that it seems proper to inscribe this book to one who might well have been the ancestor of any true American: Tiberius Cornelius Rufus.   (Anderson 1935: v)

In spite of his complicated past, which incorporates many motifs familiar in historical fictions of the ancient world (he was shipwrecked, raised by poor fisher-folk, abducted by pirates, enslaved, and trained as a gladiator), Tiberius appears in this novel as a well-educated and well-to-do patrician with a philosophical bent, clearly reminiscent of the American Founding Fathers and, given that he is tall, red-headed, and a widower, perhaps especially to be identified with Thomas Jefferson.

Like Jefferson and other Founding Fathers, Tiberius is a slave-holder, and Anderson here confronts a fact of Roman life that is also a troublesome legacy of the American past and so requires careful handling for an American audience. Anderson's approach to Roman slavery echoes the ameliorating treatment of American plantation life found in children's books of the 1920s and 1930s, although he admits more unease about the institution than some of his contemporaries.[55] Tiberius is a benign and paternalistic master and beloved by his slaves, who are admirably loyal if less intelligent than their masters. The slaves may be beaten, but not severely; they take pride in their work; and praise from Tiberius or his mother affects them deeply (25–6).

It is Tiberius who turns the book's narrator and hero, Gaius Aemilius Durus, from a dissolute young man about town to a hardy soldier in Julius Caesar's legions and a person with the intelligence to understand—at least in retrospect—the "real" reason for Caesar's conquests:

But Caesar's great plan, to which all these were merely subsidiary, of aiding the regeneration of the Republic by allowing it to expand northward into the

---

[55] On the depiction of slavery in American children's books of the 1920s and 1930s, see Connolly 2013: 134–40; Schmidt 2013: 66–71. In some cases, the condition of slavery is elided as slave characters are labeled "servants," whose position can then be portrayed as freely chosen out of a sense of "belonging." Some positive portrayals of plantation life from this period are not only ameliorating but actually nostalgic.

wide-flung agricultural lands of the Aquitani, the Celtae, and the Belgae, that our burgesses might there find homes of a nature to encourage and develop the sturdy Roman virtues of their ancestors—that vast conception was beyond me, as it was beyond any save the giant brain that conceived it, that brain which dared to alter and bend to its will the course of history, the destiny of nations. (85)

The Romans will settle and farm the "wide-flung agricultural lands" of Gaul as Americans settled the prairies; their intended regeneration of the Republic, in an alteration of Rome's destiny, similarly recalls the association of American expansion with the spread of republican institutions in what was once called "manifest destiny."[56]

We may find an echo of the controversy over slavery in the new territories of North America in Anderson's concluding "Author's Note," which again emphasizes the agricultural basis of Roman expansion and declares that Caesar hoped to create "a class of free, land-loving, patriotic burgesses" in the "North" of the book's title to compensate for the social impact of the "vast private estates operated with slave labor" (269). But Gaius himself, like Tiberius Rufus, is a slave owner, and Anderson's attempts to palliate this fact by showing him as a principled and affectionate master only go so far. When Gaius faces financial ruin in the wake of his father's death, his loyal slaves—whose loyalty is attributed both to good treatment and to the fact that they are for the most part "bred" not bought—offer their savings to him, but he informs them that his losses are too great, that he must sell all his estates, and, as an afterthought, that they must themselves be sold, including his "own personal vestiplica, Doris" and his "half-cousin" Pericles. But it is only when Gaius learns that he himself risks being sold into slavery to satisfy his creditors that he reacts with real horror: "I would fall on my sword first!" (49–52). Instead he leaves for the north to join Caesar's army as a legionary.

Some chapters later, Gaius' reaction to the mass enslavement of the rebellious Veneti displays the same mixture of feeling for and dismissal of the suffering of slaves. He has "always found something pitiful in this sale of captives," but is sure that it is "a necessary evil; the world's work could not be done without slaves, and this is the principal way to get them" (93). Furthermore, because he himself suggested the tactic that led to the defeat of the Veneti at sea, he receives as a reward a portion of the

---

[56] On the origins and usage of this term and on American expansionism, see Stephanson 1995, Johannsen 1997.

proceeds of this sale. When, at the end of his adventures, Gaius returns and buys back his father's house, the farm slaves are "too widely scattered to be found," but this is evidently unimportant because "there was not the personal feeling towards them that there was towards the *familia* of the City." As for the *familia*, on a "whim," as he tells us, Gaius first tricks them into thinking they have been bought by someone else, and then reveals himself, to their "pathetic" delight. Gaius manages to achieve this repurchase with his "share from the sale of slaves or plunder," carefully invested by Tiberius in his absence (266).

When Gaius follows Caesar to Britain, the idea of settlement as a renewal of the Republic gives way to another American narrative, the newcomer's encounter with the natives who populate the new world. At the outset of Caesar's first invasion, Gaius is captured by the British in a way that recalls the many captivity narratives of Europeans carried off by Native Americans.[57] The first chapter of this section is entitled "My Captivity among the Britanni," and as we read on, we find an obvious reminiscence of one of the earliest and most widely known of these narratives, the story of Captain John Smith. Gaius is about to be sacrificed by the Druids:

> When we were five or six paces from the Stone [of Sacrifice], my eye was caught by a flurry in the crowd to my right, and as I turned my head I saw a girl struggling with two of the Druids, trying to get way from them, and calling out in her own language ... she broke away, leaving part of her attire in the Druids' clasp, and raced out to stand in front of me, laying her hand on my arm.   (147)

Brighde, the daughter of a chieftain of the Dumnonii, thus rescues Gaius by claiming him in marriage; the episode recalls, not only in its general outline, but in certain details of wording, the story of Pocahontas in Smith's most fully embroidered version (the italics are ours):

> Having feasted him after their best barbarous manner they could, a long consultation was held, but the conclusion was, two great *stones* were brought before

---

[57] The identification of ancient Britons with Native Americans has a long history in British and European thought; on a different aspect of this comparison, see Kupperman 2000: 28–30, 59, 60–1, 94, 107, 113, 224–5; Hoselitz 2007: 31–3. In his preface to *The Eagles Have Flown*, Treece evokes by association the Indian of popular culture when he tells his reader (in italics): "*Please don't read this as a 'history' book! It is an adventure story, about people rather like ourselves—all except those who were more like Apache Indians and gangsters!*" (Treece 1965: 9).

Powhatan: then as many as could laid hands on him, dragged him to them, and thereon laid his head, and being ready with their clubs to beat out his brains, Pocahontas, the king's dearest daughter, when no entreaty could prevail, got his head in her arms, and *laid her own upon his* to save his from death.

(Smith 1907: 101)

Brighde's intervention is as successful as Pocahontas'; Gaius survives, and the two marry. When she takes him home to her own people, his father-in-law, convinced (like Henty's Beric) of the superiority of Roman military discipline, makes Gaius his war-chief, and Gaius trains the Dumnonii in tactics and leads them into war against the Silures. At this point Anderson evokes another trope of the American frontier: the contrast between the friendly natives and their hostile counterparts, or (as in James Fenimore Cooper) between the noble and the ignoble savage. The description of the Silures in battle is reminiscent of nine-teenth- and early-twentieth-century descriptions of American Indians in its depiction of primitive ferocity, "uncouth cries," and the practice of killing enemies by torture, and in its use of the adjective "fiendish":[58]

The people [the Silurians] are fierce and most dangerous fighters; rude, filthy, unkempt of hair and of dress, clad mostly in skins of wild beasts, and armed with long, crooked knives, and their delight is to get in close and fight hand to hand. And I must admit that the sight of a wild-eyed band of them rushing into battle, brandishing their knives, yelling their uncouth cries, and eager for slaughter, is no encouraging spectacle even to one who had been through as many encounters as I had. To make matters worse, anyone who is wounded and left on the scene of battle is foredoomed to a slow and agonizing end, for the Silures take their women to war with them, and after a fight these harridans go over the field, rescue such of their own men as are not to grievously hurt, dispatch those who are beyond hope, and in fiendish joy whittle a wounded enemy to bits, as slowly and painfully as they can. (214)

Gaius' marriage and his role as war-chief do not however, however, lead to any real attachment to Britain. Even Brighde, though she ultimately wins his admiration and affection, initially strikes him as little more than a temporary pastime, inferior as she seems to "the better class of Roman

[58] In his 1922 biography of Daniel Boone, Stewart Edward White cites competing views of "the Indian" as "a fiend incarnate" and as "the 'noble redman'"; he himself ascribes to "the Indians" both noble characteristics and "a deep ingrained racial cruelty," including the routine practice of torture (82, 93). On the representation of Native Americans in American children's books of the 1920s and 1930s, see Schmidt 2013: 61–6; on persistent motifs in "the idea of the Indian," Berkhofer 1978.

maids" (165). He agrees to lead the Dumnonii chiefly as a way of honing his leadership skills and gaining "insight into the Britannic mind" (200) and is careful to swear no allegiance to them, though he is briefly tempted by a vision of himself as ruler of Britain. After the defeat of the Silurians, he makes his way back to Caesar (accompanied—against his orders—by Brighde, in disguise as a boy) and ultimately to Rome, where he regains his family property. He continues to serve in the army, survives the civil wars, and ends the book "in the Golden Age of Augustus" (267–8), surrounded by his family. Brighde too survives and thrives in Rome, rather than dying an untimely death like Pocahontas in London, but she does so by a transformation into "a true Roman matron" whose grandchildren find it hard to believe she was ever anything else (268). In spite of the echo of manifest destiny in Caesar's plans, Anderson represents the new world or frontier of Britain as a place where his hero can prove himself and enrich himself, like an explorer, rather than as a place to settle in or to transform, or one that might make a lasting mark on him. As Gaius enters adult life, Britain falls away as a site of significant history.

We find a very different vision in Caroline Dale Snedeker's *The White Isle*: there Britain offers a permanent alternative to the traditional centers of the classical world. Snedeker's several historical novels set in antiquity (which we discuss both in this chapter and in Chapter 5) offer appreciative portrayals of both Greece and Rome, with Greece as a poetry-loving culture that is largely superior to Rome and the Roman Republic as the locus of true Roman virtue and of the democratic impulse, manifest above all in the martyred Gracchi. But neither country allows the freedom that, in her construction of Roman Britain, Snedeker locates in the geographical periphery of colony and province, which she aligns with new institutions such as the Early Christian Church and new possibilities in the inner life of family and individual.

In *The White Isle*, Lavinia, a Roman girl jilted by an aristocratic cad because of her looks, travels to Britain, where her father (a lover of the old republican ways) has been posted as a provincial magistrate as a result of his opposition to Hadrian's plans. After various vicissitudes, including abduction by hostile tribesmen and the loss of her brother with the Ninth Legion, Lavinia marries a young man who is half Roman, half British, and a Christian, and becomes a Christian herself. The novel, published in 1940, is in part a paean to Great Britain in its hour of peril;

the narrator evokes the white cliffs of Dover, Jane Austen's Bath, and the stories of King Arthur. And Snedeker's Romans, like Sutcliff's and Kipling's, eventually come to see themselves as belonging to Britain. But the narrative also clearly identifies Roman Britain with the American frontier, more settled than Anderson's site of exploration and battle, but still rugged. It also evokes another of America's founding myths: the New World as the site of political and religious freedom, a refuge for those like Lavinia's republican father and her Christian husband, and a world with fewer constraints for women as well.

Where Anderson's novel recalls captivity narratives and Cooper's Deerslayer series, Snedeker's recalls the frontier fiction for children that was especially popular in the period in which she was writing: her own earlier novel *The Beckoning Road* (1929) and the works of her contemporaries Laura Ingalls Wilder (1867–1957), author of a well-known series of novels based on her own family's life as settlers and homesteaders in the American Middle West and West, published from 1932 to 1943, and Carol Ryrie Brink (1895–1981), a prolific writer whose *Caddie Woodlawn* (1935) and its sequel were based on her grandmother's childhood experiences on the frontier. Written in the context of the Great Depression, such stories offered inspiring accounts of self-sufficiency and resilience as enduring American traits.[59]

Snedeker first invokes the idea of Britain as frontier when the family prepare to depart. Initially believing that Lavinia will marry and stay in Rome, her parents give her gifts:

Mother's necklace of enamel she gave to Lavinia, for what use would that be in the frontier country of Britain? Father gave her the marble carved table with the lion heads on the legs, one of the few things saved when their fortune was lost so long ago. (Snedeker 1956: 15)

In a fundamental trope of emigration narratives and frontier narratives of this period, it is the older members of the family (and particularly the women) who are most dubious about the enterprise; Laura Ingalls Wilder's Ma yearns to stay in settled places, and Caddie Woodlawn's mother imagines the lost splendors of England. Here Lavinia is eager for change, but her mother "[does] not share Lavinia's hopefulness about

---

[59] Schmidt 2013: 3–24; Abate 2008: 143–4; Murray 1998: 147–52; Marcus 2008: 116.

the new land" (33). The distance that promises safety to Lavinia simply makes her mother sad:

All would be safe there. Never in Britannia would she be asked to marry a man like Decimus. Never would there be the cruel Emperor nor the secret dangers of which even Father was afraid. In Britannia she could stay a girl for years and years. "Where is Britannia?" she asked. "Dear, it is far away—on the very edge of the world," said Aurelia sadly.   (24)

The allusion to the family's lost fortune is straight out of *Little Women*[60] but also recalls Brink's *Caddie Woodlawn*; in this narrative topos the fallen fortunes of the family make them a representative of thrifty American virtue in contrast to the Europe-derived decadence of their past.

"It's a wicked shame!" continued Mrs. Woodlawn tartly. "All that land in England, that great stone house, even the peacocks—they ought to belong in part to your father, perhaps entirely. Who knows? Think, children, all of you might have been lords and ladies!" "No, no, Harriet," said Mr. Woodlawn, growing grave again. "It was a hard struggle, but what I have in life I have earned with my own hands. I have done well, and I have an honest man's honest pride."
(Brink 1997: 86)

On Snedeker's redrawn spiritual map, Rome now stands for Britain and Britain for America.[61]

Loss of fortune does not, however, involve the loss of the family slaves, who are expected to travel to Britain too, and here Snedeker shows her twentieth-century American sensibility by giving Lavinia a degree of awakened consciousness while also flagging it as anachronistic. Lavinia finds an elderly slave woman weeping at the prospect of separation from her son and given her own "new and tender mood" she feels that "even a slave must not be weeping," especially one she loves as she loves Ino, and questions her. But Ino's answer sets her off on a different train of thought about her own life, and Ino sees that "her little mistress had forgotten her" (26–7). Her sobs not only catch Lavinia's attention afresh, but lead to an unaccustomed self-examination:

She stopped. She was ashamed of what she was about to say, that she did not know Ino could love her son. Pity, that feeling so unaccustomed to the Romans, took hold of Lavinia. She was almost angry for she saw no way out.   (27)

---

[60]   Alcott 1947: 43.

[61]   Britain's redescription as early America effects a kind of renewal, which might be compared to the premise of *St. David's Walks Again*, a 1928 novel in which an American boy with an enterprising spirit and "the pluck of American pioneers" brings new life and prosperity to a sleepy, demoralized Cornish village (MacLeod 1995: 159–61).

When Ino suggests that she might be freed, Lavinia is initially horrified at such ingratitude. But "again that queer understanding [comes] over Lavinia" (28) and she takes the request to her father, who consents, and the manumission takes place—a ceremony that moves Lavinia and her mother to tears but that also assigns freed slaves a continuing role of comic relief: Ino's son is there, "for of course he had heard. Slaves and freedmen hear everything" (30–1). And Ino herself is a figure of fun in the high felt "liberty cap."

When the journey begins, the landscape and conditions of travel through Gaul and in Britain regularly suggest the American frontier. The cavalcade depicted on the endpapers of the volume features riders accompanying a Roman version of a covered wagon; and as if to signal her own anachronistic perspective once again, Snedeker comments on the anomaly of Father's travelling on horseback:

For though Romans did not usually travel on horseback, Favonius, accustomed to long campaigns in foreign lands, preferred it. (39)

Even more surprising, Lavinia soon acquires a pony and joins her father and brother on horseback; her father is dismayed, and declares, "We're getting to be barbarians because we are away from Rome" (53). Lavinia's displacement from Rome liberates her from the actual constraints of her ancient setting, and she enjoys a freedom that is the cherished possession of the American frontier children whom she increasingly resembles.

The family travel through Provence, "the flattest country Lavinia had ever seen," where "the wiry silvery grass stretched away and away to where the sky came down" (104–5), and here we might be in the prairies of the American West as described by Snedeker's contemporary Laura Ingalls Wilder: "On every side now the prairie stretched away empty to a far, clear skyline" (Wilder 1953: 62). They see herds of wild cattle and wild horses; they encounter a bear, and one evening, in another passage that seems to acknowledge the limits for Snedeker of historicity:

They came to the flickering light of the soldiers' camp fire. The great kettle hanging over it, in soldier fashion—gypsy fashion—eternal human fashion.
(Snedeker 1956: 75)

After arriving in Britain, the family travel through miles and miles of unbroken forest and see more wild animals (including an elk); the occasional houses they pass are explicitly compared to the dwellings of the American frontier, "rude wooden houses with peaked roof, log cabins, typical then of the frontier as they are today" (143). Throughout this journey, Lavinia relishes her newfound freedom and sense of self, but her mother's reaction is that of the pioneer wife: "To her it was a homeless forest where she must try to create a home for her family" (133).

The home the family establish represents for Snedeker not only a pioneer outpost but a pre-industrial ideal:

> Now, day by day, was the new home established in Britain—a home with those multitudinous interests and industries of which machines have robbed it. And so robbing they have destroyed a precious thing in the world. This home was self-sufficient—or almost so. It afforded occupation and creative work for everybody in it... (167)

And in this home the family begin to enjoy the pleasures of frontier life:

> October brought nutting parties for the young people, who went far into the woods, duly protected by their elders. Such gathering of food would have been called slave work in Rome. But here on this frontier of the Empire, life was more natural. (170)

Not that slaves can be dispensed with. Soon after their arrival, Lavinia and her brother Marcus head to the market to find a cleaning woman, since the slave who had done that work was left behind in Rome. And here Snedeker's implicit critique of ingrained Roman attitudes gives way to the unselfconscious introduction of the stereotypical Irish servant: "Slaves from Ivernia / Best in the land" (153). As Marcus and Lavinian contemplate a filthy young woman with blue eyes, the slave merchant declares, "That kind work like devil spirits. They come from an island west of Britannia. There's nothing like 'em" (154). Buvinda joins the household and proves both a devoted servant and a source of comedy.

Under the auspices of a new and friendly governor, father and son happily join the Roman legionary forces to combat half-naked, painted "wild men" who "fight like wolves" (134); as in Anderson the description recalls familiar representations of Native Americans in frontier narratives.[62] Lavinia continues to enjoy her freedom and the out-of-doors life

---

[62] Cf. Wilder's *Little House on the Prairie* and Brink's *Caddie Woodlawn*, which depict white settlers' fear of Native Americans and include both stereotypical descriptions and distinctions between "good Indians" and others.

she never had in Rome, and even her mother ceases to miss Rome and declares, "we are Britons now" (187).

Snedeker's vision of life on the frontier is already an idealized one: the life of these pioneers, its hardships little more than inconveniences, is natural, self-sufficient, and free of the constraints of the old world. But the last part of the book goes beyond such idealization to offer a genuinely utopian vision, as Lavinia and her mother are introduced to an idyllic Christian community in Avalonia (the Arthurian Avalon) and Lavinia falls in love with and marries one of its members. Here too, however, in its depiction of a loving and non-hierarchical communal existence, *The White Isle* draws on a vision of the American frontier, this time as the locus of pioneering utopian settlements like that of New Harmony, Indiana, founded by Snedeker's great-grandfather Robert Owen, and described in detail by Snedeker both in two earlier novels (*Seth Way*, 1917, and *The Beckoning Road*, 1929) and in a non-fiction work (*The Town of the Fearless*, 1931). The utopianism of the setting further enables the element of romantic fantasy in *The White Isle*, as Lavinia, rescued from an unwanted old-world arranged marriage with a hateful suitor, falls in love almost at first sight with a young man whose open courtship and public displays of affection set the capstone on the freedoms of the new land.

As they reconceive the outpost of Empire that is Roman Britain as a version of America and the American frontier, Anderson and Snedeker offer us different versions of this new world, each appropriate to the time period of the story. Anderson's novel, set at the time of Julius Caesar's initial invasion of Britain, recalls the earlier days of European exploration and settlement in North America, although with a glance forward at the expansionism of manifest destiny; Snedeker's, set in the Romanized Britain of Hadrian's day, tends rather to invoke the movement of pioneers into the Midwest and West and the lives of these settlers.

A more significant difference may be found in the contrast noted earlier between the cyclical narrative of *Swords in the North* and the linear narrative of *The White Isle*. Gaius travels to Britain, fights, falls in love—and returns to Rome with his British wife, now a "true Roman matron." Lavinia and her family come to see themselves as Britons, for whom return to Rome is neither possible nor desirable; indeed, the characteristically Roman experiences of exile by the emperor and appointment to provincial administration, both of which could be expected to end in a return to Rome (as in Anderson's plot), are here reconceived as a story of permanent emigration. The difference may partly be a function of the contrasting eras in American history the authors choose to evoke: Gaius is an invader and explorer, Lavinia a pioneer and settler. It also has something to do with the transformative role of Christianity—something from which there is no way back—in Snedeker's novel. But the difference is, most crucially, a matter of gender—both of the characters and of the intended audience.

Anderson's hero can go out into the world, reach manhood, show what he is capable of, and return to his place of origin, the Rome of which is he now a worthy citizen. For Snedeker, however, Rome (admirable as in some respects it is) allows women little freedom, little agency, and no choice in love. In order to offer her twentieth-century girl readers a central character in whom they can see themselves, she must remove her heroine from Rome and imagine for her a home at the margins, conceived of as a space of free development and romantic love.[63] Thus, although Anderson's story can be seen as a typical boy's story in its deployment of the quest narrative, what we find here is at odds with a claim that is sometime made about boy's stories as typically the site of linear progression and girl's stories as involving circularity and a return home.[64]

Anderson seems to signal the problem posed by gender in his own resolution. As the story ends, Gaius's grandchildren have been listening to the story of his adventures:

"It is difficult," says one, when the tale ends, "to imagine Grandmother riding in armor with the Tenth Legion, or fighting with outlaws in the Great Forest of Anderida." My wife smiles at me, and I press her hand. "None the less, she did," I reply. "For all that your grandmother was born and grew to womanhood in the Island of the North, she has all the courage, all the virtues, of a true Roman matron. See to it that you are worthy of her."   (268)

The question asked by this grandchild reveals that their grandmother's adventures seem quite incompatible with her current manifestation as a

---

[63] On the creation of "agentic" heroines and the anachronism this often entails, see Wilson 2011: ch. 3 and the discussion of Snedeker and others in Chapter 5.

[64] See Nikolajeva 1996: 124–6, though she also sees the circular journey as in general fundamental to children's literature, 79–80. On the "quest romance" in boys' adventure stories, see Ferrall and Jackson 2010: ch. 2.

Roman matron. Brighde, tellingly, leaves it to her husband to reply; and his answer suggests that whatever her earlier life, it is as a Roman matron that she is to be honored and imitated by her descendants—and presumably admired by Anderson's readers.[65] Snedeker's story, in contrast, turns its back on the Roman matron, has that matron turn her back on Rome, and offers its readers as model a girl of the Roman frontier, who recalls the modern pioneer heroines whom they were also encountering in the works of Laura Ingalls Wilder and Carol Ryrie Brink.

In Chapter 5, we investigate further the ancient girl heroines of historical fiction as they fulfill their intersecting (and sometimes conflicting) roles as representatives of a very different era and as potential other selves for modern girl readers.

---

[65] Anderson here reverses the conclusion of *Beric the Briton*, in which Beric returns to Britain with his Roman wife, and reminds her that she is now in Britain, where women are equal, and that he expects her to "quite change under the influence of British air" (Henty 1892: 381).

5

Ancient History for Girls

In a memoir of the years leading up to her marriage at the age of 17 in 1914, the British writer and activist Naomi Mitchison recalls her girl-hood reading of Plato's *Republic*.

[Back volumes of *Punch*] were in the revolving bookcase in the dining room and I used to take them out and read them sitting on the end of the sofa, or even behind it... One of the other large sets of books in this bookcase was the complete Jowett translation of Plato; in the process of twirling the bookcase, the contents of which sometimes cascaded onto the floor, I picked up and began to read *The Republic* and was much taken up with the idea of being a Guardian. This, I know, started off one of my interminable inside stories, interspersed with noble sayings in the manner of Jowett. (Mitchison 1975: 40)[1]

This recollection reminds us, once again, that young readers often come upon books that are not particularly intended for them, and also that they can easily imagine themselves as characters who are not their own close counterparts. Mitchison goes on to flag the disparity between herself and Plato's Guardians specifically in terms of gender; in doing so, she calls attention to the problem that classical antiquity does not offer good models for an intellectually ambitious, egalitarian-minded modern girl to identify with. "It is odd that I was not put off by the undoubted fact that all Plato's Guardians were male and that he said many unpleasant things about the inferiority of women. But in my inside stories I don't suppose I was ever a Greek woman" (40).[2]

With her freely ranging imagination (not to mention the confidence that comes with social privilege), Mitchison was able to evade the reality

---

[1] On Mitchison's life, see, in addition to her own memoirs (1973, 1975, 1979), Benton 1990 and Calder 1997.

[2] On such cross-gender reader identification in Mitchison and others, see Hoberman 1997: 2; Mitchell 1995: 111–13, 126, 167–8; Flint 1993: 202–3.

of ancient gender arrangements and make use of classical settings for the formative "inside stories" that led eventually to her adult life as a writer and social activist.[3] A fictional account of another English girl reading a classical text at the same period paints a bleaker picture of entrapment within oppressive norms rather than of escape. In Virginia Woolf's multigenerational novel *The Years* (1937), in a section of the narrative set in 1907, Sara Pargiter encounters the most famous girl heroine of classical Greek literature. As she lies on her bed, listening out the window to the sounds of a party, she picks up a translation of *Antigone* made by her cousin Edward, an Oxford don, and inscribed to her on the flyleaf.

She skipped through the pages; then from the litter of broken words, scenes rose, quickly, inaccurately, as she skipped. The unburied body of a man lay like a fallen tree-trunk, like a statue, with one foot stark in the air. Vultures gathered . . . Then in a yellow cloud came whirling—who? She turned the page quickly. Antigone? She came whirling out of the dust-cloud to where the vultures were wheeling and flung white sand over the blackened foot.

Sara reads on, half-distracted by the party in the garden below, to the point at which Antigone is apprehended and confronts Creon.

The man's name was Creon. He buried her. It was a moonlight night. The blades of the cactuses were sharp silver. The man with the loincloth gave three sharp taps with his mallet on the brick. She was buried alive. The tomb was a brick mound. There was just room for her to lie straight out. Straight out in a brick tomb, she said. And that's the end, she yawned, shutting the book.

As Sara falls asleep, she buries herself in her bed.

She laid herself out, under the cool, smooth sheets and pulled the pillow over her ears. The one sheet and the one blanket fitted softly round her. At the bottom of the bed was a long stretch of cool fresh mattress   (Woolf 1992: 130–1)[4]

---

[3] On Mitchison's ambivalence about her own privilege, see Chapter 6. The potentially constraining effect of not only class but also race on a child's imaginative identification is underscored by the contrast with Mitchison's younger contemporary, the African American poet Gwendolyn Brooks (1917–2000). The classics were also part of Brooks's childhood furniture: she was "spellbound" by the Harvard Classics (including "Nine Greek Dramas"), the "white treasures" in her father's "dark mahogany" bookcase (Brooks 1996: 12). But in her autobiographical anti-epic "The Anniad," her childhood self dreams of being a fairy-tale princess only until she looks in the mirror and sees "unembroidered brown" and "black and boisterous hair" (Brooks 1949: 20). On Brooks's relationship to classical culture, especially in "The Anniad," see Whelan-Stewart 2014.

[4] This account echoes Woolf's own experience. In 1906, she was courted by the Cambridge classicist Walter Headlam, who proposed to dedicate his translation of the

Here the connection between the girl reader and what she finds in a Greek text is made implicitly and in the voice of the narrator, who assimilates Sara's bedtime routine to Antigone's live burial. Instead of Mitchison's cheerful bypassing of both ancient and modern gender constraints, we get Woolf's rueful evocation of a doomed tragic heroine to characterize the stifled lives of women in Victorian and Edwardian England.[5]

The fact that, in both of these passages, a girl reads a Greek text in English translation reflects a modern form of gender disparity that was of particular significance for both Mitchison and Woolf. While both were raised in prosperous, prominent literary and academic families and were themselves extremely well read, they were unhappily excluded from the educational opportunities that were the automatic prerogative of their brothers, in which learning Greek played a prominent role; they were still subject to the division assumed by Kingsley a half century earlier in his preface to *The Heroes* between his male and female readers.[6] Woolf first learned of the classical world when her older brother Thoby came home from school and introduced her to its mysteries:

Agamemnon to her (Woolf 1975: 259). Her persistent concern with the Greek language is addressed most fully in her essay "On Not Knowing Greek" (discussed in Chapter 6), which also records her fascination with a Sophoclean heroine, in that case Electra, and her sense of birds as particularly expressive of a Greek spirit.

[5] On Sara's reading of *Antigone*, see Dalgarno 2001: 98; McCoskey and Corbett 2012: 470; on the novel's several references to *Antigone* in relation to spiritual live burial, Joseph 1981: 28. In *Three Guineas*, published the following year, Woolf invokes Antigone as a more active prototype for modern women standing up to oppressive tyrants (Woolf 2006b: 98–9, 201–2).

[6] As determined feminists and members of progressive circles, both were in a position to remedy this. Woolf studied Greek at King's College London and with private tutors, notably Janet Case, and produced her own translation of *Agamemnon*. On Woolf's Greek studies, see Lee 1997: 141–2; Fowler 1999; Dalgarno 2001: 1–48; Koulouris 2011: 43–8; her brother Thoby also helped her with Sophocles (Woolf 1975: 42). Mitchison never studied Greek, but the possibility was envisioned by Andrew Lang in his response to a poem in English hexameters she had sent him: "*all* English (and German) hexameters are naturally bad; as you will understand when you can read Homer in Greek—and the sooner the better" (Mitchison 1975: 54). Her egalitarian-minded husband also encouraged her: "he was terribly keen that I should wander about the same world as his...and gave me a 'Greek Without Tears' textbook, but I didn't get far with that" (Mitchison 1990: 11). On English women of letters and their experiences with Greek in the 19th and early 20th centuries, see Fowler 1983; on English and American women of the Victorian period who performed their knowledge of Greek through translations and theatrical productions, see Prins 2017.

... he it was who first told me—handing it on as something worth knowing—about the Greeks... we went walking up and down stairs together, and he told me the story of the Greeks: about Hector and Troy... fitfully, excitedly. To do that, he had to break through the schoolboy convention about "work". (Woolf 1976: 108)

In Mitchison's case, her unequal access to schooling was linked explicitly to biology. As a child, she was sent with her brother to the Dragon School, a boy's preparatory school in Oxford, where she was the only female student. "I had enjoyed myself very much at the Dragon School. I was for all practical purposes a boy until the horrible thing happened. I was twelve... and then there was blood on my blue serge knickers. I was quickly pulled out of school and I never went back" (Mitchison 1975: 11).

Both of these girl readers are also incipient writers. In the final version of *The Years*, Sara's literary vocation is thwarted and she writes only letters to her cousin North, which themselves trail off, but in earlier drafts she is an author.[7] Mitchison was destined to become a prolific writer in numerous genres, including historical fiction for both child and adult readers.[8] Both make use of Greek texts as springboards for their own inventions. Sara conjures up scenes that occur offstage in Sophocles' play and fills in details that he does not provide. Mitchison's mind wanders off from the *Republic* into "inside stories." Yet their fantasies are also conditioned by their ancient sources. Sara's scenes from *Antigone* are reconstructions of what is implied by Sophocles' text, as Woolf makes clear through metaphors of archaeological recovery. Her image of Polyneices' body is like an ancient statue that might be unearthed in modern times; Sophocles' words are like the fragmentary rubble from which a modern archaeologist reconstructs an ancient site. Mitchison inserts herself into a role provided for her by Plato, basing her imaginings on his own counterfactual construct, in which the constraints of ordinary society are not accentuated, but rather relaxed. (In the *Republic*, women are even allowed to be Guardians, contrary to Mitchison's "undoubted fact.")

As they connect to the ancient world by freely elaborating on classical texts, these girl readers anticipate strategies adopted by the

[7] Lee in Woolf 1992: xxiii.

[8] For a list of Mitchison's publications, see Benton 1990: 177–86. Mitchison is especially honored as the first female author of science fiction. On her place among women writers of historical fiction in the early 20th century, see Cam 1961: 11–12; Trodd 1998: 114–16. On her novels of the ancient world, see Hoberman 1997; Wallace 2005: 43–52.

twentieth-century authors of history and historical fiction for girls discussed in this chapter. Those authors faced a significant challenge as they tried to stay true to the conditions of ancient history while also providing their readers with more straightforward and positive scenarios in which to find themselves—opportunities for identification that do not lead either to rebellion and premature death or to a change of gender. The ancient record offers few women who could play the role of inspiring, consequential leader that a figure like Caesar does in books for boys and little basis for female protagonists who might resemble the high-spirited, energetic girls found in novels with modern settings.[9]

Lively, active girls were a prominent feature of children's literature from the mid-nineteenth century on;[10] notable examples include Alice in Lewis Carroll's *Alice's Adventures in Wonderland* (1865) and *Through the Looking-Glass* (1871), Jo March in Louisa May Alcott's *Little Women* (1868–9), Katy in Susan Coolidge's *What Katy Did* (1872), Rebecca in Kate Douglas Wiggin's *Rebecca of Sunnybrook Farm* (1903), Roberta in E. Nesbit's *The Railway Children* (1905), Anne Shirley in Lucy Maud Montgomery's *Anne of Green Gables* (1908), Laura in Laura Ingalls Wilder's Little House on the Prairie series (1932–43), Caddie in Carol Ryrie Brink's *Caddie Woodlawn* (1935), and the protagonists in many works of popular fiction, most notably Nancy Drew in the series devoted to her exploits as a detective (introduced in 1930).[11] While the circumstances of these heroines vary widely, it is generally the case, as many critics have pointed out, that their independent adventures are confined to a delimited period of girlhood, which will end with their entry into a tamer, narrower, and largely domestic existence as conventional young women and ultimately wives.[12]

[9] Reflecting on her *Memoirs of Hadrian*, Marguerite Yourcenar observes: "Another thing virtually impossible, to take a feminine character as a central figure, to make Plotina, for example, rather than Hadrian, the axis of my narrative. Women's lives are much too limited, or else too secret" (1990: 327).

[10] Many of these books, and their heroines, were popular with adult readers as well as children (Stoneley 2003).

[11] On the energetic heroines of L. T. Meade (1844–1914), the adventurous heroines of Bessie Marchant (1862–1941), sometimes known as "the girls' Henty," and other examples from popular fiction for girls, see Mitchell 1995, Stoneley 2003, Ferrall and Jackson 2010.

[12] This phenomenon is treated in 19th-century American literature by Macleod (1994: 3–29), who finds these fictional accounts confirmed in contemporary memoirs and detects in some of them unstated regret for the loss of childhood freedom; and in relation to the tomboy as a prominent figure in 19th- and 20th-century American culture, by Abate 2008.

The Goddess of the Hearth

In an early example of this pattern of girlhood freedom curtailed, from a work by the prolific novelist and children's writer Charlotte M. Yonge (1823–1901), a narrowed scope for action coincides with yet another case of a sister's exclusion from the classical learning enjoyed by her brother. Yonge herself had a classical education and was evidently committed to the importance of such an education for girls as well as boys.[13] She was the founder and editor of a magazine (*The Monthly Packet*) aimed primarily at girls, and some of the most memorable characters in her novels are strong-minded, intelligent, and book-loving girls, including the heroine of *Countess Kate* (1862) and Ethel in *The Daisy Chain* (1856). Ethel shows her ambition by getting her brother to teach her the Latin and Greek he learns at school, but she is ultimately persuaded to sacrifice her plan of keeping up with him in order to be "a useful, steady, daughter and sister at home" (Yonge 1896: 163), to teach in a school for the poor, and to learn things more appropriate for a young woman (such as needlework and handwriting) (158–64).

The non-fictional histories of Greece and Rome for "young folk" that Yonge published in 1878 and 1879 replicate this gendered division. She privileges her boy readers, noting in one of her prefaces that one reason for giving children Greek and Roman history is "because little boys ought not to begin their classical studies without some idea of their bearing" (Yonge 1879: v–vi). In her depiction of antiquity, she offers no corrective to the lack of interesting girls and women and tends instead to suggest that women's limited place in the historical record is simply a reflection of appropriate social limits.[14] Yonge recognizes that her classical subject matter requires her to include material that is not strictly factual,[15] but

---

[13] On Yonge's own classical education and her views on the importance of some exposure to the classics for a wide range of children, see esp. Schultze 2007.

[14] For Yonge's complicated relationship to classical antiquity across the body of her work, see Schultze 2007; on her use of the Penelope myth to address the lives of modern women, Schultze 2014.

[15] See Hurst 2006: 42–4; Schultze 2007. *Young Folks' History of Greece* (1879) begins with a declaration (of a sort never made in her historical novels) that "I am going to tell you the history of the most wonderful people who ever lived. But I have to begin with a good deal that is not true...the people who descended from Japhet's son Javan, and lived in the beautiful islands and peninsulas called Greece, were not trained in the knowledge of God like the Israelites, but had to guess for themselves. They made strange stories" (Yonge 1879: 13–14).

this is due to the Greeks' own ignorance, exposed in their myths, of Christianity. She views those myths as essential reading for children because they are the sources of later art and literature, not because of the imaginative possibilities they open up, and she retells them in ways that accentuate the restricted roles of ancient women. Whether mythical or historical, the female figures who appear in these works model for Yonge's girl readers their own limited access to a wider world, constructing the kind of inhibiting relationship between ancient texts and the lives of modern girls that Woolf exposed and Mitchison managed to escape.

In the first or mythical section of her history, Yonge includes major goddesses and heroines, but presents them in ways that valorize virginity, household tasks, and devotion to family. Minerva and Diana are associated with "all that was nobly, purely and wisely lovely," whereas Venus is considered one of the "powers of ill" (Yonge 1879: 24); Juno is queen, but "the quietest and best of all the goddesses was Vesta, the goddess of the household hearth—of home, that is to say" (20). She limits or modifies the agency of mortal heroines. Her retelling of the *Odyssey* is notably detailed, but she has Odysseus simply reveal himself to Penelope with no mention of Penelope's deception over the olive-tree bed (112). She chooses the version of Agamemnon's story in which Aegisthus, not Clytemnestra, actually carries out the murder (115). The oracle Oedipus receives has him killing his father but not marrying his mother, and the woman he marries is "the king's sister," so that Jocasta is completely written out of the story (118–20). And although Yonge identifies Antigone, who acted alone and at night, as "the noblest woman of Greek imagination," she has her burying both her brothers, thus doubling the role of devoted sister and muting the element of conflict in the play (120).[16]

In the historical portion of the text, Yonge mentions a few women who play supporting roles: the wife of Leonidas, the wife of Socrates, the mother and the nurse of Alexander. Aspasia and Sappho are absent. She seems glancingly to acknowledge the scarcity of women in her ancient sources in her description of Euripides' plays as "more like those of later times, with more of story in them, and more characters, especially of women" (195). But her own—very limited—general remarks about Greek women are in keeping with the preference she expressed for

[16] Cf. *A Book of Golden Deeds* (1864), in which Antigone is "blandly represented as a good daughter who cares for her aged father" (Hurst 2006: 44).

Vesta. In her description of the typical Greek house, Yonge tells us that "There was a kind of back court for the women of the family, who did not often appear in the front one, though they were not shut up like Eastern women" (130), and in her account of Alexander's encounter with the Persian queen she has him reassure her that his offer to have her grandchildren learn to spin and weave is no insult, because "the distaff, loom, and needle were held to give honor to Greek ladies" (287). Here she acknowledges to some degree the constraints on actual Greek women (as opposed to figures like Antigone) but stresses that these constraints reflect properly Western values rather than dangerous Eastern ways.

A Strange Life, a Happy Day

A view of the ancient world as exemplifying appropriate limits on women became increasingly less tenable in the twentieth century, which brought a much greater presence for women in history, as authors, readers, and subjects. As Anthea Trodd describes it,

The early twentieth century saw the emergence of women academic historians, most of them working in the areas of social and economic history, and concerned with recovering the unrecorded lives of women and working people. The women's movement created a demand for information about the lives of women in history, and a need to understand how they had lived; history became one of the most popular subjects with women students. By the 1920s historical fiction, unpopular in the Edwardian period, had re-established its popularity and become a genre particularly associated with women readers and writers.[17]

In the 1920s and 1930s, as the prewar conditions evoked by Mitchison and Woolf underwent rapid change, more authors, both of history and of historical fiction, were writing specifically for girl readers and trying to present those readers with interesting ancient versions of themselves.[18]

[17] Trodd 1998: 110; see also Hoberman 1997 on historical novelists of the ancient world. On the upswing in active, capable heroines in children's literature, including historical fiction, in the early 20th century, see Levstik 1983; Mitchell 1995; Abate 2008: 137–44; Ferrall and Jackson 2010. New contexts for girl heroines were provided by school stories (Trodd 1998: 141–3), juvenile detective fiction (Murray 1998: 160–4), and stories about the Girl Guides, in which the heroine's vigor and initiative coincide with devotion to the Empire (Bratton 1989).

[18] On the changing conditions of American children and adolescents during the 1920s and 1930s, a period that saw smaller families, expanded enrollment in schools and colleges, an emerging youth culture, the rise of dating, and increased career opportunities for women, see Hawes 1997.

In the field of history, we find, for example, the works of Dorothy Mills (1879–1966), *The Book of the Ancient Greeks* (1925) and *The Book of the Ancient Romans* (1927), written under very different conditions and with very different assumptions than those of Charlotte Yonge half a century earlier. Mills was herself formally educated, with an LLA (Lady Literate in Arts) degree from St Andrews and an MA in Education from Columbia, and she taught at several girls' schools, including the Brearley School in New York, where she was head of the History Department (and where she tried out both books in manuscript on her students before publication).[19] As a woman writer of historical narratives for girls, and as a teacher at a school founded to offer girls an education comparable to that of their brothers, Mills had to confront the restrictions on the lives of ancient women, the prominence of misogynistic elements in ancient culture, the lack of documentary evidence on women's lives, and the virtual absence of women from the historical events recounted in her texts. In responding to this challenge, she sometimes stepped over the boundary between history and fiction or at least into the contested territory between.

Like Yonge, Mills incorporates material from antiquity that is not strictly factual, but for her the critical issue is not the difference between Greek invention and Christian truth,[20] but the more widely shared goal of capturing the spirit of ancient Greece and Rome. For this purpose, actual events and works of art are equally significant, as she explains in a credo with which she opens both works: "The aim of this book has been to use such parts of the political history of the Greeks/Romans, of their literature and of their art as seem to have been the outward and visible signs of the spirit that inspired them" (Mills 1925: v; 1937: iii). Here the difference between the historical and the mythical becomes less significant, since the events to which history refers are themselves seen, like literature and art, as pointing beyond the "real world" to a spiritual reality:

For the character of a nation is influenced by what that nation believes about its origins and by the traditions on which it brings up its youth. It is from such traditions that we can learn what a people admired and what it despised, what

---

[19] Spaeth 1927: 150. These were part of a series that included *The Book of the Ancient World* (1923), *The Middle Ages* (1935), and *Renaissance and Reformation Times* (1939).
[20] Cf. Yonge 1879: 132–3; Mills 1925: 359.

kind of heroes were held up as examples to be followed, what was considered noble and honorable, and what was held to be petty and mean.   (Mills 1937: 15)

Although they present themselves in many respects as standard works of history, reporting documented facts and complete with footnotes and bibliography, Mills's texts sometimes blur the distinction between history and fiction. While she restricts myths about the gods and heroes to a chapter on religion in *The Book of the Ancient Greeks*, and entitles the first section of *The Book of the Ancient Romans* "The Rome of Myth and Legend," she uses literary sources freely and quite uncritically throughout, citing passages from ancient authors not as evidence but in a kind of continuous narrative with her own text, often including speeches ascribed to historical characters by authors like Herodotus, Thucydides, and Plutarch. This approach gives her the means to redress, to some degree, the problem that, where the lives of women are concerned, the historical facts may undermine her depiction of the Greek spirit as intellectually, physically, and politically liberating. In two particularly striking passages in *The Book of the Ancient Greeks* she herself slips into narrative modes that evoke the language of fiction in order to give an appealing picture of female experience.

Mills includes in her account of Greece a few paragraphs on Cretan women (unsecluded and mingling freely with men) and Spartan women (trained in athletics); unlike Yonge, she mentions Sappho as well as Xanthippe (though not Aspasia). She devotes an entire section of her chapter "A Day with an Athenian" to "the Athenian Lady," and depicts the largely enclosed and house-bound life of the Athenian wife and daughter. Towards the end of this section she points with some bemusement to the apparent contradictions of this life, and quotes another woman scholar, Emily Putnam, to call attention to the Athenian woman's exclusion from the intellectual, spiritual and civic blossoming of her city:

In many ways it was a strange life that the Athenian lady lived, one that seems as if it were in contradiction to all that the Athenians held of the highest importance, for the

Athenian lady lived in the house among a people that lived out of doors. Among a people who gave great importance to physical training she was advised to take her exercise in bedmaking. At a time when the human spirit was at its freest she was enclosed on all sides. Art and thought and letters were reaching the highest development they were ever to know, but for her they hardly existed . . .

(Mills 1925: 219; cf. Putnam 1910: 13)

Mills responds to this contradiction by appealing to the "ideal of womanhood" expressed in Athenian religion, art, and literature (1925: 219). Her view that historical events are no more revelatory of Greek beliefs than works of the imagination allows her to claim that, in this particular context, what the Greeks actually do (their history) is less significant than the stories their literature tells us. This explicitly defensive theoretical turn from history to fiction is anticipated by a curious narrative turn in Mills's description of a woman's day, immediately following her account of the training of Athenian girls:

> But it was not all work for the maiden, and many a time did she sit in the swing in the courtyard and idle away a warm afternoon gently swinging to and fro, and many a merry game of ball did she have with her companions. It was she who made the fresh garlands and wreathes for the altars or the house, and who, when the moon was full, laid offering on the tomb of her grandparents   (217)

As we noted in Chapter 4, narrative modes associated with fiction are not uncommon in histories for children. But the wording here, oddly evocative of sentimental nineteenth-century fiction, is at odds with Mills's usual prose, and there is nothing like it in her description of the lives of Athenian men and boys; it is as if her own language seeks through a kindly fiction to compensate for what she is forced by history to tell her readers.

Mills adopts a similar tone in an earlier section on Crete and Mycenean Greece in which, after commenting on the absence of any written record, she undertakes what she calls a "reconstruction" of a day in ancient Crete on the basis of archaeological evidence:

> It is early dawn about the year 1500 B.C. The great palace of Knossos lies quiet and still, for the inhabitants have not yet begun to stir. When they are aroused, the noise will be like the bustle of a town, for everything used in the palace is made there, from the bronze weapons used by the King when he goes out hunting to the great clay vessels...   (16)

Both the term "reconstruction" and the obvious play of invention as the description proceeds suggest a parallel with the work of Sir Arthur Evans, who not only excavated the great palace at Knossos in Crete but also—to an extent no archaeologist now would approve—reconstructed and restored the site to what he imagined it must have looked like in Minos' day. His restoration and Mills's reconstruction are alike in being fictional edifices on an historical basis (and recall Sara Pargiter's supplements to the *Antigone,* compared by Woolf to an archaeological reconstruction). The discoveries of Evans in Crete and of Schliemann at Troy and Mycenae seem to give a general warrant to Mills's incorporation of fiction and poetry, allowing her to describe the ancient Aegean as "a world where fairy tales have come true" (6).

The opportunity to fill in experiences hinted at by material remains offsets women's relative absence from the historical record. "A Day in Crete," like the account of "the Athenian lady," is chiefly dedicated to an account of a girl's day—but not just the ordinary day of an ordinary girl.

Some of the potters are fashioning beautiful vases, the younger workmen copying the well-known patterns, the more experienced thinking of new forms, but all of them handing over the finished vessel to the artist who paints beautiful designs on them. The weavers have been very busy of late, for today is the birthday of the Princess, and great festivities are to be held in her honour...

The morning is spent in preparation for the festivities of the afternoon. The Princess is arrayed by her maidens in her new and beautiful robes; her hair is elaborately arranged, a long and tiresome process, but the time is enlivened by the merry talk of the maidens who give to their young mistress all the gossip of the palace. (17–18)

The narrative mode here—with its use of the present tense—almost sounds like an ekphrasis, and the passage actually includes an ekphrasis, since Mills embeds in her narrative a passage from the description of Achilles' shield in *Iliad* 18:

When all are ready they go out to that

dancing place, which Daedalus had wrought in broad Knossos for Ariadne of the lovely tresses. There were youths dancing and maidens of costly wooing, their hands on one another's wrists... (18–19)

Mills's "reconstruction" thus doubly illustrates the "world where fairy-tales have come true" offered by archaeology, in at once realizing the world of the Homeric poems and providing for her girl readers the story of a princess.[21]

The problem Mills faces is less stark where *The Book of the Ancient Romans* is concerned, partly because she sees the Romans primarily as conquerors and civilizers, not as liberators of the human spirit,[22] partly

---

[21] On the prominence of female royalty in works of both history and historical fiction by women writers, see Trodd 1998: 112–13; Vallone 2008.

[22] She begins her history by quoting *Aeneid* 6.847–53 (Mills 1937: 3).

because there are more noteworthy women in Roman history, and partly because "The Roman Lady" had considerably more access to the larger world than "her Athenian sister" (Mills 1937: 339). Nonetheless, she articulates the limits on Roman women in terms that take Emily Putnam's contrast between freedom and enclosure one step further.

All men rule over women, we Romans rule over all men, and our wives rule over us—Cato the Censor.

The Romans held women in greater honour than any other nation of the ancient world. The words of Cato that "all men rule over women" were quite true, however, for in the eyes of the Roman law a woman had no freedom. Before her marriage she was entirely in the hand of her father, on her marriage she passed into a similar position towards her husband, and if she remained unmarried she was under the control of her nearest male relative. Nevertheless, though legally she may have seemed to be little better than a slave, her position in the family was a very honoured one.   (338–9)[23]

Although she works hard to retract it, Mills's comparison of a Roman wife to a slave offers a bleak assessment of ancient women's lives from a modern reader's perspective. In keeping with her emphasis on the honor accorded to women, she then devotes fully half of "The Roman Lady" to a detailed narrative of a Roman girl's wedding followed by (and continuous with) one of Catullus' epithalamia (342–6). If this does not constitute quite the turn to fiction we find in "The Athenian Lady," it offers an analogous focus on the compensatory pleasures girls could expect in antiquity and an analogous shift from historical fact to poetry.

Historical Confinement, Fictive Escapes

The genre of historical fiction at once demands and allows a greater freedom in the portrayal of ancient girls than we find in Mills's historical works, while still requiring a significant degree of historical accuracy. The desired blend of fact and fiction is summed up in the admiring terms of the publisher's blurb for *The Perilous Seat* (1923), a novel by Caroline Dale Snedeker, whose *The White Isle* was discussed in Chapter 4:

Recommended for the high school age because it is an accurate picture of the ancient Greeks and Romans; because it makes that life glow with present-day reality; because of its feeling for nature; because it is a good adventure and a

---

[23] See e.g. Hallett 1984: 1–34 on the "paradox of elite Roman women."

clean, fresh love story, told with...delicate distinction of phrase and vigorous sweep of sentence.

The initial stress on accuracy signals the expectation that Snedeker's readers will be learning the facts of history, but the succeeding phrases insist not only on a poetic style but also on anachronistic elements that belong to contemporary fiction: resonance with the reader's own experience and a plot that includes both adventure and romance. The story advertised here features a protagonist who has a modern girl's opportunities for exciting experiences; it may conclude with her settling down and marrying (as do many modern stories), but her marriage will conform to the modern ideal of the love match.

Snedeker contrived to fulfill these competing requirements in three novels about girls growing into womanhood in the ancient world, which have diverse settings but use similar strategies for telling historically plausible stories of girls who lead exciting, meaningful lives. *The Perilous Seat* (1923), set in Delphi at the time of Xerxes' invasion (480 BCE), concerns Eleutheria, a visionary young woman with a gift for poetry. Eager to avoid an arranged marriage and longing to find some arena for expression and action, Theria persuades her father to have her made Pythia—prophetic priestess of Apollo—in the hope that the god will give a favorable response to Athens in its efforts to withstand the Persians; failing to enter the trance state, she herself improvises the famous oracle of the wooden walls. She is ultimately released from her role as Pythia and sent with her husband Eëtion, a former slave whose freedom she has paid for, to found a colony in Sicily.

In *The Forgotten Daughter* (1929), set in Italy at the time of the Gracchi, Chloe grows up as a slave on a country estate. Her Roman father married her mother, a Greek captive, and then apparently abandoned her to make a marriage approved by his family. At the end of the novel, after the death of his second family from the plague, her father rediscovers Chloe and she him; his initial abandonment proves to have been based on a mistaken belief that she and her mother had died. She has in the meantime fallen in love with a young neighbor, Aulus, a friend and supporter of Tiberius Gracchus, and her father approves the marriage. The last of the three is *The White Isle* (1940), discussed in Chapter 4 for its American perspective on Roman Britain, in which Lavinia escapes an arranged marriage to journey with her family from

Rome to Britain, where she settles, joins a Christian community, and marries one of its members.

Snedeker's novels mingle invented characters and historical characters in a historical setting, although their focus is on the lives of the invented characters.[24] She took seriously her own responsibility as an author of historical fiction; she had little classical background, and before embarking on her first novel she undertook with her husband's encouragement several years of independent study of the ancient world and its literature.[25] Snedeker makes explicit her stories' claims to historicity: in the preface to *The Perilous Seat* she tells her readers that "the background and details of this story have been carefully authenticated" and justifies her one departure from historical fact as nonetheless "correct in character and spirit" (Snedeker 1939: vii); similarly, in the preface to *The White Isle* she excuses the single liberty she has taken with chronology (Snedeker 1956: xiii). Within the narratives she occasionally names her authority, as when in *The Forgotten Daughter* she cites Cato in her discussion of ancient slavery (Snedeker 1933: 54–5). The most striking example of such a citation—suggesting a concern both with plausible fiction and with documentary history—occurs in *The Perilous Seat* at the moment when the Persian invaders, on the threshold of Delphi, are about to be crushed by an earthquake:

What happened now can hardly be believed, but it is recorded by the father of history and later writers bear testimony to it. This had happened time and time again in the past to the hurt of Delphi, why not happen this once to her help? Herodotus says it did happen.   (Snedeker 1939: 243)

Like Mills, Snedeker is much given to generalizations about the Greek spirit and the Roman spirit, and like Mills she generally privileges the former: she speaks of the spiritual life of the Greeks, their appreciation for beauty, and their love of intellectual interchange in conversation. Her generalizations, somewhat didactic, often fervent, seem to call for a reader prepared to be taught and ready to respond with a corresponding fervor to expatiations on the Greek spirit, the Roman way, the early

[24] The heroine of *The Perilous Seat* is herself in one sense a historical character, the Pythia who on Herodotus' account delivered the famous oracle. But Snedeker has substituted her character for the differently named Pythia in Herodotus (who also appears in the novel, as Theria's unhappy predecessor).

[25] Meigs et al. 1953: 487–8.

Christian life. But she is unsparing in her depiction of the isolation and diminution of women's lives. In the opening episode of *The Perilous Seat*, the heroine reveals that the song with which her brother has just won a prize at the Pythian games is really her song, and her family is first incredulous and then outraged.[26] The novel then takes us back to Theria's childhood and her early efforts to escape the limitations of her life, beginning with an ancient version of the modern girl's disappointing exclusion from her brother's schooling:

> She seemed in the presence of a calamity which had been approaching since all the days she had been alive, and now was come. With the vagueness of her seven years, yet very deeply, she knew that not going to school meant the closing away from her of precious things....
>
> Dryas was prancing about, hugging his lyre. He was not slow to taunt her. "Ai: I'm going to school. You can't go; you can't go!" "I can. Father said I could. I heard him." "When did he say it?" "I don't know when, but I heard him. 'Daughter, you are going to school; you are seven years old! Everybody goes to school then.'"   (27–8)

The event reveals that "everybody" does not include girls.

In the years that follow, Theria arrives at the insight that Mills advances but qualifies in her discussion of Roman women: a woman's life is no better than slavery. Offering her jewelry to help free a slave (the man she will ultimately marry), Theria tells him, "you will be free and I will be in my room again. Shut in—always shut in!" His response expresses men's failure to recognize women's desires as exceeding their circumstances: "I never thought, Despoina, that wives and maidens cared to walk abroad" (109).

If women and slaves share some restrictions in *The Perilous Seat*, in *The Forgotten Daughter* the central women characters *are* slaves, and to some extent the bitterness of women's lives is here subsumed in the even greater bitterness of slavery. But this novel also begins by commenting on the particular circumstances of ancient women, as we are introduced to two weavers: "A woman and child, we should call them, but to the Romans they were two women. The younger, twelve years old, was of the marriageable age in Roman law" (Snedeker 1933: 2). Among the

---

[26] In response to a reader's question, Snedeker wrote: "No, Theria was not a real girl. I imagined how a Greek girl must feel who inherited her father's genius but could have no education nor outlet" (Snedeker 1944). On the figure of the suppressed artist in women's historical fiction of this period, see Trodd 1998: 113–14.

restrictions on women that Snedeker depicts, it is the fact that girls are forced to become women sooner than they wish, to leave their families (beloved, though confining) against their will, and to marry men they have not chosen and may not like that she treats as the worst, genuinely terrifying rather than simply constricting. That threat is the starting point of *The White Isle*, in which the heroine Lavinia is more distressed by the prospect of her marriage to an unpleasant young man than by his insulting abandonment of her. It is only this unwanted marriage and her father's uncomprehending insistence on it that make Lavinia unhappy; she is not a natural rebel like Theria, although she enjoys glimpses of the freedom she will later attain. "Everything she had to do was in the house... For, being a girl, the house was her place, and Lavinia took that for granted. But when she was to go outdoors her heart always sang within her" (Snedeker 1956: 2–3).

Snedeker never suggests, as Mills does, that the actual circumstances of Greek women's lives are irrelevant in comparison with the nobility of their depiction and the idealization of women from which it stems. On the contrary, she suggests through an imagined childhood encounter between Theria and the young Sophocles that the nobility of women in Greek literature might reflect an undocumented reality. Sophocles is astonished to learn that Theria wishes she too could be a poet, that she reads her father's books, that she hates being confined to the house, and that women's apparent contentment is illusory.

Who shall say that when in after years this boy sang of a woman and gave her a new type of nobleness the image of this proud sweet maid of Delphi did not float before him and make his creation real? (Snedeker 1939: 76)

Snedeker acknowledges that the Greeks were particularly given to a misogyny she finds baffling but does not palliate or disregard. Nor does she suggest (as Mills does) that the delights of the wedding day are somehow a compensation for Roman girls: Lavinia goes through the rituals of her abortive wedding frozen in apathy.

In these ways, Snedeker's fictional inventions fill in the historical reality of women's lives, which is documented by historical accounts but not fully narrated; at the same time, she also allows her narratives to evade the limitations that threaten to confine her heroines, with the help of three recurrent strategies. The first of these is displacement. Each of Snedeker's heroines finds herself in some new place or role or both, and this remove constitutes both a marginalization and a kind of release. Theria first leaves her family's home to take on the role of Pythia. In so doing she becomes a figure who though female is also asexual, deprived of womanhood, and she is enabled to speak, to sing, and to influence the course of events. At the end of the book, released by the Delphian priesthood, Theria experiences another remove, as leader of a colony, proposed by an imaginative Delphian who cites the examples of Dido and of Manto. This second displacement does not desexualize Theria as the first did; with her husband, she successfully establishes the colony and attains a life of greater freedom in the West, at the edges rather than in the center of things.

In *The White Isle*, Lavinia leaves Rome with her family and finds in the provinces and especially in Britain a new openness that is comparable, as we saw in Chapter 4, to that found by American girls in the expanding West. Girls ride in public and associate more freely with young men. Her father grumbles at this, and Lavinia herself is astonished at the easygoing ways of her young Greco-Gallic friends: "No Roman girl would do so. No Roman girls she knew. Yet it was all kind, childlike almost" (Snedeker 1933: 96). She is then further liberated by her final encounter with Christianity and her conversion.

In the *Forgotten Daughter* the displacement is one of status as well as location: the condition of slavery that nearly destroys Chloe also releases her from the constraints of a properly brought up Roman girl, so that she runs free in the woods outside an isolated villa, learns quantities of Greek poetry by heart, and has both a capacity for companionship and an affection for literature the young man she loves has never seen in his respectable sisters.[27] Had she grown up as her father's acknowledged daughter in Rome, he realizes,

There would have been no companionship. Girls were stupid. They had no life outside the house . . . Aulus's own sisters could read, but what good did it do them? They never read the scrolls, only did household accounts.   (Snedeker 1933: 198)

Here Snedeker takes advantage of the significant differences between slavery in the recent American past and ancient slavery, which was not based on race and was a much more variable and mutable condition. Like

---

[27] Cf. Parton 1932, in which several stories have class settings that allow girl characters greater freedom, and Trease 1952, in which an Athenian girl of good family can join the hero in his adventures because she was exchanged at birth and raised as a servant's child. On the use of this plot device, see Trease 1976: 10; Rahn 1990: 42–4.

ancient writers, especially of comedies and novels centering on romance, who employ their characters' movements in and out of slavery as convenient plot devices (often involving dramatic twists like capture by pirates or mistaken identity), Snedeker makes use of such occasions to generate satisfying storylines for her girl heroines and to characterize them in sympathetic terms for her own modern readers.[28] Not only does Chloe have a freer life than most girls of her day, but both Lavinia and Theria take meaningful action by bringing about a slave's release, and both *The Perilous Seat* and *The Forgotten Daughter* end in marriages between free characters and former slaves. In this last respect, Snedeker's ancient setting allows her to do what would have been impossible in an American context. In novels from the same period with abolitionist themes and antebellum American settings, the focus is exclusively on the heroic white liberators and a romantic relationship between a free character and a slave or former slave is out of the question.[29]

Snedeker's second strategy involves recognition and acceptance by the father: the very individual who at first most powerfully represents and enforces the society's restrictive customs ultimately comes to appreciate his daughter's individuality and her kinship to himself.[30] At the end of *The Perilous Seat*, Theria's previously uncomprehending father comes to a new realization:

Theria was always doing the unexpected, poor child, always bringing down wrath upon her own head, and as he now saw it, doing something either interesting or noble. What a Nikander she was, how true in every instinct to her ancient race... This girl was the child of his mind and heart.... Why had he not known it before?
(Snedeker 1939: 210–11)

Similarly in *The White Isle*, the narrator comments:

It is strange how a black oblivion can rest between two minds in one house so they are practically invisible to each other. Such an oblivion had rested between

---

[28] For other uses of this motif, see Anderson 1930 and Evans 1944 (discussed in Chapter 4); stories featuring enslavement or manumission include Sterne 1929; Parton 1932: 151–67; Anderson 1939; Lawrence 1946; Sutcliff 1954; Williamson 1957.

[29] These are labeled "pseudoabolitionist" by Connolly (2013: 140–48) in part because their young male protagonists tend to outgrow their abolitionist sentiments much as female protagonists of the same period outgrow their desire for action outside the domestic sphere.

[30] On the importance to Snedeker of the father–daughter connection, see Snedeker 1944. On the role of the father in tomboy stories of this period, including the heroine of Snedeker's *Downright Dencey*, see Levstik 1983: 18. On the historical evidence for father–daughter relations in the ancient world, see Hallett 1984: 62–149.

Favonius and his daughter. And at this moment that suddenly melted. Favonius had had no idea that Lavinia was like the person he saw now...He was moved, he was proud. By the gods—the girl was a true Claudian.   (Snedeker 1956: 128)

In *The Forgotten Daughter*, this recognition is literal, since the heroine's father comes to know of the existence of a daughter he thought had died at birth, but here too the recognition confers a status unusual for a girl. Chloe takes the place not so much of the daughter (her half-sister) her father lost to the plague as of the son; indeed, she at first appears to him as that son, since her hair is cut short and she is dressed in her half-brother's cast-off clothes, a disguise in which she had tried to escape from slavery.

The final strategy involves the introduction of romantic love (often at first sight) and a freely chosen husband. All three girls fall in love with men they encounter by chance, outside the house; all have reason to worry that their parents may object both to the man they love and to the unconventional way the lovers met; in all three cases intimacy is precipitated by a rescue. In The *White Isle*, most conventionally, Govan rescues Lavinia, but in the other two books, it is the woman who is the rescuer.[31] It is made clear that these are men who appreciate the women they love in part for their difference from other women; Theria is almost incredulous to find that Eëtion actually wishes her "to find joy in something beyond...home and children" and even beyond himself (Snedeker 1939: 291).

While Snedeker's first two strategies are presented as unusual circumstances that might nonetheless be possible in the ancient world, the third is figured as an outright intrusion, especially in this passage from The *Perilous Seat*:

There in the narrow lane pure love, neglected and chilled by Greek custom and unknown to Greek sullying passion, burned high and clear like an altar flame.   (150)

The anachronistic romantic love featured in these stories is a kind of deus ex machina arrived from the world of twentieth-century fiction to

---

[31] As Mitchell points out, Bessie Marchant's formula for the girl's adventure story includes rescue as well as displacement: "her [girl] heroes can ride across country, shoot to kill, travel unprotected among rough men, and swim in their underclothing so long as they are rescuing someone, and are doing it elsewhere than in England" (1995: 117).

rescue the heroine, her tale, and the ancient world for twentieth-century girls. At the same time, Snedeker suggests that the love that modern girls dream of is a universal fact of nature, like fire, obscured by the Greeks, who neglected and sullied it (much as, for Hawthorne, they turned myth into something "cold and heartless"), but capable of shining forth even in their world under the right circumstances.

As we have seen, both historicity and universalism are characteristic of Snedeker, and her narrator's generalizations frequently make these explicit; some draw attention to features of the ancient world, while others comment on human nature and in particular on the nature of children and of adolescents (e.g., "Who can account for the hidden places of reverence that lie in a child's mind," Snedeker 1933: 38). The first type seem to reinforce the distance between the present and the past, but the second (which tend to make use of the present tense) seem to close up that distance.

Snedeker, then, uses the resources of fiction both to establish historical realities and to transcend them. Rather than turn to fantasy she seeks to find a place for women as marginalized persons through a recurrent turn to the geographical margins: Theria's "western home" (1939: 313), Lavinia's Britain "on the very edge of the world" (1956: 24), Chloe's woods outside a "remote and little known" villa (1933: 148). To return to a contrast drawn at the end of Chapter 4, all of her heroines find homes on the periphery where they can lead permanently unconventional lives, unlike Anderson's Brighde, who experiences adventure and romance in her native Britain but then settles into the role of a typical matron at Rome. Snedeker's remoter settings and their inhabitants are alike the subjects of utopian recentering: Chloe's life before marriage (in a cave in the woods, with her cherished goats) suggests the pastoral world, Lavinia finds a Christian paradise in the island of Avalonia, and Theria's colony clearly recalls for Snedeker the utopian community of New Harmony in which she herself was born:

For it is curiously true that a town will retain for hundreds of years the spirit of its founders. Men may flock in and overwhelm it in numbers, but the original subtile spirit, be it good or bad, absorbs the new comers. In this lies the immortal glory of the pioneers.   (Snedeker 1939: 314)[32]

---

[32] On women writers (including Snedeker) and utopian fictions, see Kessler 1995.

In realizing these utopian visions for her female protagonists, Snedeker does not, however, free them from dependency on and competition with the male. The heroine's own escape leaves male authority intact and, in fact, requires recognition from both father and husband. It also hinges on the elimination of a male rival, since the daughter's achievement in each of these books entails or accompanies the downfall or loss of a brother: Theria's twin brother is revealed as a weakling and near-traitor, Chloe's half-brother dies in an outbreak of plague, and Lavinia's brother is killed in Britain with the ninth legion. Were we to look for a classical analogue, we might think of Medea, who leaves her home for the man she has fallen in love with and enables their escape by killing her brother. But the violence here belongs to the author, not to her heroines, who are uniformly noble, loving, and pure. However successfully she imagines full and fulfilling lives for them, she cannot do so without acknowledging the prevailing limitations of an unequal social structure, in which a brother always has a higher claim than his sister.

Freedom at the Margins of History

Where Snedeker seeks to find a place for her heroines within the framework of the historical record but at the margins of the known world or in marginalized circumstances, her younger contemporary Erick Berry (the pen name of Allena Champlin Best 1892–1974) sets *The Winged Girl of Knossos* (1933) at the margins of history, in the world of Minoan Crete—the same world to which Dorothy Mills also turned for a past more freely available to imaginative reconstruction. Here the discoveries and hypotheses of archaeologists allow the writer a basis in material reality (assisted by modern restoration), and myth provides a familiar narrative framework, but the cultural context remains largely open to authorial invention and intervention.

Berry may be little known today, but she wrote and illustrated many books with a wide range of settings as well as illustrating the work of others, and *The Winged Girl of Knossos*, one of her first novels, was (with Snedeker's *The Forgotten Daughter*) a runner-up for the Newbery Medal in 1934. Its heroine, Inas, is the daughter of the inventor Daidalos[33] and a

---

[33] Berry suggests that this Daidalos, who invents a system of weighing and a kind of printing, is one in a line of inventors and builders; he refers to "that Daidalos who was my

Greek mother, now dead. She is independent, courageous, and athletic; as a bull-vaulter, she achieves the "almost-impossible trick" of turning "a double somersault on the back of a charging bull" (Berry 1933: 97). She assists her father in testing the wings (reconceived as gliders) he is busy inventing, takes Ariadne's thread to Theseus to help him find his way out of the Labyrinth (a palace storehouse), and escapes with her father to Sicily when his inventions (regarded by the ignorant as witchcraft) and the resentment of rivals put his life in danger. In the end, as Crete falls to invaders, Inas escapes once more, with the help of her father's wings, and sails off with her friend and would-be husband Kadmos and a faithful slave. She is uncertain of her destination, but anticipates a prophesied welcome from Ariadne, who is in Greece, married to Theseus, "the chief of a small band of half-savage herdsmen near a place called Sparta, or mayhap Athens" (229).

Berry's dedication signals the place of invention in the subsequent narrative: "For Anne, because, like me, she believes in almost everything" (v). In her introduction, she mentions the glimpses of a lost Minoan culture we get in the songs "the blinded bards of the Achaeans sang ... for their barbarian nomad listeners," notes that "some wise men" (vii) identify Crete with Atlantis, and brings us to the present:

> Then in our own time came the archaeologists, those magicians who build authentic history out of lowly potsherds. They drew from oblivion the sounds and scenes of that long stilled, almost unexpected civilization ... We have learned too that many of the ancient legends were based upon truth.   (viii)

Depending on what sort of magician Berry has in mind, the building of "authentic history" from potsherds may evoke either genuine wizardry or sleight of hand; in either case, it suggests there is something fictive about this authenticity. In the course of the novel, Berry herself generates a fictional solution to an archaeological puzzle: on her flight to Greece (where she is last heard of "near a place called Sparta"), Ariadne takes with her "the famous Bull cups" (195). These cups are now famous as the "Vaphio cups," spectacular works of Minoan goldsmithing that were found at a site near Sparta, sparking a debate among archaeologists about how they got there. Berry mentions these cups by their modern

---

grandfather" (1933: 120) as having designed the palace with its many passages (119), while a great-grandfather designed the arena for bull-vaulting (51).

name in an afterword, in which she describes the fragmentary remains of Cretan culture that license her narrative (249).

In her introduction, Berry further notes that in spite of many unanswered questions and points of disagreement,

enough is now known so that one with a fair knowledge of how civilizations are developed and of the needs that have been felt by people all the world over, may weave together a story of those days that is perhaps not too far from what really happened. (ix)

Archaeologists may reconstruct a particular history on the basis of potsherds, but the writer of historical fiction can evidently construct a story about the little-known past on the basis of universals of human society and individual human psychology. Berry's Minoan Crete can thus offer far more possibilities for action and self-expression to a girl character than Snedeker's Greece and Rome.[34]

Berry's "knowledge of how civilizations are developed" leads her to create a Crete at once primitive (its people fear science as witchcraft), advanced (its urbanized culture is possessed of many refinements), and decadent (its "effete" upper classes have begun to hand over their entertainments to foreigners and the defense of the country to mercenaries). The Greeks, in contrast, are uncultured peasants who believe in childish stories like that of the Minotaur; Theseus, whose "clumsy masculinity" (88) appeals to no one but Ariadne, simply kills bulls without playing them. Inas is unusual even among Cretan women: when we first meet her she is with the sponge fishers, diving for sport; indeed, she is an all-round athlete, good at swimming, archery, riding, and acrobatics.[35] She thinks it would be "wonderful to be a man . . . , to have adventures, to travel and see the world," and she is no good at women's tasks like weaving. But the Cretan society Berry invents can somehow accommodate Inas and her difference: other girls take part in the bull-vaulting (though no woman has ever achieved what she does), and no one seems

---

[34] For contemporaneous depictions of Minoan Crete in historical fiction for children, see Lamprey 1924 and "The Prince" in Mitchison 1931a; both feature bull-dancing as including both boys and girls.

[35] Cf. the story "Dolphin Girl" in Parton 1932, in which a fisherman's daughter uses her diving and swimming skills to help her father cut the moorings of Persian ships during the storm before Salamis, and Hildegarde Hawthorne's portrayal of Sappho, discussed later in this chapter. On the association between the tomboy and the "exercise enthusiast" in the early 20th century, see Abate 2008: ch. 4.

shocked when Inas walks through the "fair grounds" (100) unchaper-
oned with Kadmos. Portrayed as both different and admirable, a refresh-
ing anomaly, Inas is like the tomboy heroines of many children's books
of the period, including some who also belong to earlier historical
periods, such as Caddie Woodlawn and Laura Ingalls. She also resembles
her literary contemporary Nancy Drew and other girls in the series
fiction of the period; like the girl detective, she is motherless, close to
her father, independent, and clever, with a keen eye for villainy, and a
generally unromantic relationship with a boyfriend.[36]

Like Snedeker, Berry exploits the relative fluidity of ancient slavery to
construct the circumstances of her narrative. Inas has the commanding
height, blue eyes, and blond hair of the ideal twentieth-century girl
because of her Greek mother, who came to Crete as a slave but was
given to Daidalos as a gift from Minos before she could be auctioned off
(29). She also has the ability to turn "a delicious brown, that hue which
only the true blond turns in the sun" (7)—an attribute which, it has been
argued, modern American tomboys appropriate from people of African
origin, but which is here carefully distinguished from blackness by its
association with the "true blond."[37]

In her imaginary Cretan setting, Berry gives a benign, even playful
account of slavery. Inas' knowledge of Greek allows her to speak to the
young Athenians who have arrived with Theseus, here defined as foreign
slaves, and she is able to reassure them that they will not, as rumor has it,
be fed to a monster but rather sold in a special sale to honored friends of
Minos and that one day they may be free again (64–5). Cretan law allows
that "any free man or woman might sell himself or herself into slavery for
a certain time if they wished freedom from want, or needed to work off a
debt" (128); when Inas is mistaken for one of the newly arrived Greeks
and put up for sale, she knows all along that she is not really in danger,
and the episode ends as her identity is revealed and she makes a joke
about auctioning off the auctioneer (130). Thus, while Snedeker engages
with slavery by having her heroines experience its sufferings or deal
sympathetically with those who are enslaved, Berry dismisses it by

---

[36] On Nancy Drew and the forms of agency made possible by her fictional circumstances, see MacLeod 1994: 30–48; Siegel 1997; Stoneley 2003: 122–34; Nash 2006: 29–70;
and the essays in Dyer and Romalov 1995; Cornelius and Gregg 2008.
[37] On the "nonwhiteness of ostensibly white tomboys," see Abate 2008: xxiv–xxviii.

having Inas treat it as trivial or even comedic. Meanwhile, some lower-class characters are distinguished from slaves of Greek origin and portrayed in ways that reflect the racist attitudes of twentieth-century America. Inas' family has African servants: her old nurse Teeta has the "dark skin...full wide mouth...kinky hair" and affectionate but scolding manner of a stereotypical plantation "Mammy" (as seen a few years later in the book and film versions of *Gone With the Wind*); Mufu, a boy with kinky locks and flashing white teeth, is credulous, fearful, and slow-moving. The degeneration of Cretan society is manifested through dependence on black mercenaries from the south (29).

What Snedeker's heroines only gradually achieve—recognition by the father, displacement of the brother, a prospective husband who is also a friend—Inas has from the outset, and without struggle or violence. She is her father's assistant, and on more than one occasion makes suggestions that reveal a better way of going about his research. She is his only child, and has in fact taken the place of the Icarus of the traditional myth, whose story she will replay, succeeding where he failed. Kadmos is a presence from the beginning of the book, and Inas has known him all her life; it turns out at the end that their fathers have always planned their marriage, but in Berry's invented Crete, this is no frightening imposition of an unwelcome arrangement but the natural outcome of a family friendship; Inas calls Kadmos her "almost-brother." The fact that these things are givens means that they play a somewhat different role in the economy of the narrative, as the preconditions of Inas' adventures, not results that she achieves in spite of obstacles. The relative freedom from known historical conditions afforded by her prehistoric Cretan setting allows Berry to grant her heroine circumstances similar to those under which her modern counterpart, Nancy Drew, finds scope for significant action.[38]

In spite of her affection for Kadmos, however, and enough concern for traditional masculine sensitivities to regret outshooting him at an archery

---

[38] On Inas' family circumstances, compare Berry's comment, quoted on the dust jacket of *Sybil Ludington's Ride* (1952), on retelling the story of an American Revolutionary War heroine. Sybil Ludington came from a family with twelve children, but "For the story's sake...I discarded all but her father and one younger obstreperous sister. Writers are allowed liberty with facts, and for story purposes a half-orphan is so much freer to move around."

booth (107), Inas resists the traditional marriage plot as Snedeker's heroines dread arranged marriages. Kadmos, who admires her skill, her strength, and her difference (she is a girl "like no other he had ever seen"), nonetheless tries to keep her from running risks and does not welcome her plans for adventure and travel; she reacts by envisioning a future unconstrained by either marriage or gender.

> Kadmos' brows met again. "My wife must be satisfied to stay at home, like wives of other sailors. How can I be content in Thebes or Rhodes or far off Sicily if my wife is not safe here at home in Crete?"
> Inas threw back her curls with an impatient hand. "And only last night you told me Crete herself was not so safe. Besides, I'm not so sure I wish to marry you, or anyone. Why should I forgo all adventures? See, I am as strong as any boy."   (30)

When Inas and her father are forced to travel in order to seek refuge from their enemies in Sicily, she finds herself not an adventurer but an unhappy exile, restricted to the company of the princesses and their women, who do nothing but weave and gossip. This island in the West, which represents for Snedeker's Eleutheria a land of utopian possibility free from the constraints of her Greek homeland, reveals to Inas more fully the merits of the Crete she has left behind. Unable to bear this new life and her own clumsiness in it, she speaks to her father.

> "And at the end—" she laughed again but there were tears behind the laughter— "I drew my knife. No woman in this city wears a knife, it is deemed unwomanly. They were frightened, but I only slashed the warp of the loom, then turned six cartwheels from the chamber! Aiee..." She put her hands over her face and the bitter tears of homesickness trickled out between her fingers.   (221)

There is something odd about Inas' nostalgia. It's true that Cretan women perform in the bull court, and win recognition for it, but we have met no other knife-wearing, cartwheel-turning girls in this story, and the women of Sicily are not that different from Ariadne and her court, as Inas knows; the princesses and their maids talk of "just such stuff as Ariadne's maidens told, save that the names are different" (220–1). What Inas is homesick for is not so much Crete as the twentieth-century girlhood she has lived there.[39]

---

[39] Brinnaria in Edward Lucas White's 1918 *The Unwilling Vestal* (aimed at adults but certainly read by girls) is another strikingly 20th-century heroine, precocious and prone to mischief, something of an ancient flapper.

As the story draws to a conclusion, with Minos dead and his fleet burned, the world of adventure Inas has imagined as an alternative to marriage seems foreclosed; her father entrusts her to Kadmos, who alone of the fleet has survived, and the two return to warn Crete of its danger. The hostility they meet with forces them to flee again, and they successfully reenact the flight of Icarus by gliding together from a high cliff on a pair of her father's wings. Like Icarus, they land in the water, but their landing is planned and take them to safety on a waiting boat below.

Kadmos, who had distrusted the wings, joins Inas in the single pair that lies ready for them. Their shared flight is a collaborative venture with a hint of sexuality:

"Make haste," she panted. "Do as I do."
Quickly he inserted his body into the same open space, his chest tight against her back, his arms spread out like hers over the wings...
There had been no time to make delicate adjustment of balance, either that balance was right, or—The nose dived steeply. Inas threw back her legs, her body. Kadmos with swift understanding followed suit.   (244–5)

With this flight, Inas leaves behind the world of idealized girlhood Berry has made of Crete; that world now ceases to exist. The moment of transition to adulthood and to a similarly idealized marriage of equals, emblematized by the mutual comprehension of both body and mind in flight, coincides with the journey to Greece and thus from prehistory to the beginnings of history. We are still in the realm of myth, but Berry has further rewritten myth so that Ariadne makes it to Greece, her assistance to Theseus loyally repaid.

As noted in Chapter 2, several retellings of the Theseus myth, including those of Andrew Lang and Edith Hamilton, end by aligning the hero's return from Crete with the onset of Athenian history as well as his own entrance into full adulthood. In Berry's novel, two young women complete the same passage, embarking on a new phase of culture in which Cretan refinement will be fortified by the heartier if cruder qualities of the Greeks. Inas, with her hybrid lineage and adventurous spirit, is ideally suited for this future.[40]

---

[40] Inas' hybrid heritage is one of several features she shares with the heroines in Bessie Marchant's popular adventure stories (see n. 11), some of whom have hereditary rights to large estates in South America or the Middle East, which they administer in place of their ineffectual fathers (Bratton 1989: 201–6).

Lesbos for Children, Lesbos for Adults

Within the time frame of Greek history, Sappho's Lesbos sometimes plays a similar role to that of prehistoric Crete, offering a plausible setting for stories of girlhood that resonate with modern girls' experiences (especially as constructed in school stories), including schooling, sports, and friendship. The suitability of this setting was promoted by the work of nineteenth- and early twentieth-century scholars, who interpreted Sappho and her circle as a schoolmistress surrounded by her students.[41] This anachronistic reconstruction helped to neutralize features of the milieu described in Sappho's poems that would be particularly unwelcome in works for girl readers, including the celebration of erotic relations among women and the portrayal of marriage as a sad conclusion to girlhood happiness rather than as the positive telos we find even (after some negotiation) in stories of active, independent adolescent girls.

One way of avoiding unsuitable aspects of Sappho's world is to shift the focus back in time to Sappho's own girlhood; this is the strategy adopted by Hildegarde Hawthorne (Nathaniel Hawthorne's granddaughter) in her 1917 time-travel fantasy, *Girls in Bookland*. A pair of sisters, stranded on a snowbound Wyoming ranch, are transported by a fairy to a series of settings (mostly those of books they have read) where they can find adventure and the companionship of "all sorts of little girls in all sorts of places and all sorts of times" (Hawthorne 1917: 21). The first of these is a version of Sappho cast as an ideal playmate for her modern visitors: "Have you heard of Sappho, the Greek girl who wrote wonderful poems after she grew up? She was a very sweet and merry child, and I know you'll enjoy playing with her" (22). The Sappho they meet is not only friendly and good fun but also, like Berry's Inas, an outstanding athlete: the main event of the episode is a torch race, in which Sappho's new friends cheer her on ("Go it, go it, you've GOT to win", 39) to a victory in which she overcomes the cheating and poor sportsmanship of her main rival. The role of sports as an arena of significant female achievement is underscored when Sappho's mother whispers, "Sappho, my daughter, I no longer regret that I did not bear a son" (41). Like Icarus in Berry's Cretan tale, the real Sappho's actual brothers (whose importance in her life is reconfirmed by the newly

---

[41] DeJean 1989: 198–220; Parker 1993.

discovered "Brothers Poem" published in 2014) have been written out of the story.

Naomi Mitchison, who evolved from a girl reading *The Republic* into a leading figure in the flowering of historical fiction by women in the 1920s and 1930s, also uses Lesbos as a promising site in which to envision an ancient girl's experience in her children's book, *Boys and Girls and Gods*. This is a collection of short "sketches of the lives of boys and girls who lived, or might have lived" in antiquity, which appeared in 1931 in the "World of Youth" series (a publishing project that assumes the same similarity and compatibility of all children that is dramatized in Hawthorne's fantasy of transhistorical friendships). Like Hawthorne, Mitchison avoids the actual circumstances alluded to in Sappho's poetry, in this case by keeping Sappho herself out of the picture. In "The First Morning," she portrays a fictional girl, Dika, who has already learned to read and write from her mother and older sister, getting ready for her first day of school. Dika wakes early, full of excitement, and her nurse accompanies her to the house of Andromeda the poetess, the idealized version of a historical figure, who figures in Sappho's poetry as a troublesome rival. There Dika finds "a dozen other girls standing or sitting on benches, some with lyres, others with book-rolls or pen and Egyptian paper" (Mitchison 1931a: 61). Andromeda explains the poem they read, and helps them with their writing:

And then she talked to them—told them about the stars, and how the most wonderful thing in the world was to be able to understand the movements of the stars, as the Gods understood them; for understanding was the true quality of the Gods. But Dika did not quite know what she meant—only she too saw, suddenly, that it would be lovely to understand—to understand anything! She looked around the big room, at the other girls, and out into the courtyard and the spreading branches of the fig tree which grew in the middle, arching over the well-head, and she thought if she could once understand even that, it would be a possession for her whole being, for her whole life!   (64)

The chapter ends as the lesson comes to a close, with Dika eagerly looking forward to the following day.

Dika's experience offers a sharp contrast to Theria's crushing discovery that school is foreclosed to her in Snedeker's *The Perilous Seat*. By focusing on the beginning of Dika's schooling and the incipient expansion of her horizons, Mitchison avoids the painful shutting down of a girl's education that coincides in her own biography with the onset of puberty and in the poetry of Sappho with marriage. The only hint in this story that Dika faces a less satisfying future comes when we learn that she will study the lyre "and learn to make songs and tunes of her own, so that she never need be lonely even if, later on, her husband were to go away on long voyages, as so many women's husbands went..." (55).

A story for adult readers written two years later shows by contrast what Mitchison suppresses when writing for children. In "The Delicate Fire" (1933), she elaborates on Sappho's expressions of regret to portray marriage as the sad curtailment of girlhood freedom and self-expression. A grown woman, Brocheo, thinks back to a time when she traveled from her home in the hills to the city of Mitylene, where she became the student first of Andromeda and then of Sappho. Brocheo is accompanied on her journey by her widowed mother Praxinoa, whose own memories underline the contrast between life as a girl and as an adult woman. As she reminisces about her own girlhood as a friend and contemporary of Sappho, Praxinoa becomes animated, remembers how she wrote a poem for Sappho, and appears to her daughter beautiful and light-hearted as never before. She acknowledges that it was hard to be separated from her friends when she married and moved to the country, but tentatively adds that when her husband came home in the evening "with his little cloak flicking out behind him and his hands reaching out for me—oh, I suppose I forgot Sappho and the others" (21). In Praxinoa's case, as in Dika's projected future, marriage seems unsatisfactory only because of the husband's necessary absence. But when Brocheo later discusses marriage with Sappho's daughter Kleis, a familiar comparison suggests itself and they struggle to differentiate marriage from slavery: " 'that's different,' said Kleis,... 'In marriage, we give and get—don't we?' " (37).

The story includes other elements that would be omitted in a story for younger readers. Kleis has a passionate attachment to Brocheo's cousin Strymo, which is not explicitly erotic but is clearly more consuming and highly charged than ordinary friendship, and she speaks regretfully of the separation that marriage will bring. Other forms of sexuality also manifest themselves: when Brocheo and Strymo attend a louche party given by Sappho's ex-prostitute sister-in-law (Sappho's troublesome brother does figure in this narrative), they are nearly raped by some of the male guests. And while they escape from that danger to a gathering of Sappho and her students that is highly idealized, Brocheo's decision to forsake Andromeda for Sappho is implicated in the tense rivalry between the two teachers.

Bedside Books?

In a another passage in her memoirs, Mitchison explicitly addresses the difference between works that are intended for girls and those that are not, bringing us back to the point illustrated by her own encounter with Plato, that girls' reading often includes books written for adults. She is describing the games she played as a teenager with her main female friend, Frances Parkinson.

> I do remember playing prisoners and captives under one of the dark, spreading yew trees and making Frances tie my wrists, though this was perhaps a little later, at fifteen or sixteen. There was a deep excitement about this, not recognizable or at least namable at this time. If a grown-up had found us and asked: "What do you children think you are doing?" we would have collapsed into sullen shame. Sexual shame? Maybe. For me it was all connected with the stories which I still told myself and of which, I suppose, versions persisted into my earlier books and are perhaps recognized by some of the young who are given *The Conquered* to read so as to improve their ancient history. Bedside books, clearly!
>
> (Mitchison 1975: 17)

Here, as often, material intended for adults is redirected to younger readers because of its educational potential. But Mitchison suggests a more interesting hidden dynamic as the source of its actual appeal to those readers. The "inside stories" inspired by Mitchison's recognition of herself in Plato's *Republic*, and in other forms of ancient history, evolve into published historical fictions that inspire a similar recognition in her teenage readers. The ancient world serves as a medium through which sexual feelings that cannot be directly named are communicated between modern adolescents—a barely adult writer and her teenage readers—who meet at the volatile border between childhood and adulthood. In both, a passion for reading stories, or for generating them, is bound up with volatile, officially unrecognized desires.

The Conquered, which appeared in 1923, when she was 25, was Mitchison's first published work. Looking back, she situates the writing of it in the early, inchoate stages of her married life, which began at the age of 17. For her husband, this period involved "the struggle at the Bar and political interests gradually emerging," while for her, "it was attempting to be a competent wife and mother according to the ideas of the time, but above all it was the intense inward excitement out of which I wrote my first book, *The Conquered*" (Mitchison 1979: 15). This formulation hints at a tension between the impulses behind the book and Mitchison's full acculturation as a conventional wife, which the book itself bears out.

The Conquered is set in Roman Gaul, a part of the ancient world prominent in traditional education because of Caesar's role as one of the first authors to be read in Latin; it draws on Mitchison's own study of Latin in school, as well as her childhood reading of historical fiction, especially Kipling's *Puck of Pook's Hill* and G. J. Whyte-Melville's *The Gladiators*, but departs from those canonical narratives to foreground the perspective of Rome's barbarian victims. Its plot substantiates Mitchison's earlier instinct that ancient male experience provides more scope for the imagination than ancient female experience. The novel shows the effects of conquest through the story of a young Gaulish brother and sister, Meromic and Fiammar, whose island nation (deliberately reminiscent of modern Ireland) is conquered by the Romans. In the opening sections, Fiammar appears to be the protagonist, but once their land is conquered, she commits suicide rather than be enslaved, at the same time urging her brother not to do the same: "I'm quite sure it will be better for me than living as a slave... But you're a man: life may hold something for you still" (Mitchison 1923: 82). Even in conquest, the prospects for fulfillment are greater for men than for women, whose lives are more readily reduced to slavery.

Fiammar kills herself in Meromic's arms, and he lays her out in a way that anticipates Virginia Woolf's image of Antigone as a figure for the stunted lives of women both ancient and modern: "at first he could not make her lie straight, she was all tumbled by the fall, but at last he got her lying along with her arms at her sides and her hair over her shoulders, like a princess in a fairy tale" (85–6). Meromic's subsequent adventures elaborate on the conflicted emotional life of the conquered.[42] But the clearest reflection of feelings that are difficult to put into words is the marked erotic bond between brother and sister, especially evident in the scene of Fiammar's death. "Meromic, with his eyes shut, warm against his sister's soft heart-beating, felt her suddenly quiver all over; he

---

[42] The novel is well discussed by Hoberman 1997: 120–9. See also Trodd 1998: 115; Wallace 2005: 43–5.

looked up; she smiled at him with the colour ebbing out of her cheeks; her hands fluttered for a moment over his face; she fell on her side" (85).

In another of her memoirs, published in 1979, Mitchison identifies this fictional pair as a portrait of herself and her brother Jack, aligning the novel with an absorbing attachment to her family of origin that continued into the early years of her marriage. Jack was a major figure in her life, and their intense relationship resulted in a transitory episode of near-incest on a walking tour in France that they took while she was writing *The Conquered* because she was "passionately eager" to see the landscapes in which the novel was set (Mitchison 1979: 162). The heightened drama of an imagined historical incident provides cover for sexual feelings that do not correlate with traditional marriage, which would have been scandalous if openly portrayed in contemporary fiction even for adults, and would never have been made available to teenage readers if not cloaked in ancient history.[43]

Mitchison's account of Fiammar's death links two powerful strands in her relationship with her brother, one being erotic attraction and special preference, the other an awareness, often mingled with competition, of his greater opportunities. Suggestively, she has Fiammar sing as she dies a song that recalls Antigone, the figure who symbolizes for Yonge a sister's self-sacrificing devotion and for Woolf the limitations on female lives (and who has come more recently to serve as a figure for incestuous desire[44]).

> Good-bye my darling,
> Oh good-bye, my brother!
>   Husband or child would
> Be only another.
>
>   .   .   .   .
>
> Now death is chosen
> The dying is nought;
> Honour's un-ending
> But sorrow is short.

---

[43] Of another of her classical novels, W. H. Auden wrote to her, "some of the scenes... were hotter than anything I've read. My dear, how do you get away with it?" (Mitchison 1979: 121; and see Trodd 1998: 116.) For Mitchison's struggles with a series of publishers over the frank portrayal of female sexuality in *We Have Been Warned* (1935), her first full-length novel with a contemporary setting, and her reluctant agreement to cut some controversial passages, see Benton 1990: 93–5; Calder 1997: 121–4.

[44] Most prominently in the work of Judith Butler (2000).

> I must make ready,
> For soon I shall see
> Father and friends who
> Are waiting for me!
> (Mitchison 1923: 84–5)

A few years after the appearance of *The Conquered*, Mitchison was herself involved in repackaging some of her adult historical fiction for child readers.[45] A group of her earlier short stories was republished in 1929 as *The Hostages and Other Stories for Girls and Boys*. The volume collects nine stories, many of which share *The Conquered*'s concern with the divided loyalties of captives, and links them together with a continuous account of history from fourth-century BCE Greece through eleventh-century CE England. This historical account is offered apologetically, as necessary background for enjoying the stories, but the reader is assured that the stories themselves are free of didactic intent:

the stories were not written to illustrate history, or, for that matter, to illustrate my theories of history. I just wrote them, and then when they were going to be made into this book, which will I hope be read by boys and girls, my own boys read them.   (Mitchison 1929: vii)

Like *The Conquered*, the stories in *The Hostages*, as presented here, pertain to young readers because they are the unmediated expressions of a writer who has not yet left her own youth behind rather than because they are instructive about history. This can be seen in a story entitled "Cottia Went to Bibracte" about the young wife of a Roman officer. Gossiping with a friend in her luxurious Roman house, Cottia recalls the earliest days of her marriage when she went out with her husband to Noviodunum (modern Nevers), where his legion was stationed, and found herself, like Snedeker's and Berry's heroines, in a setting on the margins of mainstream classical culture.

The foreign prelude to Cottia's married life allows for unpredictable adventures that predate her comfortable establishment in that role, including an episode of captivity that recalls Mitchison's girlhood games. Captured at Noviodunum, she is taken to the remoter settlement of Bibracte, where she is nearly raped by a group of four or five Gallic chieftains. After being pushed around by all of them,

---

[45] On such repackaging, see Beckett 2009: 232–9.

I ended up in a man's arms with my hands held over my head, and he squeezing me up to him and kissing my neck; I could feel his great hot body against mine, and I didn't know what wasn't going to happen. But anyway I bit his ear as hard as I could, and he let go and swore.   (102)

This turns out to be Vercingetorix, who on further observation cuts an impressive figure:

he was the tallest of the lot, with coral brooches and great knobbly gold bracelets all up his arms ... He was drunk and standing with one hand on the table and the other on his sword hilt; he'd blue eyes and ruddy brown hair, and his ear was bleeding all down his neck, where I'd bitten it. He was half laughing and half scowling, and the others all had their eyes on him.   (101–2)

Vercingetorix has the grace to forgive Cottia for biting him, and in a soberer moment he charms her into forgiving him: "Vercingetorix made me a bow, saying, 'Will Rome forgive?' 'No!' I said, but he was smiling at me so nicely that at last I changed my mind." Finally he insists that she accept one of his coral brooches, which she does despite misgivings. "Anyhow, I did take it. It's a great thing for a man to have a smile like that!" (105). And then she is reunited with M., who says it was fine to take the brooch and it should become a family heirloom. Before settling into her proper marriage, then, Cottia has a thrilling encounter with a powerful, sexy man, who is also courtly and sympathetic. Bedside books, clearly!

In accounts of her experience writing historical fiction, Mitchison stressed that material objects from antiquity were among her chief sources of inspiration. After she saw a Viking ship in a museum in Oslo "the ship made itself into a story" (Mitchison 1935: 645). She notes the influence of Irish fairy tales and of Kipling on The Conquered, then adds: "But it was the British Museum which produced the best inspiration. The bronze weapons and shields, the great curved war-horns—the lurs (made perhaps like an auroch's horn)—all these were good and the closer one looked the more educative it became" (646). Here inspiration and education merge as concrete objects anchor Mitchison's fantasies in historical reality.

In "Cottia Went to Bibracte," Mitchison tells the story of an object that might have inspired her in this way, Vercingetorix' coral brooch, and so offers a kind of validation for the free range of her imaginings, much as Berry grounds her version of the Ariadne myth in the real Vaphio cups found at Sparta. The treasured heirloom of a prominent Roman family could be a mute witness to an experience of wilder, more wayward feelings than are expected in a respectable wife. Fictional invention is motivated by the silence of material remains—which include objects from the otherwise unrecorded sphere of domestic life as well as ships, shields, and war-horns—and finds a legitimating parallel in scholarly interpretation and conjecture, as in Mills's reconstruction of the life of a Minoan princess or in Woolf's detailed delineation of Antigone's death.

For Woolf, archaeological reconstruction is a metaphor for reading between the lines of a text. When that text is *Antigone*, she—like Mitchison in *The Conquered*—finds a sad precedent for the spiritual death that she saw as the fate of modern girls; antiquity offers only a heightened version of her own patriarchal world, in which girls were not educated to the same degree as their brothers and were expected to move swiftly into quiet adult lives of domesticity and service. Charlotte Yonge, however much she may have recognized the toll of this trajectory on her modern heroines, did also embrace it for them, and she recorded its classical precedents in her accounts of ancient women as supportive wives and secluded keepers of the house.

Other writers, such as Dorothy Mills, Caroline Dale Snedeker, and Erick Berry, who wanted both to instruct their girl readers and to offer them a positive point of entry into ancient experience, used ancient texts and objects to ground more expansive stories of creative, passionate, independent girls, contriving to make their protagonists the owners of surviving objects, or the actual authors of surviving texts or their real-life inspiration.[46] Snedeker builds on the passive role of the Pythia to envision a young woman as the active, skillful author of an especially important oracle, and also imagines her as the unacknowledged composer of one of the thousands of now-forgotten songs performed at Greek festivals. And she finds traces of the same young woman in the portraits of strong, noble women in Sophocles' plays. Mills combines textual inspiration with the authority of material culture, taking her cue

---

[46] The most successful "discovery" of a girl author of an ancient text is Samuel Butler's theory, outlined in *The Authoress of the Odyssey* (1897), that the *Odyssey* was the work of a young Sicilian woman who depicted herself within the poem as Nausicaa. Butler's theory inspired a historical novel for adults by Robert Graves, *Homer's Daughter* (1955). On the relationship of Graves's novel to the strategies for depicting active ancient girl heroines discussed in this chapter, see Murnaghan 2015a.

from a textual account of an object, the shield of Achilles. Bypassing the status of that object as a piece of weaponry made by a male god and possessed by a male warrior, she goes inside its decoration to focus on one of the young women who appears there as a dancer, animating a figure who in Homer is more an ornamental motif than a real person. Berry ties part of her story to a material fact: the undocumented transit of the Vaphio cups from Crete to Sparta. In addition to making the most of such scraps of evidence, these authors exploit what might be called less normative aspects of ancient culture: moments of historical crisis that call for dramatic action, the diversity and complexity of communities at the social and geographical margins, and ancient speculations about other ways of organizing society.

Through acts of imagination that straddle the border between historical reconstruction and free invention, these authors compensate for what is missing or unsatisfactory in the historical record and construct ancient experiences of girlhood that answer to the presumed aspirations of their modern readers—whether those experiences are sentimentalized, as in the case of Mills; or hard won, as in the case of Snedeker; or miraculously available in the undocumented space of prehistory, as in the case of Berry. In doing so, they universalize the conceptions of girlhood their readers would have encountered in other contexts, including novels with contemporary settings; they imply that girls at all times and places legitimately wish for some combination of schooling, outdoor play, success in sports, intense female friendships, special birthdays, opportunities for artistic expression, recognition as the intellectual equals of their brothers, adventures, and heterosexual romance leading to companionate marriage.[47] Finding ways to circumvent the restrictions imposed by ancient social arrangements, these writers reinforce the norms of their own period, with their greater, though hardly limitless, freedoms. As in the case of Antigone, but also of Virginia Woolf and Naomi Mitchison, their heroines' achievements and opportunities are still defined in relation to those of their brothers, whom they must displace or replace—whether this is brought about by a brother's

---

[47] For anachronistic "agentic heroines" in girls' historical fiction since the mid-20th century, see Wilson 2011: 63–101. Wilson stresses that such heroines reinforce second-wave feminist values and modern ideas of personal autonomy at the expense of an accurate picture of past realities and attitudes and of progress over time.

inadequacy or by his simple excision from the ancient record. And the future envisioned for these heroines as wives in idealized marriages is left hazy. As Naomi Mitchison testifies, both through her own reading and through the reception history of her books, for accounts of the ancient world that go beyond such limitations—to project a girl's less conventional sexual feelings or an adult's full participation in public life—an inquisitive girl of the early twentieth century had to find books that were not intended for her.

6

The Ancient Prehistory of Modern Adults

In a famous anecdote from an autobiographical narrative published in 1881, the archaeologist Heinrich Schliemann tells how he formed the desire to discover Troy.

[My father] related to me with admiration the great deeds of the Homeric heroes and the events of the Trojan war, always finding in me a warm defender of the Trojan cause. With great grief I heard from him that Troy had been so completely destroyed, that it had disappeared without leaving any traces of its existence. My joy may be imagined, therefore, when, being nearly eight years old, I received from him, in 1829, as a Christmas gift, Dr. Georg Ludwig Jerrer's *Universal History*, with an engraving representing Troy in flames, with its huge walls and the Scaean gate, from which Aeneas is escaping, carrying his father Anchises on his back and holding his son Ascanius by the hand; and I cried out, "Father, you were mistaken: Jerrer must have seen Troy, otherwise he could not have represented it here." "My son," he replied, "that is merely a fanciful picture." But to my question, whether Troy had such huge walls as those depicted in the book, he answered in the affirmative. "Father," retorted I, "if such walls once existed, they cannot possibly have been completely destroyed: vast ruins of them must still remain, but they are hidden away beneath the dust of ages." He maintained the contrary, whilst I remained firm in my opinion, and at last we both agreed that I should one day excavate Troy.   (Schliemann 1976: 3)

Schliemann traces his life's ambition to a classic childhood encounter with an ancient myth, known partly through a parent's storytelling, partly and most compellingly through an illustration, and indicates a clear progression from his early fascination with the Troy legend to adult accomplishments involving worldly success, scientific discovery, and the establishment of historical fact. The excavation of Troy confirms his childhood intuitions and refutes the discouraging, inadequate adult response against which his childhood self had to struggle. He is able to tell such a decisive story of adult achievement as the vindication of childhood conviction in part because, as is now generally recognized, the anecdote is a fiction: it appears to have been fabricated retrospectively in the context of the adult Schliemann's rivalry with his collaborator Frank Calvert over priority in the pursuit of Homeric topography.

Although Schliemann here foregrounds the goal of showing that the walls of Troy are still standing, what is really at stake is the historicity of the Trojan War, the actual occurrence of what his father dismisses as "merely a fanciful picture." Schliemann's achievement is regularly glossed as having proven that the Troy legend really happened, as in the doubly fictionalized version of his anecdote retold for child readers in Marjorie Braymer's 1960 biography, *The Walls of Windy Troy*. There Heinrich's father tells him that the picture is "all imaginary . . . No one really knows what Troy was like," and worse that "Many historians think that Troy was a myth, like the story of its war with the Greeks . . . From everything we know the *Iliad* is a wonderful story about a war and a city that did not exist—except in Homer's poetry."

"I'll find out for myself. When I grow up, I'm going to find Troy," Heinrich had replied. His father had smiled. It sounded like a child's boasting. But the desire had grown into the fabric of his will. He had longed to continue school, to learn more history and to study Greek so that one day be could prove his belief in the existence of the real Troy.   (Braymer 1960: 27–8)[1]

Schliemann's mythic account of a child's life-changing encounter with a classical myth epitomizes the experiences of many writers and thinkers who came of age in the late nineteenth and early twentieth centuries, when archaeology was having its broadest cultural impact, and who saw their own literary and scientific projects as affirming truths revealed in children's special connection to antiquity. In this chapter, we consider some of the ways in which that connection is conceptualized and elaborated in works written not for children but for other adults. We move briefly away from our Anglo-American focus to discuss Schliemann and one of Schliemann's most influential admirers, Sigmund Freud, but look

---

[1] For an incisive account of Schliemann's self-mythologizing and the critics who have exposed it, especially William M. Calder and David A. Traill (Traill 1985, Calder and Traill 1986, Traill 1995), see Gere 2009: 19–27, 236–7. For a recent overview of Schliemann's life and cultural impact, see Samida 2012. A more recent account for children acknowledges his tendency to lie, but still portrays him as an inspiring figure, who "loved stories . . . so much that he wanted them to be true" (Schlitz 2006: 2).

primarily at novelists and memoirists writing in English in the 1920s through the 1940s, including James Joyce, H.D., Mary Butts, and the two who appeared in Chapter 5 as witnesses to girls' differential relationship to the classics, Naomi Mitchison and Virginia Woolf. These writers regularly draw on the practice of archaeology and the knowledge of Greek (for Schliemann an essential preparatory step) as models through which to construe the relationships among childhood and adulthood, antiquity and modernity. In previous chapters, learning Greek has emerged as a hallmark of the advanced schooling that distinguishes boys from girls as they leave childhood behind. In this chapter, we discover not only men whose paths in life depend on the formal study of Greek but also women who reclaim the Greek language as an intuitive medium of expression that is aligned with childhood and capable of redeeming a sharply gendered world from its patriarchal, class-bound, and militaristic values.

Schliemann's trajectory from the wholehearted enjoyment of myth to the learning of Greek (a "happiness" for which as a young man just starting out he ceaselessly prayed, and to which he subsequently devoted himself for two years) to the establishment of historical fact recalls the progressive scenario envisioned by Kingsley for the young male readers of his book. The career of the American modernist poet, memoirist, and novelist H.D. (1886–1961) offers another example of a lifelong vocation formed by childhood experience of mythology that is more in the romantic spirit exemplified by Hawthorne. In *The Gift*, a book about her childhood in Pennsylvania in the last years of the nineteenth century, H.D. testifies to the currency of Hawthorne's works four decades after their publication and confirms his understanding of how the mythic fuses with the personal in a child's imagination. For the child H.D., as for the young Schliemann, the appeal of classical myth is linked to the power of illustrations and the heightened excitement of Christmas. Together with two of the most important figures of her childhood, her older brother and the family servant Ida ("our devoted friend, who did the cooking and read Grimm's tales to us at night before we went to sleep" (H.D. 1998: 35)), she eyes the cardboard carton that contains the figures of the Christmas crèche, and her thoughts travel to another box:

There was a picture of Pandora and her box in the *Tanglewood Tales* that Miss Helen read us, Friday afternoons if we were good, instead of lessons. Pandora let all evil things out of the box but there was one good thing left: Miss Helen explained it was a myth. The good thing left was hope.   (94)[2]

Contained in a book, Hawthorne's tales are nonetheless received by H.D. and her classmates as they are in his fictional scenario, orally (now through reading aloud) and as pleasurable alternatives to school-work; and they come with the added bonus of illustrations.

In H.D.'s mind, the Greek myth merges with the Christian traditions of her family. Because "it was not time to take out the animals, we did the Christmas-tree things first" (94), the children just play with the box: Ida cuts the string that keeps it closed, and they lift the lid. In this they are reenacting the myth without its disastrous ending, since Hawthorne makes a point of the knotted cord with which Pandora's box is tied, and of untying that knot, then lifting the lid "to take just one peep" (Hawthorne 1982: 1222) as the first steps towards opening it.[3] H.D. and her brother fulfill Hawthorne's vision of the Pandora myth as a story about modern American children, which is made explicit by his narrator, Eustace Bright, who also anticipates H.D.'s association of the box with Christmas.

> Just imagine, my little hearers, how busy your wits would be, if there were a great box in the house, which, as you might have reason to suppose, contained something new and pretty for your Christmas or New Year's gifts! Do you think that you should be less curious than Pandora? If you were left alone with the box, might you not feel a little tempted to lift the lid? . . . Pandora . . . felt just as anxious to take a peep, as any of these little girls, here around me, would have felt.   (1220)

Another of H.D.'s reminiscences shows that for her, as for Hawthorne with his avowed distaste for the Greek sources, the significance of a myth transcends the particular text in which it is recounted. She recalls a difficult milestone of her childhood, her family's move from the small town of Bethlehem to a suburb of Philadelphia when she was 9. As they unpack in the new house, she asks for her copy of *Grimms' Fairy Tales*

---

[2] H.D.'s attribution of the Pandora story to *Tanglewood Tales* rather than *A Wonder-Book* may be a mistake, but could also reflect the fact that the two books were sometimes described together under that name and *A Wonder-Book* was sometimes published as a first *Tanglewood Tales*.

[3] "The box, I had almost forgotten to say, was fastened; not by a lock, nor by any other such contrivance, but by a very intricate knot of gold cord" (Hawthorne 1982: 1219).

and her mother sheepishly admits that she gave it away. H.D. responds with despair and defiance. "In the new house, with everything empty and no clock ticking in the hall, I knew that something dreadful was going to be told. It was so dreadful that I really didn't care." But her indifference to the lost book turns from bravado into a deeper truth: "it did not matter. How could it? It was only an old book, it was falling to pieces, she had given it away, some other child—I forgot it then, or rather . . . [H.D.'s ellipsis] the pictures came true in my head" (H.D. 1998: 101).

H.D. then reproduces the thought process through which the illustrated myth is realized as her own inalienable birthright.

I could see the first picture, the bright princess with the ball and the frog in the corner to the left and then the large dancing-bear and the girl going up the glass-mountain with spikes she stuck in the ice-sides of the mountain.

I was part of the ice of the mountain, it had happened long ago.

I did not care. Why should I? There was the princess with the brothers, she had long hair and lilies in her arms, there were ravens and the little hut in the forest. All that had been given away—it was not possible—you can not give away yourself with a star on your forehead and your brothers flying over a tower above a forest and a hut in the woods.   (101)

While the story in question is a European fairy tale rather than a classical myth, she goes on to assert its identity with both classical and Christian traditions.

That was the book, it had gone anyway now; Grimm was the children's Bible Mama used to say. It was fairy-tales, but so was the Greek myth, *Tanglewood Tales* that Miss Helen read in school, it was the same kind of thing, it was real. It went on happening, it did not stop.   (101)

Like Schliemann, H.D. portrays herself as a child for whom the unshakeable possession of a myth is a source of strength that counters the disadvantages of childhood, underlying the child's independent self-assertion in the face of a disappointing, uncooperative parent.[4] Here too that strength is tied to a conviction that myths are real, but real in an entirely different sense: not as a facts to be established in adulthood, but as archetypes to be relived at all stages of life ("It went on happening,

---

[4] In Braymer's retelling, Schliemann's reception of the myth occurs as it does for H.D., through the direct internalization of an image: "There was a book open on his lap, and its pictures were engraved forever on his mind's eye" (Braymer 1960: 26–7; cf. "the pictures came true in my head").

it did not stop") and as keys to the inherent grandeur of ordinary experience.

For H.D., as for Schliemann, this conviction was the foundation of a lifelong project, but again in an entirely different way. Fulfilling Hawthorne's view of classical myths as belonging just as much to "a modern Yankee" as to "an old Greek," H.D. made them the basis of personal as well as national histories. Her extensive literary output, encompassing poems, novels, translations, and memoirs, was shaped by her identification of her own experiences with the landscapes and myths of ancient Greece. In brief lyrics, she used Greek settings and poetic styles to craft controlled, displaced expressions of her own emotions. In other poems, she offered pointed revisions of myths from the perspectives of such figures as Demeter, Eurydice, and Calypso, correcting the male-centered, patriarchal, and militaristic tradition through testaments to female experience and subjectivity. Towards the end of her life, she wrote "Helen in Egypt," a revisionist epic centered on the mythical figure who meant most to her (in part because she shared the name of her own mother, Helen), at once a veiled autobiography and a summation of her feminist, pacifist, and mystical vision.[5]

H.D.'s myth-infused poetics, like Schliemann's archaeological science, was an adult's advanced technique for validating an understanding of antiquity first grasped in childhood; the ongoing validity of myth was for her too a matter of scientific discovery as well as of personal experience. Looking back at her blissful love of the family dog, now appearing in her dreams, she writes:

Mythology is actuality, as we now know. The dog with his gold-brown wool, his great collar and the barrel, is of course none other than our old friend Ammon-Ra, whose avenue of horned sphinxes runs along the sand from the old landing-stage of the Nile barges to the wide portals of the temple at Karnak.

(H.D. 1998: 84)

The recent knowledge to which H.D. refers derives in particular from two disciplines that had emerged during her lifetime and by which she was herself deeply influenced, psychoanalysis and anthropology; both broke new ground by making the imagination an object of study and by

---

[5] H.D.'s Hellenism is so pervasive that virtually every discussion of her work touches on it. For overviews, see Swann 1962, Gregory 1997, Murnaghan 2008. For H.D.'s biography, see Guest 2003.

showing that childhood experiences and childlike conceptions determine beliefs and behaviors at all stages of life.

The Mythical Method

H.D.'s embrace of myth as a pattern through which to make sense of an individual life was a personal legacy from childhood but also a literary strategy broadly shared with many writers of her period. In his famous 1923 essay, "Ulysses, Order, and Myth," T. S. Eliot offered a manifesto for "the mythical method," in which he redefines classicism as a means of giving expression to a writer's own experience: not "turning away from nine-tenths of the stuff that lies at hand and selecting only mummified stuff from a museum" but rather "doing the best one can with the material at hand." His example is Joyce's identification of the experiences of contemporary Dubliners with the Odysseus myth: "In using the myth, in manipulating a continuous parallel between contemporaneity and antiquity, Mr. Joyce is pursuing a method which others must pursue after him . . . It is simply a way of controlling, of ordering, of giving a shape and a significance to the immense panorama of futility and anarchy which is contemporary history" (Eliot 1975: 176–7). As a means of ordering experience, the mythical method supplants the linear structure of narrative, replacing it with a nexus of embedded meanings that are constantly present, as in H.D.'s myth that "went on happening, it did not stop." Eliot goes on to identify Yeats as another practitioner of the "method," which also informed the work of Eliot himself and many others.

In her recreations of childhood consciousness, H.D. shows with particular vividness how the mythical method is anticipated in a child's instinctive connection to myth, but the reminiscences of other modernists give similar indications. In a conversation with his student Georges Borach, Joyce identified his interest in Ulysses as the consequence of a childhood preference: "I was twelve years old when we took up the Trojan War at school; only the *Odyssey* stuck in my memory. I want to be candid: at twelve I liked the mysticism in Ulysses . . . Why was I always returning to this theme? Now *al mezzo del camin* I find the subject of Ulysses the most human in world literature."[6] Joyce's formulation

---

[6] Borach 1954: 325. This is a slightly misquoted and misspelled version of the opening words of Dante's *Divine Comedy: nel mezzo del cammin di nostra vita*, "midway through the

captures the alignment of the personal and the cultural that underlies the modernist identification of antiquity with childhood: the adult's continual return to the most formative experiences of childhood parallels the modern world's continual return to the seminal archetypes of the classical past.

Despite its childhood roots, the mythical method is an adult project of reconstruction and reappropriation, as Joyce's return to the past from the vantage point of middle age indicates. It may sometimes be an expression of nostalgia, a longing to recover lost states of clarity and wholeness associated both with childhood and with premodern culture, but it belongs on an equal footing with forms of knowledge associated with adulthood and scientific progress. This is hinted at in Joyce's suggestion that he returns to Ulysses in a midlife quest for a definition of the human and overtly stated by Eliot, who not only uses the term "method," but also asserts that Joyce's "parallel use of the Odyssey . . . has the importance of a scientific discovery," and goes on to specify the new forms of science to which this parallelism is allied: "Psychology (such as it is, and whether our reaction to it be comic or serious), ethnology, and *The Golden Bough* have concurred to make possible what was impossible even a few years ago" (Eliot 1975: 178).

While nostalgia is undoubtedly one element in modernist uses of myth, the method identified by Eliot, and the new disciplines that support it, offer more conflicted and dynamic pictures of both childhood and the past than we find in idealizing visions such as Hawthorne's "happy era" of which "children are now the only representatives." Eliot himself saw idealized childhood reminiscences as a sign of regression and self-indulgence: in a 1927 review of a book by the Georgian poet Edmund Blunden about the metaphysical poet Henry Vaughan, he takes Blunden to task for treating "a love of one's own childhood" as "a token of greatness":

We all know the mood; and we can, if we choose to relax to that extent, indulge in the luxury of the reminiscence of childhood; but if we are at all mature or

journey of our life," through which Dante situates his autobiographical narrative in the year when he was 35. Joyce encountered the Ulysses myth in Charles Lamb's *The Adventures of Ulysses*, which he read at school. Assigned to write an essay on "My Favourite Hero," he chose Ulysses over such expected figures as Achilles and Hector (Gorman 1939: 45; S. Joyce 1958: 43).

conscious, we refuse to indulge this weakness to the point of writing or
poetizing about it. We know that it is something to be buried and done with,
though its corpse will from time to time find its way up to the surface.

(Eliot 1927: 260–1)

Making the connection between ancient myths and childhood deliberately and in maturity may involve coming to terms with a period of
turbulence and trauma, a deadly time producing corpses that refuse to lie
still, rather than returning to a time of unalloyed happiness. This is the
case with the first of Eliot's sciences, psychology, or more specifically
psychoanalysis, which reflects the conjunction, at the turn of the twentieth century, of new and less idealized conceptions of childhood with
new and less idealized conceptions of antiquity.

Freud's invention of psychoanalysis entails an especially far-reaching
and influential exercise of the mythical method: the identification of a
classical myth, the myth of Oedipus, as a universal template for ordinary
experience in all historical periods, including the present.[7] The significance of the Oedipus myth, as he presents it in *The Interpretation of
Dreams*, derives from its resonance with childhood experience, but the
child's relationship to the myth is far from the easy embrace that we have
seen repeatedly summoned up in childhood reminiscences and solicited
in successive child-friendly retellings. Children respond with horror, not
to a version of the myth itself, but to the discovery in their own personal
relations of impulses towards its signature acts of incest and parricide,
acts that make it the suitable subject of a tragedy for adults rather than
children's literature; the Oedipus myth is one of Hawthorne's "old
legends . . . amid which the Greek Tragedians sought their themes, and
moulded them into the sternest forms of grief that ever the world saw,"
which can only be presented to children if they are purified and infused
with sunshine (Hawthorne 1982: 1310). According to Hawthorne (or at
least his narrator Eustace Bright), disturbing events like those of the
Oedipus myth are inessential and fall away when myths are made to
conform to the innocent sensibility of children. But for Freud, with his
very different conception of childhood, those same features are essential

---

[7] On Freud's universalization of the Oedipus myth and the personal and cultural roots of
his interest in Oedipus, see esp. Armstrong 2005: 47–62; Bowlby 2007: 14–46; Leonard
2013; Rudnytsky 1987: 3–223; Winter 1999: 25–53. On his reading in classical literature and
scholarship, see Mitchell-Boyask 1994.

sources of the myth's lifelong power precisely because they capture children's psychic experience.

On Freud's interpretation, Oedipus' actions fulfill desires that represent—at least for men, whom he treats as normative—a universal and unwelcome birthright, in fact a curse: "His destiny moves us only because it might have been ours—because the oracle laid the same curse on us before our birth as upon him. It is the fate of all of us, perhaps, to direct our first sexual impulse toward our mothers, and our first hatred and our first murderous wish against our father" (*SE* 4: 262).[8] Those feelings are not only suffered but also repudiated and repressed within the span of childhood: as adults "we shrink back from him with the whole force of the repression by which those wishes have since that time been held down within us" (*SE* 4: 263). A childhood drama of apprehension and denial determines the structure of adult psychic experience, in which childhood memories are anything but idyllic. "Like Oedipus, we live in ignorance of these wishes, repugnant to morality, which have been forced on us by Nature, and after their revelation we may all of us well seek to close our eyes to the scenes of our childhood" (*SE* 4: 263).

In Freud's version of the familiar nineteenth-century mapping of the individual lifespan onto human history, the identification of such a childhood with classical antiquity depends on a view of the ancient world as combining warring elements of unruly emotion and determined repression.[9] This was facilitated by developments in the study of antiquity during the decades leading up to *The Interpretation of Dreams* (first published in 1900): the discovery of prehistory and of the ongoing presence of prehistoric elements within classical culture, and the emergence of archaeology as a new method of historical research. During the period of Freud's intellectual formation, deeply rooted views of an idealized classical past (associated with such earlier figures as Hegel, Winckelmann, and von Humboldt) were challenged and complicated by the recognition of inescapable traces of the primitive within the culture of classical Greece, revealed both in the archaeological remains

[8] Unless otherwise noted, references to Freud's works are from the *Standard Edition* (*SE*), ed. and trans. James Strachey (1953–74).

[9] On Freud's relationship to biologically-oriented recapitulation theory (according to which "ontogeny recapitulates phylogeny"), see S. J. Gould 1977: 155–61; Sulloway 1992; Ritvo 1990: 74–98.

of prehistory in such sites as Mycenae and in the evident affinities between Greek religion, myth, and poetry and expressions of primitive culture everywhere.[10] The Greek world, which had been cordoned off from previous history and constructed as a pure point of origin for Western culture, was now directly impinged upon by a primitive past; this past asserted itself in remnants and survivals, often revealed in connection with civilization's efforts to control and suppress them.

How well this vision of ancient history suits Freud's model of child-hood as a series of developmental stages can be seen in his application of the theory, first proposed by the Swiss anthropologist and legal historian Bachofen, that the patriarchal order of the historical era was preceded by a period of prehistoric matriarchy. The historical transition from matri-archy to patriarchy was understood as an advance in civilization that brought the invention of law and the rule of reason—as Freud puts it, "a victory of intellectuality over sensuality." This transition had been com-pleted by the classical period but "an echo of this revolution seems still to be audible in the *Oresteia* of Aeschylus" (*Moses and Monotheism, SE* 23: 114)—a trilogy in which the passionate attachments and violent conflicts of the family are overcome through the establishment of law and the elevation of paternity and connection to the father over the claims of maternity and connection to the mother.

On this interpretation, echoes of the primitive in competition with civilization are similarly audible in *Oedipus the King,* where the sensual impulses of nature are also in tension with the hero's unsuccessful efforts to deny and master them by avoiding his fated actions. Oedipus is undone by his failure to escape a destiny of incest and patricide, but both Aeschy-lus' trilogy and Sophocles' play record a similar cultural struggle, corres-ponding in each case to the same developmental challenge for the individual who must negotiate the formative stages of childhood. Both reflect the male protagonist's need to leave his mother behind and identify positively with his father in the interests of order, rationality, and progress. In the case of Orestes, this work is accomplished within the ancient myth; in the case of Oedipus, it is left to the individual to negotiate the stage of development that is defined by the Oedipus complex and to make a successful transition to adult life, entering (if they are male) into a wider

---

[10] Armstrong 2005: 29.

sphere that corresponds to modern life.[11] Either way, the textual record of Greek antiquity is a privileged witness because the proximity of the Greeks to prehistory means that the call of primordial emotion can still be heard in their myths.[12]

The fact that Greek prehistory was hidden from view and had to be rediscovered by means of excavation and fresh interpretations of the classical sources made it an especially apt parallel for a period of childhood involving feelings that are necessarily repressed and only later accessed through vague memories or, when insufficiently repressed, through mysterious neurotic symptoms. Freud famously compared his own discovery of the true nature of childhood experience to the revolutionary new findings of ancient historians and archaeologists.[13] As he refined his view of the Oedipus complex to account for female development, he noted that, "Our insight into the early, pre-Oedipus, phase in girls comes to us as a surprise, like the discovery, in another field, of the Minoan-Mycenean civilization behind the civilization of Greece" (*SE* 21: 226). And, in a letter to his friend Fliess, he drew an explicit parallel between himself and Schliemann as both having proven the truth of what had been dismissed as fantasy: when a breakthrough with a patient involved discovering "buried beneath all of his fantasies . . . a scene from his primal period (before twenty-two months)," he proclaimed, "It is everything at the same time—sexual, innocent, natural, and the rest. I scarcely dare believe it yet. It is as if Schliemann had once more excavated Troy, which had hitherto been deemed a fable" (Freud 1985: 391–2).

Archaeology corresponds most closely to the work of analysis when archaeological excavation is understood, not as scraping away the gradual residue of a long, indifferent span of time (as is generally the case), but as undoing a form of concealment that belongs, like the repression built into the Oedipus myth, to antiquity itself. One of Freud's clearest

---

[11] The different prospects for girls and boys in relation to Freud's deployment of classical mythology are discussed in Bowlby 2007: 146–68.

[12] Thus Freud notes in *The Interpretation of Dreams* that Oedipal themes are treated more opaquely in *Hamlet* because Shakespeare belongs to a later historical period, which reflects "the secular advance of repression in the emotional life of mankind" (*SE* 4: 264).

[13] On Freud's extensive use of archaeology as an analogue to psychoanalysis, see esp. Armstrong 2005: 39, 46, 109–17, 183–200; Colby 2009: 87–139; and on the influence of Schliemann in particular, Gay 1988: 172.

articulations of the parallel involves an episode of wholesale burial that occurred within ancient history, the disappearance of Pompeii through the eruption of Vesuvius. This occurs in his analysis of Wilhelm Jensen's novella *Gradiva*, the story of an archaeologist, Norbert Hanold, who is blind to his own erotic desires.[14] Hanold's interest is aroused only by an ancient relief depicting a woman with a beautiful gait. In his obsession with this relief, he feels a mysterious compulsion to visit Pompeii. There he imagines that he meets the original of the relief, a girl who died in the eruption of Vesuvius now returned to life, but he comes to realize that he is actually reencountering a contemporary young woman, his childhood love Zoe Bertgang. In childhood, Hanold had repressed his feelings for Zoe and replaced them with a single-minded devotion to archaeology. The novella's plot corrects this wrong turn as Hanold and Zoe are reunited and become engaged. As antiquarian inquiry turns into self-discovery, an ancient artifact reveals the archaeologist's own forgotten childhood self rather than forgotten truths about antiquity: as Freud puts it, the marble sculpture "tore our archaeologist away from his retreat from love and warned him to pay off the debt to life with which we are burdened from our birth" (*SE* 9: 49). Zoe herself registers this shift of attention as she thinks about the "childhood friend who had been dug out of the ruins." With this metaphor, Freud notes,

the author has presented us with the key to the symbolism of which the hero's delusion made use in disguising his repressed memory. There is, in fact, no better analogy for repression, by which something in the mind is at once made inaccessible and preserved, than burial of the sort to which Pompeii fell a victim and from which it could emerge once more through the work of spades. Thus it was that the young archaeologist was obliged in his phantasy to transport to Pompeii the original of the relief that reminded him of the object of his youthful love.   (*SE* 9: 40)

In Jensen's fable, the link between the burial of the past within antiquity and the childhood roots of adult difficulties is brought to light through the protagonist's instinctive responses to his own obsessions and delusions. This fictional scenario earns Jensen Freud's professional respect: in constructing Hanold's delusion, Jensen "was well justified, indeed, in

---

[14] On Freud's interpretation of *Gradiva*, see Armstrong 2005: 12–25; Bowlby 1992: 157–80; Rudnytsky: 1994; Colby: 2009, 103–10, and esp. 104 for the archaeological motif as a metaphor for lost and recovered love in other fictional works of the same period.

lingering over the valuable similarity which his delicate sense had perceived between a particular mental process in the individual and an isolated historical event in the history of mankind" (*SE* 9: 40). Jensen has intuited the parallel between individual experience and human history—the recapitulation of phylogeny by ontogeny—that Freud has discovered through scientific research.

As Freud presents it, the tight link between childhood experience and antiquity is inescapable but so disturbing that it is generally and purposefully ignored. Most adults do not stop to ask why they are especially moved by Sophocles' play; only those who undergo psychoanalysis or accept its guiding principles understand the hidden power of the Oedipus myth. Children too are inattentive to the significance of classical myths: in *The Question of Lay Analysis*, as he considers the myth of Cronus swallowing his children, a vivid account of violent intergenerational conflict, Freud observes "How strange this must have sounded to you when you first heard it! But I suppose none of us thought about it at the time" (*SE* 20: 211). The full meaning of ancient myths emerges in the hard-won and often painful discoveries (comparable to the archaeologist's "work of spades") of the adult researcher, who stands apart from childhood and recognizes it as a recurrent reenactment of the collective human past—the anthropologically-informed myth expert, the psychoanalyst, or the finely sensitive novelist. As Freud goes on to say in the same essay, "it was only through the knowledge of infantile sexuality that it became possible to understand mythology and the world of fairy tales. Here then something has been gained as a by-product of analytic studies" (*SE* 20: 211).

The Romance of Archaeology

Wilhelm Jensen may earn Freud's respect for his intuitive understanding of the parallel between childhood repression and the burial of Pompeii, but his vision differs significantly from Freud's. In his story, what is denied in childhood is something precious, and its rediscovery is a source of joy (even if Freud describes the protagonist's erotic fulfillment as a debt and a burden). In this respect, Jensen resembles Schliemann, who also portrays archaeology as the means by which childhood desires are gladly fulfilled. Freud himself remarked on this in one of his letters to Fliess: "I gave myself a present, Schliemann's *Ilios*, and greatly enjoyed the account of his childhood. The man was happy when he found

Priam's treasure, because happiness comes only with the fulfillment of a childhood wish" (Freud 1985: 353). Accepting the narrative as authentic, Freud saw Schliemann's achievement as a rare exception to his own conclusion that childhood fantasies are so grand and voracious that they are virtually impossible to sustain or realize in adult life; subjected to a "reality principle," they are inevitably tempered by taking "into account the conditions imposed by the real external world" (*SE* 20: 201).

Freud's reaction highlights the fictional nature of Schliemann's narrative and shows just how much Schliemann is able to enhance the value of his archaeological achievements by giving them a childhood genesis. In locating the wish to discover Troy in a dispute with his father, Schliemann also constructs a scenario that invites analysis in Freud's own terms, as a classic case of Oedipal conflict. He turns his triumph over his father in a debate about ancient history into a far-reaching victory that makes up for other childhood disappointments, for which his father is also responsible.

In constructing this account of Oedipal triumph, Schliemann had the advantage of a genuinely inadequate father as well as a flair for narrative. Ernst Schliemann was a Lutheran pastor in the small German village of Ankershagen, whose career was shadowed and eventually derailed by personal and financial indiscretions. On the death of his wife, when Heinrich was 9, he began an open affair with one of the family servants; his parishioners responded with public displays of disgust (banging pots and pans outside the house on Sundays) and Heinrich and his siblings were banned from contact with other children. Heinrich was sent away to live with an uncle and began studies at a classical gymnasium, but then his father was suspended from his position because of an embezzlement charge, and Heinrich moved to the vocational *Realschule*; as a result he had to make his own fortune in business and to learn Greek and other languages on his own.

As he elaborates on his childhood vocation, Schliemann presents archaeology as the means of regaining everything that his father's failings deny him. As a child with "a natural disposition for the mysterious and the marvelous," he is highly responsive to romantic legends about Ankershagen.

Vast treasures were said to be buried close to the ruins of a round tower in the garden of the proprietor of the village. My faith in the existence of these treasures was so great that, whenever I heard my father complain of his poverty, I always expressed my astonishment that he did not dig up the silver bowl or the golden cradle, and so become rich.   (Schliemann 1976: 1–2)

For all its childish credulity, Heinrich's suggestion anticipates the steps he himself will take to overcome his impoverished beginnings, first by becoming rich, then by digging up gold and silver artifacts.

As in Jensen's novella, archaeology is also bound up with the loss and recovery of romantic love. As a boy, Schliemann shares his dream with a neighbor girl, Minna Meincke, who takes it as seriously as he does, and at the age of 9 they exchange "vows of eternal love." Their feelings for each other are channeled into historical research as they use the occasion of dancing lessons to examine interesting relics, visit a nearby cemetery, study the church register, or interview old-timers, all of which "increased our passion for the mysterious." Their intention is that "as soon as we were grown up we would marry, and then set about to explore all the mysteries of Ankershagen . . . and lastly Troy; nay we could imagine nothing pleasanter than to spend all our lives in digging for the relics of the past" (5). In this fantasy of married happiness, the unearthing of ancient artifacts goes hand in hand with another way of discovering hidden treasure, through the satisfaction of erotic desires repressed in childhood.

After the death of his mother, his father's disgrace deprives him of Minna, who is no longer allowed to associate with him. "The future appeared dark to me; all the wonders of Ankershagen and even Troy itself lost their interest for a time." But his belief in Troy is unquenchable, so that he reaches his goal even though—thanks to his feckless father— "it was not destined for me to realize till in the autumn of my life, and then without Minna—nay, far from her—the sweet dreams of fifty years ago" (5–6). When he goes on to describe that excavation, Minna's place is filled by his second wife Sophia.

At length, on the 27th of September, I made my way to the Dardanelles, together with my wife, Sophia Schliemann, who is a native of Athens and a warm admirer of Homer, and who, with glad enthusiasm, joined me in executing the great work which, nearly half a century ago, my childish simplicity had agreed on with my father and planned with Minna.   (21)

Sophia's double role as archaeological accomplice and erotic object is captured in a famous photograph in which she appears adorned with "Priam's treasure." In another of Schliemann's fabricated anecdotes, the two of them unearth the treasure alone together, with the workmen conveniently sent away on a lunch break, and she carries it out in her shawl (like the secret baby conceived in an illicit tryst).[15]

The fantastic nature of Schliemann's narrative is thrown into relief, not only by Freud's comment, but also by its inverse relation to a famous episode in Freud's own biography. While Schliemann traveled to Troy to affirm the reality of the events he had always believed to be true, Freud's own travels to Greece had the opposite effect.[16] When he climbed the Acropolis during his first visit to Athens in 1904, his response to finding himself at the actual site of ancient events was not satisfaction but surprise: "So all this really *does* exist, just as we learned at school." Years later, Freud was still puzzling over this reaction, with its counterfactual implication that as a child he had doubted the existence of the Acropolis. In his analysis of the event, in a letter to Romain Rolland written in 1936 (*SE* 22: 238–48), he concludes that this "disturbance of memory" was a way of displacing onto the remoter past an unwillingness to believe that the Acropolis was real that he felt at the time of his visit, and he interprets that conviction of unreality as an attempt to separate himself from the very wish to visit Greece.

For Freud, the wish to visit Greece has to be repudiated because, like Schliemann's wish to find Troy, it represents a desire to outdo his father, from which he recoiled. The ambition to leave home and travel is "rooted . . . in dissatisfaction with home and family"; the adult traveler's guilt at his "satisfaction in having gone such a long way" is inspired by the child's forbidden criticism of his father. "It seems as though the

---

[15] As Schliemann himself later admitted, Sophia was in Athens at the time. See Traill 1995: 112. Schliemann makes it clear that the loss of Minna eclipsed the trauma that led to it, the death of his mother. In an episode involving Sir Arthur Evans, the excavator of Crete, the archaeologist's "discovery" compensated for the childhood loss of his mother. Evans accepted as real finds an assemblage of forged objects that brought together figurines of a boy-god and a mother-goddess and that resembled a set of objects he had buried in his garden as a boy of seven after the death of his mother. On this episode, see Gere 2009: 132–9.

[16] In his earlier autobiographical writings, composed before his dispute with Calvert, Schliemann identifies his own childhood ambitions simply with travel to Greece: "At last I was able to realize the dream of my life, and to visit at my leisure . . . the country of the heroes whose adventures had delighted and comforted my childhood" (Schliemann 1976: 18). Even such tourism involves outdoing his father, who "often told me with warm enthusiasm of the tragic fate of Herculaneum and Pompeii, and seemed to consider him the luckiest of men who had the means and the time to visit the excavations that were going on there" (3).

essence of success was to have gotten further than one's father, and as though to have excelled one's father was still something forbidden" (*SE* 22: 247). The specific destination of Athens makes the voyage yet more transgressive, because an interest in Greece reflects a level of education that Freud's own father never reached. With a father who is merely poor and not an embarrassing failure, Freud cannot allow himself unalloyed pleasure in an action that implies childhood disloyalty. A different attitude towards his father generates different feelings about arriving at the site of ancient glory, which lead in turn to a different reconstruction of his childhood views about the reality of ancient history. But Freud and Schliemann are alike in that for both, as products of a culture in which classical learning represented high achievement and in which boys regularly met ancient legends at home and ancient history at school, contact with the material reality of a classical site was a sign of arrival; whether asserted by Schliemann or accepted with guilty hesitation by Freud, the realness of the ancient setting confirms a successful passage from the mere dreams of childhood to efficacious adult achievement.[17]

For a fictional project of a different kind that also makes a "mystical" myth known in childhood correspond to reality, we return to Joyce's *Ulysses*, which provides a further example of Schliemann's cultural impact. Joyce built on his childhood love of the Odysseus myth to produce a fictional narrative in which a realistic and entirely human version of the hero, together with other figures from his legend, are situated in a meticulously realistic recreation of turn-of-the-century Dublin. Joyce manifests Schliemann's influence by emulating, not Schliemann himself (in the manner of Freud), but Homer as Schliemann's excavations had defined him: the reliable guide to a lost city.

"I want," said Joyce, as we were walking down the Universitätstrasse, "to give a picture of Dublin so complete that if the city one day suddenly disappeared from the earth it could be reconstructed out of my book."[18]

---

[17] Whether or not they confirm the universal validity of Freud's views, the resemblances between Freud's reminiscence and Schliemann's autobiography reflect this shared historical context. On the Oedipus complex as naturalizing and universalizing the classical education and professional formation of Freud's own Viennese milieu, see Winter 1999: 40–53. For an insightful account of "Freud's modeling of his own scientific improvisation on Schliemann's biomythography," see Armstrong 2005: 114–17.

[18] Budgen 1934: 67–68.

Like Schliemann, the "warm defender of the Trojan cause," Joyce pro-
leptically saves his threatened city through feats of memory and research
and the faithful recording of topographical landmarks and domestic
details. Ordinary objects are endowed with further value as clues for a
Schliemann of the future as the familiar terrain of Joyce's youth is
implicitly equated with the landscapes of classical legend.

   In making that equation, Joyce was inspired in part by another, and
less widely accepted, late nineteenth-century image of Homer: the authoress of the *Odyssey* as reconstructed by Samuel Butler.[19] Like Schliemann,
and under the influence of his discoveries, Butler approached the Homeric
epics as records of real experience, from which objects could be identified,
buildings reconstructed, and places recognized. In addition, he argued on
the basis of extensive, first-hand topographical research (backed up by
photographs), that the *Odyssey* had been written by a young Sicilian
woman, who put herself into the poem as the princess Nausicaa and
used the geographical details of her own small city of Trapani and the
waters surrounding Sicily as the basis for the *Odyssey*'s far-flung and often
fantastic settings. Butler attributes this procedure to the authoress' particular aesthetic "which consists in wise selection and judicious application
of materials derived from life" and adds that "no artist can reach an ideal
higher than his own best actual environment" (S. Butler 1967: 208). But
the circumstances he imagines for the *Odyssey*'s genesis also suggest the
imaginative tendencies of childhood, since children often equate the settings of stories with their own surroundings and invest those surroundings
with the mystery and importance of legendary scenes, viewing the first
places they know as both paradigmatic and magical.

   Following an aesthetic similar to that praised by Butler, Joyce achieved
in *Ulysses* a considered, adult refinement of this child's vision of home.
The novel captures the world of Joyce's own childhood at the point at
which he left it behind: the date of its events, June 16, 1904, tallies with
Joyce's early twenties and with the period when he left Ireland to live
abroad for the rest of his life. Unlike the hypothetical authoress of the
Odyssey, Joyce keeps the fictionalized version of his home entirely nat-
uralistic; rather than making his childhood world the basis of a fantasy,
he memorializes it in its actuality; at the same time, through an extended

---

[19] On the influence of both Schliemann and Butler on Joyce, see Kenner 1969;
1971: 41–50.

classical allusion, he also grants it the stature and significance of myth. While Joyce's Dublin is transformed in this way by identification with the *Odyssey* myth, that myth is also transformed: no longer, as in his childhood, the sign of otherworldly mysteries, it is now a pattern that matches the real-world experiences of ordinary people, who unknowingly confirm its validity as they go about their lives.

H.D.'s Mythical Childhood

Freud's interpretation of myth was a significant factor in H.D.'s many reworkings of the childhood legacy evoked in her autobiographical writings. H.D. was herself a student of Freud, with whom she worked, and by whom she was analyzed, during a difficult period of writer's block in 1933–4, an experience that she memorialized in a memoir, *Tribute to Freud*. There she presents a memory from her own childhood through an analytic lens that highlights the discrepancy between an adult's mythically informed retrospection and the immediate experiences of children. Summoning up a traumatic incident of Oedipal conflict, in which her brother is in trouble for taking the magnifying glass from their father's study, she contrasts the hapless ignorance of that moment with her current knowledge of the mythical pattern that was being played out— actually but unconsciously.

I do not know, he does not know that this, besides being the magnifying glass from our father's table, is a sacred symbol . . . I did not know this when I stood beside my brother in the garden. It is only now that I write this that I see how my father possessed sacred symbols, how he, like the Professor [H.D.'s name for Freud], had old, old sacred objects on his study table. But the shape and form of these objects, sanctified by time, were not so identified. They were just a glass paper-weight, just a brass paper-knife or the ordinary magnifying glass that my brother is still holding in his hand.

What will my brother say? He cannot say, "I brought fire from heaven." He cannot answer father Zeus in elegant iambics and explain how he Prometheus, by his wit and daring, by his love of the unknown, by his experimentation with occult, as yet unexplainable forces, has drawn down fire from the sky. It is an actual fact. But my brother has never heard of Prometheus, he doesn't know any Greek. (H.D. 1984: 25)

In *The Gift*, as we have seen, the child H.D. identifies herself and her brother with Hawthorne's child versions of Pandora and Epimetheus, but here the adult H.D. identifies her brother with the adult Prometheus, and he gains in retrospect an adult's dignity and stature, transformed from a powerless, disobedient child with nothing to say for himself into a self-assertive adult who answers his father on equal terms and who, like his astronomer father, is an intellectual explorer fascinated by the heavens (with an interest in the occult that also assimilates him to Freud and to H.D. herself).

Like Freud, H.D. uses a classical myth to reinterpret a child's traumatic experience and to rescue him in retrospect from its debilitating effects, but she chooses a more optimistic mythical analogue. Prometheus is, like Oedipus, a rebel and an intellectual explorer, but he does not destroy the father figure he defies; Zeus is not actually Prometheus' father (but his cousin), and the two are destined to be reconciled in the end. Yet H.D.'s transformation and rescue of her brother is only notional, confined to the revised understanding she shares with her readers. In this respect, her written memory is less efficacious than Freud's therapeutic practice, in which the expert deployment of mythology transforms and heals the traumatized child still present within the struggling adult. Or, as she puts it in another passage in which she compares Freud to Hercules rescuing Alcestis from death, "he himself has . . . made the dead live, has summoned a host of dead and dying children from the living tomb" (74). Freud's discoveries provide a solution to Eliot's identification of childhood as a lethal time that produces living corpses. But this solution is not available to H.D.'s brother, since by the time she writes he is truly dead, one of many young victims of World War I.

H.D.'s brother cannot rescue himself from his child's predicament because "he doesn't know any Greek," a suggestive phrase that indicates both his stage of life as a not-yet-educated boy and a more metaphorical lack of access to the mythical. Knowing Greek would have been for him, as for the young Schliemann who vows to study Greek in order to find Troy, an adult accomplishment, acquired through formal schooling, which would have put him on an equal footing with his learned father and might have led to scientific achievements of his own. But H.D.'s sophisticated understanding of Greek myths as keys to individual experience is also an adult accomplishment: "it is only now that I write this" that she can see the mythic significance of her childhood memory. Her use of knowing Greek as a figure for the passage from inarticulate helplessness to self-knowledge and self-preservation echoes Freud's own use of translation as a metaphor for the therapeutic process, in which unconscious thoughts are converted into conscious ones,[20] and also his view of psychoanalytic insight as a professional skill that draws on various forms of specialized knowledge, both classical and scientific. The "sacred objects" in H.D.'s father's study, like the archaeological relics in Freud's study, may have occult significance, but they are also tools of a trade, emblems of adult professional achievement.

For H.D., however, the idea of a child's knowledge of Greek, in the sense of a child's personal identification with figures from myth, also had its own undeniable power. The ongoing importance of childhood experience was essential to her Hellenism. Asked about the place of Greece in her early poetry, she explained: "It is nostalgia for a lost land. I call it Hellas. I might, psychologically just as well, have listed the Casco Bay islands off the coast of Maine" (which she visited in one of the summers of her childhood) (H.D. 1938: 1287). When she traveled to Greece, the journey did not signify escape from childhood, victory over the father, worldly achievement, and the display of cultural capital as it did for Schliemann and Freud, but rather a return to origins and a reunion with her mother, whose name was Helen—as Freud himself explained, interpreting the strange visions that she experienced there.

The Professor translated the pictures on the wall, or the picture-writing on the wall of a hotel bedroom in Corfu, that I saw projected there in the spring of 1920, as a desire for union with my mother. I was physically in Greece, in Hellas (Helen). I had come home to the glory that was Greece.   (H.D. 1984: 44)

And yet H.D.'s desire for union with her mother was also bound up with strongly held beliefs on which she disagreed with Freud: she rejected his views of normative human development, in which bisexuality and universal attraction to the female were stages to be left behind rather than, as in her own experience, powerful lifelong constants, and she had a mystical view of myths as pointing to real spiritual forces.[21] When she wrote about her own childhood in *The Gift*, she was trying to awaken a spiritual power rooted in her own early life in Bethlehem, Pennsylvania and in the personal maternal legacy of which Greece was one symbol.

---

[20] "[I]t may be pointed out that the interpretations made by psycho-analysis are first and foremost translations from an alien method of expression into the one which is most familiar to us" (*The Claims of Psycho-Analysis to the Interest of the Non-Psychological Sciences, SE* 13: 176). On this point, see Bowlby 2007: 216.

[21] H.D.'s points of disagreement with Freud are discussed in Friedman 1981: 87–154.

The book is not a straightforward childhood memoir or an expression of nostalgia, but an active response to the terrors of World War II, which H.D. experienced by living through the London Blitz. To cope with those terrors, she undertakes a journey in memory that resembles the work of psychoanalysis, sparked by associations between her present trials and the darkest moments of her childhood (for example, the book begins by linking the threat of incendiary bombing to a horrifying incident in which a girl caught on fire and was burned to death). Yet her goal is not (or not only) the personal cure of psychoanalysis, but the recovery of a tool with which to heal her shattered world.[22]

One event relived in this backward journey is experienced through another classical myth, which is known from reading Hawthorne but also understood in a way that affirms Freud's views of the sexual feelings of children. A child who simultaneously represents H.D's mother and herself visits a fortune teller's tent and starts to think of a trapdoor. Once again, a classical myth comes true in her imagination.

> The thought of dead leaves reminded her of the matted fern on the path and the thought of a trap-door; it was happening now, under her feet, as if the folding-stool she sat on, like the stools they carried on their sketching trips, might simply drop through a hole in the floor, a hole in the earth, like that Greek myth in the *Tanglewood Tales* that they used now as a reader in some of the special classes; there was a girl who was raped away—raped, yes, the word somehow sounding like something out of the Bible—by the darkness, by Dis, by death.   (H.D. 1998: 78)

In this child's mind, Hawthorne's tale is fused with elements from other sources that restore what Hawthorne suppresses as alien to the "childish purity of his auditors": the provocative word "rape," imported (possibly from the title of another version of the story that she has encountered) and turned into a verb; darker biblical associations suggesting sin and punishment. As her train of thought continues, being raped away is associated with sensations of self-surrender: "That was the feeling . . . that back-rose of despair when one was happiest . . . if one were happy, swept quite, quite away, melted away so that even your name was forgotten."

---

[22] *The Gift*'s purposes and technique are well discussed by Jane Augustine in her introduction (H.D. 1998: 1–28) and by Susan Stanford Friedman under the rubric of "the writing cure" (1990: 329–54). The definitive influence of psychoanalysis was stressed by H.D. herself (1986: 192).

The conflicted sexual feelings that are suggested but not named by the expression "raped away" are conveyed through a return to the Bible and in particular to the story of Eve's fall: "a whole set of poetical and biological emotions that there were no names for, that were things having to do with the Tree of the Knowledge of Good and Evil and that were not right."

It is impossible to disentangle the recollected child from the recollecting adult in this reconstruction of a child's mentality for an adult audience. The circumvention of Hawthorne's sanitizing testifies both to the capacity of children to intuit and restore the unsuitable material that adults hide from them, and to the readiness of a twentieth-century adult attuned to psychoanalysis to recognize the sexual feelings (encompassing both pleasure and shame) of children, as well as the spiritual death those feelings can inspire. H.D. might not have remembered childhood this way if she had not engaged with the ideas of Freud and others who shared his views of childhood; at the same time, she confirms via her reconstruction of a child's sensibility the reality of emotions that Freud recognized only as an adult, illustrating the link between mythology and infantile sexuality that he came to as "a by-product of analytic studies."[23]

This memory is one step on a spiritual journey that culminates in the merging of H.D.'s childhood self Hilda into another myth, which signifies the "gift" of the book's title, a spiritual legacy passed down through the female line in H.D.'s maternal family, descendants of the original Moravian settlers of Bethlehem, founded in 1741. This legacy derives from the Holy Spirit as a female force and is linked to female creativity; it belongs to the shared unconscious and universal language that underlies all religions; it forges connections between disparate peoples and is the

---

[23] The views of Freud, the sexuality of children, classical associations, and the utopianism we have seen in historical fiction, also come together in the works of Guy Davenport, in a somewhat later period than that of this study. Davenport's fictions portray the free and various sexual experiences of prepubescent and pubescent children. These have classical precedents (especially in idealized Greek accounts of erotic relations among men) and are identified with utopian settings that include the arcadian realm of ancient pastoral. The collection *Eclogues* (1981) includes the story of a summer of experimentation entitled "On Some Lines of Virgil" (borrowing the title of an essay by Montaigne in which sexual openness is also associated with antiquity). The novella *Wo Es War, Soll Ich Werden*, which takes its title from a statement of Freud's about incorporating elements of the id into the ego, is set in a contemporary utopian Danish school, but it is the classics master who teaches the protagonist to recover and act upon his childhood feelings. See Furlani 2004.

source of peace. The Moravians manifested this gift in their harmonious relations with their Native American neighbors, epitomized in a ceremony in which the Moravian leader's wife, a German noblewoman named Anna von Pahlen, was identified with the Indian princess "Morning Star," who had been baptized by the Moravians. But the truce between the Moravians and the Indians was broken, and the gift had gone dormant in the intervening time, its potential unfulfilled but preserved in H.D.'s maternal line. The book combines detailed, carefully researched information about the history and religion of these ancestors with H.D.'s gradual recognition of her own status as a bearer of the gift.

To arrive at this recognition, H.D. has first to come to terms with betrayal by her mother, whose treacherous side is indicated in the passage already quoted in which she gives away the book of fairy tales but finds its worst expression in her declaration that none of her own children has inherited the gift. As a child, H.D., who equates the gift with musical talent, assumes that her mother has given the gift away to her own brother Fred, the accomplished founder of the Bach choir for which the Moravians of Bethlehem were celebrated. Probing the past as an adult, H. D. comes to understand that her mother was herself the victim of inhibiting patriarchal disapproval: one day she was overheard singing by her father, who made a spontaneous disparaging comment, after which she never sang again. Restored to harmonious identification with her mother, H.D. arrives in memory at a key episode, in which she is herself identified as a bearer of the gift by her mother's mother Mamalie.

H.D.'s consecration by Mamalie occurs as Mamalie speaks garbled, confusing words, like those of a prophet or oracle, in the course of which she tells H.D. about the pact between the Moravians and the Native Americans and calls her by the name "Agnes." In the final section of the book, the significance of this name finally reveals itself to H.D. as she thinks about her miraculous survival of the Blitz.

I had gone down under the wave and I was still alive, I was breathing. I was not drowning though in a sense, I had drowned; I had gone down, been submerged by the wave of memories and terrors, repressed since the age of ten and long before, but with the terrors I had found the joys, too.

The gate that opens to let out the Old Witch serves, this is the odd thing, to release Saint Nicholas and the Princess with the Star on her forehead who was Mamalie's Morning Star whose name was Angelica and Aunt Agnes' name was Angelica, so when Mamalie called me Agnes, I was Morning Star or I was Anna von Pahlen who had been a sort of Princess in Europe. So Europe and America had at last been reconciled in the very depth of my subconscious being.

(H.D. 1998: 219)

Through the local family history that she absorbed as a child, H.D. arrives at the same identity that she affirmed, also as a child, by internalizing a widely-read fairy tale, concluding that "you can not give away yourself with a star on your forehead," while also asserting that this fairy tale, like Greek myths, "was real. It went on happening, it did not stop."[24] Her personal quest clarifies what she means in declaring myth "real" and highlights the difference between her idea of reality and the reality which Schliemann established by excavating Troy. For H.D., myth points to a real spiritual power that can be activated at any point. By regaining contact with that power in wartime London, the adult H.D. keeps alive the possibility of peace, to be realized when Europe and America once again join forces and achieve victory.

The impressionistic technique of *The Gift*, with its associative patterns and representations of childhood consciousness, is more than a stylistic feature shared with other modernist writers. The adult H.D. must be reconnected with, and inspired by, her childhood self Hilda; as she put it in a later comment on the book, "the Child actually returns to that world, she lives actually in those reconstructed scenes, or she watches them like a moving picture" (H.D. 1986: 192). The adult's success depends on this reconnection and is a matter of suspense until the end of the book, which concludes with Hilda's vocation in the past and the "all clear" announced by H.D.'s companion Bryher in the present.

A visionary gift like H.D.'s never leaves those who possess it, but it is most readily accessed in childhood, in a child's instinctive sense of myth as full of wonder, as pointing to mysterious, otherworldly truths. Greek myths have the advantage of wide currency, offering a shared repository of mythic knowledge but, on this understanding, their value does not lie in their particular geographical or historical origins, or in facts to be discovered through the study of ancient Greek—a point on which Hawthorne and H.D. converge in their identification of Greek myths with their own American settings. As H.D. puts it in one of her unpublished notes on

---

[24] In a later discussion, she also connects the story of her conversation with her grandmother to the Greek world, identifying it as a reworking of the episode of the writing on the wall in Corfu. Sword 1995: 354.

Euripides, "I know that we need scholars to decipher and interpret the Greek, but we also need poets and mystics and children to rediscover this Hellenic world, to see *through* the words."[25]

Ancient History and the Language of Childhood

H.D.'s sense of Greek as words to be seen through, as imperfect signs of the ineffable, is echoed in the strikingly similar prefaces to two historical novels, both by English women writing in the 1920s and 1930s, set in ancient Greece. The first is *Cloud Cuckoo Land*, published in 1925, the story of a young couple's adventures in late fifth-century Greece, by Naomi Mitchison, who appeared in Chapter 5 reading Plato in the family dining room and writing historical fiction that surreptitiously communicates the sexual feelings of girls. Between comments on the perennial problem of transliterating Greek names and indications of her historical sources, Mitchison explains:

Occasionally I have used Greek words when there is no exact or easy English equivalent. A Ker, for instance, is not quite a ghost or spirit. It is more definitely queer and hungry and winged: there are love-keres and death-keres. But we are so steeped in the traditions of a different religion that they are rather hard to get at. I suppose Jane Harrison knows as well as anyone.   (Mitchison 1926: iv)

The second comes from Mary Butts's *The Macedonian*, a novel based on the life of Alexander the Great, written in 1931.

I have used two greek words which may be unfamiliar, but for which English has no exact equivalent—daimôn and kêr. Daimôn—from which our "demon" but with a specifically bad sense—is a potency, never a god; though some of the great daimônes attained personality and became gods. A daimôn is sometimes as definite as a season personified, such as Winter and Spring; but usually it is the sheer force that lies behind the manifestations of life—the "mana" even of a dead man or a tree or the sea or the wind, or an idea such as Plenty or Nemesis or Luck.
(Butts 1994: 4)

---

[25] From "Notes on Euripides, Pausanias, and Greek Lyric Poets," unpublished MS in the Beinecke Library, Yale, quoted in Gregory 1997: 68 (emphasis original). Cf. Yeats's fanciful unsent letter to his son's schoolmaster, in which he suggests that he be taught Greek by the Berlitz method (as opposed to the traditional method of schoolmasters who "read Greek with Latin eyes") so he can read the *Odyssey* right away, adding that "Greece, should we but approach it with eyes as young as its own, might renew our youth" (1962: 320–1).

Butts's preface ends with a note listing her main sources for the novel, including "J.E. Harrison, *Prolegomena to the Study of Greek Religion and Themis.*"

By fixing on *ker* and *daimon* as key terms of Greek culture and giving Jane Harrison a prominent place among their sources for Greek history, Butts and Mitchison align themselves with a pioneering and unconventional classical scholar who was one of the most influential exponents of a primitivist view of early Greece.[26] In order to become a professional classicist, Harrison (1850–1928) had to struggle against the cultural expectation that girls would not learn classical languages. In a reminiscence of herself as "a very happy little girl [who] secretly possessed herself of a Greek grammar," she recalled the "chill, cutting words" of a "much-adored aunt": "I do not see how Greek grammar is to help little Jane to keep house when she has a home of her own" (Harrison 1915: 117). Because she lacked the early linguistic training of her male counterparts, Harrison avoided traditional philologically-based topics in her scholarship, turning instead to innovative studies of material culture and religion, in which she also developed an original approach to the Greek language.

Like Freud (of whom she was an early supporter), Harrison was inspired by a conception of the Greek world as having developed through a series of stages culminating in the historical era, a time of law, rationality, Olympian religion, and patriarchy within which the traces of an earlier, pre-Olympian, matriarchal world were still discernible. But she differed sharply from Freud, and from the earlier anthropologists, such as Tylor and Lang, who were important influences, in seeing primitive culture as a superior time of transcendent wholeness rather than an inferior stage in the development of civilization; for her, as for H.D., the spiritual legacy of a mother-centered past was a source of salvation to be reclaimed, not a threat to be suppressed. Her major works, *Prolegomena to the Study of Greek Religion* (1903) and *Themis* (1912), give detailed and appreciative accounts of Greek prehistory as marked by fusion with nature, instinctive connection to the divine, and collective freedom from the limitations of rationality and individuation. The

---

[26] On Harrison's life, see Peacock 1988, Robinson 2002; on her legacy within classics, Beard 2000. Harrison's influence on Mitchison, Butts, and other female authors of historical fiction set in antiquity is traced in Hoberman 1997 (esp. 17–23, 47–9, 53–4); on H.D. in Gregory 1997: 108–25; on Woolf in Shattuck 1987, J. Mills 2014; and on Joyce, Eliot, and Woolf in Carpentier 1998.

transition to the Olympian order of the historical period, with its clear, fixed categories, was the renunciation of "all life and that which is life and reality—Change and Movement" in favor of "a brazen lifeless immutability" (Harrison 1912: 468).

For Harrison, prehistoric Greece was also closer to a prelinguistic time, when complex concepts were captured in their full significance by "holophrases," "utterances in which subject and object have not yet got their heads above water" that predate "our familiar 'Parts of Speech,'" which are "abstracted from the stream of warm conscious human activity in which they were once submerged" (473–4). This idea anticipates subsequent feminist theorizing, notably that of Julia Kristeva, about pre-Oedipal, maternally focused utterances in the early stages of individual development (Carpentier 1998: 176-8; Mills 2014: 34). It also recalls Freud's view of the symbols generated by the unconscious and used in dreams as an archaic quasi-language that has to be translated "into the [mode] that is familiar to us" (*SE* 13: 176–7). Freud compares the universal "language of dreams" to ancient writing systems, such as hieroglyphics, and the more obscure learned languages, such as Sanskrit ("this is . . . as if you were to discover that your housemaid understood Sanskrit," *SE* 15: 165), but not Greek, the language of the more advanced classical period and the adult accomplishment of educated men of his day.

Harrison, however, finds traces of the holophrase in the Greek language, in words like the ones singled out by Mitchison and Butts. *Ker* and *daimon* are terms for the expansive primitive spirits that came to be replaced by the more narrowly defined Olympian gods; these manifestations of "a protoplasmic fullness and forcefulness not yet articulate into the diverse forms of its ultimate births" are impossible to understand through "our modern habit of clear analytic thought" (Harrison 1922: 164). In a survey of the "various shifting notions that cluster around the term Ker," she identifies it as "perhaps the most untranslatable of all Greek words" (212), but also points out that its full meaning was already occluded in the more abstract and literary Greek of our surviving classical texts, which register only its association with fate and death and not its beneficent side.[27]

---

[27] Harrison herself identified so closely with the term *ker* that she used it as her signature in many of her letters to her fellow ritualist and close collaborator Gilbert Murray (Stewart 1959: 35).

As we have already seen with Freud, a vision of Greek culture as bringing together powerful instincts with ideas and institutions designed to civilize them provides a productive analogue for childhood as a time of division, a period when sensual impressions and instinctive desires confront systems of thought that tame and alter them. For Harrison, followed by Mitchison and Butts, language figures as a carrier of primitive elements within Greek culture, through the survival of specific Greek terms for elemental spiritual forces belonging to the earlier strata of prehistory. The designation of those terms as untranslatable captures their strangeness within historical Greek culture, their connection to forces that could not be contained within Olympian religion, but also transposes that strangeness to the authors' anglophone present.

To know of things that can only be expressed in Greek is to be in touch with primordial feelings and powers that are lost to the modern world, in part (to follow Mitchison's suggestion) because of the obfuscating influence of Christianity. The result is a vision of history in which the most salient division is not between earlier and later Greek culture, but between Greek prehistory as a period of natural spontaneity and all subsequent time, including the present. This vision offers an analogue to childhood that is different from Freud's (and closer to the romantic vision represented by Hawthorne), one in which antiquity represents the natural milieu of the child and modernity the adult world of rules and conventions into which the child is born.

Because both Mitchison and Butts wrote memoirs as well as novels, it is possible to read their versions of ancient history together with their accounts of personal history and to see how their constructions of antiquity are shaped by the legacies of childhood.[28] Both recall the process of growing up as one of encountering names and conventions—English terms—that do not exactly match a child's felt experience. Each records a first memory in which her own impulses are, in effect, mistranslated by an adult.

For Butts, "The first thing that I remember is a puddle of yellow mud." This mud is so alluring that she deliberately hurls herself face-first into

---

[28] The classical novels of both Butts and Mitchison are well studied from the perspective of gender in Hoberman 1997, to which the following discussion is indebted throughout. For the lives of these writers, see in addition to their memoirs, the biographies of Butts by Blondel (1998) and of Mitchison by Benton (1990) and Clader (1997).

the puddle in order to taste it, which teaches her the difference between appearance and taste ("I put out my tongue. No good and not so soft. Gritty. So that was mud-taste, the lovely yellow mud that gravel makes"), swiftly followed by her nurse's misinterpretation: "Miss Mary! Can't you see where you are going? . . . there's your fine coat ruined" (Butts 1988: 1). Butts's sensuality, longing for experience, and connection to nature are misnamed in an idiom of caution and materialism that she would seek all her life to escape. In response, she reveals herself as already (at an age somewhere between 3 and 6) bilingual, speaking both the foreign language of adults and the native "nonsense" of her own strong sensations.

Cook was severe: "We'll have our work cut out, getting that off." I was the tiniest bit sorry at this. I said the kind of things that grown-up people expect, but I had a question to ask. As we went up to tea in the nursery I ran back to the kitchen: "Are you really and truly sure that you never cook with mud?" (Butts 1998: 2).

Mitchison opens her memoir with an account of how adult misnaming introduces her to the painful topic of status. Her first memory is of sitting in her pram, from which she then graduates to a mail-cart.

Sometimes (or perhaps once), grown-ups, speaking of me in my mail-cart, called it a pram. I became terribly indignant. My new status had been denigrated: how could I bear it? Certainly I couldn't explain. I think I screamed. Status—essential for all gregarious animals, essential in the farmyard. Now I knew it and would always know it. (Mitchison 1973: 9)

Soon afterwards, staying at the seaside resort of Studland, Mitchison learns something of status from another angle as she is reprimanded for making contact with a "tripper." Looking back, she comments, "Guilt was duly aroused, though I never knew quite what I had done. This, however, was the beginning of class-consciousness," then goes on to consider the word "tripper" as a term of snobbery peculiar to the world of her childhood.

That curious word "tripper," probably right out of the current vocabulary! It dates from the time when most people could only afford a few days' holiday but when they did they came irritatingly into the very same places which those who could afford longer holidays had claims on and when they got there they made uncouth noises and wore unsuitable townee clothes. (11)

Untranslatable words for powerful spiritual forces, like *ker* and *daimon*, mark ancient Greece as preserving something of the ineffable experience of childhood that is sadly distorted in such expressions of adult English as "your fine coat ruined" or "pram" or "tripper" or "townee." In its combining and recombining of different cultural strands, Greek history offers a magnified version of the individual experience of learning the language of adulthood while still remembering the instincts and sensations of childhood, and so writing a novel set in the Greek world offers another way for an adult to realize antiquity in order to revisit, and possibly resolve, the conflicts of childhood. Mitchison and Butts both use Greek settings to restate their own childhood dilemmas within a privileged era of world history, where those dilemmas can be given, for a general audience, the clarity and consequence that they had for the writer herself when first encountered.

In transposing her own experiences to antiquity, Butts focuses on powerful figures of large historical significance (recapturing the child's conviction of her own importance) whom she presents as transcending the rift between social identity and connection to nature because they occupy moments of cultural transition: Alexander the Great in *The Macedonian* and Cleopatra in her subsequent *Scenes from the Life of Cleopatra*, published in 1935. Butts is especially drawn to the Hellenistic period as a time of intensified contact between Greece and other cultures, and of a renewed interest in mysticism that reanimates the Greek world's prehistoric heritage. For her, Alexander's personal triumph and historical significance stem from the way he combines two cultural eras.

There are men who sum up an epoch, and men who begin another. Alexander did both. Almost the last of the original creating Greeks, he was the first to carry over that energy into the second state of its activity, shaping it into an instrument by which the world's growing civilizations could express themselves without loss or distinction of race.   (Butts 1994: 3)

This vision of Alexander recapitulates the personal legacy that Butts struggled to wrest from her own childhood. Her memoir, *The Crystal Cabinet*, records her efforts to create for herself a version of that synthesis of energy and civilization that she finds in Alexander. She recalls her upbringing in an eighteenth-century house, Salterns, in Poole in Dorset, in surroundings of great natural beauty always under attack from suburban development, which represented for her the vulgar, philistine direction of modern life. Her childhood is defined by a sharp sense of division between her parents. Her much older father (56 when she was born) represents history, tradition, and the arts, summed up in a set of paintings by Blake inherited from his grandfather. Her mother stands for materialism, ignorant conventionality, and a focus on sexuality and sexual attractiveness accompanied by prudishness. The death of Butts's father when she is 14 leads to a series of betrayals by her mother: swift remarriage, to a man she has probably already been involved with; sale of the Blake paintings to pay death duties; and a bonfire of Butts's father's books, many of them classic works of French literature, on the grounds that they are pornographic.

As she negotiates this terrain, Butts forges—out of the passionate connection to nature that sends her plunging into the yellow puddle, and the inspiration and sustenance gained from a rich mix of myth and literature—a high-minded vision of the connectedness of all forms of life. This vision is always under assault from the vulgar, piously Christian, and crudely sexual outlook that she associates with the modern world and especially with her mother. That conflict surfaces in several episodes in which Butts's responses to poetry meet with soul-crushing responses. At the age of 12, she recites a romantic poem by Kipling, which leads her mother to connect romance with "the love of Lancelot and Guinivere . . . one of those disappointing moments when, about poetry and other things, grown-up people had just got it wrong" (32). On another occasion, her mother interprets thrilling lines from Macaulay about "the priest who slew the slayer, | and shall himself be slain," as "a kind of heathen prophecy about Our Lord" (41)—an example of that occlusion of the classical by Christianity deplored by Mitchison.

Butts's memoir culminates in a series of confirmatory visions that allow her to carry the impressions and intuitions of childhood permanently into her adult life. These visions center on the landscape near her home, especially the Badbury Rings, prehistoric remains which are the scene of a blissful initiation that brings the book to a close.[29] Her experiences of particular places are spiritually fortifying and uncontaminated by the poisonous adult world, now asserting itself in the form of

---

[29] "That afternoon, I was received. Like any candidate for ancient initiations, accepted. Then in essence, but a process that time after time would be perfected in me. Rituals whose objects were knitting up and setting out, and the making of correspondence, a translation which should be ever valid, between the seen and the unseen . . . Here it came with a radiant bliss. Bliss of light, bliss of green, bliss of birds" (266).

vicious sexual accusations made by her mother (who charged Butts with inappropriate designs on both her brother and her stepfather).

Or motoring inland with my mother or walking there alone—one way or another I was seized of those places, the process by which one comes to possess utterly one part of the earth. Possesses and is possessed. The work of my childhood knit up on the edge of my maturity. The one thing my family could not mind, to which they could not—nor did they try to—give any bad interpretation. (261–2)

A decade later, now separated from the scenes of her childhood, and after a difficult early adulthood, Butts validated and memorialized her formative visionary experience by giving the same experience to Alexander. The high point of *The Macedonian* is Alexander's visit, while in Egypt, to Siwa, where he visits the temple of the Egyptian god Amen-Ra and is identified as the god's son, undergoing the kind of encounter with age-old pre-rational religious tradition that is made possible by a classical setting. Alexander's visit to Siwa is a moment of conscious union with the spirit that works through him to shape world events, but which is also the same force connecting all of life by which Butts was so powerfully touched at Badbury Rings. Alexander feels it as a companion, but also as something beyond any individual. This spirit is captured, so far as is possible, by the Greek term *daimon* glossed by Butts in her preface as "the sheer force that lies behind the manifestations of life—the 'mana' even of a dead man or a tree or the sun" (4).

"Tell me more what I am," he whispered to himself: to the sand. He had never been so far from man before, not in the thracian wilderness nor the mountains of Taurus nor at sea. "I am the man who holds Persia as a man holds a cup. After Persia—what shall I do after Persia? I shall find out." He tried to put even such thoughts aside, trying to reach, not at doing, but being. And all that he was sure he understood was that he had been alone, and that now he was not alone. Who was the Companion, who had never left him, and whom he met now, for the first time, riding out into silence across Africa? His daimôn? The ghost of Achilles? a god?
     It was not that. It was not a person. It was something that shaped equally the Universe and an acorn, and It called him friend. (39)

Butts situates Alexander's epiphany in different historical circum-stances and in a different literary structure than she does her own. She presents Alexander's historical moment as a time of transition, as we have seen, but it remains nonetheless wholly classical, not marred by the prurience, vulgarity, and greed that she associated with her own modern age.[30] Alexander's coming of age, which coincides with the historical developments of his epoch, is not the hard-won culmination of a painful, tortuous inner journey such as Butts describes in *The Crystal Cabinet* but the one real glimpse we get of the subjective experience of a figure who is otherwise seen only from the outside. The novel is structured as a series of intermittent scenes from Alexander's life, from his birth to his death, presented through the eyes of others: his sharply opposed parents (pragmatic, rational Philip and intense, Dionysiac, Thracian Olympias), his tutor Aristotle, his ambitious companions, a Persian satrap, the priests of Seleucus. Alexander himself remains throughout largely mysterious, but always invested with singular power and grace. This deployment of diffuse, partial perspectives that the reader must integrate is what makes this work interesting in formal terms and constitutes the main basis of its claim on a continuing readership. But what may be viewed as an ambitious aesthetic experiment also represents a creative resolution to the cognitive struggles imposed by Butts's own difficult initiation into life.

The vision that Butts labored to refine and preserve as she came to adult consciousness is embodied in the figure of Alexander, who transcends particular circumstances and is spared the painful process of becoming himself. Just before his vision at Siwa, we learn that "He was a little boy, he remembered, who had never been anything but what he was now; who, from his first instant of memory, had sprung at life, and was still traveling on that spring" (39). Earlier, Alexander and Ptolemy are described, in notable contrast to Butts's remembered self, as "both in the perfection of youth which has grown without hindrance of circumstance or heredity" (28). The bewildering profusion of perspectives that complicated and sometimes thwarted Butts's own arrival at transcendence are disentangled, parceled out to the various observers through whom we see Alexander, each of whom is associated with distinctive strands within the cultural fabric of the Hellenistic world. Alexander's

---

[30] This vision of antiquity is spelled out in Butts's review of Mitchison's *The Corn King and the Spring Queen* (discussed later in this section), which appeared in 1931, when she was writing *The Macedonian*. The influences of archaeology, *The Golden Bough*, and the innate Hellenism of British culture, she claims, have enabled "a book whose quick, entrancing life makes us free of that new world which writers ask for and people who read" (*The Bookman* 81/482 (Nov. 1931), 137, quoted in Blondel 1998: 268).

parents embody the cultural difference that Butts found in her own parents in a reconfigured form: Philip represents rationality and a version of modernity, while Olympias represents passion, instinct, and connection to the gods of an earlier time; Olympias is explicitly linked to the "daimôn" of pre-Olympian Greece, which speaks to Alexander through her (25–6).[31]

In her novels with ancient settings, Naomi Mitchison also draws on the cultural complexity of classical culture to project the inner conflicts of her childhood onto a broad historical screen, with the difference that her concerns are social as well as personal. As we have seen, Mitchison's earliest memories were bound up with the consciousness of status, both as something that must be defended for those who are deprived of it (the child whose milk cart is demoted to a pram) and as something that is savored and prized by those who enjoy it at the expense of others (the adults who stigmatize less well off holiday-makers as "trippers"). In her account of growing up in a prosperous academic family in Oxford, Mitchison portrays her development as shaped by these conflicting identifications with those who possess privilege and those who are denied it. Her early encounter with the tripper is followed by puzzling relations with servants: "It was a funny business, really. Here were people living in the same house, walking through the same rooms, but thought of differently" (Mitchison 1973: 104).

To return to the passage discussed in Chapter 5 in which Mitchison evokes her adolescent responses to Plato, there her identification with Plato's Guardians clearly represents the empowering freedom of the imagination, the escape from second-class citizenship expressed in the statement, "in my inside stories I don't suppose I was ever a Greek woman." But Mitchison is also troubled by Plato's connection to the imperialistic jingoism favored by her mother.

---

[31] For Alexander's combination of his father's and mother's traits as projecting a longed-for world, see Foy 2000: 120–2. Butts's other classical novel, *Scenes from the Life of Cleopatra*, is a similarly fragmented portrait of a powerful figure who lives at a time of cultural transition and unites opposing cultural forces, in this case Greek and Egyptian. Cleopatra is infused with the spirit of Isis and can see beyond ordinary speech and action. Like Butts herself, she belongs to a family in decline, whose moment in history is passing, and she suffers the restrictions and prejudices that come with being a woman. Drawing on historical research to deny charges of sexual licentiousness that go back to antiquity, Butts becomes Cleopatra's champion, protesting "the kind of legend the vulgar mind loves" (Butts 1994: 342) in a way that recalls the high-minded adolescent purist of *The Crystal Cabinet*.

I am sure, however, that in common with only too many upper-class British, I got
a lot of curious ideas from Plato. Some fitted in excellently with my mother's view
of politics and the superiority of the State (in her case the Empire) over any
individual. (Mitchison 1975: 40)

And she finds her eventual salvation in the gender status that she had
escaped in her imaginary experience of being Greek.

Perhaps I only escaped the Platonic net, so widely spread in Oxford, by being one
of those inferior creatures of the wrong sex, born, not to be leaders, but perhaps
with luck, like Socrates (not to be confused with his caricature in *The Republic*) to
be a gadfly. (41)

Recalling this formative experience, Mitchison can only make sense of
her past self through ambivalence—a confident embrace of the advantages of education and culture associated with Plato, in tension with
egalitarian sympathies derived from her gender.

As an adult, Mitchison presents herself as never free of this ambivalence, which is permanently fostered by the association of privilege with
the arts and the intellectual tradition symbolized by Plato. She spells this
out in a later volume of her autobiography entitled *You May Well Ask*—
an allusion to the fact that she was often asked how she could reconcile
the progressive political views that she shared with her husband, a left-
wing lawyer and Member of Parliament, and her comfortable way of
life—in a passage that veers between self-accusation and self-defense.

So there we were and rooms were clean and tidy, the meals were cooked and
served, orders to shops were delivered on time and there were at least three posts
a day, all based on our being at the top end of the class structure. We could
presumably have sat back and enjoyed it but we filled up all that lovely spare time
which nobody seems to have today with our friends and children, ours and our
friends' love affairs, our good causes and committees, Dick's Bar work, my
writing, interest in the other arts, letters, trips abroad, and as time went on the
growth of social conscience. The last didn't go as far as doing without Lev, nurse,
cook, housemaid and the rest, which would of course also have meant giving up
our home, dependent as it was on them. But at least we found ourselves living
into a frame of mind where the class structure began to look very unreal.
(Mitchison 1979: 28)

In *Cloud Cuckoo Land*, Mitchison restates this dilemma through the
political and cultural conflicts of late fifth-century Greece. The story
concerns a young man, Alxenor, from a small fictional Ionian island,
Poieëssa, whose story involves him in the real events of his time,

sometimes bringing him into contact with known historical figures, such as Theramenes. Alxenor is caught between the oligarchic, pro-Spartan views of his rich older brother Eupaides and the democratic pro-Athenian views of his best friend Chromon; Chromon is also himself the brother of Moiro, the woman with whom Alxenor is in love. In the wake of an oligarchic coup, Alxenor flees Poieëssa, taking Moiro with him in an impulsive expression of a love that seemingly overrides all political concerns. This romantic beginning leads, not to a story of joint adventure and ultimate triumph, but to a more realistic account of the hardships encountered by this couple, hardships that prove quickly destructive to their incipient love and that ultimately lead to their estrangement and Moiro's death. True to her early understanding of the limited scope of Greek women's lives, Mitchison portrays Moiro as hopelessly limited by her upbringing and circumstances. And the one female "gadfly" she includes is quickly silenced and marginalized.[32]

The more meaningful experiences are those of the male protagonist Alxenor, who travels from city to city in the last days of the Peloponnesian War, spending time both in Athens, with its exhilarating freedoms and self-defeating excesses, and in Sparta, with its appealing but also oppressive order and coherence. When we see him back in Poieëssa at the end of the novel, he is struggling with a conundrum that is strongly reminiscent of Mitchison's own.

As the weeks went by, Alxenor found himself in a curious position. The oligarchs were all very friendly; no one seemed to remember the old days. And they were mostly pleasant people, who gave the nicest parties, the only houses where he could see, and talk over, the newest books, a painting or vase by some master from the mainland, a foreign embroidered hanging, or what-not. There was music too, better than he had heard for years; Tolmaios had taken to it as he grew older—there were always flute and harp players, or singers, among his guests. It was so kind and lovely after the chill of Sparta, and all the arts frozen to death there!

But all the same, he wanted to go to meetings of the democrats, the Club that met by the Temple of Poseidon at the little harbour; he wanted to hear Chromon speak, and become completely persuaded himself that this was the right way. But the democrats were shy of him. His relationship with Chromon was not, after all, perfectly plain sailing. They wanted him to say straight out that he was one of

---

[32] On the portrayal of women and women's lives in *Cloud Cuckoo Land*, see Benton 1990: 46–8; Hoberman 1997: 27–33.

them, and would follow their leaders through blood and fire. And he would have liked to be able to say it; he would have liked to rest his troubled mind in a party. Only, always at the last moment he could not agree with everything. He kept thinking of the Athenian democracy, the cleverest people in the world, and yet they had almost come to ruin, and even in the end—well, it was hard to tell what Athens was like nowadays. (Mitchison 1926: 302-3)

The historical conditions of classical Greece, in which a single culture comprised, at the same time, discrete political entities with different political tendencies and which involved frequent factional clashes along class lines, gave Mitchison a setting in which she could externalize and dramatize her own inner struggles. What she presents in her memoirs as a personal birthright acquired in her first remembered moments of consciousness is recast as the inevitable outcome of a thoughtful adult's participation in the heightened atmosphere of late fifth-century Greece. Mitchison reconfirms the inescapable nature of this legacy of ambivalence by having Alxenor impose it on his son Timas. Before going off to join the mercenary expedition to Persia that we know from Xenophon's *Anabasis*, Alxenor leaves Timas in Poieëssa to be raised jointly by his two uncles: the oligarchic Eupaides and the democratic Chromon. "He was to see two sides of life: and try to be fair" (309).

This note of inevitability receives a challenge, however, in the novel's title, which alludes to the utopian fantasy land of Aristophanes' *Birds*. This otherwise unexplained reference marks as unreal a world that, in the details of its portrayal, is studiously realistic and diligently researched, much as Mitchison seeks to mitigate her participation in the British class structure by claiming that it "began to look very unreal."[33] Paradoxically, Mitchison's quest for a narrative that would satisfy her sense of reality led a few years later to a very different novel set in the classical past, *The Corn King and the Spring Queen*, published in 1931, in which the historian's version of antiquity is juxtaposed to another version derived, as her title suggests, from the reconstructions of anthropologists.

The novel is set, like Butts's two classical novels, in the Hellenistic period (specifically in 228–187 BCE), which appears to offer Mitchison a similar freedom to imagine the interpenetration of Greek and other cultures. But instead of envisioning individuals who combine and

---

[33] On Mitchison's several uses of the idea of "Cloud Cuckoo Land" or "Cloud Cuckoo Borough," see Hoberman 1997: 29–30.

integrate disparate forces, as Butts does, Mitchison envisions two distinct cultures, between which the central characters move in the course of the plot. One is historical Sparta, as known from classical sources, especially Plutarch, in which the king Cleomenes attempts a series of egalitarian reforms (based, on Mitchison's own admission, on the Soviet Union) that fail, leading to a dead end similar to that reached in the wholly historical *Cloud Cuckoo Land*. The other is Marob, a fictional kingdom set in Scythia, on the margins of the Greek world, and based on the prehistoric cultures projected in Frazer's *Golden Bough*.

In the inclusive, ritualistic, and nature-oriented culture of Marob, Mitchison is able to resolve the contradictions that have plagued her since childhood. She presents a central female character, the Spring Queen Erif Der, who is at once powerful, sensual, and maternal (like Butts's Cleopatra) and who eventually realizes married happiness with her husband, the Corn King Tarrik. The privilege of exalted status is put at the service of the group through the ritual actions of the royal pair, including the self-sacrifice of the king. The artistic expression of the community is not divorced from the rhythms of popular life, but implicated in ritual performance and reflected in a series of paintings that document the underlying myth of royal self-sacrifice that ultimately unites Marob and Sparta.

As in the fictions for girls explored in Chapter 5, Mitchison is able to tell a satisfying story because she constructs a utopian society based on the fragmentary evidence of prehistory and the suggestive witness of surviving artifacts. As she explains in a prefatory note, "The place called Marob is not historically real, but people on the shores of the Black Sea, and thereabouts, made very beautiful things, of the kind which Berris Der made" (Mitchison 1931b). By making that society contemporaneous with the historical Spartan society that reflects her own present, and by recounting her characters' movements between the two, Mitchison suggests that the more integrated realm of Marob remains present for modern people in the same way that childhood, with its intuitive, prelinguistic sense of wholeness, remains present for adults. In this respect, her fictional world resembles Freud's model of the human psyche, which variously combines elements ascribed to prehistory and to history.

In the same note, Mitchison goes on to compare all historical reconstruction to a childrens' game:

...it is scarcely possible that Kleomenes of Sparta was really at all like the Kleomenes I have made, though I doubt whether, in the present state of knowledge, anyone else's idea is inherently more probable—it is all a game of hide-and-seek in the dark and if, in the game, one touches a hand or a face, it is all chance; so Marob is just as likely, or unlikely, as the rest of the world.

Moments of success in the course of research, whether it involves reading texts or decoding objects, are like fleeting moments of unmediated physical contact, experienced in the haphazard course of a game. In introducing Marob in the opening section of the narrative, Mitchison designates her construction as at once imaginary and real by labeling the section "Kataleptike Phantasia," which refers to a doctrine of ancient Stoicism (an important element in the novel) locating truth in an impression on the mind derived from what actually exists, but which might be loosely translated "realistic fantasy." And she further indicates the basis of that fantasy in childhood by prefacing the section with a familiar nursery rhyme, in which the adult assumption of powerful social roles is a matter of innocent play.

> Lavender's blue, dilly, dilly!
> Rosemary's green;
> When I am king, dilly, dilly!
> You shall be queen...

Children's Greek

The most famous early twentieth-century discussion of what it means to know Greek is a meditation on its opposite, Virginia Woolf's 1925 essay, "On Not Knowing Greek."[34] While Woolf's title seems to indicate the condition of women and others who are excluded from elite male education, she quickly redefines not knowing Greek as a debility of modern people in general, all of whom "should be at the bottom of any class of schoolboys" and yet "feel for ever drawn back to" a language, and with it a whole culture, that is essential and familiar but imperfectly knowable (Woolf 1925: 24). In this way, Woolf casts the modern longing

---

[34] Accounts of Woolf's lifelong engagement with the Greeks and their language can be found in Herman 1983, Fowler 1999, Dalgarno 2001, Koulouris 2011, Prins 2017. On this essay in relation to contemporary debates about translation, see Dalgarno 2012: 18–37.

for Greek and Greece in terms that suggest nostalgia for a cherished childhood.[35] For her, the Greeks possess qualities of freshness, straight-forwardness, and completeness that have been lost in the modern world. In a conception that recalls Mary Butts's vision of Alexander as an adult untainted by the struggles of growing up, Woolf's Greeks combine an adult's capacities with a child's instincts and lack of reserve. The *Odyssey* may be a tale of adventure that we read "quickly in the spirit of children wanting amusement to find out what happens next," but "here is nothing immature; here are full-grown people, crafty, subtle, and passionate." And yet their long tradition—their uncomplicated cultural birthright—"makes them no more self-conscious than children" (39).[36]

Like other people construed as primitive (including those found in "villages . . . in the wilder parts of England," 25), Woolf's Greeks stand in a paradoxical, privileged relation to time, blessed by tradition but freed from history. The longstanding regularity of their ways endows them with clarity and confidence; frozen in the past ("in a fastness of their own," 24), they maintain their distinctiveness and authenticity, sheltered from the leveling repetitions of history: "Here we meet them before their emotions have been worn into uniformity" (29). This account of Greece as the locus of "the stable, the permanent, the original human being" (28) chimes with a vision of childhood that is expressed elsewhere by one of Woolf's characters (and that also recalls Mary Butts and her puddle of yellow mud):

Don't you remember in early childhood when, in play or talk, as one stepped across the puddle or reached the window on the landing, some imperceptible shock froze the universe to a solid ball of crystal which one held for a moment—I have some mystical belief that all time past and future too, the tears and powdered ashes of generations clotted to a ball; then we were absolute and entire; nothing then was excluded; that was certainty—happiness.[37]

---

[35] In more personal terms, Woolf, like H.D., identified the physical terrain of Greece with the cherished lost landscape of her own childhood. During a visit in 1932, she wrote in her diary, "And I could love Greece, as an old woman, so I think, as I once loved Cornwall, as a child" (Woolf 1982: 97).

[36] This view of the *Odyssey* as appealing to children is anticipated in Woolf's unpublished Greek reading notebook, where she assimilates the Cyclops episode to a fairy tale: "This is precisely like a traditional fairy tale of a man's great cunning . . . I imagine how the child would have liked the dreadful plight that Odysseus was in" (Koulouris 2011: 95).

[37] Woolf 1989: 98–9. On this passage as epitomizing a quest for wholeness registered throughout modernist literature, see Mahaffey 2007: 16. In a diary entry for 1903, Woolf

Woolf's Greeks are like adults who have grown up without losing the wholeness and ahistoricity of childhood. This may be what she means by labeling them "full-grown," a condition that seems unattainable for many of her fictional characters, for whom entering adulthood means becoming more conflicted and inhibited, more constricted by habit and cultural expectations. In her ringing final sentence—"It is to the Greeks that we turn when we are sick of the vagueness, of the confusion, of the Christianity, and its consolations, of our own age (39)"—the final phrase "our own age" suggests personal as well as cultural history.

The elusiveness of the Greeks is encapsulated in the difficulty of their language, which provides only a partial means of contact with them. The occlusion brought by modernity and adulthood is reflected in the modern English into which Greek is inadequately translated, which "can but offer us a vague equivalent . . . necessarily full of echoes and associations" (37). In its untranslated form, Greek, epitomized by tragedy and especially by Sophocles' *Electra*, is direct and open (in contrast to the "slow reserve, the low half-tones, the brooding introspective melancholy" (26) of English) and, like the consciousness of children, allied with prelinguistic forms of expression rooted in nature and the body. Electra's words resemble the songs of birds or inarticulate vocalizations of pure feeling, "mere cries of despair, joy, hate" (27). Greek, which Woolf labeled "magic" in the title of one essay (Woolf 1990: 252) and "The Perfect Language" in another, resembles the more adequate medium sought by the writer Bernard at the end of *The Waves*: "I need a little language such as lovers use, words of one syllable such as children speak when they come into the room and find their mother sewing . . . I need a howl; a cry" (Woolf 2006a: 219).

This conception of the Greek language (shared with Harrison, H.D., Mitchison, Butts, and others) as the key to what is timeless, childlike, and free of modern convention, surfaces throughout Woolf's fiction, counterpoised with the traditional idea of learning Greek as the cornerstone of elite male education. That traditional idea is evoked, mocked, and finally rendered tragic in *Jacob's Room*, her elegiac novel about a young man killed in

associates the "delicious sensation" of intense reading with transhistorical identification with the Greeks: "I think I see for a moment how our minds are all threaded together—how any live mind today is of the very same stuff as Plato's & Euripides" (Woolf 1990: 178).

World War I published in 1922.[38] For Jacob Flanders, knowing some Greek
is bound up with the confidence that comes with masculine privilege. As
recent graduates of 22, he and a friend affirm the superiority of Greek by
shouting quotations from Aeschylus and Sophocles on Haverstock Hill,
and he opines that "Probably . . . we are the only people in the world who
know what the Greeks meant," even though, we are told, "Jacob knew no
more Greek than served him to stumble through a play" (Woolf 2000: 102).
    This limited yet exhilarating knowledge of Greek is identified with
complacency and blindness to the ways in which the classics are implicated in the imperialistic and militaristic values underlying England's
pursuit of the war and thus Jacob's early death. On a trip to Greece,
disillusioned by the messy vulgarity of modern Greek life, Jacob begins to
intuit the deformations associated with idealized views of the Greeks,
which begin with the earliest training and are inculcated by women as
well as men: "But it is the governesses who start the Greek myth," he
thinks—or "something in this fashion" (189). But he has no chance to
develop these nascent thoughts or act on them. His life is lost in action,
never described or placed on the map, but obliquely rendered by the
sentence, "Darkness drops like a knife over Greece" (245).
    The location of the Gallipoli campaign in fabled classical terrain
(confirmed as such by Schliemann's excavations) was a much-observed
coincidence of World War I, and participation in that campaign was yet
another version of the adult realization of a childhood fantasy through
travel to an ancient site.[39] This was spelled out in a letter from Rupert
Brooke to Violet Asquith as he set out in February 1915, "I suddenly
realize that the ambition of my life has been—since I was two—to go on a
military expedition against Constantinople" (Brooke 1968: 662–3). As he
wrote this, Brooke was, of course, unaware that this expedition would
lead to his premature death, unable to foresee the dark fulfillment of a
classical ideal absorbed in childhood that Woolf indicates and laments in
Jacob's Room. But, in the best known poem of World War I, Wilfred

[38] On the significance of Greek in *Jacob's Room*, see Dalgarno 2001: 53–66; Koulouris
2011: 216–22; Flack 2014: 141–8; on Woolf's critical, sometimes satiric stance towards
traditional Greek scholarship throughout her works, Fowler 1999: 219–20; on the ways in
which Woolf's approach to the language differed from that of the professional scholar,
Nagel 2002; McCoskey and Corbett 2012.
[39] On the Great War as "The Second Trojan War" in the works of British poets, see
Vandiver 2010: esp. 228–80.

Owen underscores the same point: participation in the war was induced
by a classically inflected fable that thrived on the credulity and inexperi-
ence of men who were essentially children:

> If you could hear, at every jolt, the blood
> Come gargling from the froth-corrupted lungs,
> Obscene as cancer, bitter as the cud
> Of vile, incurable sores on innocent tongues,
> My friend, you would not tell with such high zest
> To children ardent for some desperate glory,
> The old lie: Dulce et decorum est
> Pro patria mori.[40]

Woolf brings her different sense of Greek, as an elusive yet insistent
expression of what traditional education suppresses, to her depiction of
the Great War's wreckage in the story of Septimus Smith, the shell-
shocked survivor of *Mrs Dalloway*. In an experience of madness that
echoes Woolf's own (Woolf 1976: 162), Septimus hears sparrows singing in Greek. Their message is redemptive—one sparrow sings "freshly
and piercingly in Greek words how there is no crime" and, joined
by another, "how there is no death"—but unable to save Septimus,
who goes on to kill himself (Woolf 1981: 24–5). There is more to be
hoped for from the Greek sung by a pair of children at the end of
The Years, the novel in which we have already encountered another
young person's death—in this case a metaphorical, spiritual death—in
conjunction with a Greek ideal: Sara Pargiter's mimesis of the death of
Antigone.

A long intergenerational family chronicle beginning in 1880, *The
Years*, written in 1934–6 and published in 1937, concludes with a party
set in "The Present Day," at the end of which two caretaker's children
(whose sex is never specified) come in and are given cake by the hostess
(Woolf 1992: 407–9). One of the guests offers them a coin and asks them
to "sing a song for sixpence." Very awkwardly, they suddenly burst into a
song composed of unrecognizable words or nonsense syllables, containing elements that are clearly reminiscent of Greek.[41]

---

[40] *Wilfred Owen: The War Poems*, edited by Jon Stallworthy (Chatto & Windus, 1994).
On the fame of this poem, and for the important point that it represents only one of many
responses to World War I in British poetry, see Vandiver 2010: 4, 393–404.
[41] Amy Richlin, singling out the monosyllables *hai, to, kai, gar, par, chree* as particularly
evocative of Greek, notes that "most are articles, conjunctions, syntactic links adrift" but

Etho passo tanno hai,
Fai donk to tu do,
Mai to, kai to, lai to see.
Toh dom to tuh do—

Fanno to par, etto to mar,
Timin tudo, tido,
Foll to gar in, mitno to par,
Eido, teido, meido—

Chree to gay ei,
Geeray didax . . .

At first no one knows what to say. "There was something horrible in the noise they made. It was so shrill, so discordant, and so meaningless." One of the male characters comments on its incomprehensibility, "Cockney accent, I suppose . . . What they teach them at school, you know." But then two of the most sympathetic female characters agree that it was somehow extraordinarily beautiful (though one then doubts whether the other had the same thing in mind as she did).[42]

Coming at the novel's end, as some of the characters are struggling to break free of inherited patterns, this enigmatic song seems to point to the future and to a new form of art. It is one manifestation of Woolf's aspiration of bringing into the novel a version of the Greek chorus, the medium of a timeless, collective, impersonal perspective or, as she puts it in "On Not Knowing Greek," "the undifferentiated voices

---

adds that "*didax-* . . . is the future stem of the verb 'to teach'" (1992: 268). Cf. the song of an old woman outside the Regent's Park tube station in *Mrs Dalloway*: "a frail quivering sound, a voice bubbling up without direction, vigour, beginning or end, running weakly and shrilly and with an absence of all human meaning into

ee um fah um so
foo swee too eem oo

the voice of no age or sex, the voice of an ancient spring spouting from the earth" (Woolf 1981: 80).

[42] Critics too have found varying ways of glossing the song: "a suggestion of something beyond, outside history, some unknown or more authentically divine spirit borne in through a speaking in tongues" (Lipking 1977: 144); "the vatic voice of the Delphic oracle" and "a mystical communion between women and children like mother's understanding of baby talk [or] . . . the social worker's solidarity with immigrants" (Marcus 1987: 28); "the working classes' song of freedom" (Marcus 1987: 49); "fragments not only of an ancient tongue, but of a future tongue, meaningful both despite and because of their fragmentation" (Richlin 1992: 268).

who sing like birds in the pauses of the wind" (Woolf 1925: 30).[43] In *Mrs Dalloway*, as we have seen, and in *The Waves* (Woolf's most thoroughly choral novel), a choral voice is identified with the actual singing of birds; in other works that voice is identified with lower-class characters, the charwoman Mrs McNabb in *To The Lighthouse* and villagers putting on a pageant in *Between the Acts*. As children, the lower-class amateur performers of *The Years* redouble the incomplete absorption into the social structure of other marginal characters whom Woolf invests with mysterious potential.[44] They are undifferentiated, not only as a group, but also over time, with successive generations playing the same games and singing the same songs.

The performing children at the end of the novel are the final instantiation of a perennial chorus of street children whose voices recur throughout as background noise, heard but not registered as meaningful speech.[45] They are first met in the opening pages, set in 1880, as indifferent bystanders absorbed in their game while the family patriarch, Colonel Pargiter, pays his regular, clandestine visits to his mistress:

Every time he approached the little street...the street where the muffin man seemed always to be ringing his bell, where children screamed and hopped in and out of white chalk marks on the pavement, he paused, looked to the right, looked to the left; and then walked very sharply to Number Thirty and rang the bell.

(Woolf 1992: 6)

When Colonel Pargiter visits his sister-in-law eleven years later, similar children encroach on her garden, again associated with a kind of demotic chorus-leader; this time their play suggests an ancient ritual.

They were silent for a moment. There were shouts of laughter from the garden.

[43] On Woolf's attempts to develop a choral voice within the novel and the influence of Harrison on her understanding of the Greek chorus, see Fowler 1999: 228–32; Shattuck 1987: 291–4.

[44] On Woolf's fascination with marginal figures who "not only have their own mysterious histories, but appear timeless, outside the precise stratification of contemporary class organization," see Flint, in Woolf 2000: xxii.

[45] The location of these children in the street connects them with a suggestion Woolf recorded in her notebook while writing *Mrs Dalloway*: "Why not have an observer in the street at each critical point who acts the part of chorus?" (*Mrs Dalloway*, holograph notes, 19 Nov. 1922, Berg Collection of the New York Public Library). But this chorus is so absorbed in its own timeless games that it leaves the protagonists unobserved, subtly mocking their seeming importance.

"Oh those children!" she exclaimed. She rose and went to the window. The colonel followed her. The children had stolen back into the garden. The bonfire was burning fiercely. The little girls were laughing and shouting as they danced round it. A shabby old man, something like a decayed groom to look at, stood there with a rake in his hand. Eugénie flung up the window and cried out. But they went on dancing. The Colonel leant out too; they looked like wild creatures with their hair flying. He would have liked to go down and jump over the bonfire, but he was too old.   (119)[46]

When the children finally come out of the street into the house, their cries are resolved into words. Jarring and incomprehensible, but beautiful to some, those words hint at a life other than that which the characters already know. Woolf locates this song and its singers in the actual place and time, England of the 1930s, in which the novel was written—not turning away, as Mitchison, Butts, and H.D. variously do, to ancient Greece (real or imagined) or to a magically-charged remembered childhood. But, as a form of Greek, however fragmentary and nonsensical, the song bears the weight of ancient tradition; it carries the hope of circumventing the recent past and returning to the freshness and directness of the classical world. But being children's Greek, it also portends the future, joining the elusive past with possibilities still unrealized, as children ideally do.

---

[46] Such children appear when a philanthropic character visits a poor family (Woolf 1992: 93), or better-off Pargiters visit poorer cousins (164–5, 298) or two characters walking through Hyde Park see a madwoman giving a speech while "a chorus of little boys imitated her" (229); thirty years after the first such occasion, the screaming children are again "playing a game with chalk marks on the pavement" (165).

7

Pan in the Alps
Child and Adult in H.D.'s
The Hedgehog

In a recollection of a book not read by someone who was *not* a child, H.D.'s daughter Perdita Schaffner describes the moment at which she first heard about *The Hedgehog*, a work written by her mother sometime between the two world wars.[1]

> She revealed—casually, over the teacups—that she had a manuscript, a story, well not exactly a story, too long, not exactly a novel, too short. A little book for children set in Switzerland, no not really for children, but about a child, about me, well sort of.
>
> Oh dear, would she ever stop thinking of me as a child? I was a full-fledged adult now at 14 or thereabouts. Those summer excursions to Alpine pastures were very sweet and wholesome, but kid stuff. I'd long since put Heidi behind me, exchanged her for the persona of a potential movie starlet. H.D. and Bryher were so cerebral, above such things as make-up and hairstyles. I set out to be flamboyant. I listened to jazz by the hour, spent my allowance on lipstick and eye shadow, fiddled with my hair. I was impossible.
>
> Now, having raised teenagers of my own, I realize I was normal. She didn't offer to show me the manuscript; I didn't ask to see it. We left it at that.
>
> (H.D. 1988: viii–ix)

H.D. began working on the book in the mid-1920s, but this scene, if it occurred when Schaffner was about 14, would have taken place in 1933.[2] Compared to H.D.'s other works, *The Hedgehog* has never had a wide readership, and its limited circulation and fame may be due to its

---

[1] An earlier version of parts of this chapter appeared in "Armies of Children: War and Peace, History and Myth in Children's Books After World War One," in K. Marciniak (ed.), 2016. *Our Mythical Childhood . . . : The Classics and Literature for Children and Young Adults.* Leiden: Brill.

[2] The first printed edition, published in 1936, is dated "Vaud, 1925" on the title page.

indeterminate status ("not exactly a novel . . . not really for children"). It was initially commissioned by Houghton Mifflin, which then rejected it,[3] and first appeared instead in 1936 in an edition of 300 copies for H.D.'s friends; it was only issued in a mass market edition (published by New Directions, with the "Introduction" by Schaffner quoted above) in 1988, after H.D. had been rediscovered by feminist criticism.

In the case of the 1936 edition, one decision was driven by the book's ostensible child audience. The publishers were family friends, of whom Schaffner recalls: "A book for children, they agreed, should be illustrated" (ix). And so *The Hedgehog* was accompanied by a series of woodcuts by another family friend, George Plank. But Plank's illustrations in their own way reinforce the uncertain identity of the text in that they depict the adventures of a child but are not marked stylistically as being particularly for children. As Schaffner thinks about her own copy out of those 300, lost in the course of many moves, she adds "I wonder what became of [the others] . . . and whether any were read by children" (xi).

The unclassifiable character of *The Hedgehog* makes it, like Jacqueline Rose's famous "case" of *Peter Pan*, a work that unsettles the category of children's literature, highlighting questions that are anticipated in H.D.'s own vacillating description: What, aside from length, is the difference between a children's "story" and an adult's "novel"? Are books with child characters really *about* children? Are so-called children's books really *for* children? Schaffner's rebellious thoughts supply the implicit negative response: that adults write for children of their own imagining, invested in the idea of childhood as a permanent and idealized state charged with an unreal wholesomeness, epitomized by the Alpine idyll *Heidi*. Perry Nodelman in particular has shown how the imperatives of the adult author tend to haunt all children's literature, producing a "shadow" story that answers to the needs of a "hidden adult," but here H.D.'s own attunement to the issue is reflected in a work in which the hidden adult is more plainly in view than usual. As a result, this is an especially fruitful text for exploring what an adult in pursuit of her own aims might gain by writing in the genre of "children's literature" and what space might be left for the child reader in such a project. Furthermore, since

---

[3] Friedman 1990: 20–1. H.D. recalled the episode in a 1960 memoir: "I was asked by a well-known Boston publisher about 1924, to write a children's story about Switzerland; Of course they didn't like the *Hedgehog* when I sent it" (2012: 181).

The Hedgehog offers a version of the scenario described in Schaffner's anecdote—forceful, high-minded mother and quietly defiant daughter—in which the mother's success in teaching her daughter about classical mythology is a crucial factor, the book also reveals what is at stake when an adult undertakes to transmit the classics to a child.

The Hedgehog's Swiss setting is one obvious reason for the thought that the book might be, in some sense, "about" Perdita. It tells the story of a girl named Madge (and nicknamed Alpen-Rose), whose American mother Bett is raising her in a village in the Swiss Alps, after the death of her English father in World War I. Bett and Madge are under pressure from Madge's paternal relatives to return to England, but Bett has chosen to remain in Switzerland out of a romantic pacifism: "Other people made wicked wars, but here people waited in their hills" (20). Bett is a thinly disguised version of H.D. herself, unconventional in her manner of life, her thinking, and her dress, and the situation is a fictionalized account of H.D.'s and Perdita's actual circumstances. By the 1930s, the two of them were spending much of their time in Switzerland, but rather than living alone together in a mountain village, they were part of a larger household that included H.D.'s partner Winifred Ellerman, usually known by her assumed name "Bryher," and Bryher's husband (and H.D.'s sometime lover) Kenneth Macpherson; in 1928, Perdita was officially adopted by the Macphersons. Perdita's father was an absent Englishman, but he had not died in World War I; rather, his brief relationship with H.D. was already over by the time Perdita was born (and she only met him once, by chance, many years later). Perdita actually lived with her mother only part of the time; she was placed in a nursing home for infants soon after she was born and was usually away at school. H.D. has taken advantage of the idealizing, euphemistic tendencies of children's fiction to imagine a version of Perdita's upbringing that is at once more conventional and more romantic than reality.[4]

The plot of *The Hedgehog* begins with a minor falling-out between mother and daughter. The trouble starts (as Schaffner's anecdote does) over tea, when a do-gooding Englishwoman unexpectedly drops by. As

---

[4] On autobiographical elements, including H.D.'s unconventional maternity, in *The Hedgehog*, see Friedman 1990: 72, 226–7. For Schaffner's memories of life with her mother, including her assumption as a small child that "fathers were absentee figures" (7), see Schaffner 1986.

Madge later explains, "It was that old Miss Hayes who made me angry, coming and interrupting my own tea with mamma" (50–1). To tease Miss Hayes, Madge pretends that a little snake sighted in their garden is just one of "a whole nest of adders" (9). This lie backfires, because her mother then insists that she has to wear shoes, which she hates. A neighbor suggests that the remedy for snakes in the garden is to get an "*hérisson*." Although Madge is fluent in French, she does not recognize the word for hedgehog and has no idea what an *hérisson* might be. But she sets off down the mountainside to visit a Dr Blum, who lives below on the shore of a lake and who is said to have one. After getting stranded on a dangerously steep path, Madge is rescued—not for the first time—in a state of panic, by her friend André, the son of a woodcutter. They make their way down to the doctor's house, where Madge has tea and returns towards evening with the hedgehog in a box.

This simple narrative rehearses what was, for H.D., a kind of master-plot: a daughter's escape to the mountains from her disappointing mother.[5] One version appears in H.D.'s account in *The Gift*, discussed in Chapter 6, of her own defiant thoughts when her mother gives away her copy of *Grimms' Fairy Tales*. There H.D. identifies both with the princess on the glass mountain ("the girl going up the glass-mountain") and the mountain that she climbs ("I was part of the ice of the mountain, it had happened long ago"). An even closer parallel is another passage from *The Gift*, in which H.D. again evokes an imaginative flight from her treacherous mother, this time bound up with the significance of names: those of her mother Helen and of the family servant Ida.[6]

"Can I help you wash clothes, Ida?" This is Ida, this is that mountain, this is Greece, this is Greek, this is Ida; Helen? Helen, Hellas, Helle, Helios, you are too bright, too fair, you are sitting in the darkened parlor, because you "feel the heat," you who are rival to Helios, to Helle, to Phoebus the sun. You are the sun and the sun is too hot for Mama, she is sitting in the sitting room with Aunt Jennie and they are whispering like they do, and they hide their sewing when I come in. I do not care what they talk about. They leave me out of everything. Ida does not leave

---

[5] For *The Hedgehog* as epitomizing another of H.D.'s recurrent plots, the female quest for freedom through mastery of mysterious signs controlled by men (such as the enigmatic *hérisson*), see Gubar 1990: 297–8; as one of a cluster of works from roughly the late 1920s that deal with issues of adolescence and separation from the mother, see Milicia 1986: 574.

[6] Murnaghan 2008: 65–6.

me out, "Here take this," says Ida. "Now squeeze it harder, you can get it drier than that." I am helping Ida wring out the clothes. (H.D. 1998: 114)

Here the mother's treachery, like Bett's, involves gossiping with another adult and making her daughter feel left out, and the daughter's escape to the mountains is identified with comfort offered by a friend from a lower social class, like the comfort Madge gains from André. If the *Hedgehog* is, in some sense, "about" Perdita, H.D. has given her daughter a story that is also very much her own.[7] And while the inner scenarios of *The Gift* here assume a literal, externalized form more suitable for a parable-like children's book, the story is still infused with a sense of fluid identification between people and landscapes and of ordinary experiences as manifestations of mythical paradigms.

Within *The Hedgehog*, H.D. reinforces Madge's connection to herself by stressing the close resemblance between Madge and Bett, the mother who also stands in for H.D. herself. In her "Introduction," Schaffner describes Madge both as "me, in appearance and general concept" and as "Bett's alter-ego, junior grade," and within the narrative Madge herself makes the identification:

Madge called her mother Bett because she hadn't any brothers and sisters, and Bett had short hair anyhow, and didn't look like the mothers of the Girl Guides who had come out from England at their school vacations. Bett wore a pull-on woolly most of the time, like Madge's pull-on woolly, only with longer arms, and Bett had the same kind of short hair that had to be brushed all the time to keep it out of your eyes. Bett was a very good friend, though she didn't seem like other people's mothers, and she did spoil things terribly. (4)

The only significant point of difference between Madge and Bett stems from Bett's attention to her maternal role: her insistence on thoughtfulness (giving tea to Miss Hayes, scolding Madge for stealing fruit from villagers who need the money it brings) and her concern for Madge's safety (making her wear shoes, foreseeing dangers in the forest or the lake). And that conflict is resolved in the course of Madge's adventures, which teach her the wisdom of Bett's views and inspire a renewed allegiance to her mother.

---

[7] H.D. acknowledges this in her memoir *Thorn Thicket* (1960), where she recalls Perdita's presence during her last visit to Freud: "This is the little girl, or am I the little girl, Madge or Mad?" (2012: 183).

Several central chapters are devoted to the critical moments when Madge finds herself trapped on the mountainside. A distant sound—a cry of "who—eee" that proves to be the voice of André—interrupts Madge's downward progress, causing her to be overcome by fear and dizziness, and precipitates a train of thought that at once affirms Bett's outlook and exemplifies a mode of mythical thinking that Madge has learned from Bett. When Madge hears the sound again, she recognizes an echo and thinks at once of "the story of the boy who was turned into a flower and the girl he loved called Echo," then remembers that "when Bett told that story, Bett was the most lovely sort of mother" (19) and begins to think with greater tenderness not only of her mother's story-telling but also of the life her mother has chosen for them, and wishes she had not quarreled with her.

Bett has taught Madge to recognize the mythical in her own surround-ings and also to understand myths as symbolic, using the metaphor of a lamp, infused with light as a mythic narrative is infused with a deeper, less literal meaning:

Bett made Madge understand that the stories weren't just stories, but that there was something in them like the light in the lamp that isn't the lamp. Bett would say to Madge, when she was a very little girl, "Now what is the lamp side of the story and what is the light side of the story?" so Madge could see very easily (when she was a very little girl) that the very beautiful stories Bett told her, that were real stories, had double meanings.   (20)

While Bett has a special fondness for classical myths, which she treats as paradigmatic, her vision is also syncretic. She stresses the fundamental identity of myths from multiple traditions, highlighting common elem-ents that transcend differences of language and religion. This is reflected in Madge's thoughts when the reverberating "whoo—eee" reminds her of a frightening thunder cloud and makes her see "the rightness of Bett in being frightened sometimes":

Madge tried to hold on to something that would bring her comfort. Bett said, in those lamp-and-light stories, that the thunder was the voice of Zeus, and Zeus in those lamp-and-light Greek stories was the father of everyone, so Bett said he was like the other God our Father which art in Heaven, only the Greek light-in-lamps people called him by another name.   (24)

Here Bett equates Zeus with the god of Christianity, evoked through the opening words of the Lord's Prayer (in the version current among English speakers of her day): "Our Father, which art in Heaven." The thought of Zeus/Our Father precipitates a prayer for forgiveness and a prayer that her mother not be angry; as she prepares to meet with the God she thinks is calling to her, Madge has "a little bout of reconciliation with everything," and this reconciliation consists chiefly of admitting to herself that her mother is right in questioning Madge's common sense and moral judgment. But the same thought also leads, beyond this acceptance of Bett's immediate maternal fears, to Bett's conception of Madge's place in history.

As she considers Bett's decision to distance herself from England, Madge's thoughts turn to the way Bett has appealed to the "father in heaven" in another sense, to explain Madge's own circumstances to her and to enlist Madge in her own pacifist vision: the father in heaven becomes a figure for the human father who has died, and specifically the father who has died in World War I. Because Madge has a father in heaven in this sense, she stands in a momentous relation to other such war orphans.

There were so many, many children, Bett said, who had that kind of "Father who art in Heaven" for a father, and such children, Bett said, were (must be) just a tiny, tiny bit different from other children. Now there was a great army of children all over the world—French children and German children and Serbian children and Turkish children and American children and Armenian children and Russian children. And all, all of these children, though they might never know one another, were all sort of odd little brothers and sisters (Bett said) and they must never, never hate each other, and they must never hate each other's countries, because every one of them had a sort of "Father which art in Heaven" for a father, and they must feel differently about wars and about soldiers killing each other than other children. (27–8)

H.D. draws on the universality of a mythical archetype—the father in heaven, identified as both the Greek Zeus and the Christian god—to address a particular historical situation. Through Madge's fictional circumstances and a narrative in which Madge channels her mother's thoughts, she expresses the hopes that she and other adults who had lived through the war invested in children: children had not yet formed the hostile allegiances of recent history and their shared relationship to a mythic archetype might prevent them from doing so. Madge knows hardly anything about the war, only that Bett lives in Switzerland in order "to forget a wicked war" (21), but she becomes the vehicle for a vision born out of H.D.'s own traumatic experiences. H.D. was living in England during the war and endured, along with generally shared hardships, the death of her brother in action, the sudden death of her grief-stricken father, estrangement from her shell-shocked English husband, and the birth of her daughter under difficult circumstances.[8]

Bett's vision of war orphans united through the mythic paradigm of the human child with a divine father reflects the hope of many in that period that international understanding could be fostered through children's shared connections to storytelling and myth; these hopes were founded both on longstanding ideas of myths as a common heritage and of children as uncontaminated by adult hatreds and on more recent discoveries by folklorists and anthropologists about the universality of story types.[9] One prominent expression of this view, which focuses specifically on classic works of European children's literature rather than wider mythic patterns, is Paul Hazard's *Les Livres, les enfants et les hommes* (published in 1932 and translated into English towards the end of the Second World War in 1944 as *Books, Children and Men*), which was mentioned in Chapter 2 for Hazard's celebration of Kingsley.[10] Hazard's study is in part an account of children's literature as forging national identities within distinct European traditions, but he lays even more stress on the ability of children's books to cross borders:

Yes, children's books keep alive a sense of nationality; but they also keep alive a sense of humanity. They describe their native lands lovingly, but they also describe faraway lands where unknown brothers live. They understand the essential quality of their own race; but each of them is a messenger that goes beyond mountains and rivers, beyond the seas, to the very ends of the world in search of new friendships. Every country gives and every country receives—innumerable are the exchanges—and so it comes about that in our first impressionable years the universal republic of childhood is born.   (Hazard 1944: 146)

Hazard's book-centered vision requires an emphasis on translation as an indispensable factor in international exchange, and he makes a great

---

[8] On H.D.'s literary career as shaped by "a series of formative tragedies between 1915 and 1919," see DuPlessis 1986: 72–3; on the impact of her World War I experiences on her fiction for adults, see Tate 1997.

[9] For a discussion of this phenomenon in relation to other, more positively martial responses to World War I in writing for children, see Murnaghan and Roberts 2016.

[10] For Hazard's contribution in the larger context of internationalist views of children's literature, and for a contemporary critique of those views, see O'Sullivan 2004. For a somewhat earlier expression of similar views by an American children's librarian, see Hunt 1924.

point of the many languages into which such children's classics as *Robinson Crusoe, The Swiss Family Robinson,* and *The Wonderful Adventures of Nils* have been translated.[11] Myths and fairy tales, however, can be seen as escaping the need for translation, since they in effect translate themselves, appearing in varied but recognizable forms in every national tradition, serving in their unchanging outlines as a timeless, universal language.

This conception of myth can be found in the introduction by Katherine Lee Bates (1859–1929) to the myth collection "retold and pictured" by Margaret Evans Price published in the United States in 1924 (and often reprinted afterwards, although without Bates's introduction), which was discussed in Chapter 3. Bates was a professor of English at Wellesley College, a prolific author (now remembered mostly for the lyrics to the popular patriotic song "America the Beautiful"), and after World War I an ardent advocate of the League of Nations.[12] Bates presents the universality of mythic archetypes, defined by their Greek exemplars, as something that unifies children of all nations and races.

All the world loves a story. Millions of children, in all countries, in all ages, have lifted eager little faces, white, black, tawny, yellow, brown, to the grandmother telling of a runner swifter than the wind, like Atalanta, or a young hero slaying the dragon that would have devoured a lovely maiden, as Perseus rescued Andromeda, or of a tiny people no bigger than clothes-pins, like the Pygmies, who fought the cranes.   (Price 1924: 7)

For Bates, the commonalities signaled by love of myth cross boundaries of class as well as of race and culture (a sentiment echoed in Hazard's image of an international children's "republic"); an example designed to illustrate continuity over time also subtly corrects an ethnic prejudice of early twentieth-century America: "the tale of Romulus and Remus was first told in Latin to black-eyed little Italians not so very, very, very long

---

[11] Hunt (1924: 6) calls for a "philanthropist of international outlook" to fund the translation into many languages of the books that she particularly recommends.

[12] In 1924, Bates refused to support the Republican nominee for president, Calvin Coolidge, despite her lifelong allegiance to the party, because of his opposition to the League ("Republican Women Declare for Davis," *New York Times,* October 20, 1924). For Bates's life, see Burgess 1952: esp. pp. 200–3 for her responses to World War I, which included admiration of Woodrow Wilson, refusal to boycott German scholarship, and rejection of pacifism coupled with the conviction that "the only program before the world today for ending war is to end *this* war by disarming Prussia."

ago" (7). While Bates does not share H.D.'s full-blown pacifism, her archetypal vision of myth is also linked to hatred of the recent war and to peace as a cherished goal. To counter the objection that myths involving self-sacrifice, such as those of Alcestis and Orpheus, "are too beautiful to be true," she insists that "They are too beautiful *not* to be true," and points to newspaper accounts of parents who try to save their children from burning houses and boys who drown trying to rescue their play-mates, then adds:

Sometime we shall forget the angers of the terrible war that has just shaken the world almost to its overthrow, but God remembers forever the soldiers who fell for their buddies, for their flags, for mercy and righteousness, for their faith in a blessed peace to come at last out of all their strife and suffering.   (8)

The connection between Bett's vision for Madge and such wider currents of internationalism in children's literature of the period is brought out by one of George Plank's woodcuts (Fig. 7.1): despite the different origins indicated by their native dress, boys and girls hold hands around a globe, joining in a circular dance that suggests simple, inclusive, and universal forms of play; their traditional, premodern clothing identifies them with the protagonists of the many books about children in foreign lands

Fig. 7.1. Illustration by George Plank from *The Hedgehog* by H.D. (Hilda Doolittle).

designed to promote international understanding in young readers,[13] while their joint dance recalls the informal, polyglot children's chorus of Woolf's *The Years*.

Bett's teaching has endowed Madge with qualities that support these hopes, including the refusal of an exclusive national identity. Despite her American and British parentage, Madge is comfortably at home in Switzerland and conversant in the various forms of French spoken in her village. In this she is contrasted to the myopic English tourists who visit the region, especially her own counterparts, Girl Guides, who say "quite solemnly, that England should, and must, fight its enemies," while Madge says "England has no enemies but its own hearts" (H.D. 1988: 28). Madge plays out the connection between a heightened attunement to myth and the ability to see beyond differences of nationality and class in her response to being rescued by André. In her fear, as she clings to the mountainside, she prays to a trio of interchangeable powers, variously invoked in German, Greek, and English: among them is the *Weltgeist*, a spirit that her mother has told her is a lovely idea of the Germans for which there is no translation, but which can be compared to the Greek god Pan.

Weltgeist was a sort of Pan, a god of terror and of woods, who belonged to everybody, and that Greek word stays the same too, since the Greeks have such lovely thoughts and such different thoughts that no words were ever found to translate them afterwards. Pan in Greek means everything, or everywhere, and God who was god of everyone, of all, all the wild things, was called Pan. *Weltgeist* and Pan were very much alike, and shivering and trembling, clutching at the berry bushes, Madge cried, "O *Weltgeist*, O Pan, O our-Father-which-art, please somebody come to help me."   (31)

When André then appears, Madge sees him as Pan answering her prayer, for to her André is "a smallish Pan person, someone who knew everything, who was everywhere at all times" (38). This treatment of André connects *The Hedgehog* with those English children's books from the earlier twentieth century in which, as we noted in Chapter 3, some version of Pan appears in the world of modern children: *Peter Pan*, *The Wind in the Willows*, *The Secret Garden*, and *Puck of Pook's Hill*.[14]

---

[13] A bibliography of such books is included in Hunt 1924.

[14] On this phenomenon, see Lerer 2008: 253–73; Nodelman 2008: 274–5; and esp. Bazovsky 2018. On the Edwardian fascination with Pan in relation to the period's interest in mysticism and the occult, in which H.D. was herself deeply involved, see Hynes 1968: 146.

The prominence of Pan in Edwardian children's books is a legacy of his widespread presence in nineteenth-century literature on both sides of the Atlantic, where he appears in works by Keats, Shelley, Robert Browning, Elizabeth Barrett Browning, Wilde, Stevenson, Hawthorne, Thoreau, and many others as a figure for paganism, rustic earthiness, erotic passion, poetic inspiration, and mystic knowledge. In works for children, Pan is inevitably somewhat tamed, most often assuming his traditional protective function as he presides over a gentle transition to greater maturity rather than playing an aggressive, disruptive role, but his presence also reflects a sense that children are inherently anarchic as well as more closely attuned to nature than adults.[15]

Among those Pan figures, H.D.'s André most closely resembles Dickon of *The Secret Garden*; like Dickon, he is a real boy of lower social status than the heroine, with a somewhat comical appearance, and he is heard before he is seen. André's "Who—ee" precedes him as does Dickon's "low, peculiar whistling sound" (Burnett 1911: 120) (which itself recalls Keats's appeal to Pan in *Endymion* as "Strange ministrant of undescribed sounds" (1. 285)). André also resembles Dickon in his role as mediator between wild and domestic spaces: he escorts Madge from the mountainside to Dr Blum's house, where he waits outside in the garden, then back to her own home. But H.D.'s version of Pan lacks the erotic dimension that appears in barely displaced form in the regenerative power of Dickon's skillful gardening. And in Madge's chastened understanding, the nature-worshipping impulses inspired by Pan must be carefully controlled out of concerns for safety and civility:

Pan was the thing that got hold of you and made you wild and made you rush up hills and along river-beds all alone, crying and swishing at the bushes for sheer joy. But all this joy is of no use if it leads you into danger, and all this joy turns a wicked thing (like some sprite or gnome or pixie) if it makes you hurt other people. (42)

What sets H.D.'s treatment of this motif apart from other examples is the way in which Pan's presence is not a given of the story (as, for example, in *The Wind in the Willows*) or an analogy suggested by nomenclature or traditional symbols but a discovery made in the child protagonist's own imagination. Madge connects André to Pan especially through his

---

[15] Nodelman 2008: 274.

dialect. Among the several levels of French that she commands (in contrast to visiting English and American schoolgirls, who learn only one standard version of the language),

> She loved best what she called André-French, and looking up now she knew that André-French was the sort of French the Greek god Pan would speak if he spoke French and not Greek. The Greek god Pan must have spoken a funny kind of Greek, just as André spoke a funny kind of French. (35–6)

By making André's demotic speech the key to his mythic identity, H.D. stresses the link between myth and the culture of ordinary people. Not only does Madge befriend André across barriers of both language and class, but she sees in him a symbol of everyone. She redefines his particular dialect of French as the idiom of a figure who transcends language, uniting ideas expressed in multiple languages, notably those of the recent war's antagonists, German and English. Here, as in other such formulations of the period, Greek mythology and the Greek language retain their privileged position, but the myths are definitive archetypes of universal phenomena rather than the starting point for a specific historical tradition, and Greek is a master language that captures the prelinguistic purity of childhood. As Madge interprets her world through the lens of myth, she embodies a transcendent brotherly and sisterly spirit needed for a new, more peaceful world. The ensuing collaboration between Madge and André, in which André scolds and teases Madge but also helps her carry out her mission of finding a hedgehog, briefly enacts the new order in which Bett has invested her hopes.[16] At the same time, André's identification with Pan recalls the childhood-resembling prewar period which that new order will reinstate.

The Hedgehog follows a pattern often found in children's books, in which the child protagonist's desires are fulfilled only to be revealed as foolish and trumped by adult wisdom. Here the desires fulfilled and corrected are relatively trivial, involving small departures from common sense such as wanting to go without shoes or to take a steep short-cut down the mountainside. Madge's newfound wisdom serves mainly as the occasion for her full scale reaffirmation of a broader outlook, instilled by her mother, which she has already internalized before the story begins. Madge's gesture of independence yields quickly to her demonstration

---

[16] On Dickon in *The Secret Garden* as a democratizing figure, see Bazovsky 2018.

that she is truly her mother's creation. Furthermore, the role of the adult author in constructing the child protagonist is built into the text through H.D.'s barely disguised inclusion of herself in the figure of Bett. The predetermined nature of Madge's experience is also signaled by the mysterious object of her quest, the *hérisson,* which when apprehended in its English form as a "HeDgehog" turns out to be one more version of H.D.'s own name, a variation on the combination of letters with which she entitled not only herself but also many of her other inescapably autobiographical works as well.[17]

As H.D. recounts her child character's embrace of an identity generated by the adult author, she exemplifies the paradoxical conception of myth that we have traced throughout this study: children are understood to be the natural possessors of myth, but they have to be told about it by better-informed adults, who are versed in the classical tradition. Like many others, H.D. softens this discrepancy by displacing the transmission of myth through books and learned authorities onto informal maternal storytelling. In making Madge learn about myth directly from Bett, H.D. bypasses the role of Hawthorne's works in her own childhood, much as Hawthorne disguises his own transmission of material derived from Anthon's *Classical Dictionary* (1841) and other bookish sources as the spontaneous storytelling of a more childlike narrator, which itself replicates a scene of primordial narration to "our great-grandmother the Earth."[18]

H.D. takes this paradox one step further by having Bett convey to Madge, not only the stories themselves, but also a sophisticated understanding of their universal symbolic significance; in this Bett departs from the worldwide grandmothers invoked, for example, by Bates. This added instruction allows Madge to seize her birthright more fully and corrects the patronizing assumption that children are inferior beings, unable to grasp what adults understand, but it also turns Madge into an atypical, precocious version of a child.

H.D. draws on her central mythical archetype to raise and then finesse the question of Madge's singularity in the episode of Madge's meeting

---

[17] Other such titles include *Hedylus, Heliodora and Other Poems; Hermetic Definition.* Schaffner's "Introduction" to *The Hedgehog* begins, "'All books are about oneself,' my mother used to say" (H.D. 1988: vii.)

[18] H.D.'s tailoring of myth for a child audience in *The Hedgehog* nonetheless reveals the influence of Hawthorne. Swann 1962: 160–1.

with Dr Blum. Struck by something Madge says, Dr Blum exclaims, "Röselein, I often wonder who really was your father. You come out with things like one of the fortunate half-children of Olympus." Dr Blum's words hint at complicating questions about the actual identity and possible legacy of Madge's absent father and construe the paradigm of the child with one divine parent as signaling individual election rather than a collective destiny. But, after a moment's hesitation, Madge reasserts Bett's more inclusive and generally beneficial interpretation of the myth.

> Now what did Doctor Blum mean by fortunate half-children? "You mean God and men, or God and women having children—like—like . . . " Then it seemed to Madge quite clear. "You mean like all of us who have only a Father-which-art-in-Heaven for a father?" (69)

Madge is also distinguished from her playmate André, who has no awareness of the mythic world in which Madge situates him. When he tells her that eagles sometimes snatch up children, Madge is reminded of a story, but André hasn't "much use at the moment for Ganymede" (40) and is concerned only to rescue Madge from her predicament. And when Madge tries to tell him about the Naiads, the Oreads, Echo, and Narcissus, he is stubbornly resistant, though this is manifested in a "stubborn little goat expression" (44) that itself reaffirms his connection to Pan in Madge's mind. André's French may be in one sense comparable to Greek, but he also resembles H.D.'s unwitting brother as she looks back at him in *Tribute to Freud*, unable to access his resemblance to Prometheus because "he doesn't know any Greek."

At the same time, Madge is assimilated to an adult who is herself notably childlike, distinguished from other adults by a sympathy for her daughter that is especially evident when she tells her about the inherently childish subject of myth. In this she resembles Hawthorne's youthful surrogate Eustace Bright and evokes the more general image of the children's writer as an adult who retains an ability to see with childlike eyes. If the knowledge of myth she transmits is more an adult's than a child's, that knowledge is also distinguished from traditional learning, which is represented by Dr Blum. When Madge asks Dr Blum whether *hérissons* are "mixed up like eagles with stories out of Greek books?" (63) his response is to turn to his own books, where he uncovers the information that at different periods the Greeks used hedgehogs' skins as caps and for combing wool.[19] In his scholarship, Dr Blum is contrasted to Bett and Madge, but he also has a full appreciation of myths as stories, so that he combines and harmonizes the forms of knowledge that are opposed in Hawthorne's confrontation between Eustace Bright and Mr Pringle.

Fending off the practical claims of England (where "there was a lot of money put away that depended on something, trustees or wards or chanceries or something like that" (27)), Bett has created a life for both herself and Madge that resembles a permanent, Edenic childhood, in a natural setting untouched by the divisions and dislocations of history, a place where "everyone knows . . . that everyone is as good everyone else" (37). The entire landscape in which Madge's flight and return is played out is a space of safety, where there are hedgehogs to deal with vipers and a friendly woodcutter to rescue the errant heroine. There Madge can stand apart from time as Bett has ordained that she should: "You must be no year at all, Alpen-Rose, but part of everything" (21). As Madge finds herself "clinging, part of sky, part of lake, part of rocks and very much part of everything, to the side of a cliff," she thinks:

All the small stones had slipped down long since, ages and ages since, before even Hannibal crossed the Alps (these Alps), before even Napoleon marched right straight through their valley (this valley) on his way to Italy. Long and long and long ago, as long ago, Madge thought, as the beginning of the first narcissus on their hills, the little stones had slipped down; Madge saw now that she was the tiniest little part of everything . . .   (23–4)

Madge associates the terrain in which she is trapped with two historical episodes that recall some of the heroic actions celebrated in historical fiction, but views them simply as random signposts in the long unbroken span of geological time, which stretches back to a mythic "long ago," when the narcissus first grew. For her the unchanging realm of myth is more real even than the inevitable changes registered in her own body. When she suddenly reaches the endpoint of her quest in Dr Blum's back garden, where "Nothing was changed, nothing had ever changed,"

---

[19] The distinction made here between the dry realm of historical fact (with its practical uses for hedgehog skin) and Madge's myth-making, which infuses the living hedgehog with new meaning, echoes a distinction H.D. makes elsewhere: "we need scholars to decipher and interpret the Greek, but we also need poets and mystics and children to rediscover this Hellenic world, to see *through* the words" (emphasis original). From "Notes on Euripides, Pausanias, and Greek Lyric Poets," unpublished MS in the Beinecke Library, Yale, quoted in Gregory 1997: 68.

Madge wondered what had happened. Yesterday, to-day? Spring, winter, summer? Growing up and last year's shoes that didn't fit this year—these were things
that were part of a dream, not part of a reality. Reality was the Erlking and the
moonlight on Bett's room wall. Reality was the water that rose and fell, that rose
and fell. (55)

By staying in Switzerland, by adopting a child's hairstyle and mode of
dress, and by creating for Madge a separate myth-based reality, Bett joins
Madge in a kind of perennial childhood, in which she keeps the world of
England, with its political and financial concerns, at arm's length. In this,
Schaffner suggests, she is like H.D. and Bryher, who are idealistically
cerebral and remain attached to Heidi (itself a story in which "excursions
to Alpine pastures" are contrasted to a more corrupt, less wholesome
urbanized world), while Schaffner herself has moved on to the movies,
jazz, and lipstick. Switzerland is both itself an idealized place and comparable to Greece, source of beautiful stories with double meanings and
birthplace of Pan, the embodiment of inclusiveness and benign nature.[20]
The outer world intrudes on Bett, but in ways she is able to manage, such
as occasional visits from Madge's buffoonishly conventional Uncle Harry
or the slightly tedious presence of Miss Hayes, who collects outworn
clothes for English orphans. Translating their circumstances into terms
she thinks Madge will understand allows Bett to "forget a wicked war" in
a country whose complex history of political neutrality can be glossed as
"people waited in their hills."[21] Here too, we see a recurrent paradox: the
innocence of children equips them to redeem the broken modern world
but also requires that they remain oriented to a timeless, primordial state,
spared knowledge of the conditions they must repair.

The Hedgehog's persistent collapsing of child and adult is evident in
the numerous ways that adult perspectives pervade its account of a
child's experience. In describing Madge's circumstances, the narrating
voice sometimes suggests an adult talking down to a child, often with

---

[20] In identifying the setting of her daughter's childhood with Greece, H.D. replicates her
approach to the American setting of her own childhood. Writing in 1937, she observed of
her early poems, "It is nostalgia for a lost land. I call it Hellas. I might, psychologically, just
as well, have listed the Casco Bay islands off the coast of Maine" (1938: 1287; see also
Pearson 1969: 437).

[21] Swiss neutrality is also obliquely indicated by the book's title, since the Swiss were said
to display the "hedgehog syndrome," a tendency to curl up and show only their prickles to
outsiders. Debo 2012: 13.

a patronizing "now" (rhetorical rather than temporal): "Now old Doctor Blum, as Madge well knew, had the little villa...down on the lake drive" (11–12). Passages focalized through Madge employ a stock version of childish diction ("Madge, who understood most anybody's French, somehow for the moment couldn't remember just what was a *hérisson*," 11) or, while adopting a simplified child-friendly tone marked by repetition and short sentences, fluctuate between Madge's thoughts and the impression she makes on adults:

> Madge sauntered toward Madame Beaupère, swinging her little too-short blue skirt. Her little too-short-skirt showed incredibly grubby knees, incredibly scratched and incredibly valiant. Madge never paid any attention to her knees. If you begin to think about them they defeat you. Madge had her funny little old philosophy, she knew so many little odd things. She was certain Bett was quite wrong this time.   (5)

Madge's sense of herself is manifestly shaped by adult expectations of children, which she simultaneously fulfills and transcends, as when she recalls Bett's teaching: "so Madge could see very easily (when she was a very little girl) that the very beautiful stories Bett told her, that were real stories, had double meanings" (20). When confronted with the benighted adult world of Uncle Harry, she deploys that understanding with self-conscious irony:

> Uncle Harry always pinched her cheeks and asked Madge if she had learned her a, b, c yet, and if she had forgotten English. Madge politely let her cheeks be pinched, and made up the sort of baby-answer that she thought would please Uncle Harry, but she knew in her heart that Uncle Harry was what Bett called a hypocrite and an old fraud. "Harry considers it patriotic to have his children speak French like *Punch* cartoon jokes of the year 1880."   (21)

As we move at the end of this passage into Bett's directly quoted comment, we enter with her into a more historically specific grown-up realm, and the narrative speaks over the heads of its child readers to an adult audience: the joke, like the jokes in *Punch*, is for grown-ups.

These narrative modes call attention to an adult presence that is arguably inescapable in any writing for children but that here manifests itself in a particularly obtrusive and prescriptive way. It is not surprising that H.D. herself was far from certain that her book was really either "for children" or "about a child" and that she did not, in the end, show it to her daughter. Nor is it surprising that, when her hopes for a more peaceful future were shattered by the arrival of World War II, she turned in *The Gift* to an experiment of a different kind: a return to her own childhood with all of its actual violence and sexuality and its more arduously resolved conflict between mother and daughter, as well as its highly particular promise of peace; this text is frankly addressed to adults, but cast in a stream of consciousness that attempts, as in the passage about Ida and her mother quoted above, to capture directly the unmediated thoughts of a child.

Looking back at *The Hedgehog* from the later vantage of 1960, H.D. deploys a metaphor from the geopolitics of that time to sum up her earlier project: "All that sentiment, security was this Swiss side of the iron-curtain, as I call it, and behind it, the other side of my consciousness, there was the whole War I sequence waiting to be written" (2012: 181). In an observation that chimes with the claims of such theorists as Jacqueline Rose, H.D. recognizes her construction of a sharply demarcated and idealized childhood as a defensive response to adult concerns (which she herself subsequently addressed in a number of works for adults).

In keeping with this agenda, *The Hedgehog* appropriates the inner life of a child and a daughter as the medium for a mother's vision, drama-tizing a strengthened bond between two characters who are already versions of each other. This merging of the child with the mother and author seems to foreclose any authentic depiction of the actual experience of a child or of the relationship of a mother and daughter as distinct people. Yet H.D. does not entirely evade the question of the daughter's need for autonomy and a distinct subjectivity. In the course of the narrative, she both acknowledges the problem she has created and points to an escape, drawing in each case on the language of myth.

When Madge first recalls the story of Echo, her version of it (which may or may not be an accurate recollection of Bett's) contains a surpris-ing mistake; she speaks of "the boy who was turned into a flower and the girl he loved [rather than the girl who loved him] called Echo" (19). We are offered this reversed version of the myth at the very moment when the daughter (Bett's alter ego, and H.D.'s fictionalized daughter and self) begins to think more kindly of her mother. The self-love of Narcissus is reworked as love of another, but another who is an imitation of Narcissus himself. Madge's slip opens up questions about the autonomy of mother and daughter. Is Bett's loving instruction of Madge simply the creation of an Echo? Is Madge's newly strengthened love for Bett really a form of imitation and mirroring?

When Madge retells this story to André, another mythological paradigm is introduced.

Some of the light-in-lamp people you look for and never find. Echo is easy to find, and the boy Narcissus. The boy Narcissus is the white flowers on the slopes in late spring . . . His breath is the breath of the narcissus, and when spring comes he rises from the black earth to tell us that there is a life after this life for everyone. Echo is the answer of our own hearts, like the singing in a sea-shell. (44)

Narcissus is here figured as a version of Persephone, returning each spring to bring the promise of the mysteries. The myth that Madge here invokes functions throughout the text as an analogue to her own experience. Her journey down the mountain to consult Dr Blum is a kind of charmed *katabasis*, a descent to the underworld in search of guidance from a wise prophet and a magic talisman, like those of such adult male heroes as Odysseus and Aeneas. But as a girl's story, involving departure from and return to her mother, it particularly evokes the adventures of Persephone.

The Persephone myth has already emerged in earlier chapters as one of the most frequently retold for children, despite its troublesome themes of sexuality and death, and we have seen those themes occluded by Hawthorne in *Tanglewood Tales* and restored by the child H.D. in *The Gift*.[22] In *The Hedgehog's* romanticized Swiss version, H.D. follows the lead of Hawthorne, whose retelling has itself invited comparison to *Heidi* for its depiction of a delightful child who brings cheer to a lonely old man. In her own retelling, H.D. replaces the dangerous and lustful Hades with two benign and helpful male figures, the Teiresias-like Dr Blum and André.

When Madge arrives in Dr Blum's garden, he himself greets her as Persephone: interrupting Madge's meditation on myth as reality, he calls out, "Why, dear me, it's Alpen-rose, come back with summer's coming." In his combination of mythic and scientific knowledge and his beneficence, Dr Blum resembles "the Professor," Freud as recalled by H.D. in

[22] On the prominence of the Persephone myth in late 19th- and early 20th-century British literature, see Radford 2007, Louis 2009; on the katabasis motif in English and French children's literature, Vaclavik 2010; on the Persephone myth in girls' fantasy literature, Blackford 2012.

Tribute to Freud;[23] the king of the dead has been replaced by the figure who "has summoned a host of dead and dying children from the living tomb." Dr Blum performs for Madge a mild version of the talking cure, helping her to understand her naughty rebellion by analogy to the inevitable thorns that come with the rose, as part of her nature as "Alpen-Rose" (a trait that links her to the prickly but helpful hedgehog). This too is an episode of mutual understanding across the linguistic divisions of the recent war. As a German-speaking Swiss from Berne, Dr Blum makes his point with a German proverb (*Bei die Rosen gleich die Dornen stehn*), which Madge comprehends through its French near-equivalent (*tout épine a sa rose*) (59).

Dr Blum's wisdom mostly reinforces Bett's teaching. His gentle chiding causes Madge to regret the hostility to Miss Hayes that set her journey in motion, nudging her towards a more adult conception of social obligations. But his house is also a space, like Persephone's under-world, where the daughter has experiences that divide her from her mother and keep her there. When Dr Blum welcomes her in his garden, Madge has been thinking about a version of reality that suggests Per-sephone as a figure for separation and freedom, "Reality was the moment that spring turns and waves farewell to summer" (55). While Dr Blum consults his books for information about ancient Greek uses of hedge-hogs, Madge examines a mirror that reflects a plume of grass in a vase; when he calls her to join him in the library, she leaves behind a part of herself: "the other Madge shut up in a gray-green surface behind a feathery gray-and-silver plume of swamp grass" (65).

The Persephone myth is also played out as a story of partial inde-pendence in Madge's alliance with André, her "wild-wood friend and wild companion" (76). André represents the threatening figure of Hades somewhat more than Dr Blum does, but even his Pan-like wildness is linked to a protective, non-sexual love:[24]

---

[23] Gubar 1990: 297. H.D. herself recalled with satisfaction that at their last meeting Freud acknowledged the book, which Bryher had sent him, by addressing Perdita with the question, "are you the heroine of the *Hedgehog*?" (2012: 183).

[24] The absence of erotic love from the book is reflected in Madge's strong identification with Artemis, in a prayer to the moon before she leaves Dr Blum's garden (75–6). In this she can be contrasted with another young figure with whom H.D. was concerned during the same period: Hippolytus, painfully caught between Artemis and Aphrodite.

There is a kind of wood-lore or wood-love that drags people into the heart of woods, but there must be a kind of love to balance it that is just natural love, the sort of love that made André rush down the dangerous cliff after a foreign girl who had been very naughty. (41–2)

Far from dragging Madge down the cliff, he follows her on her downward course, and snatches her up "half lifting, half jerking, half pulling" (40) in order to rescue her. Helping her on her way to Dr Blum's house, he resembles Pan's father Hermes, the god who provides humans with an escort to the underworld. André is most threatening for the way he teases Madge, laughing at her ignorance about the *hérisson*, hiding her lost shoes before giving them back, and promising to tell her mother "*this* time" (42) about the trouble she got herself into.

At the very end of the story, when Madge is safe at home, she falls asleep. Unsure whether or not she is dreaming, she overhears André, not in fact telling her mother of her dangerous adventure but instead making excuses and concealing the truth:

I would not scold her too much, we were late because we—because I got stuck on the hill-path. We were—we were late because we got lost, you see—we got lost, you see—going to find the hedgehog. (77)

With these words, which end the book, Madge is once again rescued by her own Pan, who takes responsibility both for the expedition and for its difficulties. Bett is evidently not to know the true story of Madge's quest; the narrative concludes with the daughter returned to the mother yet granted a space of privacy, a separate life to which the mother has no access.

In *The Hedgehog*, then, H.D.'s myth-inflected meditation on mothers and daughters brings together the inevitable mirroring and self-love that so complicate this relationship with the promise that recovery and reunion are not incompatible with separation and growth. The depiction of classical myth as a form of maternal heritage reveals the adult's absorption of the child into a set of attitudes and values that are not of the child's own making, throwing into relief the adult agendas that drive many retellings of myths for children. But myth is here not just a shared language that binds daughter to mother, child audience to adult storyteller; it is also a set of tools with which the child can herself explore, interpret, and reimagine the world in which she finds herself.

Epilogue

In *The Ordinary and the Fabulous*, a tribute to myths and fairy tales as indispensable reading for children first published in 1968, the English educator Elizabeth Cook evokes the power of "archetypal and anonymous" stories to inspire creative play.

I have seen two ten-year-olds playing at Theseus and the Minotaur in a solitary orchard with no grown-up, as they thought, within sight or hearing.

(Cook 1976: 9)

The grownups who figure in this book share Cook's fascination with what they see or remember as a child's distinctive experience of the classical past—playful, direct, unselfconscious, and absorbing. In their many and various works, they seek to stimulate and channel that experience for child readers or return to it in memory as they address their own ongoing concerns for adult audiences.

The alliances these authors construct between classics and childhood are sometimes rooted in actual playacting like the scene that Cook observed. Nathaniel Hawthorne's groundbreaking retellings of Greek myths for modern children were preceded by games in which his wife Sophia acted out the same myths with their own children. Edith Hamilton, telling the myths again a century later, was building on a legacy stretching back to her own childhood in Indiana in the 1870s, in which she and her siblings reenacted the Trojan War. Even more pervasive is the assumption that children are especially given to, and especially enjoy, the kind of identification and immediacy involved in reenactment. We have seen that assumption affirmed in many adult reminiscences, from Heinrich Schliemann taking on Hector's mission to defend Troy, to Frederic Macdonald who "knew the pyramids and the Colosseum" by the time he was 12, to Robert Lowell insisting that Hawthorne's version of the Heracles story was the right one because "I was there."

Children's identification with figures from ancient mythology and history is actively promoted by adult writers who work to make classical figures easier for modern children to see as versions of themselves. Myth-retellers like Hawthorne or the Crawfords refashion Pandora or Persephone to resemble modern girls; authors of historical fiction insert ancient girls and boys with modern outlooks into ancient history; other authors invent modern child avatars of ancient figures, such as James Daugherty's Andy or H.D.'s André. This fostering of identification is designed to activate children's presumed pleasure in the past, fueling their imagination and sense of wonder, and also to bring other, more useful benefits: that pleasurable involvement is enlisted in the cause of education, laying the groundwork for cultural literacy and paving the way for more formal training in classical languages or the documented facts of ancient history.

Acting out the story of Theseus, the boys observed by Cook are engaging with a figure whose own transition from youth to adulthood traverses the border between the inspiring fictions of myth and the instructive lessons of history, as he progresses from his fantastic Cretan adventures to a new role as a statesman, in which he is presented by Andrew Lang as a shrewd diplomat forging a strategic alliance between the Athenians and the Dorians and by Edith Hamilton as the founder, through the unification of Attica, of a federation of states devoted to liberty for all. Erick Berry imagines a parallel trajectory for her "winged girl of Crete," who undergoes along with Theseus' wife Ariadne a final displacement from mythical Crete to historical Athens; in the case of Berry's girl heroine, however, the change from myth to history, girlhood to womanhood, entails a loss of freedom and autonomy with her departure from the public stage into the narrowed world of womanhood and marriage.

In the preceding chapters, we have observed the century-long development of a tradition of classics for children, initiated in the mid-nineteenth century and repeatedly updated to supply new, more timely scripts for children's imaginative lives. Over that span of time there was a significant expansion in the range of children envisioned as the natural audience for classical material, with writing for children playing a continuing role as a leading form of popularization. Hawthorne and Kingsley were addressing their groundbreaking myth collections to affluent, leisured New Englanders on vacation from school or to English boys who would soon be learning Greek and Latin and English girls who would be expected in their future lives to recognize classical allusions. But as the myths and legends of Greece and Rome were increasingly recognized as forms of universal folklore, largely through the anthropological investigations of the late nineteenth century, they were more readily seen as the property of all children, regardless of status or nationality, a view articulated with particular clarity by Padraic Colum in his equation of children with the audiences of popular storytelling.

In the first half of the twentieth century, classical myth and ancient history were addressed to a broader range of children, most of whom would not go on to more specialized forms of classical learning. As educational opportunities expanded for girls, fictionalized history and historical fiction offered them more active, self-directed ancient counterparts. With efforts to forge a distinctive American children's literature, the classical heritage was appropriated for pointedly ordinary, down-to-earth, white middle-class children like Robert McCloskey's Homer Price; the experiences of such children were projected onto imagined classical equivalents like the Roman farm boy recruits of Reuben Wells's *With Caesar's Legions*.

For some writers, children's affinity to a universal heritage embodied in classical myth was not just a spur to never-ending new publications but also a source of hope for the human race, especially in response to the twentieth century's two world wars. We see this in the works of H.D., both in her vision of war orphans brought together across national divisions by their shared relationship to the myth of the semi-divine child and in her attempt to access her own childhood connection to myth as an antidote to the destructive hostilities of World War II. The possibility that children's universal connection to myth could also transcend divisions of class was recognized, not just by writers like James Daugherty and Robert McCloskey, but also by educators like Elizabeth Cook, who argued (echoing a point made by Charlotte Yonge a century earlier) that myths and fairy tales were more accessible to the economically and ethnically diverse British school population of the 1970s than realistic novels that assumed an understanding of specific social conditions and conventions (Cook 1976: 8). Among the most purposeful promoters of this link between children's experience of Greco-Roman classics and an increasingly inclusive vision was Virginia Woolf. Woolf herself first learned of the Greeks when her brother came home from school and, "handing it on as if it was something worth knowing" (Woolf 1976: 108), told her about Hector and Troy, but decades later she herself claimed the heritage of Greece for a very different vision in the final episode of *The Years*, in which lower-class children who are not differentiated by gender and who represent an unknown but undoubtedly changing future instinctively incorporate fragments of Greek into their song.

In the period since the mid-1960s there has been no falling-off of efforts to make the classics accessible to children, pursued under expanding definitions of inclusiveness and answering to children's evolving tastes and modes of consumption. In the United States, the conservatism inherent in much home-schooling has led to the reissuing of many of the older books we have treated here: myth collections, histories, biographies and historical novels dating back to the middle of the nineteenth century are available in print or on the Internet, and pagan myth and history have a paradoxically important place among "the best of the children's books first published a century ago when a Christian worldview and high standard of literary excellence were the norm."[1] But fresh representations of the ancient world for modern children are also appearing in ever-increasing numbers and in a wider range of genres and media. And though adult nostalgia continues to play an important role, many of the most recent works strive for a striking contemporaneity, offer revisionist or subversive readings, or seek to speak to children in what is meant to be their own idiom.

In spite of the generally diminished role of the classical languages and of ancient history in secondary education, mythology has remained a staple of both school curricula and pleasure reading, regularly cited by college students as the basis of their interest in classical studies, and the supply of new myth books for children seems endless.[2] Some of these are collections of stories like Hawthorne's and Kingsley's, either sharing their focus on Greek myth (Reeves 1969a, 1969b; Lines 1973; Russell 1989; Blaisdell 1995), or presenting Greek myth in a global context (Untermeyer 1968; Horowitz 1985). But in the years following the publication of *D'Aulaires' Book of Greek Myths* (1962), the influence of this collection has made itself felt in a long series of copiously

---

[1] http://www.yesterdaysclassics.com/, accessed Dec. 15, 2016.
[2] On this continuing tradition, see Murnaghan and Roberts 2017; see also Murnaghan and Roberts 2018; Murnaghan 2015b; Roberts 2009, 2015; Weinlich 2015.

illustrated books and picture books. Among these are Mary Pope Osborne's *Favorite Greek Myths* (1989), Geraldine McCaughrean's *Greek Myths* (1992), Heather Amery's *Usborne Greek Myths for Young Children* (1999), Lucy Coats's *Atticus the Storyteller* (2002), Heather Alexander's *A Child's Introduction to Greek Mythology* (2011), and Donna Jo Napoli's *Treasury of Greek Mythology* (2011).[3] Single-story picture books are also common.[4]

The myths in these new versions are familiar ones, and they undergo familiar modifications: sexuality and violence are obscured and heroic bad behavior is often omitted or palliated.[5] The retelling of myth continues to be justified in part by its foundational and continuing role in Western culture. At the same time, however, many new versions of myth reflect contemporary anxieties about the capacity of material from the distant past to appeal to modern children. The introduction to Shari Lewis's 1987 *One-Minute Greek Myths* advises parents not to "let [children] know that they're getting 'classical' Greek mythology" (Lewis 1987: 6), and the jacket of Michael Townsend's *Amazing Greek Myths of Wonder and Blunders* (2010) promises readers that "these aren't your parents' Greek myths." Readers are emphatically assured that myths are worth reading simply because they are such terrific stories: "People still tell these myths because they are good. *Really* good. We're talking keep-reading-them-thousands-of-years-later good" (Alexander 2011: 8).

The language of Heather Alexander's self-advertisement reflects an increasing tendency to talk to children about myth in language that imitates the colloquial speech of contemporary childhood. If there is a governing model for the modern myth collection, it is the cartoon or comic, which like the (now largely abandoned) fairy-tale comparison of earlier generations seems intended to appeal to children—and perhaps also to reassure adults that there will be nothing inappropriate or too frightening in such a setting. Some retellings of myth actually take the form of comic books (Williams 1991; Townsend 2010), while in others we find cartoon-like drawings (Spires 2001; McCaughrean 1992), and many

---

[3] Cf. Oldfield 1988, Vinge 1999, Kimmel 2008.

[4] See e.g. Hodges 1973; Weil 1986; Hawthorne 1987, 1990; Simons and Simons 1991.

[5] Some versions reflect new concerns about what children ought to read; they may for example comment on or attempt to mitigate ancient sexism or misogyny (Vinge 1999:11).

emphasize monsters—favorites in films and TV shows for children—over heroes, as in John Harris's *Greece! Rome! Monsters!* (2002).[6] Retellings of myth may also allude to or adopt the language of assorted phenomena of popular culture: science fiction, sports writing, and film.[7]

Recent versions of myth also display an ever-increasing freedom in the use of the original sources. In some, the ancient myth is virtually effaced, leaving only the most basic cultural associations; in others, the received story is fundamentally subverted. Retellings that attempt to reach the very young may be so simplified and so reductive that all sense of the original and of its historical distance is lost. The "Mini Myths" board book, *Be Patient, Pandora!* (Holub 2014) is the story of a little girl whose mother forbids her to open a cardboard box full of cupcakes; she is predictably unable to resist. There are glancing allusions to the myth for those who know the story (the cupcakes fly out of the box, and Pandora expresses the "hope" that her mother will still love her), but the small children for whom this series seems to be intended will presumably experience the story of the cupcakes purely on its own terms—unless or until an adult reads to them the very brief version of the myth itself on the last page of the book.[8] In contrast, retellings designed to appeal to older children who might otherwise find myth boring or antiquated offer versions that clearly rely on readers to have the kind of prior knowledge that makes revision and parody both apparent and enjoyable. In her "Myth-o-mania" books (2002–14) Kate McMullan cheerfully overturns familiar myths; her narrator, Hades, depicts these new versions as corrections of the misleading accounts in the dull and canonical *The Big Fat Book of Greek Myths*. In *Phone Home, Persephone!*, for example, we learn that the heroine was simply trying to escape her overprotective mother (McMullan 2002). The reader is presumed to be sufficiently well informed—as a result of reading some big fat myth book or other— to appreciate the humor.[9]

---

[6] For example, Sara Fanelli's *Mythological Monsters of Ancient Greece* (2002). See Roberts 2009.

[7] See Swinburne and Swinburne 1977; Bryant 2010a, 2010b; Harris 2002.

[8] Rosemary Wells's versions of Greek myth in her Max and Ruby series (Wells 1993, 1995) are also directed at the very young, but the changes she introduces are less drastic and the illustrations anchor her anachronistic versions in the ancient world.

[9] See Townsend 2010 for further retellings which retain the basic plot but introduce copious anachronisms and new features: Arachne has a fan club, and Icarus is busy training a monkey army.

A similar playfulness in the retelling of myth may be found in the relationship between verbal and visual narrative, especially in picture books and comic books, sometimes accompanied by the kind of self-reflective experimentation characteristic of the modern picture book. Marcia Williams tells her reader that "The Labyrinth was a confusing maze of cold, dark, passages," but then pictures the Labyrinth as a full-page puzzle-maze such as the reader might find (and try to negotiate) in a book of puzzles (Williams 1991). The text of Sara Fanelli's *Mythological Monsters* provides a playfully scary account of mythical beings, but the incorporation of photographs of human eyes in her collage-like representations of both monsters and heroes has an uncanny effect that is at once monstrous and humanizing. (Fanelli 2002).[10]

Historical fiction for children and young adults set in classical antiquity has also continued to flourish. Rosemary Sutcliff and Geoffrey Trease went on writing fiction set in the ancient world through the last decades of the twentieth century, and many other writers have followed in their footsteps.[11] There have been several noteworthy series, from Mary Ray's sequence of five novels, published between 1971 and 1980, which spans the Roman world in the early days of Christianity,[12] to Jack Mitchell's *The Roman Conspiracy* (2005), *The Ancient Ocean Blues* (2008), and *Chariots of Gaul* (2011), and Caroline Lawrence's hugely successful Roman Mysteries series, with seventeen novels published between 2001 and 2009. Lawrence picks up on the mystery theme, generally popular in children's literature, and featured in a number of earlier works set in classical antiquity.[13]

Historical novels set in antiquity have undergone predictable shifts in response to cultural and political change: female characters and characters who belong to other marginalized groups (the enslaved, the disabled, the non-Roman or non-Greek) are more likely to play central roles.

[10] On the "interanimation of word and image" in Fanelli and in Harris 2002, see Weinlich 2015.

[11] Examples include Dillon 1977, Banks 2004, Geary 2006, Bradman 2010. On recent fictions of Roman Britain, see Butler and O'Donovan 2012: ch. 2. Some (Sutcliff 1972, 1973; Trease 1972, 1997) are shorter works, often aimed at younger children, but see also Sutcliff 1978, 1980.

[12] Ray 1971, 1974, 1975, 1977, 1980. Ray has also written stand-alone or paired novels set in Crete and Greece during the Mycenean period.

[13] e.g. Williams 1943, 1944, 1948, 1960, and Winterfeld 1956 and 1971, translated from German. On Caroline Lawrence's series, see Lovatt 2016.

Currently acceptable attitudes are anachronistically promoted in ancient settings, and aspects of daily life once glossed over are now included. In *Reading History in Children's Books* (2012) Catherine Butler and Hallie O'Donovan describe such developments in recent children's novels about Roman Britain. The Roman occupation is no longer valued even for the material and cultural advances it has introduced, but is depicted as simply cruel and oppressive; the British resistance to or critique of Roman practices is in some novels associated with Celtic patriotism, in others with a New Age version of Druidism whose ecologically sound relationship to the land (as sacred) contrasts with the Romans' mere ownership and their (once admired) engineering projects.[14] A more playful, less heavy-handed anachronism may be found in comically subversive works like Steve Barlow and Steve Skidmore's *The Lost Diary of Julius Caesar's Slave* (1997), which makes use of cartoon illustrations and plentiful allusions to popular culture.

Over the last half century, there has been a progressive blurring of the generic distinction between retold myth and historical fiction, driven in large part by the proliferation of various forms of fantasy for young readers. In her preface to the second edition of *The Ordinary and the Fabulous*, published in 1976, Cook comments on the emergence of "an art form that did not exist before the 1960's . . . virtually teenage or even adult romances built upon plots taken from myth, legend, or fairy tale" (xiv–xv). Most of Cook's examples belong to the world of post-Tolkien, post-Lewis fantasy fiction which Michael Levy and Farah Mendlesohn call "mythopoeic fantasy" (though she includes examples of "soberly historical romance," like Rosemary Sutcliff's version of *Tristan and Iseult*) and draw on non-classical sources: Celtic legend, Egyptian and Israelite legend, German fairy tales.[15] But Cook also sees as instances of this genre Leon Garfield and Edward Blishen's retellings of Greek myth, *The God Beneath the Sea* (1970) and *The Golden Shadow* (1973), which reflect developing conceptions of how classical myths might be presented not to the D'Aulaires' child audience but to adolescents or "young adults," increasingly identified as a distinct category of reader (xv–xvi).[16]

---

[14]   Butler and O'Donovan 2012: ch. 2. Examples include Eldridge 2008, Chandler 2008, Webb 2006.

[15]   Levy and Mendlesohn 2016: ch. 7.

[16]   Eyre 1973 (1st pub. 1971); Marcus 2008: 185.

Rather than create an anthology of myths, or include subordinate myths as clearly demarcated stories within a larger mythical frame story (as in Colum's *Golden Fleece*), Garfield and Blishen weave together a selection of myths from the earliest days of gods and mortals into a work of fiction that begins with Hephaestus' first casting out of Olympus, moves both forward and backward in time, and is open to difficult "adult" themes like sexuality and death, palliating little that is disturbing. One child reader of that period, Francis Spufford (1964–), looking back as an adult, recalled what an exciting innovation this was. Compared to Roger Lancelyn Green's "useless" versions of the myths, which made "all their highs and lows smoothly, mildly reasonable," Garfield and Blishen offered a revelation of "beauty and terror."[17]

Contemporary novelists have produced a stream of classics-based versions of Cook's "romances," addressing the concerns of contemporary young readers through fictions set in the world of ancient legend, especially Minoan Crete and the Trojan War with its various aftermaths, in which the experiences of mythical figures are reimagined. Retellings by Tracy Barrett (*King of Ithaka*, *Dark of the Moon*), Adèle Geras (*Troy*, *Ithaka*, and *Dido*), Ursula Le Guin (*Lavinia*), and Clemence McClaren (*Inside the Walls of Troy* and *Waiting for Odysseus*) are typically both decentered and revisionist, and often feature female narrators or protagonists.[18] These are also, like many adult novels in the tradition of Mary Renault, rationalized and historicizing versions of the legends on which they depend: the supernatural is typically an object of belief rather than a mover of events, and a creature like the Minotaur appears (for example) as a disabled human being rather than a mythical monster. Other writers, however, maintain the supernatural framework of the mythical work; Doris Orgel's *The Princess and the God* (1996) retells the Cupid and Psyche story from Psyche's point of view, but with all the magical elements of the original, and Donna Jo Napoli intertwines the stories of Philoctetes and the Sirens (*Sirena*, 1998) and of Pan and Iphigenia (*The Great God Pan*, 2003).[19]

The loosening of distinctions among myth, history, and fantasy has given rise to a range of hybrid forms. Historical fiction set in antiquity

---

[17] Spufford 2002, 125.
[18] Barrett 2010, 2011; Geras 2001, 2005, 2009; LeGuin 2008; McClaren 1996, 2000.
[19] Cf. Kindl 2002 in which the Minotaur is a man-beast hybrid on the model of a centaur.

may include fantastic elements, as in Ann Lawrence's *The Forest and the Hills* (1977), which features an invented province in late Roman Britain, a mysterious cup, Woden in human form, and several whimsical anachronisms including a performance of the Hallellujah Chorus and an intrusion of the three bears into the story of St Perpetua.[20] Time-slip novels in which modern children encounter the ancient world (anticipated by E. Nesbit's *Story of the Amulet* and Kipling's *Puck of Pook's Hill*) include Lynne Ellison's *The Green Bronze Mirror* (1966); Phyllis Reynolds Naylor's *Shadows on the Wall* (1980) and *Faces in the Water* (1981); Julia Jarman's *The Time Travelling Cat and the Roman Eagle* (2001); and Tracy Barrett's *On Etruscan Time* (2005). In N. M. Browne's *Warriors of Alavna* (2000), time travel, fantasy, and alternative history meet as two British teenagers are transported to a past world that resembles but is not in fact Roman Britain.[21] Fantasy novels fully set in antiquity freely invent new plots and engage in transpositions of every kind: Lloyd Alexander's *The Arkadians* (1995) and Paul Shipton's *The Pig Scrolls* (2004) and *The Pig Who Saved the World* (2007) playfully allude to and rework stories from the *Odyssey* to *The Golden Ass*, and Tobias Druitt's Corydon trilogy (2005, 2006, 2007) makes monsters like Medusa, the Minotaur, and the protagonist Corydon (son of Pan, with one goat leg) sympathetic figures and turns traditional heroes into villains.[22]

At the same time, the classical past continues to play a major role in fantasy fiction set in the modern world.[23] Two of the most popular recent fantasy series—J. K. Rowling's Harry Potter books and Philip Pullman's *His Dark Materials* trilogy—follow C. S. Lewis in incorporating figures from classical mythology and other allusions to the ancient world.[24] But another bestselling fantasy sequence, Rick Riordan's Percy Jackson series, is even more centrally engaged with ancient myth. Riordan tells the story of a 12-year-old boy in modern America, to which the classical

---

[20] Discussed in Wood 2018.   [21] See Butler and O'Donovan 2012: ch. 2.

[22] See also Joan Holub and Suzanne Williams's "Goddess Girls" series (beginning with *Athena the Brain*, 2010) in which the Greek goddesses appear as teens attending Mount Olympus Academy.

[23] See e.g. Hale 2016 on the *katabasis* motif, Blackford 2012 on the Persephone myth, and Kümmerling-Meibauer 2016 on Tony Abbott's "Underworlds" series (2011–12).

[24] On Pullman and Rowling, see Spencer 2015, Hodkinson 2016, Olechowska 2016, Walde 2016.

gods have migrated as they follow the progress of world historical political dominance. Percy discovers that his learning disabilities (and assorted mysterious events in his life) are the result of his unusual heritage: he is the son of the god Poseidon, who had a brief affair with Percy's mortal mother. He joins other demigods at Camp Half-Blood and finds himself caught up in an ongoing struggle among gods, titans, and monsters that plays out in various contemporary settings.[25]

Riordan's works are explicitly rooted in the tradition of myth books for children stretching back to the nineteenth century that we discuss in our opening chapters. In contrast to his exact contemporary Francis Spufford, Riordan declares himself to have been inspired by Lancelyn Green's *Tales of the Greek Heroes*. But in his introduction to a new edition issued in 2009, Riordan recommends that book to contemporary readers by transforming it from a nostalgic and poetic encounter with the Greek past into an action-packed adventure in the here-and-now.

> Ready to get started? Fasten your armour. Grab your shield. Make sure your sword is sharpened. Within these pages are monsters that have been waiting 3000 years to fight you. It's time you showed them who's boss.
>
> (Lancelyn Green 2009: vi)

Riordan's formulation is in part a nod to the video game as a format that may be more appealing than books to many contemporary children and adolescents, especially boys. The cultural impact of new media is reflected in the various spinoffs generated by his own books, which include not only video games, but a film, multiple websites, and a Camp Half-Blood where children can enact their own quests—alternative ways of encountering the world of myth that supplement, compete with, and influence traditional printed books.[26] But he is also appealing to children's perennial tendency to respond to what they read by treating it as real and making it their own. This is a feature of

---

[25] On Riordan's use of classical motifs to address contemporary American issues, see Morey and Nelson 2015. Riordan has also written several other series, featuring the Egyptian gods, the Roman versions of the Greco-Roman pantheon, and the Norse gods.

[26] On classical myth in video games, see McMenomy 2015. Children's exposure to the ancient world through a variety of media is not new: Victorian children enjoyed scenes from ancient history in popular performances and in toy theatres, Disney was already making animated versions of myth in the 1930s, and there were comic strips with classics subjects in the 1950s, when *Astérix* got its start (see Bryant Davies 2018, Keen 2015, Almagor 2015).

childhood that is repeatedly recalled by adults, for many of whom, including Heinrich Schliemann, H.D., Robert Lowell, and Louise Glück, it forms the basis of a uniquely valued lifelong relationship to the classics.

Ever since the mid-nineteenth century, adult authors, illustrators, and publishers have acted on a broadly held conviction that children will enjoy and benefit from Greco-Roman myth and history, which can and should be rewritten for children's pleasure and understanding. In doing so, they may hope to sell books, to lay the ground for future education, to provide children with models for understanding the world, to stimulate children's imaginations, or to recreate a pleasure of their own childhood. Meanwhile, their child audiences have taken possession of the versions produced for them by adults and converted them into new stories of their own, as in the case of Leigh Hunt's erotic reading of Tooke's dry-as-dust handbook, or Penelope Lively's strategic transformation of Lang's *Tales of Troy and Greece* into a book primarily about mythical heroines, or the version of Theseus and the Minotaur enacted by two boys in an English orchard. The Internet age has generated a new far-reaching public medium for such stories in the genre of fan fiction, in which a global and multilingual community of young readers has produced over the last three decades an outpouring of revisionary responses to classical mythology. While the material reworked in fan fiction has diverse sources both ancient and modern, contemporary retellings like Riordan's Percy Jackson books play a dominant role, forming a new classical canon that has displaced traditional myth collections much as the myth collections of Hawthorne and Kinsgley and their successors displaced the myth-tellers of antiquity.[27] The long-term impact of fan fiction is still uncertain, but this new genre clearly adds yet another chapter to the ongoing history of interactions between adults and children through which children have received the legacy of classical antiquity.

[27] Marciniak 2016b.

Bibliography

Abate, M. A. 2008. *Tomboys: A Literary and Cultural History.* Philadelphia: Temple University Press.

Ackerman, R. 1991. *The Myth and Ritual School: J. G. Frazer and the Cambridge Ritualists.* London: Routledge.

Adams, J. T. 1931. *The Epic of America.* Boston: Little, Brown & Co.

Adler, E. 2015. "Kipling's Rome in *Puck of Pook's Hill.*" *Classical Receptions Journal* 7: 159–76.

Alderson, B. 1995. "Heroic Reading." *Children's Literature in Education* 26/1: 73–82.

Alcott, L. M. 1947. *Little Women.* New York: Grosset & Dunlap. First published 1868.

Alexander, H. 2011. *A Child's Introduction to Greek Mythology.* Illus. M. Hamilton. New York: Black Dog and Leventhal.

Alexander, L. 1995. *The Arkadians.* New York: Dutton.

Almagor, E. 2015. "Bridging the Gap between Generations: Astérix between Child and Adult, Classical and Modern," in L. Maurice, ed., *The Reception of Ancient Greece and Rome in Children's Literature: Heroes and Eagles.* Leiden: Brill. 291–307.

Amery, H. 1999. *Usborne Greek Myths for Young Children.* Illus. L. Edwards. London: Usborne.

Andersen, H. C. 1846a. *Wonderful Stories for Children.* Trans. M. Howitt. London: Chapman and Hall.

Andersen, H. C. 1846b. *Danish Fairy Legends and Tales.* Trans. C. Peachey. London: Pickering.

Andersen, H. C. 1846c. *A Danish Story Book.* Trans. C. Boner. London: Cundall.

Andersen, H. C. 1846d. *The Nightingale and Other Tales.* Trans. C. Boner. London: Cundall.

Andersen, H. C. 1850. *Wonderful Tales from Denmark.* Trans. C. Boner. New York: C. S. Francis.

Anderson, P. L. 1929. *With the Eagles.* New York: Appleton.

Anderson, P. L. 1930. *A Slave of Catiline.* New York: Appleton.

Anderson, P. L. 1931. *For Freedom and for Gaul.* New York: Appleton.

Anderson, P. L. 1935. *Swords in the North.* New York: Biblo and Tannen.

Anderson, P. L. 1939. *Pugnax the Gladiator.* New York: Biblo and Tannen.

Anthon, C. 1841. *A Classical Dictionary: Containing an Account of the Principal Proper Names Mentioned in Ancient Authors and Intended to Elucidate All the*

Important Points Connected with the Geography, History, Biography, Mythology, and Fine Arts of the Greeks and Romans: Together With an Account of Coins, Weights, and Measures, with Tabular Values of the Same. New York: Harper.

Antler, J. 1987. *Lucy Sprague Mitchell: The Making of a Modern Woman.* New Haven: Yale University Press.

Arbuthnot, M. H. 1947. *Children and Books.* Chicago: Scott, Foresman.

Arizpe, E., and Styles, M. 2003. *Children Reading Pictures: Interpreting Visual Texts.* London: Routledge.

Armstrong, R. H. 2005. *A Compulsion for Antiquity: Freud and the Ancient World.* Ithaca, NY: Cornell University Press.

Artzybasheff, B., ed. 1933. *Aesop's Fables.* Illus. with 20 wood engravings. New York: Viking Press.

Attebery, B. 1980. *The Fantasy Tradition in American Literature: From Irving to LeGuin.* Bloomington, IN: Indiana University Press.

Austen, J. 1953. *Mansfield Park.* London and Glasgow: Collins. First published 1814.

Avery, G. 1994. *Behold the Child: American Children and Their Books 1621–1922.* Baltimore: Johns Hopkins University Press.

Avery, G., and Kinnell, M. 1995. "Morality and Levity: 1780–1820," in P. Hunt, ed., *Children's Literature: An Illustrated History.* Oxford: Oxford University Press. 46–76.

Bacon, H. H. 1980. "Edith Hamilton," in B. Sicherman and C. H. Green, eds., *Notable American Women: The Modern Period.* Cambridge, MA: Harvard University Press. 306–8.

Bader, B. 1976. *American Picturebooks from Noah's Ark to the Beast Within.* New York: Macmillan.

Baikie, J. 2008. *Peeps at Many Lands: Ancient Greece.* Chapel Hill, NC: Yesterday's Classics. First published 1920.

Baldwin, E. [Godwin, W.] 1806. *The Pantheon: or Ancient History of the Gods of Greece and Rome. For the Use of Schools, and Young Persons of Both Sexes.* London: Godwin.

Baldwin, J. 1905. *A Story of the Golden Age of Greek Heroes.* New York: Scribner's. First published 1887.

Banks, L. R. 2004. *Tiger, Tiger.* London: HarperCollins.

Barlow, S., and Skidmore, S. 1997. *The Lost Diary of Julius Caesar's Slave.* Mahwah, NJ: Troll Communications.

Barnhouse, R. 2000. *Recasting the Past: The Middle Ages in Young Adult Literature.* London: Heinemann.

Barrett, T. 2005. *On Etruscan Time.* New York: Henry Holt.

Barrett, T. 2010. *King of Ithaka.* New York: Henry Holt.

Barrett, T. 2011. *Dark of the Moon.* New York: Houghton Mifflin Harcourt.

Baughman, R. 1967. *The Centenary of Arthur Rackham's Birth*. New York: Columbia University Libraries.

Baym, N. 1973. "Hawthorne's Myths for Children: The Author Versus His Audience." *Studies in Short Fiction* 10/1: 35–46.

Bazovsky, G. 2018. "The Paradox of Pan as a Figure of Regeneration in Children's Literature," in H. Lovatt and O. Hodkinson, eds., *Classical Reception and Children's Literature: Greece, Rome and Childhood Transformation*. London: I. B. Tauris. 120–41.

Beale, D., Soulsby, L. H. M., and Dove, J. F., eds. 1898. *Work and Play in Girls' Schools by Three Head Mistresses*. London: Longmans, Green.

Beard, M. 2000. *The Invention of Jane Harrison*. Cambridge, MA: Harvard University Press.

Bechtel, L. S. 1930. Macmillan Department of Books for Boys and Girls catalog for 1930. Louise Seaman Bechtel Collection, box 17, folder 206, Vassar College Library.

Bechtel, L. S. 1969. *Books in Search of Children: Speeches and Essays*, ed. Virginia Haviland. New York: The Macmillan Company.

Beckett, S. L. 2009. *Crossover Fiction: Global and Historical Perspectives*. New York: Routledge.

Beckett, S. L. 2010. "Artistic Allusions in Picturebooks," in T. Colomer, B. Kümmerling-Meibauer, and C. Silva-Díaz, eds., *New Directions in Picturebook Research*. New York: Routledge. 83–98.

Beckett, S. L., ed. 2012a. *Transcending Boundaries: Writing for a Dual Audience of Children and Adults*. New York: Routledge. First published 1999.

Beckett, S. L. 2012b. *Crossover Picturebooks: A Genre for All Ages*. New York: Routledge.

Beckwith, H. 1896. *In Mythland*. Boston: Educational Publishing Co.

Benson, S. 1940. *Stories of the Gods and Heroes*. New York: The Dial Press.

Benton, J. 1990. *Naomi Mitchison: A Biography*. London: Pandora.

Berkhofer, R. F. 1978. *The White Man's Indian: Images of the American Indian from Columbus to the Present*. New York: Knopf.

Berry, E. 1933. *The Winged Girl of Knossos*. New York: D. Appleton-Century.

Betts, R. F. 1971. "The Allusion to Rome in British Imperialist Thought of the Late Nineteenth and Early Twentieth Centuries." *Victorian Studies* 15: 149–59.

Billman, C. 1982. "National Hawthorne: 'Revolutionizer' of Children's Literature." *Studies in American Fiction* 10/1: 107–14.

Blackford, H. V. 2012. *The Myth of Persephone in Girls' Fantasy Literature*. London and New York: Routledge.

Blaisdell, B. 1995. *Favorite Greek Myths*. New York: Dover.

Blamires, D. 2003. "A Workshop of Editorial Practice: The Grimms' Kinder- und Hausmärchen," in H. E. Davidson and A. Chaudhri, eds., *A Companion to the Fairy Tale*. Cambridge: Brewer. 71–93.

Blondel, N. 1998. *Mary Butts: Scenes from the Life*. Kingston, NY: McPherson & Company.

Blyton, E. 1930. *Tales of Ancient Greece*. London: Latimer.

Blyton, E. 1939. *The Watchman with 100 Eyes and Other Greek Tales*. London: Johnston.

Borach, G. 1954. "Conversations with James Joyce." Trans. J. B. Prescott. *College English* 15/6: 325–7.

Bowen, Z. 1970. *Padraic Colum: A Biographical-Critical Introduction*. Carbondale, IL: Southern Illinois University Press.

Bowen, Z. 1973. "Ninety Years in Retrospect: Excerpts from Interviews with Padraic Colum." *Journal of Irish Literature* 1: 14–34.

Bowlby, R. 1992. *Still Crazy After All These Years: Women, Writing and Psychoanalysis*. London: Routledge.

Bowlby, R. 2007. *Freudian Mythologies: Greek Tragedy and Modern Identities*. Oxford: Oxford University Press.

Bowler, P. J. 1989. *The Invention of Progress: The Victorians and the Past*. Oxford: Blackwell.

Boyer, P. S. 1968. *Purity in Print: The Vice-Society Movement and Book Censorship in America*. New York: Scribner's.

Bradman, T. 2010. *Spartacus: The Story of the Rebellious Thracian Gladiator*. London: A & C Black.

Bratton, J. S. 1989. "British Imperialism and the Reproduction of Femininity in Girls' Fiction, 1900–1930," in J. Richards, ed., *Imperialism and Children's Literature*. Manchester: Manchester University Press. 195–215.

Braymer, M. 1960. *The Walls of Windy Troy*. New York: Harcourt, Brace & World.

Brazouski, A., and Klatt, M. J. 1994. *Childrens' Books on Ancient Greek and Roman Mythology: An Annotated Bibliography*. Westport, CT: Greenwood Publishing Group.

Bridge, H. 1893. *Personal Recollections of Nathaniel Hawthorne*. New York: Harper & Brothers.

Briggs, J., and Butts, D. 1995. "The Emergence of Form (1850–1890)," in P. Hunt, ed., *Children's Literature: An Illustrated History*. Oxford: Oxford University Press. 130–66.

Brink, C. R. 1997. *Caddie Woodlawn*. New York: Simon & Schuster. First published 1935.

Bristow, E. J. 1977. *Vice and Vigilance: Purity Movements in Britain since 1700*. Dublin: Gill and Macmillan.

Brittain, V. 1933. *Testament of Youth*. London: Gollancz.

Brooke, R. 1968. *The Letters*. Ed. G. Keynes. New York: Harcourt, Brace.

Brooks, G. 1949. "The Anniad," in *Annie Allen*. New York: Harper. 19–32.

Brooks, G. 1996. *Report from Part Two*. Chicago: Third World Press.

Brown, G. 2004. "Hawthorne's American History," in R. H. Millington, ed. *The Cambridge Companion to Nathaniel Hawthorne*. Cambridge: Cambridge University Press. 121–42.

Brown, S. A. 2017. "The Classical Pantheon in Children's Fantasy Literature," in B. M. Rogers and B. E. Stevens, eds., *Classical Traditions in Modern Fantasy*. Oxford: Oxford University Press. 189–208.

Browne, N. M. 2000. *Warriors of Alavna*. London: Bloomsbury.

Bruce, M. 1925. *Maro the Lion-Keeper: A Tale of Ancient Rome*. London: George Harrap.

Bryant, M. 2010a. *Oh My Gods! A Look-It-Up Guide to the Gods of Mythology*. New York: Scholastic.

Bryant, M. 2010b. *She's All That: A Look-It-Up Guide to the Goddesses of Mythology*. New York: Scholastic.

Bryant Davies, R. 2018. "Through the Proscenium Arch," in A. Buckland and S. Qureshi, eds., *Time Travellers: Victorian Perspectives on the Past*. Chicago: University of Chicago Press.

Buckley, E. F. 1908. *Children of the Dawn: Old Tales of Greece*. London: Wells, Gardner, Darton.

Budgen, F. 1934. *James Joyce and the Making of Ulysses*. London: Grayson & Grayson.

Bulfinch, T. 1855. *The Age of Fable; or Beauties of Mythology*. Boston: J. E. Tilton.

[Bulfinch, T.] 1942. *A Book of Myths: Selections from Bulfinch's Age of Fable with Illustrations by Helen Sewell*. New York: Macmillan.

Burgess, D. 1952. *Dream and Deed: The Life of Katharine Lee Bates*. Norman, OK: The University of Oklahoma Press.

Burnett, F. H. 1911. *The Secret Garden*. New York: Frederick A. Stokes and Company.

Butler, C. 2015. "The 'Grand Tour' as Transformative Experience in Children's Novels about the Roman Invasion," in L. Maurice, ed., *The Reception of Ancient Greece and Rome in Children's Literature: Heroes and Eagles*. Leiden: Brill. 259–79.

Butler, C., and O'Donovan, H. 2012. *Reading History in Children's Books*. Houndmills: Palgrave MacMillan.

Butler, J. 2000. *Antigone's Claim: Kinship Between Life and Death*. New York: Columbia University Press.

Butler, S. 1967. *The Authoress of the Odyssey*. Repr. with a new introduction by David Grene. Chicago: University of Chicago Press. First published 1897.

Butts, D. 1995. "The Beginnings of Victorianism (*c.*1820–1850)," in P. Hunt, ed., *Children's Literature: An Illustrated History*. Oxford: Oxford University Press. 77–101.

Butts, M. 1988. *The Crystal Cabinet: My Childhood at Salterns*. Boston: Beacon Press. First published 1937.

Butts, M. 1994. *The Classical Novels: The Macedonian, Scenes from the Life of Cleopatra*. Kingston, NY: McPherson & Company.

Calder, J. 1997. *The Nine Lives of Naomi Mitchison*. London: Virago.

Calder, W. M., and Traill, D. A. eds. 1986. *Myth, Scandal and History: The Heinrich Schliemann Scandal and a First Edition of the Mycenean Diary*. Detroit: Wayne State University Press.

Cam, H. 1961. *Historical Novels*. London: Routledge and Kegan Paul.

Carpentier, M. C. 1998. *Ritual, Myth, and the Modernist Text*. Amsterdam: Gordon and Breach.

Carroll, L. 1953. *Alice's Adventures in Wonderland*. London: Macmillan. First published 1865.

Casazza, J. 2003. "Taming the Savageness of Man: Robert Kennedy, Edith Hamilton, and Their Sources." *Classical World* 96: 197–9.

Cather, K. D. 1916. *Pan and His Pipes and Other Tales for Children*. Camden, NJ: Victor Talking Machine Co.

Chandler, P. 2008. *The Mark of Edain*. Oxford: Oxford University Press.

Church, A. J. 1887. *The Count of the Saxon Shore*. London: Seeley.

Church, A. J. 1960. *Lucius: The Adventures of a Roman Boy*. New York: Biblo and Tannen. First published as *Two Thousand Years Ago: the Adventures of a Roman Boy*, 1885.

Clarke, A. C. 1890. *Fabiola's Sisters: A Tale of the Christian Heroines Martyred at Carthage in the Commencement of the Third Century*. New York: Benziger.

Coats, L. 2002. *Atticus the Storyteller*. Illus. A. Williams. London: Orion.

Cohn, D. 1999. *The Distinction of Fiction*. Baltimore and London: Johns Hopkins University Press.

Colby, S. 2009. *Stratified Modernism: The Poetics of Excavation from Gautier to Olson*. Bern: Peter Lang.

Collins, F. M., and Graham, J. 2001. *Historical Fiction for Children: Capturing the Past*. London: David Fulton.

Colloms, B. 1975. *Charles Kingsley: The Lion of Eversley*. London: Constable.

Colomer, T., Kümmerling-Meibauer, B., and Silva-Diáz, C. 2010. *New Directions in Picturebook Research*. New York: Routledge.

Colum, P. 1916. *The King of Ireland's Son*. Illus. W. Pogany. New York: Macmillan.

Colum, P. 1918. *The Adventures of Odysseus or The Children's Homer*. New York: Macmillan.

Colum, P. 1920. *The Children of Odin*. New York: Macmillan.

Colum, P. 1921. *The Golden Fleece and the Heroes Who Lived Before Achilles*. Illus. Willy Pogany. New York: Macmillan.

Colum, P. 1928. *The Forge in the Forest*. Illus. B. Artzybasheff. New York: Macmillan.

Colum, P. 1968. *Story Telling New & Old*. New York: Macmillan. First published 1927.

Colum, P. 2004. *The Golden Fleece and the Heroes Who Lived Before Achilles*. New York: Simon & Schuster. First published 1921.

Compton, C. H. 1935. *Who Reads What? Essays on the Readers of Mark Twain, Hardy, Sandburg, Shaw, William James, the Greek Classics*. New York: H. W. Wilson. First published 1934.

Connolly, P. T. 2013. *Slavery in American Children's Literature, 1790–2010*. Iowa City: University of Iowa Press.

Cook, E. 1976. *The Ordinary and the Fabulous: An Introduction to Myths, Legends, and Fairy Tales*. 2nd edition. Cambridge: Cambridge University Press.

Coolidge, O. 1962. *Men of Athens*. Boston: Houghton Mifflin.

Cornelius, M. G., and Gregg, M. E., eds. 2008. *Nancy Drew and Her Sister Sleuths: Essays on the Fiction of Girl Detectives*. Jefferson, NC: McFarland.

Cox, G. W. 1861. *Tales from Greek Mythology*. London: Longman, Green, Longman, and Roberts.

Cox, G. W. 1862. *Tales of the Gods and Heroes*. London: Longman, Green, Longman and Roberts.

Cox, G. W. 1867. *A Manual of Mythology in the Form of Question and Answer*. London: Longmans, Green, and Co.

Cox, G. W. [1913.] *Dwellers on Olympus: Selected Stories from Cox's "Tales of the Gods and Heroes."* London: Thomas Nelson and Sons.

Crawford, J. R. 1929. *Greek Tales for Tiny Tots*. Illus. P. A. Crawford. Bloomington, IL: Public School Publishing Company.

Crew, H. C. 1927. *The Singing Seamen*. Chicago: E. M. Hale.

Crew, H. C. 1928. *The Trojan Boy*. New York: Century.

Crew, H. C. 1929. *The Lost King*. New York: Century.

Culler, A. D. 1985. *The Victorian Mirror of History*. New Haven: Yale University Press.

Cunningham, H. 2005. *Children and Childhood in Western Society since 1500*. Abingdon: Routledge.

D'Aulaire, I. and E. P. 1931. *The Magic Rug*. New York: Doubleday.

D'Aulaire, I. and E. P. 1936. *George Washington*. New York: Doubleday.

D'Aulaire, I. and E. P. 1939. *Abraham Lincoln*. New York: Doubleday.

D'Aulaire, I. and E. P. 1940. "Working Together on Books for Children." *The Horn Book* 16/4: 247–55.

D'Aulaire, I. and E. P. 1962. *D'Aulaires' Book of Greek Myths*. New York: Delacorte Press.

D'Aulaire, O. 1996. "Introduction," in N. Hawthorne, *A Wonder Book for Girls and Boys*. Illus. W. Crane. Oxford: Oxford University Press. 5–7.

Dalgarno, E. 2001. *Virginia Woolf and the Visible World*. Cambridge: Cambridge University Press.

Dalgarno, E. 2012. *Virginia Woolf and the Migrations of Language*. Cambridge: Cambridge University Press.

Darlington, W. 1832. *A Catechism of Mythology*. Baltimore: William R. Lucas.

Darton, F. J. H. 1982. *Children's Books in England: Five Centuries of Social Life*. Rev. B. Alderson. Cambridge: Cambridge University Press.

Daugherty, J. 1938. *Andy and the Lion: A Tale of Kindness Remembered or the Power of Gratitude*. New York: Viking Press.

Daugherty, J. 1940. "Children's Books in a Democracy." *The Horn Book* 16/4: 231–7.

Daugherty, J. 1943. "Comment on *Homer Price*." *The Horn Book* 19/6: 425–6.

Davenport, G. 1981. *Eclogues*. San Francisco: North Point Press.

Davidson, H. E., and Chaudhri, A. 2003. *A Companion to the Fairy Tale*. Cambridge: Brewer.

Debo, A. 2012. *The American H.D.* Iowa City: University of Iowa Press.

DeJean, J. 1989. *Fictions of Sappho, 1546–1937*. Chicago: University of Chicago Press.

Demos, J. 2005. "Afterword: Notes from, and about, the History/Fiction Borderland." *Rethinking History* 9: 329–35.

Dillon, E. 1977. *The Shadow of Vesuvius*. Nashville: Thomas Nelson.

Donahey, M. D. 1924. *Peter and Prue*. New York: Rand McNally and Co.

Donovan, E. B. 2002. "'Very Capital Reading for Children': Reading as Play in Hawthorne's *A Wonder Book for Girls and Boys*." *Children's Literature: Annual of The Modern Language Association Division on Children's Literature and The Children's Literature Association* 30: 19–41.

Doudna, M. K. 1985. "Hawthorne's Pandora, Milton's Eve, and the Fortunate Fall." *Emerson Society Quarterly* 31: 164–72.

Druitt, T. 2005. *Corydon and the Island of Monsters*. London: Simon and Schuster.

Druitt, T. 2006. *Corydon and the Fall of Atlantis*. London: Simon and Schuster.

Druitt, T. 2007. *Corydon and the Siege of Troy*. London: Simon and Schuster.

DuPlessis, R. B. 1986. *H.D.: The Career of that Struggle*. Bloomington, IN: Indiana University Press.

Dyer, C. S., and Romalov, N. T., eds. 1995. *Rediscovering Nancy Drew*. Iowa City: University of Iowa Press.

Eldridge, J. 2008. *Roman Invasion (My Story)*. London: Scholastic.

Eliot, T. S. 1927. "The Silurist." *The Dial* 9: 259–63.

Eliot, T. S. 1975. *Selected Prose of T. S. Eliot*. Ed. F. Kermode. New York: Harcourt Brace Jovanovich.

Eliott, L. S. 1953. *Ceva of the Caradocs*. London: Frederick Warne & Co.

Ellison, L. 1966. *The Green Bronze Mirror*. London: Blackie.

Evans, I. O. 1944. *Gadget City*. London: Frederick Warne & Co.

Evans, J., ed. 2009. *Talking Beyond the Page: Reading and Responding to Picturebooks*. London: Routledge.

Eyre, F. 1973. *British Children's Books in the Twentieth Century*. New York: E. P. Dutton & Co. First published 1971.

Fadiman, C. 1959. *The Voyages of Ulysses*. New York: Random House.

Fadiman, C. 1960. *The Adventures of Hercules*. New York: Random House.

Falconer, R. 2009. *The Crossover Novel: Contemporary Children's Fiction and Its Adult Readership*. New York: Routledge.

Fanelli, S. 2002. *Mythological Monsters of Ancient Greece*. Cambridge, MA: Walker Books.

Farwell, B. 1999. *Over There: The United States in the Great War, 1917–1918*. New York: Norton.

Feldman, B., and Richardson, R. D., Jr. 1972. *The Rise of Modern Mythology: 1680–1860*. Bloomington, IN: Indiana University Press.

Felmingham, M. 1988. *The Illustrated Gift Book, 1880–1930*. Aldershot: Scolar Press.

Fenn, G. M. 1904. *Marcus, the Young Centurion*. London: Ernest Nister.

Ferrall, C., and Jackson, A. 2010. *Juvenile Literature and British Society, 1850–1950*. New York: Routledge.

Field, E. M. 1892. *The Child and His Book: Some Account of the History and Progress of Children's Literature in England*. 2nd edn. London: Wells Gardner, Darton & Co.

Fields, J. T. 1900. *Yesterdays with Authors*. Cambridge: Riverside. First published 1871.

Flack, L. C. 2014. "1922's 'UnUlyssean' Ulysses: Modernist Revisions of the Homeric *Nostos*," in H. Gardner and S. Murnaghan, eds., *Odyssean Identities in Modern Cultures: The Journey Home*. Columbus, OH: Ohio State University Press. 133–49.

Flanders, J. 2001. *A Circle of Sisters: Alice Kipling, Georgiana Burne-Jones, Agnes Poynter and Louisa Baldwin*. London: Viking.

Fletcher, A. 2008. *Growing Up in England: The Experience of Childhood 1600–1914*. New Haven: Yale University Press.

Flint, K. 1993. *The Woman Reader 1837–1914*. Oxford: Clarendon Press.

Foster, M. L. 1970. "Ingri and Edgar Parin D'Aulaire." *Catholic Library World* 41/6: 347–51.

Fowler, R. 1983. "'On Not Knowing Greek': The Classics and the Woman of Letters." *Classical Journal* 78: 337–49.

Fowler, R. 1999. "Moments and Metamorphoses: Virginia Woolf's Greece." *Comparative Literature* 51/3: 217–42.

Foy, R. R. 2000. *Ritual, Myth, and Mysticism in the Works of Mary Butts.* Fayetteville, AR: University of Arkansas Press.

Freud, S. 1953–74. *The Standard Edition of the Complete Psychological Works of Sigmund Freud.* Ed. and trans. J. Strachey et al. London: Hogarth Press. (Individual volumes cited as *SE*.)

Freud, S. 1985. *The Complete Letters of Sigmund Freud to William Fliess, 1887–1904.* Ed. and trans. J. M. Masson. Cambridge, MA: Harvard University Press.

Friedman, S. S. 1981. *Psyche Reborn: The Emergence of H.D.* Bloomington, IN: University of Indiana Press.

Friedman, S. S. 1990. *Penelope's Web: Gender, Modernity, H.D.'s Fiction.* Cambridge: Cambridge University Press.

Frost, R. 1915. *A Boy's Will.* New York: Henry Holt.

Furlani, A. 2004. "Guy Davenport's Pastorals of Childhood Sexuality," in S. Bruhm and N. Hurley, eds., *Curiouser: On the Queerness of Children.* Minneapolis: University of Minnesota Press. 225–44.

G.G. [Grote, G.] 1843. "Grecian Legends and Early History." *Westminster Review* 39: 285–328.

Gardner, A. 1891. *Friends of the Olden Time.* London: Edward Arnold.

Garfield, L., and Blishen, E. 1970. *The God Beneath the Sea.* Illus C. Keeping. London: Longman.

Garfield, L., and Blishen, E. 1973. *The Golden Shadow.* London: Longman.

Gassman, P. 2016. *Play for Me, Pan: Exploring Pan as a Guiding Spirit and Troubled Adolescent in Children's Literature.* Senior Thesis, Bryn Mawr College.

Gay, P. 1988. *Freud: A Life for Our Times.* New York: Norton.

Geary, J. 2006. *The Eagle and the Bull: A Celtic Adventure in Ancient Rome.* Boone, NC: Ingalls.

Geras, A. 2001. *Troy.* London: Scholastic.

Geras, A. 2005. *Ithaka.* Oxford: David Fickling.

Geras, A. 2009. *Dido.* Oxford: David Fickling.

Gere, C. 2009. *Knossos and the Prophets of Modernism.* Chicago: University of Chicago Press.

Gessert, G. S. 2017. "The Mirror Crack'd: Fractured Classicisms in the Pre-Raphaelites and Victorian Illustration," in B. M. Rogers and B. E. Stevens, eds., *Classical Traditions in Modern Fantasy.* Oxford: Oxford University Press. 63–91.

Ginsberg, L. 1993. " 'The Willing Captive': Narrative Seduction and the Ideology of Love in Hawthorne's *A Wonder Book for Girls and Boys.*" *American Literature* 65: 255–73.

Glück, L. 1994. *Proofs & Theories: Essays on Poetry.* Hopewell, NJ: Ecco.

Goldhill, S. 2011. *Victorian Culture and Classical Antiquity: Art, Opera, Fiction, and the Proclamation of Modernity*. Princeton: Princeton University Press.

Goldman, P. 1994. *Victorian Illustrated Books, 1850–1870: The Heyday of Wood Engraving*. Boston: Godine.

Goodman, J. 2005. "Fictional History." *Rethinking History* 9: 237–53.

Goodrich, S. G. 1832. *A Book of Mythology for Youth: Containing Descriptions of the Deities, Temples, Sacrifices and Superstitions of the Ancient Greeks and Romans: Adapted to the Use of Schools*. Boston: Richardson, Lord and Holbrook.

Goodrich, S. G. 1839. *Peter Parley's Tales about the Mythology of Greek and Rome*. London: Thomas Tegg.

Goodrich, S. G. 1856. *Recollections of a Lifetime, or Men and Things I Have Seen: In a Series of Familiar Letters to a Friend, Historical, Biographical, Anecdotical, and Descriptive*. 2 vols. New York: Miller, Orton and Mulligan.

Gorman, H. 1939. *James Joyce*. New York: Rinehart & Company, Inc.

Gould, F. J. 1910a. *The Children's Plutarch: Tales of the Greeks*. New York: Harper & Bros.

Gould, F. J. 1910b. *The Children's Plutarch: Tales of the Romans*. New York: Harper & Bros.

Gould, S. J. 1977. *Ontogeny and Philogeny*. Cambridge, MA: Harvard University Press.

Grahame, K. 1982. *The Wind in the Willows*. New York and Toronto: Bantam. First published 1908.

Graves, R. 1955. *Homer's Daughter*. New York: Doubleday.

Graves, R. 1962. *Myths of Ancient Greece*, 2nd edn. London: Cassell. First published as *Greek Gods and Heroes*, 1960.

Greenway, B., ed. 2005. *Twice-Told Children's Tales: The Influence of Childhood Reading on Writers for Adults*. New York and London: Routledge.

Gregory, E. 1997. *H.D. and Hellenism: Classic Lines*. Cambridge: Cambridge University Press.

Grenby, M. O. 2011. *The Child Reader, 1700–1840*. Cambridge: Cambridge University Press.

Grimm, J., and Grimm, W. 1823. *German Popular Stories*. Trans. E. Taylor. London: C. Baldwyn.

Gubar, S. 1990. "The Echoing Spell of H.D.'s *Trilogy*," in S. S. Friedman and R. B. DuPlessis, eds., *Signets: Reading H.D.* Madison: University of Wisconsin Press. 297–317. First published 1978.

Guerber, H. A. 1896. *The Story of the Greeks*. New York: American Book Company.

Guest, B. 2003. *Herself Defined: H.D. and Her World*. Tucson: Schaffner Press, Inc.

Gugler, E. 1943. "Comment on *Homer Price*." *The Horn Book* 19: 424–5.

Gullick, M. E. 1926. *The Dipping Well: A Story of Roman Bath*. London: Sir Isaac Pitman & Sons.

H.D. 1938. "A Note on Poetry," in W. R. Benét and N. H. Pearson, eds., *The Oxford Anthology of Modern Literature*, vol. 2. New York: Oxford University Press. 1287–8.

H.D. 1984. *Tribute to Freud*. New York: New Directions.

H.D. 1986. "H.D. by Delia Alton." *Iowa Review* 16: 180–221.

H.D. 1988. *The Hedgehog*. With an Introduction by Perdita Schaffner and woodcuts by George Plank. New York: New Directions. (Privately printed in 1936, London: Curwen Press.)

H.D. 1998. *The Gift: the Complete Text*. Ed. with notes by J. Augustine. Gainesville, FL: University Press of Florida.

H.D. 2012. *Magic Mirror, Compassionate Friendship, Thorn Thicket*. Ed. N. J. Christodoulides. Victoria: ELS Editions.

Haaren, J. H., and Poland, A. B. 1904. *Famous Men of Rome*. New York: American Book Company.

Hale, E. 2015. "Classics, Children's Literature, and the Character of Childhood, from *Tom Brown's Schooldays* to *The Enchanted Castle*," in L. Maurice, ed., *The Reception of Ancient Greece and Rome in Children's Literature*. Leiden and Boston: Brill. 17–29.

Hall, E. 2016. "Our Fabled Childhood: Reflections on the Unsuitability of Aesop to Children," in K. Marciniak, ed., *Our Mythical Childhood . . . : The Classics and Literature for Children and Young Adults*. Leiden: Brill. 171–82.

Hall, E. 2018. "Aesop the Morphing Fabulist," in O. Hodkinson and H. Lovatt, eds., *Classical Reception and Children's Literature: Greece, Rome and Childhood Transformation*. London: I. B. Tauris. 89–107.

Hallett, J. P. 1984. *Fathers and Daughters in Roman Society: Women and the Elite Family*. Princeton: Princeton University Press.

Hallett, J. P. 2009a. "Edith Hamilton and Greco-Roman Mythology," in G. Staley, ed., *American Women and Classical Myths*. Waco, TX: Baylor University Press. 105–30.

Hallett, J. P. 2009b. "The Anglicizing Way: Edith Hamilton (1867–1963) and the Twentieth-Century Transformation of Classics in the U.S.A.," in J. P. Hallett and C. Stray, eds., *British Classics Outside England: The Academy and Beyond*. Waco, TX: Baylor University Press. 149–65.

Hamilton, E. 1930. *The Greek Way to Western Civilization*. New York: W. W. Norton & Company.

Hamilton, E. 1942. *Mythology*. Boston: Little, Brown and Company.

Hamnett, B. 2011. *The Historical Novel in Nineteenth-Century Europe: Representations of Reality in History & Fiction*. Oxford: Oxford University Press.

Harding, C. H., and Harding, S. B. 1906. *Stories of Greek Gods, Heroes, and Men: A Primer of the Mythology and History of the Greeks.* Chicago: Scott, Foresman.

Harris, J. 2002. *Greece! Rome! Monsters!* Los Angeles: J. Paul Getty Museum.

Harrison, J. E. 1912. *Themis: A Study of the Social Origins of Greek Religion.* Cambridge: Cambridge University Press.

Harrison, J. E. 1915. *Alpha and Omega.* London: Sidgwick & Jackson, Ltd.

Harrison, J. E. 1922. *Prolegomena to the Study of Greek Religion.* 3rd edn. Cambridge: Cambridge University Press. First published 1903.

Harthan, J. P. 1981. *The History of the Illustrated Book: The Western Tradition.* New York: Thames & Hudson.

Hartley, C. G. 1909. *Stories from the Greek Legends.* Philadelphia: Lippincott.

Hathaway, R. D. 1961. "Hawthorne and the Paradise of Children." *Western Humanities Review* 15/2: 161–72.

Hawes, J. 1997. *Children Between the Wars: American Childhood, 1920–1940.* New York: Twayne Publishers.

Hawthorne, H. 1917. *Girls in Bookland.* New York: George H. Doran Company.

Hawthorne, J. 1885. *Nathaniel Hawthorne and His Wife.* 2 vols. Boston: Osgood.

Hawthorne, N. 1851. *A Wonder-Book for Girls and Boys.* With engravings by Baker from designs by Billings. Boston: Ticknor & Fields.

Hawthorne, N. 1853. *Tanglewood Tales: Another Wonder-Book.* Boston: Ticknor, Reed, and Fields.

Hawthorne, N. 1885a. *The Wonder-Book for Girls and Boys.* Illus. F. S. Church: Houghton, Mifflin, and Company.

Hawthorne, N. 1885b. *The Letters, 1843–1853.* Ed. T. Woodson, L. N. Smith, and N. H. Pearson. Columbus, OH: Ohio State University Press.

Hawthorne, N. 1897. *Hawthorne's Works*, with Introductions by Katharine Lee Bates. Vol. 14. New York: Thomas Y. Crowell & Co.

Hawthorne, N. 1906. *Tanglewood Tales, Told to the Children by C. E. Smith.* London: T. C. and E. C. Jack.

Hawthorne, N. 1913. *Tanglewood Tales.* Illus. M. Winter. New York: Rand McNally & Company.

Hawthorne, N. 1922. *A Wonder-Book for Girls and Boys.* Illus. A. Rackham. London: Hodder & Stoughton.

Hawthorne, N. 1963. *Pegasus the Winged Horse.* Introduced by R. Lowell. New York: Macmillan.

Hawthorne, N. 1982. *Tales and Sketches, A Wonder Book for Girls and Boys, Tanglewood Tales for Girls and Boys.* The Library of America. New York: Viking Press.

Hawthorne, N. 1985. *The Letters, 1843–1854.* Ed. T. Woodson, L. N. Smith, and N. H. Pearson. Columbus: Ohio State University Press.

Hawthorne, N. 1987. *The Golden Touch*. Illus. R. Salvucci. New York: St Martin's Press.

Hawthorne, N. 1990. *King Midas*. With selected sentences in American Sign Language. Illus. D. Majewski. Line drawings by S. Cozzolino. Washington, DC: Gallaudet University Press.

Hawthorne, N. 1996. *A Wonder-Book for Girls and Boys*. Illus. W. Crane. Introduction by O. D'Aulaire and Afterword by J. Pfister. New York: Oxford University Press.

Hazard, P. 1944. *Books, Children and Men*. Trans. M. M. Mitchell. Boston: The Horn Book Inc. First published as *Les Livres, les enfants et les hommes*, 1932.

Hearn, M. P. 1986. *The Best of the Andrew Lang Fairy Tale Book*. New York: Signet Classics.

Hearn, M. P. 1996. "Discover, Explore, Enjoy," in M. P. Hearn, T. Clark, and H. N. B. Clark, *Myth, Magic, and Mystery: One Hundred Years of Children's Book Illustration*. Boulder, CO: Roberts Rinehart Publishers. 3–44.

Hearne, B. 1988. "Booking the Brothers Grimm: Art, Adaptations, and Economics," in J. M. McGlathery, ed., *The Brothers Grimm and Folktale*. Urbana and Chicago: University of Illinois Press. 220–33.

Henty, G. A. 1892. *Beric the Briton*. London: Blackie and Son.

Herman, W. 1983. "Virginia Woolf and the Classics: Every Englishman's Prerogative Transmuted into Fictional Art," in E. K. Ginsberg and L. M. Gottleib, eds., *Virginia Woolf: Centennial Essays*. Troy, NY: The Whitston Publishing Company. 257–68.

Hewins, C. M. 1926. *A Mid-Century Child and Her Books*. New York: Macmillan.

Hingley, R. 2000. *Roman Officers and English Gentlemen: The Imperial Origins of Roman Archaeology*. London: Routledge.

Hoberman, R. 1997. *Gendering Classicism: The Ancient World in Twentieth-Century Women's Historical Fiction*. Albany, NY: State University of New York Press.

Hodgdon, J. R. 1922. *The Enchanted Past: True Stories of the Lands Where Civilization Began*. Boston: Ginn & Co.

Hodges, M. 1973. *Persephone and the Springtime*. Boston: Little, Brown.

Hodkinson, O. 2016. "'His Greek Materials': Philip Pullman's Use of Classical Mythology," in K. Marciniak, ed., *Our Mythical Childhood . . . : The Classics and Literature for Children and Young Adults*. Leiden: Brill. 267–90.

Hodkinson, O., and Lovatt, H. 2018. *Classical Reception and Children's Literature: Greece, Rome and Childhood Transformation*. London: I. B. Tauris.

Hodnett, E. 1982. *Image and Text: Studies in the Illustration of English Literature*. London: Scolar Press.

Hodnett, E. 1988. *Five Centuries of English Book Illustration*. Aldershot: Scolar Press.

Hoffman, D. 1964. "Myth, Romance, and the Childhood of Man," in R. H. Pearce, ed., *Hawthorne Centenary Essays*. Columbus, OH: Ohio State University Press. 197–219.

Holt, E. S. 1887. *The Slave Girl of Pompeii; or, by a Way They Knew Not: A Tale of the First Century*. London: Shaw.

Holub, J. 2014. *Be Patient, Pandora*. New York: Abrams.

Holub, J., and Williams, S. 2010. *Goddess Girls: Athena the Brain*. New York: Simon and Schuster.

Horn, J. 2013. "'Legends Malleable in His Intellectual Furnace': Nathaniel Hawthorne's *Wonder Book*, Mythological Adaptation, and Children's Literature." Senior Thesis, Haverford College.

Horowitz, A. 1985. *The Kingfisher Book of Myths & Legends*. London: Kingfisher.

Hoselitz, V. 2007. *Imagining Roman Britain: Victorian Responses to a Roman Past*. Woodbridge, UK: Royal Historical Society/The Boydell Press.

Hunt, C. H. 1924. *International Friendship Thru Children's Books*. New York: League of Nations Non-Partisan Association.

Hunt, Leigh. 1850. *Autobiography*. London: Smith, Elder and Co.

Hunt, P., ed. 1990. *Children's Literature: The Development of Criticism*. London: Routledge.

Hunt, P., ed. 1995. *Children's Literature: An Illustrated History*. Oxford: Oxford University Press.

Hurst, I. 2006. *Victorian Women Writers and the Classics: The Feminine of Homer*. Oxford: Oxford University Press.

Hutchinson, W. M. L. 1925. *The Golden Porch*. London: Longmans, Green.

Hyland, P., and Sammells, N., eds. 1992. *Writing & Censorship in Britain*. London: Routledge.

Hynes, S. 1968. *The Edwardian Turn of Mind*. Princeton: Princeton University Press.

Idol, J. L. Jr. 1999. "Mary Russell Mitford: Hawthorne as the Best Living Writer of Prose Fiction," in J. L. Idol Jr. and M. M. Ponder, eds., *Hawthorne and Women: Engendering and Expanding the Hawthorne Tradition*. Amherst, MA: University of Massachusetts Press. 144–50.

Idol, J. L. Jr., and Jones, B., eds. 1994. *Nathaniel Hawthorne: The Contemporary Reviews*. Cambridge: Cambridge University Press.

Jackson, M. V. 1989. *Engines of Instruction, Mischief, and Magic: Children's Literature in England from its Beginning to 1839*. Lincoln, NE: University of Nebraska Press.

Jacobs, L. B. 1952. "Some Observations on Children's Historical Fiction." *Elementary English* 29: 185–9.

Jacobs, L. B. 1961. "Historical Fiction for Children," *Reading Teacher* 14: 191–4.

Janka, M., and Stierstorfer, M. eds. 2017. *Verjüngte Antike: Griechisch-römische Mythologie und Historie in zeitgenössischen Kinder- und Jugendmedien.* Heidelberg: Universitätsverlag Winter.

Jarman, J. 2001. *The Time Travelling Cat and the Roman Eagle.* London: Andersen.

Jensen, W. 1956. *Gradiva: A Pompeiian Fancy.* Trans. H. M. Downey. In S. Freud, *Delusion and Dream and Other Essays.* Ed. P. Rieff. Boston: Beacon Press. 147–235. First published 1902.

Jiang, M. 2011. "The Blue Fairy Book." http://onceonatyme.wordpress.com/2011/12/23/the-blue-fairy-book/>. Accessed July 22, 2012.

Johannsen, R. W. 1997. "The Meaning of Manifest Destiny," in S. W. Haynes and C. Morris, eds., *Manifest Destiny and American Antebellum Expansionism.* College Station, TX: Texas A&M University Press. 7–20.

Johnson, R. 2010. "Is Beric a Briton? The Representation of Cultural Identity in G. A. Henty's *Beric the Briton* (1893) and Rosemary Sutcliff's *The Outcast* (1955)." *Journal of Children's Literature Studies* 7: 75–85.

Jones, L. 2013. "Writing and Righting History: Henty's Nation," in C. Kelen and B. Sundmark, eds., *The Nation in Children's Literature: Nations of Childhood.* New York: Routledge. 161–74.

Joseph, G. 1981. "The *Antigone* as Cultural Touchstone: Matthew Arnold, Hegel, George Eliot, Virginia Woolf, and Margaret Drabble." *PMLA* 96: 22–35.

Joyce, S. 1958. *My Brother's Keeper: James Joyce's Early Years.* New York: The Viking Press.

Kaufman, R. 1884. *Our Young Folk's Plutarch.* Philadelphia: J. B. Lippincott & Co.

Keen, R. 2015. "'Wulf the Briton': Resisting Rome in a 1950s British Boys' Adventure Strip," in L. Maurice, ed., *The Reception of Ancient Greece and Rome in Children's Literature: Heroes and Eagles.* Leiden: Brill. 280–90.

Keene, J. 2003. *Doughboys, the Great War, and the Remaking of America.* Baltimore: Johns Hopkins University Press.

Keeping, C. 1970. "Illustration in Children's Books." *Children's Literature in Education* 1/1: 41–54.

Keightley, T. 1828. *The Fairy Mythology.* London: Ainsworth.

Keightley, T. 1831. *The Mythology of Ancient Greece and Italy, Intended Chiefly for the Use of Students at the Universities and the Higher Classes in Schools.* London: Whittaker, Treacher.

Keightley, T. 1838. *The Mythology of Ancient Greece and Italy.* 2nd edn. London: Whittaker.

Keightley, T. 1866. *The Mythology of Ancient Greece and Italy.* 3rd edn. New York: Appleton.

Kenner, H. 1969. "Homer's Sticks and Stones." *James Joyce Quarterly* 6: 285–98.

Kenner, H. 1971. *The Pound Era.* Berkeley and Los Angeles: University of California Press.

Kennon, P. 2007. "F(r)ictional Masculinities: The Representation of Manhood in Rosemary Sutcliff's Roman Britain Series of Historical Novels for Young Adults," in M. S. Thompson and V. Coghlan, eds., *Divided Worlds: Studies in Children's Literature*. Dublin: Four Courts Press. 76–85.

Kessler, C. F. 1995. *Daring to Dream: Utopian Fiction by United States Women before 1950*. 2nd edn. Syracuse, NY: Syracuse University Press.

Kimmel, E. A. 2008. *The McElderry Book of Greek Myths*. New York: Simon & Schuster.

Kincaid, C. A. 1915. *The Indian Heroes*. London: Humphrey Milford.

Kindl, P. 2002. *Lost in the Labyrinth*. Boston: Houghton Mifflin.

Kingsley, C. 1855 (postdated to 1856). *The Heroes: or, Greek Fairy Tales for My Children*. Cambridge: Macmillan.

Kingsley, C. 1859. *The Heroes; or, Greek Fairy Tales for My Children*. Cambridge: Macmillan.

Kingsley, C. 1875. *The Heroes, or, Greek Fairy Tales for My Children*. New edn. London: Macmillan.

Kingsley, C. 1899. *Letters and Memories*. Ed. F. Kingsley. New York and London: Cooperative Publication Society.

Kingsley, C. 1905. *The Heroes*, told to the children by M. MacGregor. London: Nelson.

Kingsley, C. 1912. *The Heroes, or Greek Fairy Tales for my Children*. Illustrated after watercolor drawings by W. Russell Flint. London and Boston: Medici Society.

Kingsley, C. 1915. *The Heroes, or Greek Fairy Tales for My Children*. Illus. S. Tawse. London: A. & C. Black.

Kingsley, C. 1928. *The Heroes, or Greek Fairy Tales for My Children*. Illus. H. M. Brock. London: Macmillan.

Kingsley, C. 1961. *The Heroes*. Ed. M. W. and G. Thomas. Illus. C. Keeping. London: Hutchinson Educational.

Kingsley, C. 1963. *The Heroes, or Greek Fairy Tales for My Children*. Illus. J. Kiddell-Monroe. London: J. M. Dent.

Kingsley, C. 1964. *Theseus*. Illus. F. Castellon. Afterword by M. Renault. New York: Macmillan; London: Collier-Macmillan.

Kingsley, C. 1968. *The Heroes*. Santa Rosa, CA: Classic Press.

Kingsley, C. 2013. *The Water-Babies*. Ed. B. Alderson. Oxford: Oxford University Press.

Kinnell, M. 1995. "Publishing for Children (1700–1780)," in P. Hunt, ed., *Children's Literature: An Illustrated History*. Oxford: Oxford University Press. 26–45.

Kipling, R. 1993. *Puck of Pook's Hill, and Rewards and Fairies*. Oxford: Oxford University Press. First published 1906, 1910.

Klaver, J. M. I. 2006. *The Apostle of the Flesh: A Critical Life of Charles Kingsley.* Boston: Brill.

Knuth, R. 2012. *Children's Literature and British Identity: Imagining a People and a Nation.* Lanham, MD: Scarecrow Press.

Kooistra, L. J. 2002. *Christina Rossetti and Illustration.* Athens, OH: Ohio University Press.

Koulouris, T. 2011. *Hellenism and Loss in the Work of Virginia Woolf.* Farnham: Ashgate.

Kümmerling-Meibauer, B. 2006. "Illustrations," in J. Zipes, ed., *The Oxford Encyclopedia of Children's Literature*, vol. 2. Oxford: Oxford University Press. 276–81.

Kümmerling-Meibauer, B. 2008. "Images of Childhood in Romantic Children's Literature," in G. Gillespie, M. Engel, and B. Dieterle, eds., *Romantic Prose Fiction*. Philadelphia: John Benjamins. 183–203.

Kümmerling-Meibauer, B. 2012. "Children's and Young Adults' Literature," in Brill online: *Brill's New Pauly.* http://referenceworks.brillonline.com/entries/brill-s-new-pauly/childrens-and-young-adults-literature-ct-e1408880.

Kümmerling-Meibauer, B., ed. 2014. *Picturebooks: Representation and Narration.* New York: Routledge.

Kümmerling-Meibauer, B. 2016. "Orpheus and Eurydice: Reception of a Classical Myth in International Children's Literature," in K. Marciniak, ed. *Our Mythical Childhood . . . : The Classics and Literature for Children and Young Adults.* Leiden: Brill. 291–306.

Kümmerling-Meibauer, B., ed. 2017. *The Routledge Companion to Picturebooks.* New York: Routledge.

Kupperman, K. O. 2000. *Indians and English: Facing Off in Early America.* Ithaca, NY: Cornell University Press.

Kutzer, M. D. 2000. *Empire's Children: Empire and Imperialism in Classic British Children's Books.* New York and London: Garland.

LaCapra, D. 1985. *History & Criticism.* Ithaca, NY and London: Cornell University Press.

LaCapra, D. 1987. *History, Politics, and the Novel.* Ithaca, NY and London: Cornell University Press.

Laffrado, L. 1992. *Hawthorne's Literature for Children.* Athens, GA and London: University of Georgia Press.

Lamprey, L. 1922. *Children of Ancient Rome.* Boston: Little, Brown.

Lamprey, L. 1924. *Children of Ancient Greece.* Boston: Little, Brown.

Lancelyn Green, R. 1946. *Andrew Lang: A Critical Biography.* Leicester: Edmund Ward.

Lancelyn Green, R. 1958. *Old Greek Fairy Tales.* London: G. Bell and Sons.

Lancelyn Green, R. 1959. *Mystery at Mycenae.* New York: A. S. Barnes.

Lancelyn Green, R. 1961. *The Luck of Troy*. London: Bodley Head.

Lancelyn Green, R. 1965. *Tales the Muses Told*. London: Bodley Head.

Lancelyn Green, R. 1980. "Andrew Lang in Fairyland," in S. Egoff, G. T. Stubbs, and L. F. Ashley, eds., *Only Connect: Readings in Children's Literature*. 2nd edn. Toronto: Oxford University Press. 244–57.

Lancelyn Green, R. 1994. *Tales of the Greek Heroes*. London: Penguin Books. First published 1958.

Lancelyn Green, R. 2009. *Tales of the Greek Heroes*. With an introduction by Rick Riordan. London: Penguin Books.

Lang, A. 1884. *Custom and Myth*. London: Longmans, Green, and Co.

Lang, A. 1895. "Introductory Essay," in F. van Eeden, *Little Johannes*. Trans. C. Bell. London: William Heinemann. v–xix.

Lang, A. 1901. *Essays in Little*. New York: J. J. Little & Co.

Lang, A. 1904. *The Brown Fairy Book*. London: Longmans, Green, and Co.

Lang, A. 1913. *Myth, Ritual and Religion*. 2 vols. London: Longmans, Green and Co. First published 1887.

Lang, A. 1965. *The Blue Fairy Book*. New York: Dover Publications. First Published 1889.

Lang, A. 2006. *Tales of Troy and Greece*. Mineola, NY: Dover Publications. First published 1907.

Langstaff, E. D. 1987. *Andrew Lang*. Boston: Twayne Publishers.

Lathey, G. 2010. *The Role of Translators in Children's Literature: Invisible Story-tellers*. New York: Routledge.

Lawrence, A. 1977. *Between the Forest and the Hills*. New York: Viking.

Lawrence, C. 2001–9. Roman Mysteries series: vols. 1–17. London: Orion.

Lawrence, I. 1946. *The Gift of the Golden Cup*. Indianapolis: Bobbs-Merrill.

Le Guin, U. K. 2008. *Lavinia*. New York: Harcourt.

Lee, H. 1997. *Virginia Woolf*. New York: Alfred A. Knopf.

Leigh Fermor, P. 2005. *A Time of Gifts*. New York: New York Review of Books. First published 1977.

Lemon, E. 1907. *Stories from Greek History*. New York: Dutton.

Leonard, M. 2013. "Freud and Tragedy: Oedipus and the Gender of the Universal." *Classical Receptions Journal* 5/1: 63–83.

Lerer, S. 2008. *Children's Literature: A Reader's History from Aesop to Harry Potter*. Chicago: University of Chicago Press.

Leslie, E. 2007a. *The Captives: or, Escape from the Druid Council*. Emmaus, PA: Salem Ridge Press. First published 1873.

Leslie, E. 2007b. *Glaucia the Greek Slave: A Tale of Athens in the First Century*. Emmaus, PA: Salem Ridge Press. First published 1874.

Leslie, E. 2007c. *Out of the Mouth of the Lion: or, The Church in the Catacombs*. Emmaus, PA: Salem Ridge Press. First published 1875.

Lesnik-Oberstein, K. 1994. *Children's Literature: Criticism and the Fictional Child*. Oxford: Clarendon Press.

Lesnik-Oberstein, K. 1999. "Essentials: What is Children's Literature? What is Childhood?," in P. Hunt, ed., *Understanding Children's Literature*. London and New York: Routledge. 15-29.

Levstik, L. S. 1983. " 'I Am No Lady!': The Tomboy in Children's Fiction." *Children's Literature in Education* 14: 14–20.

Levy, M., and Mendlesohn, F. 2016. *Children's Fantasy Literature: An Introduction*. Cambridge: Cambridge University Press.

Lewis, C. S. 1966. "On Three Ways of Writing for Children," in *On Stories: and Other Essays on Literature*. London: Harcourt. 31–44.

Lewis, D. 2001. *Reading Contemporary Picturebooks: Picturing Text*. London: Routledge/Falmer.

Lewis, F. F. 1976. *Literature, Obscenity, & Law*. Carbondale, IL: Southern Illinois University Press.

Lewis, S. 1987. *One-Minute Greek Myths*. New York: Doubleday.

Lindner, R. 1984. *Der Raub der Persephone in der Antiken Kunst*. Würzburg: Konrad Triltsch Verlag.

Lines, K., ed. 1973. *The Faber Book of Greek Legends*. London and Boston: Faber.

Lipking, J. 1977. "Looking at the Monuments: Woolf's Satiric Eye." *Bulletin of the New York Public Library* 80/2: 141–5.

Lively, P. 2005. *Making It Up*. London: Penguin Books.

Locke, J. 1889. *Some Thoughts Concerning Education*. Cambridge: Cambridge University Press. First published 1693.

Louis, M. K. 2009. *Persephone Rises, 1860–1927*. Farnham: Ashgate.

Lovatt, H. 2016. "East, West, and Finding Yourself in Caroline Lawrence's 'Roman Mysteries,' " in K. Marciniak, ed., *Our Mythical Childhood . . . : The Classics and Literature for Children and Young Adults*. Leiden: Brill. 411–27.

Lovelace, M. H. 1955. *Betsy's Wedding*. New York: HarperCollins.

Lovelace, M. H. 1979. *Betsy and Tacy Go Downtown*. New York: HarperCollins. First published 1943.

Lucas, A. L. 2003. "Introduction: The Past in the Present of Children's Literature," in A. L. Lucas, ed., *The Presence of the Past in Children's Literature*. Westport, CT: Praeger. xiii–xxi.

Lukács, G. 1982. *The Historical Novel*. Trans. H. Mitchell and S. Mitchell. London: Merlin. First published 1937.

Mabie, H. W. 1905. *Heroes Every Child Should Know*. Boston: Houghton Mifflin.

Mabie, H. W. 1913. *Myths Every Child Should Know: A Selection of the Classic Myths of All Times for Young People*. Garden City, NY: Doubleday, Page, & Company.

McBratney, J. 2002. *Imperial Subjects, Imperial Space: Rudyard Kipling's Fiction of the Native-Born*. Columbus, OH: Ohio State University Press.

McCaughrean, G. 1992. *Greek Myths*. Illus. E. Chichester Clark. New York: McElderry.

McClaren, C. 1996. *Inside the Walls of Troy*. New York: Bantam.

McClaren, C. 2000. *Waiting for Odysseus*. New York: Simon Pulse.

MacClintock, P. L. 1907. *Literature in the Elementary School*. Chicago: University of Chicago Press. First published 1897.

McCloskey, J. 2011. *Robert McCloskey: A Private Life in Words and Pictures*. Kittery Point, ME: Seapoint Books.

McCloskey, R. 1940. *Lentil*. New York: Viking Press.

McCloskey, R. 1943. *Homer Price*. New York: Viking Press.

McCloskey, R. 1951. *Centerburg Tales: More Adventures of Homer Price*. New York: Viking Press.

McCoskey, D., and Corbett, M. J. 2012. "Virginia Woolf, Richard Jebb, and Sophocles' *Antigone*," in K. Ormand, ed., *A Companion to Sophocles*. Malden, MA: Blackwell. 462–76.

MacCulloch, J. A. 1905. *The Childhood of Fiction: A Study of Folktales and Primitive Thought*. New York: Dutton.

Macdonald, F. W. 1907. *In a Nook with a Book*. London: Horace Marshall & Son.

Macdonald, F. W. 1919. *As a Tale that is Told*. London: Horace Marshall & Son.

McGavran, J. H. Jr., ed. 1991. *Romanticism and Children's Literature in Nineteenth Century England*. Athens, GA: University of Georgia Press.

McGavran, J. H. Jr., ed. 1999. *Literature and the Child: Romantic Continuations, Postmodern Contestations*. Iowa City: University of Iowa Press.

McGavran, J. H. Jr., ed. 2012. *Time of Beauty, Time of Fear: The Romantic Legacy in the Literature of Childhood*. Iowa City: University of Iowa Press.

Macgregor, M. 1914. *The Story of Greece*. London: T. C. and E. C. Jack.

MacKenzie, C. 1972. *Golden Tales of Greece: The Stories of Perseus, Jason, Theseus, and Achilles*. London: Aldus.

MacKenzie, N. 1931. *Children of Athens, London and Rome*. Ed. C. B. Firth. London: Ginn and Co.

MacLeod, A. S. 1994. *American Childhood: Essays on Children's Literature of the Nineteenth and Twentieth Centuries*. Athens, GA: University of Georgia Press.

MacLeod, A. S. 1995. "Children's Literature in America: from the Puritan Beginnings to 1870," in P. Hunt, ed., *Children's Literature: An Illustrated History*. Oxford: Oxford University Press. 102–29.

McMenomy, M. 2015. "Reading the Fiction of Video Games," in L. Maurice, ed., *The Reception of Ancient Greece and Rome in Children's Literature: Heroes and Eagles*. Leiden: Brill. 105–38.

McMullan, K. 2002. *Phone Home, Persephone!* New York: Scholastic.

McPherson, H. 1969. *Hawthorne as Myth-Maker: A Study in Imagination*. Toronto: University of Toronto Press.

Mahaffey, V. 2007. *Modernist Literature: Challenging Fictions*. Malden, MA: Blackwell.

Mahoney, B. 1928. "The First Children's Department in Book Publishing." *The Horn Book* 4 (August): 3–4.

Mahoney, B., and Mitchell, M. 1940. "Ingri and Edgar Parin D'Aulaire." *The Horn Book* 16/4: 256–64.

Majeed, J. 1999. "Comparativism and Reference to Rome in British Imperial Attitudes to India," in C. Edwards, ed., *Roman Presences: Receptions of Rome in European Culture, 1789–1945*. Cambridge: Cambridge University Press. 88–109.

Malouf, D. 2009. "A Mirror for Our Times." *Australian National University Reporter*. Summer: 13.

Malvern, G. 1958. *Rhoda of Cyprus*. Philadelphia: Macrae Smith.

Marciniak, K., ed. 2016a. *Our Mythical Childhood . . . : The Classics and Literature for Children and Young Adults*. Leiden: Brill.

Marciniak, K. 2016b. "Create Your Own Mythology: Youngsters for Youngsters (and Oldsters) in Mythological Fan Fiction," in K. Marciniak, ed., *Our Mythical Childhood . . . : The Classics and Literature for Children and Young Adults*. Leiden: Brill. 428–50.

Marciniak, K., Olechowska, E., Klos, J., and Kucharski, M., eds. 2013. *Polish Literature for Children & Young Adults Inspired by Classical Antiquity: A Catalogue*. Warsaw: Artes Liberales.

Marcus, J. 1987. *Virginia Woolf and the Languages of Patriarchy*. Bloomington & Indianapolis: Indiana University Press.

Marcus, L. S. 1980. "Life Drawings: Some Notes on Children's Picture Book Biographies." *The Lion and the Unicorn* 4/1: 15-31.

Marcus, L. S. 1992. *Margaret Wise Brown: Awakened by the Moon*. Boston: Beacon Press.

Marcus, L. S. 2008. *Minders of Make-Believe: Idealists, Entrepreneurs, and the Shaping of American Children's Literature*. Boston and New York: Houghton Mifflin Company.

Marrs, E. W. 1975. *The Letters of Charles and Mary Anne Lamb*, vol. 2: *1801–1809*. Ithaca, NY: Cornell University Press.

Martin, D. 1989. *The Telling Line: Essays on Fifteen Contemporary Book Illustrators*. New York: Delacorte.

Martin, D. 1993. *Charles Keeping: An Illustrator's Life*. London: Julia MacRae.

Massee, M. 1935. "Ingri and Edgar Parin D'Aulaire: A Sketch." *The Horn Book* 11/5: 265–70.

Matthews, B. 1901. *The Historical Novel and Other Essays*. New York: Charles Scribner.

Mattingly, M. 1928. *Marcus the Briton: A Romance of Roman London*. London: Humphrey Milford.

Maurice, L., ed. 2015a. *The Reception of Ancient Greece and Rome in Children's Literature*. Leiden: Brill.

Maurice, L. 2015b. "From Chiron to Foaly: The Centaur in Classical Mythology and Fantasy Literature," in L. Maurice, ed., *The Reception of Ancient Greece and Rome in Children's Literature*. Leiden: Brill. 139–68.

Maxwell, R. 2009. *The Historical Novel in Europe, 1650–1950*. Cambridge: Cambridge University Press.

Meigs, C., Eaton, A., Nesbitt, E., and Viguers, R. H. 1953. *A Critical History of Children's Literature*. New York: Macmillan.

Mickenberg, J. L. 2006. *Learning from the Left: Children's Literature, the Cold War, and Radical Politics in the United States*. New York: Oxford University Press.

Milicia, J. 1986. "H.D.'s 'Athenians': Son and Mother in *Hedylus*." *Contemporary Literature* 27/4: 574–94.

Mills, D. 1925. *The Book of the Ancient Greeks*. New York: Putnam's.

Mills, D. 1937. *The Book of the Ancient Romans*. New York: Putnam's. First published 1927.

Mills, J. 2014. *Virginia Woolf, Jane Ellen Harrison, and the Spirit of Modernist Classicism*. Columbus, OH: Ohio State University Press.

Mintz, S. 2004. *Huck's Raft: A History of American Childhood*. Cambridge, MA: Harvard University Press.

Mitchell, J. 2005. *The Roman Conspiracy*. Toronto: Tundra.

Mitchell, J. 2008. *The Ancient Ocean Blues*. Toronto: Tundra.

Mitchell, J. 2011. *Chariots of Gaul*. Toronto: Tundra.

Mitchell, L. S. 1921. *Here and Now Story Book: Two-to Seven-Year-Olds*. New York: E. P. Dutton & Co.

Mitchell, S. 1995. *The New Girl: Girls' Culture in England 1880–1915*. New York: Columbia University Press.

Mitchell-Boyask, R. 1994. "Freud's Reading of Classical Literature and Classical Philology," in S. L. Gilman, J. Birmele, J. Geller, and V. D. Greenberg, eds., *Reading Freud's Reading*. New York: New York University Press. 23–46.

Mitchison, N. 1923. *The Conquered*. London: Jonathan Cape.

Mitchison, N. 1926. *Cloud Cuckoo Land*. New York: Harcourt, Brace and Company. First published 1925.

Mitchison, N. 1929. *The Hostages, and Other Stories for Boys and Girls*. London: Jonathan Cape.

Mitchison, N. 1931a. *Boys and Girls and Gods*. London: Watts & Co.

Mitchison, N. 1931b. *The Corn King and the Spring Queen*. New York: Soho Press, Inc.

Mitchison, N. 1933. *The Delicate Fire: Short Stories and Poems*. New York: Harcourt Brace.

Mitchison, N. 1935. "Writing Historical Novels," *Saturday Review of Literature* 11 (April 27): 645–6.

Mitchison, N. 1973. *Small Talk: Memories of an Edwardian Childhood*. London: Bodley Head.

Mitchison, N. 1975. *All Change Here: Girlhood and Marriage*. London: Bodley Head.

Mitchison, N. 1979. *You May Well Ask: A Memoir 1920–1940*. London: Gollancz.

Mitchison, N. 1990. *A Girl Must Live: Stories and Poems*. Glasgow: Richard Drew Publishing.

Moebius, W. 1996. "Introduction to Picturebook Codes." *Word & Image* 2/2: 141–58.

Mohr, L. M. 1933. *Greeks and Persians of Long Ago*. New York: Rand McNally.

Monsigny, M. 1794. *Mythology, or, a History of the Fabulous Deities of the Ancients; Designed to Facilitate the Study of History, Poetry, Painting, etc.* London: Richardson.

Moore, A. C. 1939. *My Roads to Childhood*. New York: Doubleday, Doran & Company.

Morey, A., and Nelson, C. 2015. " 'A God Buys Us Cheeseburgers': Rick Riordan's Percy Jackson Series and America's Culture Wars." *The Lion and the Unicorn* 39: 235–53.

Morrison, J. 1976. *Children of the Northlights: A Portrait of Ingri and Edgar D'Aulaire*. Weston, CT: Weston Woods Studios. VHS film.

Moyers, B. 2002. "Bill Moyers Interviews Mary Zimmerman on NOW. 3.22.02." <http://www.pbs.org/moyers/faithandreason/print/zimmerman_print.html>. Accessed Sept. 17, 2015.

Murnaghan, S. 2007. "The Memorable Past: Antiquity and Girlhood in the Works of Mary Butts and Naomi Mitchison," in C. Stray, ed., *Remaking the Classics: Literature, Genre and Media in Britain, 1800–2000*. London: Duckworth. 125–39.

Murnaghan, S. 2008. "H.D., Daughter of Helen: Mythology as Actuality," in G. A. Staley, ed., *American Women and Classical Myths*. Waco, TX: Baylor University Press. 63–84.

Murnaghan, S. 2009. "Myths of the Greeks: The Origins of Mythology in the Works of Edith Hamilton and Robert Graves." *Classical Bulletin* 84/1: 81–9.

Murnaghan, S. 2011. "Classics for Cool Kids: Popular and Unpopular Versions of Antiquity for Children." *Classical World* 104: 339–53.

Murnaghan, S. 2015a. "*Homer's Daughter*: Graves' *Vera Historia*," in A. Gibson, ed., *Robert Graves and the Classics*. Oxford: Oxford University Press. 57–76.

Murnaghan, S. 2015b. "Men into Pigs: Circe's Transformations in Versions of *The Odyssey* for Children," in L. Maurice, ed., *The Reception of Greece and Rome in Children's Literature: Heroes and Eagles*. Leiden: Brill. 195–212.

Murnaghan, S., and Roberts, D. H. 2016. "Armies of Children: War and Peace, Ancient History and Myth in Children's Books After World War One," in K. Marciniak, ed., *Our Mythical Childhood: The Classics and Literature for Children and Young Adults.* Leiden: Brill. 219–40.

Murnaghan, S., and Roberts, D. H. 2017. "Myth Collections for Children," in V. Zajko and H. Hoyle, eds., *A Handbook to the Reception of Classical Mythology.* Oxford: Wiley-Blackwell. 87–104.

Murnaghan, S., and Roberts, D. H. 2018. "Arachne's Web: The Reception of an Ovidian Myth in Works for Children," in O. Hodkinson and H. Lovatt, eds., *Classical Reception and Children's Literature: Greece, Rome, and Childhood Transformation.* London: I. B. Tauris. 141–61.

Murray, G. S. 1998. *American Children's Literature and the Construction of Childhood.* New York: Twayne Publishers.

Nagel, R. 2002. "Virginia Woolf on Reading Greek." *Classical World* 96: 61–75.

Napoli, D. J. 1998. *Sirena.* New York: Scholastic.

Napoli, D. J. 2003. *The Great God Pan.* New York: Random House.

Napoli, D. J. 2011. *Treasury of Greek Mythology: Classic Stories of Gods, Goddesses, Heroes, and Monsters.* Illus. C. Balit. Washington, DC: National Geographic.

Nash, I. 2006. *American Sweethearts: Teenage Girls in Twentieth-Century Popular Culture.* Bloomington: Indiana University Press.

Naylor, P. R. 1980. *Shadows on the Wall.* New York: Scholastic.

Naylor, P. R. 1981. *Faces in the Water.* New York: Scholastic.

Neale, J. M. 1847. *Stories from Heathen Mythology and Greek History for the Use of Christian Children.* London: Joseph Masters.

Nesbit, E. 1959. *The Story of the Amulet.* London: Puffin. First published 1906.

Nesbit, E. 1979. *The Enchanted Castle.* London: Penguin. First published 1907.

Newberry, F. 1987. *Hawthorne's Divided Loyalties: England and America in His Works.* Rutherford, NJ: Fairleigh Dickinson University Press.

Niebuhr, B. G. 1843a. *Stories of the Gods and Heroes of Greece, told by Berthold [sic] Niebuhr to His Son.* [Trans. L. Duff Gordon]. London: Parker.

Niebuhr, B. G. 1843b. *Heroic Tales of Ancient Greece, Related by Berthold [sic] Niebuhr to His Little Son Marcus.* Trans. "Felix Summerly" [aka Henry Cole]. London: Chapman.

Niebuhr, B. G. 1903. *The Greek Heroes: Stories Translated from Niebuhr,* with additions. Illus. A. Rackham. London: Cassell.

Niebuhr, B. G., et al. 1854. *The Life and Letters of Barthold Georg Niebuhr: With Essays on His Character and Influence.* Trans. S. Winkworth. New York: Harper.

Nield, J. 1911. *A Guide to the Best Historical Novels and Tales.* 4th edn. London: Elkin Mathews. First published 1902.

Nikolajeva, M. 1996. *Children's Literature Comes of Age.* New York: Garland.

Nikolajeva, M. 2006. "Picture Books," in J. Zipes, ed., *The Oxford Encyclopedia of Children's Literature*, vol. 3. Oxford: Oxford University Press. 247–51.

Nikolajeva, M., and Scott, C. 2006. *How Picturebooks Work*. London: Routledge. First published 2001.

Nodelman, P. 1988. *Words About Pictures*. Athens, GA: University of Georgia Press.

Nodelman, P. 2008. *The Hidden Adult: Defining Children's Literature*. Baltimore: Johns Hopkins University Press.

O'Malley, A. 2003. *The Making of the Modern Child: Children's Literature and Childhood in the Late Eighteenth Century*. New York: Routledge.

O'Sullivan, E. 2004. "Internationalism, the Universal Child and the World of Children's Literature," in P. Hunt, ed., *International Companion Encyclopedia of Children's Literature*, 2nd edn. London: Routledge. 13–25.

Oldfield, P. 1988. *Tales from Ancient Greece*. New York: Doubleday.

Olechowska, E. 2016. "J. K. Rowling Exposes the World to Classical Antiquity," in K. Marciniak, ed., *Our Mythical Childhood . . . : The Classics and Literature for Children and Young Adults*. Leiden: Brill. 384–410.

Orgel, D. 1996. *The Princess and the God*. London: Orchard.

Osborne, M. P. 1989. *Favorite Greek Myths*. Illus. T. Howell. New York: Scholastic.

Panofsky, D. and E. 1956. *Pandora's Box: The Changing Aspects of a Mythical Symbol*. New York: Pantheon Books.

Paris, M. 2000. *Warrior Nation: Images of War in British Popular Culture, 1850-2000*. London: Reaktion.

Parker, H. 1993. "Sappho Schoolmistress." *Transactions of the American Philological Association* 123: 309–51. Reprinted in E. Greene, ed., 1996. *Reading Sappho: Reception and Transmission*. Berkeley and Los Angeles: University of California Press. 146–83.

Parton, E. 1932. *The Mule of the Parthenon, and Other New Stories of Ancient Greece*. New York: Doubleday, Doran.

Paul, J. 2015. " 'Time is only a mode of thought, you know': Ancient History, Imagination, and Empire in E. Nesbit's Literature for Children," in L. Maurice, ed., *The Reception of Ancient Greece and Rome in Children's Literature*. Leiden and Boston: Brill. 30–55.

Peabody, J. P. 1897. *Old Greek Folk Stories Told Anew*. Boston: Houghton Mifflin.

Peacock, S. J. 1988. *Jane Ellen Harrison: The Mask and the Self*. New Haven: Yale University Press.

Pearce, R. H. 1972. "Historical Introduction," in *The Centenary Edition of the Works of Nathaniel Hawthorne*, vol. 6. Columbus, OH: Ohio State University Press. 287–311.

Pearson, N. H. 1969. "Norman Holmes Pearson on H.D.: An Interview," with L. S. Dembo. *Contemporary Literature* 10: 435–6.

Peck, E. 1985. "Hawthorne's Nonsexist Framework: The Real Wonder of *A Wonder Book.*" *Children's Literature Association Quarterly* 10: 116–19.

Peppin, B. 1975. *Fantasy: The Golden Age of Fantastic Illustration.* London: Watson-Guptill.

Perrin, N. 1969. *Dr. Bowdler's Legacy: A History of Expurgated Books in England and America.* New York: Atheneum.

Pfister, J. 1996. "Afterword," in N. Hawthorne, *A Wonder Book for Girls and Boys.* Illus. W. Crane. Oxford: Oxford University Press. 243–54.

Plotz, J. 2001. *Romanticism and the Vocation of Childhood.* New York: Palgrave.

Pollard, E. F. 1892. *Avice: A Story of Imperial Rome.* London: S. W. Partridge.

Pomey, F. 1659. *Pantheum mythicum seu fabulosa deorum historia.* Lyons.

Powers, A. 1944. *Hannibal's Elephants.* New York: Longmans, Green.

Price, M. E. 1924. *A Child's Book of Myths.* With an Introduction by Katherine Lee Bates. Chicago: Rand McNally and Company.

Prins, Y. 2017. *Ladies Greek: Victorian Translations of Tragedy.* Princeton: Princeton University Press.

Putnam, E. J. 1910. *The Lady: Studies of Certain Significant Phases of Her History.* New York: Sturgis & Walton.

Radford, A. 2007. *The Lost Girls: Demeter-Persephone and the Literary Imagination.* Amsterdam and New York: Rodopi.

Rahn, S. 1990. " 'It Would Be Awful Not to Know Greek': Rediscovering Geoffrey Trease." *The Lion and the Unicorn* 14: 23–52.

Rahn, S. 1991. "An Evolving Past: The Story of Historical Fiction and Nonfiction for Children." *The Lion and the Unicorn* 15: 1–26.

Randall, D. 2000. *Kipling's Imperial Boy: Adolescence and Cultural Hybridity.* New York: Palgrave Macmillan.

Ransome, A. 1937. "A Letter to the Editor." *Junior Bookshelf* 1/4: 3–5.

Ray, G. 1976. *The Illustrator and the Book in England from 1790–1914.* New York: Dover.

Ray, M. 1971. *A Tent for the Sun.* Faber and Faber.

Ray, M. 1974. *The Ides of April.* London: Faber and Faber.

Ray, M. 1975. *Sword Sleep.* London: Faber and Faber.

Ray, M. 1977. *Beyond the Desert Gate* London: Faber and Faber.

Ray, M. 1980. *Rain from the West.* London: Faber and Faber.

Reeves, J. 1969a. *Gods and Voyagers.* London: Blackie.

Reeves, J. 1969b. *Heroes and Monsters.* London: Blackie.

Reid, D. F. 1967. *Edith Hamilton: An Intimate Portrait.* New York: Norton.

Resinski, R. 2009. "Revising Pandora (and Rewriting Eve) in Nathaniel Hawthorne's *Wonder Book.*" Paper delivered at conference on "Asterisks and Obelisks: Classical Receptions in Children's Literature," Lampeter, July 6–10.

Resinski, R. 2011a. "Painting the Statues: Subversion and Authority in Nathaniel Hawthorne's *Wonder Book*." Paper delivered at the Annual Meeting of the American Philological Association.

Resinski, R. 2011b. "The Education of the Spirit in Nathaniel Hawthorne's *Wonder Book*." Paper delivered at the Annual Meeting of the South Atlantic Modern Languages Association.

Reynolds, K. 1990. *Girls Only? Gender and Popular Children's Fiction in Britain 1880–1910*. Philadelphia: Temple University Press.

Reynolds, K. 2009. "Words about War for Boys: Representations of Soldiers and Conflict in Writing for Children before World War I." *Children's Literature Association Quarterly* 34: 255–71.

Richards, J., ed. 1989. *Imperialism and Juvenile Literature*. Manchester: Manchester University Press.

Richardson, A. 2009. "Wordsworth, Fairy Tales, and the Politics of Children's Reading," in J. H. McGavran, ed., *Romanticism and Children's Literature in Nineteenth-Century England*. Athens, GA: University of Georgia Press. 34–55.

Richardson, R. D. Jr. 1979. "Myth and Fairy Tale in Hawthorne's Stories for Children." *Journal of American Culture* 2: 341–6.

Richlin, A. 1992. "Striking Back at the (Roman) Empire: The Artist as Classicist in Stead and Others." *Tulsa Studies in Women's Literature* 11: 265–87.

Riordan, Rick. 2005. *Percy Jackson & The Olympians: The Lightning Thief*. New York: Hyperion Books.

Riordan, Rick. 2006. *Percy Jackson & The Olympians: The Sea of Monsters*. New York: Hyperion Books.

Riordan, Rick. 2007. *Percy Jackson & The Olympians: The Titan's Curse*. New York: Hyperion Books.

Riordan, Rick. 2008. *Percy Jackson & The Olympians: The Battle of the Labyrinth*. New York: Hyperion Books.

Riordan, Rick. 2009. *Percy Jackson & The Olympians: The Last Olympian*. New York: Hyperion Books.

Ritvo, L. B. 1990. *Darwin's Influence on Freud: A Tale of Two Sciences*. New Haven: Yale University Press.

Rivet, A. L. F. 1976. "Rudyard Kipling's Roman Britain: Fact and Fiction." An Inaugural Lecture Given in the University of Keele on Thursday, Nov. 6, 1976. University of Keele.

Robbins, E. 1830. *Elements of Mythology, or Classical Fables of the Greeks and Romans: to which are Added Some Notices of Syrian, Hindu, and Scandinavian Superstitions: together with those of the American Nations: the Whole Comparing Polytheism with True Religions: For the Use of Schools*. Philadelphia: Towar and Hogan.

Roberts, D. H. 2007. "Reconstructed Pasts: Rome and Britain, Child and Adult in Kipling's *Puck of Pook's Hill* and Sutcliff's Novels of Roman Britain," in C. Stray, ed., *Remaking the Classics*. London: Duckworth. 107–23.

Roberts, D. H. 2009. "From Fairy Tale to Cartoon: Collections of Greek Myth for Children," *Classical Bulletin* 84: 58–73.

Roberts, D. H. 2010. "Water-Jug and Plover's Feather: Rudyard Kipling's India in Rosemary Sutcliff's Roman Britain," in E. Hall and P. Vasunia, eds., *India, Greece, and Rome 1757–2007*. London: Institute of Classical Studies. 117–29.

Roberts, D. H. 2015. "The Metamorphosis of Ovid in Retellings of Myth for Children," in L. Maurice, ed., *The Reception of Ancient Greece and Rome in Children's Literature: Heroes and Eagles*. Leiden: Brill. 233–56.

Robertson, C. L. 2001. *An American Poet in Paris: Pauline Avery Crawford and the* Herald Tribune. Columbia, MO: University of Missouri Press.

Robinson, A. 2002. *The Life and Work of Jane Ellen Harrison*. Oxford: Oxford University Press.

Roe, N. 2003. "Leigh Hunt: Some Early Matters," in N. Roe, ed., *Leigh Hunt: Life, Politics, Poetics*. London: Routledge. 19–31.

Rogers, B. M., and Stevens, B. E., eds. 2015. *Classical Traditions in Modern Fantasy*. Oxford: Oxford University Press.

Rose, J. 1992. *The Case of Peter Pan, or the Impossibility of Children's Fiction*, 2nd ed. Philadelphia: University of Pennsylvania Press. First published 1984.

Rouse, W. H. D. 1957. *Gods, Heroes and Men of Ancient Greece*. New York: Signet. First published 1934.

Rowland, A. W. 2012. *Romanticism and Childhood: The Infantilization of British Literary Culture*. Cambridge: Cambridge University Press.

Rudd, D. 2010. "Deus ex Natura or Nonstick Pan?: Competing Discourses in Kenneth Grahame's *The Wind in the Willows*," in J. C. Horne and D. R. White, eds., *Kenneth Grahame's* The Wind in the Willows: *A Children's Classic at 100*. Lanham, MD: Scarecrow Press. 3–21.

Rudd, D. 2013. *Reading the Child in Children's Literature: An Heretical Approach*. Basingstoke: Palgrave Macmillan.

Rudnytsky, P. L. 1987. *Freud and Oedipus*. New York: Columbia University Press.

Rudnytsky, P. L. 1994. "Freud's Pompeiian Fantasy," in S. L. Gilman, J. Birmele, J. Geller, and V. D. Greenberg, eds., *Reading Freud's Reading*. New York: New York University Press. 211–31.

Russell, W. F. 1989. *Classic Myths to Read Aloud*. New York: Broadway.

Rutherford, A. 1964. "Officers and Gentlemen," in A. Rutherford, ed., *Kipling's Mind and Art*. Edinburgh: Oliver and Boyd. 171–96.

Sagon, A. 1907. *Under the Roman Eagles*. London: S. W. Partridge.

Saintsbury, G. 1975. *The Historical Novel*. Norwood, PA: Norwood Editions. First published 1895.

Samida, S. 2012. *Heinrich Schliemann*. Tübingen: A. Francke Verlag.

Sánchez-Eppler, K. 2004. "Hawthorne and the Writing of Childhood," in R. H. Millington, ed., *The Cambridge Companion to Nathaniel Hawthorne*. Cambridge: Cambridge University Press. 143–61.

Schacker, J. 2003. *National Dreams: The Remaking of Fairy Tales in Nineteenth-Century England*. Philadelphia: University of Pennsylvania Press.

Schaffner, P. 1986. "Running." *Iowa Review* 16/3: 7–13.

Schliemann, H. 1976. *Ilios: The City and Country of the Trojans*. New York: Arno Press. First published 1881.

Schlitz, L. A. 2006. *The Hero Schliemann: The Dreamer Who Dug for Troy*. Cambridge, MA: Candlewick Press.

Schmidt, G. D. 1990. *Robert McCloskey*. Boston: Twayne Publishers.

Schmidt, G. D. 2013. *Making Americans: Children's Literature from 1930 to 1960*. Iowa City: University of Iowa Press.

Schultze, C. 2007. "Charlotte Yonge and the Classics," in J. Courtney and C. Schultze, eds., *Studies in Charlotte M. Yonge*. Abingdon: Beechcroft Books. 159–88.

Schultze, C. 2014. "Absent Fathers and Faithful Wives: Penelope-Figures in the Novels of Charlotte Yonge," in H. S. Gardner and S. Murnaghan, eds., *Odyssean Identities in Modern Culture: The Journey Home*. Columbus, OH: Ohio State University Press. 64–85.

Schwarcz, J. H. 1982. *Ways of the Illustrator: Visual Communication in Children's Literature*. Chicago: American Library Association.

Schwarcz, J. H., and Schwarcz, C. 1991. *The Picturebook Comes of Age*. Chicago: American Library Association.

Scott, C. 2010. "Frame-Making and Frame-Breaking in Picturebooks," in T. Colomer, B. Kümmerling-Meibauer, and C. Silva-Diáz, eds., *New Directions in Picturebook Research*. New York: Routledge. 101–12.

Seaby, A. W. 1943. *The Ninth Legion*. London: George G. Harrap.

Serraillier, I. 1965. *The Way of Danger and The Gorgon's Head*. Oxford: Heinemann Educational Books.

Shahan, T. J. 1901. *A Book of Famous Myths and Legends*. Boston: Hall and Locke.

Shattuck, S. D. 1987. "The Stage of Scholarship: Crossing the Bridge from Harrison to Woolf," in J. Marcus, ed., *Virginia Woolf and Bloomsbury: A Centennial Celebration*. London: Macmillan. 278–98.

Shaw, C. D. 1903. *Stories of the Ancient Greeks*. Boston: Ginn & Co.

Shaw, H. E. 2005. "Is There a Problem with Historical Fiction (or with Scott's *Redgauntlet*)?" *Rethinking History* 9: 173–95.

Shipton, P. 2004. *The Pig Scrolls, by Gryllus the Pig*. Cambridge, MA: Candlewick.

Shipton, P. 2007. *The Pig Who Saved the World, by Gryllus the Pig*. Cambridge, MA: Candlewick.

Siegel, D. L. 1997. "Nancy Drew as New Girl Wonder: Solving It All for the 1930s," in S. A. Inness, ed., *Nancy Drew and Company: Culture, Gender, and Girls' Series*. Bowling Green, OH: Popular Press. 159–86.

Simons, J., and Simons, S. 1991. *Why Spiders Spin: A Story of Arachne*. Englewood Cliffs, NJ: Silver Press.

Slater, N. W. 2015. "Classical Memories in C. S. Lewis' Chronicles of Narnia, " in L. Maurice, ed., *The Reception of Ancient Greece and Rome in Children's Literature*. Leiden: Brill. 169–91.

Slotkin, R. 2005. "Fiction for the Purposes of History." *Rethinking History* 9: 221–36.

Smith, J. 1907. *General Historie of Virginia, New-England, and the Summer Isles*. Glasgow: Maclehose. First published 1624.

Smith, V. 2009. "Making and Breaking Frames: Crossing the Borders of Expectation in Picturebooks," in J. Evans, ed., *Talking Beyond the Page: Reading and Responding to Picturebooks*. London: Routledge. 81–96.

Snedeker, C. D. 1912. *The Spartan*. Garden City, NY: Doubleday.

Snedeker, C. D. 1917. *Seth Way: A Romance of the New Harmony Community*. Boston: Houghton Mifflin.

Snedeker, C. D. 1929. *The Beckoning Road*. Garden City, NY: Doubleday, Doran.

Snedeker, C. D. 1931. *The Town of the Fearless*. Garden City, NY: Doubleday.

Snedeker, C. D. 1933. *The Forgotten Daughter*. Garden City: Doubleday. First published 1929.

Snedeker, C. D. 1939. *The Perilous Seat*. New York: Doubleday, Doran. First published 1923.

Snedeker, C. D. 1944. Letter to Shirley Herndon (née Pomeroy), January 29. On deposit at the deGrummond Children's Literature Collection, University of Southern Mississippi Libraries.

Snedeker, C. D. 1956. *The White Isle*. Garden City: Doubleday. First published 1940.

Spaeth, J. Jr. 1927. Review of *The Book of the Ancient Romans* by Dorothy Mills. *Classical Journal* 23: 150–2.

Speare, E. G. 1961. *The Bronze Bow*. Boston: Houghton Mifflin.

Spencer, R. A. 2015. *Harry Potter and the Classical World: Greek and Roman Allusions in J. K. Rowling's Modern Epic*. Jefferson, NC: McFarland.

Spickelmire, C. 1911. *Stories of Hellas*. Indianapolis: Bobbs-Merrill.

Spires, E. 2001. *I am Arachne: Fifteen Greek and Roman Myths*. New York: Square Fish.

Sprague, R. 1947. *Northward to Albion*. New York: Roy.

Spufford, F. 2002. *The Child that Books Built*. London: Faber and Faber.

Stallworthy, J. ed. 1994. *Wilfred Owen: The War Poems*. London: Chatto & Windus.

Stephanson, A. 1995. *Manifest Destiny: American Expansionism and the Empire of Right*. New York: New York University Press.

Stephens, J. 1992. *Language and Ideology in Children's Fiction*. London: Longman.

Stephens, J., and McCallum, R. 1998. *Retelling Stories, Framing Culture: Traditional Story and Metanarratives in Children's Literature*. New York: Garland.

Sterne, E. G. 1929. *Blue Pigeons*. New York: Duffield.

Sternlicht, S. 1985. *Padraic Colum*. Boston: Twayne Publishers.

Stevens, B. E. 2017. "Ancient Underworlds in J. R. R. Tolkien's *The Hobbit*," in B. M. Rogers and B. E. Stevens, eds., *Classical Traditions in Modern Fantasy*. Oxford: Oxford University Press. 121–44.

Stewart, J. G. 1959. *Jane Ellen Harrison: A Portrait from Letters*. London: Merlin.

Stoneley, P. 2003. *Consumerism and American Girls' Literature, 1860–1940*. Cambridge: Cambridge University Press.

Stray, C. 1998. *Classics Transformed: Schools, Universities, and Society in England, 1830–1960*. Oxford: Clarendon Press.

Sulloway, F. J. 1992. *Freud, Biologist of the Mind: Beyond the Psychoanalytic Legend*. Cambridge, MA: Harvard University Press.

Sutcliff, R. 1954. *The Eagle of the Ninth*. London: Oxford University Press.

Sutcliff, R. 1955. *Outcast*. Oxford: Oxford University Press.

Sutcliff, R. 1960. *Rudyard Kipling*. London: Bodley Head.

Sutcliff, R. 1959. *The Lantern Bearers*. London: Oxford University Press.

Sutcliff, R. 1961. *Dawn Wind*. New York: Henry Z. Walck, Inc.

Sutcliff, R. 1963. "Gods and Heroes: Classical Legends Retold." *Times Literary Supplement* 3198 (June 14): 431.

Sutcliff, R. 1965. *The Mark of the Horse Lord*. London: Oxford University Press.

Sutcliff, R. 1972. *Heather, Oak, and Olive*. New York: Dutton. First published as *The Truce of the Games*, 1971.

Sutcliff, R. 1973. *The Capricorn Bracelet*. Oxford: Oxford University Press.

Sutcliff, R. 1978. *Song for a Dark Queen*. London: Pelham.

Sutcliff, R. 1980. *Frontier Wolf*. Oxford: Oxford University Press.

Sutcliff, R. 1993. *The Silver Branch*. Farrar, Straus & Giroux. First published 1957.

Swann, T. B. 1962. *The Classical World of H. D.* Lincoln, NE: University of Nebraska Press.

Sweeney, M. M. 2005. "Checking Out America: Libraries as Agents of Acculturation in Three Mid-Century Girls' Books." *Children's Literature* 33: 41–65.

Swinburne, L., and Swinburne, I. 1977. *Ancient Myths: The First Science Fiction*. Milwaukee, WI: Heinemann.

Sword, H. 1995. "H.D.'s *Majic Ring*." *Tulsa Studies in Women's Literature* 14: 347–62.

Sypher, F. J. 2015. *Charles Anthon: American Classicist*. Ann Arbor: Scholars' Facsimiles & Reprints.

Tappan, E. M. 1907. *Stories from the Classics*. Boston: Houghton, Mifflin.

Tatar, M. 1987. *The Hard Facts of the Grimms' Fairy Tales*. Princeton: Princeton University Press.

Tatar, M. 2009. *Enchanted Hunters: The Power of Stories in Childhood*. New York: Norton.

Tate, T. 1997. "HD's War Neurotics," in S. Raitt and T. Tate, eds., *Women's Fiction and the Great War*. Oxford: Clarendon Press. 240–62.

Thorp, M. F. 1937. *Charles Kingsley, 1819–1875*. Princeton: Princeton University Press.

Tolkien, J. R. R. 1994. "On Fairy Stories," in *Poems and Stories*. Boston: Houghton, Mifflin. 113–88. First published 1964.

Tooke, A. trans. 1781. *The Pantheon: Representing the fabulous histories of the heathen gods and most illustrious heroes, in a short, plain and familiar method by way of dialogue*. London: Bathhurst, Rivington, Law, Keith, Robinson, Baldwin. First published 1694.

Tooke, A, trans. 1819. *The Pantheon: Representing the fabulous histories of the heathen gods and most illustrious heroes, in a plain and familiar method*. 34th edn. London: Rivington et al.

Tooke, A., trans. 1825. *Tooke's pantheon of the heathen gods and illustrious heroes: Revised for a classical course of education, and adapted for the use of students of every age and of either sex*. Baltimore: E. J. Coale.

Towle, E. 1906. *John Mason Neale D.D.: A Memoir*. London: Longmans, Green.

Townsend, M. 2010. *Amazing Greek Myths of Wonder and Blunders*. New York: Puffin.

Traill, D. A. 1985. "Schliemann's Dream of Troy: The Making of a Legend." *Classical Journal* 81: 13–24. Reprinted in *Excavating Schliemann*. Atlanta, GA: Scholar's Press: 29–40.

Traill, D. A. 1995. *Schliemann of Troy: Treasure and Deceit*. London: John Murray.

Treadwell, M. 1985. "Benjamin Motte, Andrew Tooke and Gulliver's Travels," in H.J. Real and H.J. Vienken, eds., *Proceedings of the First Münster Symposium on Jonathan Swift*. Munich: Wilhelm Fink Verlag. 287–304.

Trease, G. 1952. *Web of Traitors*. New York: Vanguard. (Published in England as *The Crown of Violet*. London: Macmillan.)

Trease, G. 1955. *Word to Caesar*. London: Macmillan.

Trease, G. 1964. *Tales Out of School*, 2nd edn. London: Heinemann.

Trease, G. 1972. *A Ship to Rome*. London: Heinemann.

Trease, G. 1973. "Old Writers and Young Readers," in J. Lawlor, ed., *Essays and Studies*. London: John Murray. 99–112.

Trease, G. 1976. "The Historical Novelist at Work." *Children's Literature in Education* 7: 5–16.

Trease, G. 1997. *Mission to Marathon*. London: A & C Black.

Treece, H. 1954. *The Eagles Have Flown*. London: Bodley Head.

Treece, H. 1965. *Legions of the Eagle*. Harmondsworth: Penguin. First published 1954.

Trilling, L. 1956. "Mr. Colum's Greeks." *The Griffin* 5 (Christmas Issue): 4–15.

Trodd, A. 1998. *Women's Writing in English: Britain, 1900–1945*. London: Longman.

Tucker, N., ed. 1976. *Suitable for Children? Controversies in Children's Literature*. London: Chatto and Windus.

Tuerk, R. 2007. *Oz in Perspective: Magic and Myth in the L. Frank Baum Books*. Jefferson, NC and London: McFarland.

Unsworth, B. 2005. "Pictures First," in B. Greenway, ed., *Twice-Told Children's Tales: The Influence of Childhood Reading on Writers for Adults*. London: Routledge. 99–102.

Untermeyer, L. 1968. *The Firebringer and Other Great Stories: Fifty-Five Legends that Live Forever*. New York: Evans.

Vaclavik, K. 2010. *Uncharted Depths: Descent Narratives in English and French Children's Literature*. London: Legenda.

Valenti, P. D. 1996. "Sophia Peabody Hawthorne's 'American Notebooks.' " *Studies in the American Renaissance*: 115–85.

Vallone, L. 2008. "History Girls: Eighteenth and Nineteenth-Century Historiography and the Case of Mary, Queen of Scots." *Children's Literature* 36: 1–23.

Van Doren, M. ed. 1929. *Correspondence of Aaron Burr and His Daughter Theodosia*. New York: Covici-Friede.

Van Emden, R. 2005. *Boy Soldiers of the Great War*. London: Headline.

Van Slyck, A. A. 1995. *Free to All: Carnegie Libraries & American Culture 1890–1920*. Chicago: University of Chicago Press.

Vance, N. 1997. *The Victorians and Ancient Rome*. Oxford: Blackwell.

Vandiver, E. 2010. *Stand in the Trench, Achilles: Classical Receptions in British Poetry of the Great War*. Oxford: Oxford University Press.

Vasunia, P. 2005. "Greater Rome and Greater Britain," in B. Goff, ed., *Classics and Colonialism*. London: Duckworth. 38–64.

Viguers, R. H., Dalphin, M., and Miller, B. M. 1958. *Illustrators of Children's Books 1946–1956*. Boston: The Horn Book.

Vinge, J. 1999. *The Random House Book of Greek Myths*. New York: Random House.

Wadsworth, S. 2000. "Nathaniel Hawthorne, Samuel Goodrich, and the Transformation of the Juvenile Literature Market." *Nathaniel Hawthorne Review* 26: 1–24.

Walde, C. 2016. "Graeco-Roman Antiquity and Its Productive Appropriation: the Example of Harry Potter," in K. Marciniak, ed., *Our Mythical Childhood . . . : The Classics and Literature for Children and Young Adults*. Leiden: Brill. 362–83.

Wallace, D. 2005. *The Woman's Historical Novel: British Women Writers, 1900–2000*. Houndmills: Palgrave Macmillan.

Warner, M. 2010. Review of L. Maguire, *Helen of Troy: From Homer to Hollywood* (Wiley-Blackwell: 2009). *London Review of Books* 32: 24–6.

Watson, J. 2009. " 'The Raven: A Christmas Poem': Coleridge and the Fairy Tale Controversy," in J. H. McGavran, ed., *Romanticism and Children's Literature in Nineteenth-Century England*. Athens, GA: University of Georgia Press. 14–33.

Webb, B. 2006. *Star Dancer*. London: Macmillan.

Weil, L. 1986. *Pandora's Box*. New York: Athenaeum.

Weinlich, B. 2015. "The Metanarrative of Picture Books: 'Reading' Greek Myth for (and to) Children," in L. Maurice, ed., *The Reception of Greece and Rome in Children's Literature: Heroes and Eagles*. Leiden: Brill. 85–104.

Wells, R. 1993. *Max and Ruby's First Greek Myth: Pandora's Box*. New York: Dial.

Wells, R. 1995. *Max and Ruby's Midas: Another Greek Myth*. New York: Dial.

Wells, R. F. 1925. *On Land and Sea with Caesar, or Following the Eagles*. Boston: Lothrop, Lee & Shepard.

Wells, R. F. 1960. *With Caesar's Legions: The Adventure of Two Roman Youths in the Conquest of Gaul*. New York: Biblo and Tannen. First published 1923.

Welty, E. 1984. *One Writer's Beginnings*. Cambridge, MA: Harvard University Press.

Weston, W. H. 1900. *Plutarch's Lives for Boys and Girls*. New York: Thomas Nelson.

Whalley, J. I. 2004. "The Development of Illustrated Texts and Picture Books," in P. Hunt, ed., *International Companion Encyclopedia of Children's Literature*, 2nd edn. London: Routledge. 318–27.

Whelan-Stewart, W. 2014. "Penelope in Bronzeville: The Theme of *Nostos* in Gwendolyn Brooks's 'The Anniad,' " in H. Gardner and S. Murnaghan, eds., *Odyssean Identities in Modern Cultures: The Journey Home*. Columbus, OH: Ohio State University Press. 153–72.

White, A. T. 1959. *The Golden Treasury of Myths and Legends*. Illus. A. and M. Provensen. New York: Golden Press.

White, E. L. 1918. *The Unwilling Vestal: A Tale of Rome Under the Caesars*. New York: E. P. Dutton & Co.

White, H. 1978. *Tropics of Discourse: Essays in Cultural Criticism*. Baltimore: Johns Hopkins University Press.

White, H. 2005. "Introduction: Historical Fiction, Fictional History, and Historical Reality." *Rethinking History* 9: 147–57.

White, S. E. 1922. *Daniel Boone: Wilderness Scout*. Garden City, NY: Doubleday.

Whitehead, A. C. 1914. The *Standard Bearer: A Story of Army Life in the Time of Caesar*. New York: American Book Company.

Whyte-Melville, G. J. 1906. *The Gladiators: A Tale of Rome and Judaea*. London: George Routledge & Sons. First published 1863.

Wilder, L. I. 1953. *By the Shores of Silver Lake*. Rev. edn. New York: Harper Collins. First published 1939.

Williams, J. 1943. *The Stolen Oracle*. London: Oxford University Press.

Williams, J. 1944. *The Counterfeit African*. London: Oxford University Press.

Williams, J. 1948. *The Roman Moon Mystery*. New York: Oxford University Press.

Williams, J. 1960. *Medusa's Head*. Illus. S. Savage. New York: Random House.

Williams, M. 1991. *Greek Myths for Young Children*. Cambridge, MA: Candlewick.

Williamson, J. S. 1957. *The Eagles Have Flown*. New York: Knopf.

Wilson, K. 2011. *Re-visioning Historical Fiction for Young Readers: The Past through Modern Eyes*. London: Routledge.

Wilson, R. 1928. *Green Magic: A Collection of the World's Best Fairy Tales from All Countries*. London: Jonathan Cape.

Wilson, R. 1929. *Silver Magic*. London: Jonathan Cape.

Winter, S. 1999. *Freud and the Institution of Psychoanalytic Knowledge*. Stanford, CA: Stanford University Press.

Winterer, C. 2002. *The Culture of Classicism: Ancient Greece and Rome in American Intellectual Life, 1780–1910*. Baltimore: Johns Hopkins University Press.

Winterer, C. 2007. *The Mirror of Antiquity. American Women and the Classical Tradition, 1750–1900*. Ithaca, NY: Cornell University Press.

Winterfeld, H. 1956. *Detectives in Togas*. Trans. R. and C. Winston. New York: Harcourt Brace & Company.

Winterfeld, H. 1971. *Mystery of the Roman Ransom*. Trans. E. McCormick. New York: Harcourt Brace Jovanovich.

Wood, A. 2018. "Perspective Matters: Roman Britain in Children's Novels," in O. Hodkinson and H. Lovatt, eds., *Classical Reception and Children's Literature: Greece, Rome and Childhood Transformation*. London: I. B. Tauris. 108–18.

Woolf, V. 1925. *The Common Reader: First Series*. New York: Harcourt, Brace and Company.

Woolf, V. 1975. *The Letters of Virginia Woolf*, vol. 1. *1888–1912*. Ed. N. Nicolson and J. Trautmann. New York and London: Harcourt Brace Jovanovich.

Woolf, V. 1976. *Moments of Being: Unpublished Autobiographical Writings*. Ed. J. Schulkind. New York and London: Harcourt Brace Jovanovich.

Woolf, V. 1981. *Mrs. Dalloway*. New York: Harcourt Inc. First published 1925.

Woolf, V. 1982. *The Diary of Virginia Woolf*, vol. 4. *1931–1935*. Ed. Ann Olivier Bell, assisted by Andrew McNeillie. New York: Harcourt Brace Jovanovich.

Woolf, V. 1989. *The Complete Shorter Fiction*. Ed. S. Dick. New York: Harcourt Brace & Company.

Woolf, V. 1990. *A Passionate Apprenticeship: The Early Journals 1897–1909*. Ed. M. A. Leaska. New York: Harcourt Brace Jovanovich.

Woolf, V. 1992. *The Years.* Ed. H. Lee. Oxford: Oxford University Press. First published 1937.

Woolf, V. 2000. *Jacob's Room.* Ed. K. Flint. Oxford: Oxford University Press. First published 1922.

Woolf, V. 2006a. *The Waves.* New York: Harcourt, Inc. First published 1931.

Woolf, V. 2006b. *Three Guineas.* New York: Harcourt, Inc. First published 1938.

Yeats, W. B. 1962. *Explorations.* New York: Macmillan.

Yonge, C. M. 1869a. *A Book of Worthies: Gathered from the Old Histories and Now Written Anew.* London: Macmillan.

Yonge, C. M. 1869b. "Children's Literature of the Last Century." *Macmillan's Magazine* (July): 229–37; (August): 302–310; (September): 448–56.

Yonge, C. M. 1878. *Young Folks' History of Rome.* Boston: Lothrop. First published as *Aunt Charlotte's Stories of Roman History for the Little Ones,* 1877.

Yonge, C. M. 1879. *Young Folks' History of Greece.* Boston: Lothrop. First published as *Aunt Charlotte's Stories of Greek History for the Little Ones,* 1876.

Yonge, C. M. 1887. *What Books to Lend and What to Give.* London: National Society's Depository.

Yonge, C. M. 1896. *The Daisy Chain, or Aspirations: A Family Chronicle.* New York: Macmillan. First published 1856.

Yonge, C. M. 1890. *The Slaves of Sabinus: Jew and Gentile.* London: National Society's Depository.

Yount, S. 1976. *Maxfield Parrish, 1870–1966.* New York: Abrams.

Yourcenar, M. 1990. *Memoirs of Hadrian.* Trans. G. Frick. New York: Noonday Press.

Zipes, J. 1988. *The Brothers Grimm: From Enchanted Forests to the Modern World.* New York: Routledge.

Zipes, J. 1994. *Fairy Tale as Myth/Myth as Fairy Tale.* Lexington: University of Kentucky Press.

Index

241, 249, 278. *See also* education;
  historical fiction; language
Compton, C. H. 135n12
Connolly, P. T. 185n29
constraints, on women 167–9, 171–2,
  174–5, 179, 182–4, 192–4,
  197–200, 231, 244, 278
  compared to slavery 179, 182–3, 197
  See also education; gender
Cook, Elizabeth 128–9, 277–8, 279, 284
Cooper, James Fenimore 157, 159
Cox, George William 48, 87n15
Crane, Walter 69
Crawford, John Raymond 103–7, 278
Crawford, Pauline Avery 103–7, 119, 278
Crete 188–94, 278. *See also* archaeology;
  Evans, Arthur; Knossos; Minotaur;
  Theseus
Cruikshank, George 59

D'Aulaire, Ingri and Edgar Parin 10, 95,
  119–23, 280–1, 284
daimon:
  meaning of 233–5, 240–1
  mystical 241–2
  as untranslatable 236–8
Darlington, William 19
Daugherty, James 108–12, 119, 278
Davenport, Guy 230n23
Donahey, Mary Dickerson 107–8
Dove, J. F. 133, 135–6
Duff Gordon, Lucie 22

Echo 273–4
education:
  and class 242–3, 247–8, 249–50
  and classical languages 1–3, 10,
    13–14, 20, 42–3, 53, 150, 169, 172,
    221, 232–4, 279
  and gender 2, 16, 43, 169, 172, 182,
    196–7, 203, 209, 224, 234, 243,
    247–8, 279–80
  historical fiction as 150
  myth's role in 2–3, 16–19, 39, 42–3,
    82, 128, 269–70
  and Oedipal conflict 224, 226–8
  Romantic views of 39
  in the United States 100
  See also brothers; gender; Greek;
    language
Electra 249
Eliot, T. S. 213–15, 228

Eliott, Lydia 146–7
emigration narratives 159–60. *See also*
  historical fiction; margins
Europa 33
Evans, Arthur 56, 88, 135, 177–8, 223.
  See also archaeology; Crete
Evans, I. O. 146, 148

fairy tales:
  audiences for 16, 19, 22, 88
  and fairies 24
  literary influence of 202
  and myth 8, 22–5, 26–7, 29–30, 40, 51,
    65–7, 83–90, 101, 126, 211
  as paradigm 232
  suitability for children 16–20
  See also myth
fan fiction 288
Fanelli, Sara 283
fantasy:
  childhood experience of 220–1
  in children's literature 17–18, 83,
    100–1, 128, 284–6
  See also imagination; magic
fathers:
  absent 32, 269
  as archetype 260–2, 269
  and daughters 33–4, 42, 98, 158–62,
    179, 183–6, 188–9, 191–4, 238–9
  and sons 17, 77, 98, 142–3, 173, 207–9,
    216–17, 221–4, 227–8
Fenn, G. G. Manville 142, 145–6
Fénelon, Abbé 17
fiction:
  in autobiography 221, 223
  resemblance to history 132–3, 175–7
  See also fan fiction; historical fiction
Flint, K. 253n44
Flint, W. Russell 72–3, 75
folklore 9, 82–4, 86, 94–6, 101–2, 262, 279
  Romantic views of 17
  See also fairy tales; myths
Ford, Henry Justice 89–90, 98–9
Freud 10, 208, 215–21, 223–4, 229–30,
  234–6, 246, 274–5
  and H. D. 226–8, 230, 274–5
frontiers:
  American 150, 153, 157–8, 161–3
  Britain as 159–60
  as utopia 162–3
  See also margins
Frost, Robert 107